John Briscoe
Valerius Maximus, *Facta et dicta memorabilia*, Book 8

Untersuchungen zur antiken
Literatur und Geschichte

—

Herausgegeben von
Marcus Deufert, Heinz-Günther Nesselrath
und Peter Scholz

Band 141

John Briscoe

Valerius Maximus, *Facta et dicta memorabilia*, Book 8

Text, Introduction, and Commentary

DE GRUYTER

ISBN 978-3-11-076369-0
e-ISBN (PDF) 978-3-11-066433-1
e-ISBN (EPUB) 978-3-11-066437-9
ISSN 1862-1112

Library of Congress Control Number: 2019938936

Bibliografische Information der Deutsche Nationalbibliothek
Die Deutsche Nationalbibliothek verzeichnet diese Publikation in der Deutschen Nationalbibliografie; detaillierte bibliografische Daten sind im Internet über http://dnb.dnb.de abrufbar.

© 2021 Walter de Gruyter GmbH, Berlin/Boston
This volume is text- and page-identical with the hardback published in 2019.
Satz/Datenkonvertierung: Meta Systems Publishing & Printservices GmbH, Wustermark
Druck und Bindung: CPI books GmbH, Leck

www.degruyter.com

Preface

Since 1989, when I accepted an invitation by Heinrich Krämer, the Head of B. G. Teubner (Stuttgart) to undertake a new edition of Valerius Maximus, replacing that of Carl Kempf, published in 1888, Valerius has been my second author (I was aware that friends on the Continent regarded me as the supreme example of the British one author scholar). The edition was published in 1998, but my publications on Valerius since then have been limited to two reviews and an article in *Oxford Bibliographies Online*, published by the OUP New York office. In 2016, however, when I was waiting for the final stages of the production of my *Oxford Classical Texts* edition of Livy books 21–25, I decided to embark on a commentary on Book 8 of Valerius, though with little confidence that it was a viable project. It grew, however, and by the time that *Liviana*, the companion volume to my OCT, was published in August 2018, it was almost complete.

My commentaries on Livy Books 31–45 were all published by OUP and my initial instinct was to offer the work to them. It soon occurred to me, however, that since my only previous major publication on Valerius was the Teubner edition and in 2006 De Gruyter had purchased the firm of K. G. Saur and their entire publishing range, including the Biblioteca Teubneriana, De Gruyter would be an appropriate home; in addition, since De Gruyter own the copyright to the Biblioteca Teubneriana, including a text and apparatus largely identical with that of my edition would be unproblematic. I therefore approached Marcus Deufert, with whom I had had many enjoyable conversations at conferences of the Academia Europaea, to which we were both elected in 2014, and he encouraged me to offer the work to *Untersuchungen zur antiken Literatur und Geschichte*, of which he is one of the Editors. I am most grateful to Marcus and his colleagues for accepting it for publication and for their helpful comments on the typescript, which eliminated a number of errors.

My edition was published at a time of renewed interest in Valerius, once an extremely popular author but largely ignored for most of the twentieth century. In particular, it saw the first modern commentaries on his work, on book 1 by David Wardle, in 1998, on book 2 by Andrea Themann-Steinke, ten years later: the former is part of the *Clarendon Ancient History* series and therefore deals only with matters of content, with the lemmata in English; the latter, a doctoral dissertation submitted to the Ruhr-Universität Bochum, is more ambitious but naturally constrained by the requirements of a thesis. Since it is unlikely that any one scholar will contemplate writing a commentary on the whole of Valerius' work, progress will consist of further volumes dealing with individual books. I chose Book 8 largely because of the interest of its variegated subject matter, the first five chapters dealing with different aspects of trials but also containing long series of non-Roman *exempla*. All commentaries are second-hand to some extent but *non omnia possumus omnes*, and this is particularly the case with the Greek artists in chapter 11 (I lack visual imagination). As in my Livy commentaries, my aim is to give equal attention to content, textual criticism, language and style, and literary matters.

As in the Preface to *Liviana*, I must thank Jim Adams for much expert advice on matters of Latinity, the staff of both the main University of Manchester Library, where the book was written, and the John Rylands Library for their friendly help, and the Library based members of the University of Manchester IT services for assistance with computer problems. I would also like to thank everyone at De Gruyter who has contributed to the publication of the book, particularly Classics Editor Torben Behm and Production Editor Karola Seitz.

Manchester   J. B.
June 2019

Contents

Preface —— v

Abbreviations —— ix

Introduction —— 1

Text —— 31

Commentary —— 67

Appendix —— 241

Addenda —— 243

Indexes —— 245

Abbreviations

This is a list of modern works referred to in an abbreviated form: it is not a full bibliography. For the authors of emendations not listed here see pp. xxxiii–xlii of my edition. Abbreviations of periodicals are those used in *L'Année philologique* and *Bibliographie de l'antiquité classique 1896–1914*. The abbreviations of the names and works of Greek and Latin authors are, with a few variations, those of Liddell–Scott–Jones and *TLL* respectively. With the exception of those listed here, abbreviations for collections of inscriptions are also those of Liddell–Scott–Jones and *TLL*. The numbers in bracket following the names of individual Romans, given on their first appearance in book 8, are those of the article concerned in *RE*.

Adams, *Bilingualism*	J. N. Adams, *Bilingualism and the Latin Language* (Cambridge, 2003)
Adams, *Informal Latin*	J. N. Adams, *An Anthology of Informal Latin, 200 BC–AD 900* (Cambridge, 2016)
Alexander	M. C. Alexander, *Trials in the Late Roman Republic* (Toronto–Buffalo, NY–London, 1990).
ANRW	H. Temporini and W. Haase (eds.), *Aufstieg und Niedergang der römischen Welt* (Berlin–New York, 1972–98)
Astin, *Cato*	A. E. Astin, *Cato the Censor* (Oxford, 1978)
Astin, *SA*	A. E. Astin, *Scipio Aemilianus* (Oxford, 1967)
Badian, *Studies*	E. Badian, *Studies in Greek and Roman History* (Oxford, 1964)
Barrington Atlas (followed by grid reference)	R. J. A. Talbert (ed.), *Barrington Atlas of the Greek and Roman World* (Princeton, NJ–Woodstock, Oxon., 2000)
Bloomer	W. M. Bloomer, *Valerius Maximus and the Rhetoric of the New Nobility* (Chapel Hill, NC, 1992)
Brennan	T. C. Brennan, *The Praetorship in the Roman Republic* (New York, 2000)
Briscoe, *Bibliography*	J. Briscoe, 'Valerius Maximus', in *Oxford Bibliographies Online* (New York, 2017)
CAH	*Cambridge Ancient History*
Carter	C. J. Carter, 'Valerius Maximus' in T. A. Dorey (ed.), *Empire and Aftermath*, *Silver Latin ii* (London, 1975), 26–56
Cichorius, *RS*	C. Cichorius, *Römische Studien* (Leipzig, 1922)
Continuity or Change	J. N. Adams and N. Vincent (eds.), *Early and Late Latin: Continuity or Change?* (Cambridge, 2016)
Crook	J. A. Crook, *Law and Life of Rome* (London, 1967)
Devine–Stephens	A. M. Devine and L. D. Stephens, *Latin Word Order: Structured Meaning and Information* (New York, 2006)
D–K	H. Diels and W. Kranz, *Die Fragmente der Vorsokratiker*, 9th edn. (Berlin, 1960)
Dyck	A. R. Dyck, *A Commentary on Cicero*: de officiis (Ann Arbor, MI, 1996)
Dyck, *Sex. Rosc.*	A. R. Dyck, *Cicero pro Sexto Roscio* (Cambridge, 2010)
ed.	J. Briscoe (ed.), *Valeri Maximi facta et dicta memorabilia* (Stuttgart–Leipzig, 1998)

Ernout–Meillet	A. Ernout and A. Meillet, *Dictionnaire étymologique de la langue latine*, 3rd edn. (Paris, 1951)
Faranda	R. Faranda, *Detti e fatti memorabili di Valerio Massimo* (Turin, 1971)
FRHist	T. J. Cornell (ed.) *et alii*, *The Fragments of the Roman Historians* (Oxford, 2013)
Goodyear	F. R. D. Goodyear, *The Annals of Tacitus, Books 1–6* (Cambridge, 1972–81)
Greenidge–Clay–Gray	A. H. J. Greenidge and A. M. Clay, *Sources for Roman History 133–70 BC*, 2nd edn., rev. E. W. Gray (Oxford, 1960)
Gruen, *LGRR*	E. S. Gruen, *The Last Generation of the Roman Republic* (Berkeley, CA, 1974)
Holford-Strevens, *Aulus Gellius*	L. A. Holford-Strevens, *Aulus Gellius: An Antonine Scholar and his Achievement* (Oxford, 2003)
H–S	J. B. Hofmann and A. Szantyr, *Lateinische Syntax und Stilistik* (Munich, 1965)
I.I.	*Inscriptiones Italiae*
ILLRP	A. Degrassi (ed.) *Inscriptiones Latinae liberae rei publicae*, 2 vols. (Florence, i, 2nd edn. 1965, ii, 1963)
ILS	H. Dessau (ed.), *Inscriptiones Latinae selectae* (Berlin, 1892–1916)
Jacoby	F. Jacoby, *Apollodors Chronik* (Berlin, 1902)
Kajanto	I. Kajanto, *The Latin cognomina* (Helsinki, 1965)
Kempf	K. Kempf, Teubner edn. (Leipzig, 1888)
Kempf (1854)	K. Kempf, edn. (Berlin, 1854)
Kirk–Raven	G. S. Kirk, J. E. Raven, and M. Schofield. *The Presocratic Philosophers*, 2nd edn. (Cambridge, 1983)
Kraus	C. S. Kraus, *Livy Ab urbe condita, book vi* (Cambridge, 1994)
Krenkel	W. Krenkel, *Lucilius, Satiren* (Leiden, 1970)
K–St	R. Kühner and C. Stegmann, *Ausführliche Grammatik der lateinischen Sprache*, 3rd edn., rev. A. Thierfelder (Leverkusen, 1955)
Leeman–Pinkster–Nelson	A. D. Leeman, H. Pinkster, and H. L. W. Nelson, *M. Tullius Cicero, de oratore libri iii*, ii–iii (Heidelberg, 1985–9)
Leeman–Pinkster–Wisse	A. D. Leeman, H. Pinkster, and J. Wisse, *M. Tullius Cicero, de oratore libri iii*, iv (Heidelberg, 1996)
Lewis	R. G. Lewis, *Asconius, Commentaries on Speeches by Cicero* (Oxford, 2006)
LGPN	P. M. Fraser, E. Matthews *et al.*, *A Lexicon of Greek Personal Names* (Oxford, 1987–2013)
Liviana	J. Briscoe, *Liviana* (Oxford, 2018)
L–S–J	H. G. Liddell, R. Scott, and H. S. Jones, *A Greek–English Lexicon* (Oxford, 1940)
LTUR	E. M. Steinby (ed.), *Lexikon topographicum urbis Romae* (Rome, 1993–2000)
Magie	D. Magie, *Roman Rule in Asia Minor* (Princeton, NJ, 1950)
Marshall	B. A. Marshall, *A Historical Commentary on Asconius* (Columbia, MO, 1985)
Mommsen, *StR*	T. Mommsen, *Römisches Staatsrecht* (Leipzig, i–ii, 3rd edn., 1887, iii. 1887–8)

MRR	T. R. S. Broughton, *The Magistrates of the Roman Republic* (New York–Atlanta, GA, 1951–86)
Münzer, *Plinius*	F. Münzer, *Beiträge zur Quellenkritik der Naturgeschichte des Plinius* (Berlin, 1897)
Münzer, *RA*	F. Münzer, *Römische Adelsparteien und Adelsfamilien* (Stuttgart, 1920); references are also given to T. Ridley (tr.), *Roman Aristocratic Parties and Families* (Baltimore, MD–London, 1999)
Naiden	F. S. Naiden, *Ancient Supplication* (New York, 2006)
Neue–Wagener	F. Neue and C. Wagener, *Formenlehre der lateinischen Sprache*, 3rd edn. (Leipzig, 1892–1905)
Nisbet	R. G. M. Nisbet, *M. Tulli Ciceronis in L. Calpurnium Pisonem oratio* (Oxford, 1961)
Nisbet and Hubbard	R. G. M. Nisbet and M. Hubbard, *A Commentary on Horace, Odes 1, 2* (Oxford, 1970, 1978)
Oakley	S. P. Oakley, *A Commentary on Livy Books vi–x* (Oxford, 1997–2005)
$OCD^{2, 3, 4}$	*Oxford Classical Dictionary*, 2nd edn., ed. N. G. L. Hammond and H. H. Scullard, 3rd edn., ed. S. Hornblower and A. Spawforth, 4th edn., ed. S. Hornblower, A. Spawforth, and E. Eidenow (Oxford, 1970, 1996, 2012)
Ogilvie	R. M. Ogilvie, *A Commentary on Livy, Books 1–5* (Oxford 1965)
OLD	P. G. W. Glare (ed.), *The Oxford Latin Dictionary* (Oxford, 1968–82)
ORF	E. Malcovati (ed.), *Oratorum Romanorum fragmenta*, 4th edn. (Turin, 1976)
Otón Sobrino	E. Otón Sobrino, *Léxico de Valerio Máximo* (Madrid, 1977–91)
Packard	D. W. Packard, *A Concordance to Livy* (Cambridge, MA, 1968)
Pease	A. S. Pease, *M. Tulli Ciceronis de diuinatione libri duo* (Darmstadt, 1973)
Pinkster	H. Pinkster, *The Oxford Latin Syntax*, i (Oxford, 2015)
Powell	J. G. F. Powell, *Cicero, Cato maior de senectute* (Cambridge, 1988)
RE	*Real-Encyclopädie der classischen Altertumswissenschaft*
Rhodes	P. J. Rhodes, *A Commentary on the Aristotelian* ATHENAION POLITEIA (Oxford, 1981)
RRC	M. H. Crawford, *Roman Republican Coinage* (Cambridge, 1974)
RS	M. H. Crawford (ed.), *Roman Statutes* (London, 1996)
Schullian, *CTC*	D. Schullian, 'Januarius Nepotianus', 'Julius Paris', 'Valerius Maximus', in F. E. Cranz and P. O. Kristeller (eds.), *Catalogus Translationum et Commentariorum* v (Washington, DC, 1984), 251–2, 253–5, 287–403
Scullard, *SA*	H. H. Scullard, *Scipio Africanus: Soldier and Politician* (London, 1970)
Shackleton Bailey	D. R. Shackleton Bailey, Loeb edn. (Cambridge, MA–London, 2000) (translations of individual passages are cited as 'SB')
Shackleton Bailey (1996)	D. R. Shackleton Bailey, 'On Valerius Maximus', *RFIC* 124 (1996) 175–84
Shackleton Bailey (2003)	D. R. Shackleton Bailey, 'New Readings in Valerius Maximus', *HSPh* 101 (2003), 473–81
Sherk	R. K. Sherk, *Roman Documents from the Greek East* (Baltimore, MD, 1969)

Sherwin-White, Roman Foreign Policy	A. N. Sherwin-White, *Roman Foreign Policy in the East, 168 B.C. to A.D. 1* (London, 1984)
Sileno	J. Briscoe, 'Some notes on Valerius Maximus'. *Sileno* 19 (1993), 395–408
Skidmore	C. Skidmore, *Practical Ethics for Roman Gentlemen: The Work of Valerius Maximus* (Exeter, 1996)
Skutsch	O. Skutsch, *The Annals of Q. Ennius* (Oxford, 1985)
Stadter	P. A. Stadter, *A Commentary on Plutarch's Pericles* (Chapel Hill, NC–London, 1989)
Stewart	A. Stewart, *Greek Scuplture: An Exploration* (New Haven, CT–London, 1990)
Suerbaum	W. Suerbaum (ed.), *Die archaische Literatur von den Anfängen bis Sullas Tod* (Munich, 2002)
SVF	H. F. A. von Arnim (ed.), *Stoicorum ueterum fragmenta* (Leipzig, 1903–24)
Syme, *AA*	R. Syme, *The Augustan Aristocracy* (Oxford, 1986)
Syme, *RP*	R. Syme, *Roman Papers* (Oxford, 1979–91)
Syme, *RR*	R. Syme, *The Roman Revolution* (Oxford, 1939)
Syme, *Sallust*	R. Syme, *Sallust* (Berkeley–Los Angeles, CA, 1964)
Texts and Transmission	L. D. Reynolds (ed.), *Texts and Transmission* (Oxford, 1983)
Themann-Steinke	A. Themann-Steinke, *Valerius Maximus: Ein Kommentar zum zweiten Buch der* Facta et dicta memorabilia (Trier, 2008)
TLL	*Thesaurus linguae Latinae*
vol. i, ii, iii. iv	J. Briscoe, *A commentary on Livy, Books xxxi–xxxiii, xxxiv–xxxvii, 38–40, 41–45* (Oxford, 1973, 1981, 2008, 2012)
Walbank	F. W. Walbank, *A Historical Commentary on Polybius* (Oxford, 1956–79)
Wardle	D. Wardle, *Valerius Maximus: Memorable Deeds and Sayings, Book I* (Oxford, 1998)
Wisse–Winterbottom–Fantham	J. Wisse, M. Winterbottom, and E. Fantham, *M. Tullius Cicero, de oratore libri iii*, v (Heidelberg, 2008)

Introduction

1 The Author

We know nothing of the life of Valerius Maximus (henceforward 'V.') beyond what can be gleaned from his work, and that is limited to the fact that he dedicated his work to the Emperor Tiberius (1 praef.), the references to his close friendship with Sex. Pompeius, discussed in section 2 (below), and the implication of 11 line 27 *tenet uisentes* and 12 lines 13–14 that he had visited Athens (see nn. ad locc.).

It is unlikely in the extreme that, as argued by Skidmore,[1] our author belonged to the patrician *gens* of the Valerii: no patrician, even if he had become one by adoption, would have talked of *mea paruitas* (1 praef. line 18), portrayed himself as a *cliens* of Sex. Pompeius (4.7. ext. 2),[2] or talked of the *gens Valeria* as he does at 8.15.5. Nor is it probable, though it cannot be totally excluded, that he was a freedman of a Valerius: one would not expect a freedman to identify himself as completely as V. does with the Roman people and their history; nor, one imagines, would a patrician Valerius have looked with favour on one of his former slaves taking a *cognomen* which had belonged to consuls in the early centuries of the Republic.[3] Alternatively, and less open to these objections, one of V.'s ancestors could have owed his enfranchisement to a Valerius in the period before the Social War; or V. could have been a descendant of a plebeian Valerius, L. Valerius Tappo, tribune in 195 and praetor in 192, C. Valerius Tappo, tribune in 188,[4] or one of the Valerii Triarii active in the late Republic.[5]

In the first chapter of book 8 V. displays a lack of understanding of Republican public law and the procedures of criminal trials;[6] his knowledge of private law, however, seems much better: perhaps he had some legal training and experience.

---

[1] Skidmore, 113–17; cf. Shackleton Bailey, i. 1.
[2] See pp. 2–3.
[3] Cf. *MRR* ii. 630.
[4] Cf. vol. ii. 43–4, iii. 124.
[5] Cf. *MRR* ii. 631.
[6] See 1. absol. 2, 3, 11, 12, damn. 3, 7, 2 lines 25–6, 6 lines 21–3, 7 lines 10–12 nn.

2 The Time of Writing

In his 1854 edition (pp. 3–8) Kempf argued that V. composed his work between AD 27 and 31. He based this on three passages. (i) 2.6.8: V. describes his visit to the island of Ceos, accompanying Sex. Pompeius, who was on his way to Asia; a nonagenarian lady was determined to end her life by poison in the presence of Pompeius. The latter will be the consul of AD 14 and Kempf argued that he was proconsul of Asia in 27. (ii) 6.1 praef.: V. refers to Julia (i.e. Livia; for *Iulia* alone meaning Livia cf. Tac. *ann.* 1.14.1, Dio 56.46.1) in a way that implies that she is still alive; Livia died in 29. (iii) 9.11. ext. 4 contains an address to someone who has been killed after plotting an act of *parricidium* against the emperor, which appears to be a reference to the condemnation of Sejanus in 31.

For over 120 years Kempf's view was unchallenged.[7] In 1975, however, Carter[8] tried to untie his argument and the process was taken further by Bellemore.[9] Carter argued that Sex. Pompeius was not necessarily proconsular governor of Asia when V. accompanied him to Ceos and that he may not be the consul of AD 14 but another Sex. Pompeius – he suggests the *eques* of Tacitus *ann.* 6.14.1 and Suetonius *Tib.* 57.2 (it is uncertain whether they are identical).

It must be acknowledged that the only clear evidence for the consul of 14 governing Asia is precisely 2.6.8, though we should expect him to have governed either Asia or Africa, the two senatorial provinces assigned to consulars. An Athenian inscription honouring Σέξτον Πομπήιον ἀνθύπατον,[10] which has been seen as marking a visit to Athens by the consul of 14 on his way to or from Asia, is as well, if not better, placed during an earlier governorship of Macedonia, apparently alluded to by Ovid in four passages of the fourth book of the *epistulae ex Ponto*.[11] Carter's doubts, however, are most implausible: V. says that the old lady thought that her death would be *Pompei praesentia clariorem* and describes Pompeius as *ut omnibus uirtutibus ita humanitatis laudibus instructissimus*. At 4.7. ext. 2, recording Pompeius' death,[12] V. compares Pompeius to Al-

---

7 It was restated by Helm, *RE* viiiA. 90–3.
8 Carter, 30–3.
9 J. Bellemore, *Antichthon* 23 (1989), 67–80.
10 *IG* ii², 4171.
11 *Pont.* 4.1.1–2, 5.33–8, 15.3–4, 41–2.
12 Carter's notion that by *iactura* (Shackleton Bailey proposed *iunctura* – in his edition he printed *iactura*, not mentioning the conjecture –, Watt *cultura*) V. may mean 'bankruptcy' or

---

Note: I here largely repeat what I wrote in *Sileno*, 398–402. Shackleton Bailey (i. 2) was kind enough to describe my arguments as conclusive, but Themann-Steinke (17–28) supports the position of Carter and Bellemore.

exander and himself to Hephaestion and says *cuius in animo uelut in parentum amantissimorum pectore laetior uitae meae status uiguit, tristior adquieuit, a quo omnium commodorum incrementa ultro oblata cepi, per quem tutior aduersus casus steti, qui studia nostra ductu et auspiciis suis lucidiora et alacriora reddidit.* Syme, comparing the language of 2.6.8 with *mea paruitas* at 1 praef. line 18, rightly says 'the language reflects the spirit of the client'.[13] Pompeius is a great man, not an *eques*.

Carter also claims that if Pompeius had indeed been the consul of 14, V. would have mentioned his 'distinguished connections and career'. But his name, including the *praenomen*, says enough about the latter,[14] and there was no reason to refer to the fact that Pompeius was consul in the year of Augustus' death, and that he and his colleague were the first to swear allegiance to Tiberius and then to administer the oath to the prefects of the praetorian guard and the *Annona*, senate, soldiers, and people.[15]

It is, then, extremely probable that Pompeius visited Ceos as proconsul of Asia, but 27 may be too late a date. Syme first chose 24/25, while allowing for the possibililiity of 23/24 or of a *biennium*,[16] but later thought that the two possible years were 24/25 and 25/26.[17]

Carter, followed by Bellemore, thought that in the preface to book 6 ch. 1 V. is referring not to Livia but to the fact that Tiberius, after being forced by Augustus to divorce Julia,[18] did not remarry, i.e. that the *sanctissimum Iuliae genialem torum* was the one shared by Tiberius and Julia, and asserts that 'Tiberius is ... Valerius' supreme invocation of Chastity'. Carter proceeds to tie himself in knots: 'An invocation to Chastity that explicitly embraced such a flagrant example of the very opposite would be tasteless and inept. But Valerius was a tasteless and inept writer and provincial enough not to have known of or forgotten a *cause célèbre* of fifteen or twenty years past'. That is absurd: the scandal of Julia, on which Velleius Paterculus waxed so eloquent,[19] cannot have been unknown to V. The same objection tells against the palaeographically attractive conjecture, found in three manuscripts used by Pighius,[20] gen<tis gen>ialem: V.

'loss of favour' is ludicrous: the perfects that precede and the beginning of the following chapter make it clear that Pompeius is dead.
13 *AA* 437.
14 His grandfather was first cousin of Pompeius Magnus. His relationship to Augustus (Dio 56.29.5) was not close enough for V. to feel any need to allude to it (cf. Syme, *AA* 414).
15 Tac. *ann.* 1.7.2.
16 *History in Ovid* (Oxford, 1978), 161, *ZPE* 53 (1983), 193.
17 *AA* 237–8.
18 Suet. *Tib.* 11.4.
19 2.100.3–5.
20 See p. 24.

cannot have praised *Pudicitia* for something she had so conspicuously failed to do. Carter's *pis-aller*, that even if the reference is to Livia, it does not follow that she is still alive, will not do either. V. could scarcely have referred to her so baldly if that were not the case.

We thus have a *terminus post quem* of 24 to 26 for book 2 and a *terminus ante quem* of 29 for book 6; I come now to the apostrophe in 9.11. ext. 4. Carter says that it stands awkwardly among the *externa exempla* of book 9 and suggests that it was a later addition, whether by V. himself or by someone else. The former view was adopted by Syme[21] 'a patent insertion, perhaps added on a second edition'. Perhaps: one may compare similar solutions to the problems of Livy's 'discovery' that Cornelius Cossus was consul, not a military tribune when he won the *spolia opima* and the final sentence of Tacitus *ann.* 2.61.[22] It is, though, not clearly the case that it is an *externum exemplum*. Carter's assertion results, I suspect, from the fact that the passage appears in editions as part of 9.11. ext. 4: if one looks at chapter 11 as a whole, one finds that after a brief preface, it contains seven Roman and three foreign *exempla* and concludes with the passage with which we are concerned, which is a conclusion to the whole chapter, not an ill-fitting addition to the non-Roman items.[23] The only reason, then, for regarding the passage as a later addition is that if V. was writing book 6 before the death of Livia in 29, he cannot have still been at work on book 9 in 31 or later. Since, of course, we have no idea of the rate at which he composed, that must be sheer speculation.

For Bellemore, however, all this is irrelevant. Accepting Carter's arguments about 2.6.8 and 6.1 praef., she believes that V. wrote in the early years of Tiberius' reign, arguing that 9.11. ext. 4 refers not to Sejanus but to Libo Drusus, whose trial for *maiestas* and subsequent suicide is described at length by Tacitus (*ann.* 2.27–32). She argues (i) that Libo was accused of plotting to murder the emperor himself, while the formal charge against Sejanus was conspiracy against the children of Germanicus, (ii) that *sidera suum uigorem obtinuerunt* is a reference to the accusation that Libo had consulted astrologers. There is a fatal argument against this: the object of V.'s wrath was *omni cum stirpe sua populi Romani uiribus obtritus*: Sejanus' children were killed, Libo's were not; Bellemore's claim that *omni cum stirpe sua* is 'empty rhetoric' smacks of desperation.[24]

---

21 *ZPE* loc. it. (n. 16).
22 Cf., respectively and conveniently, Badian in W. Schuller (ed.), *Livius* (Konstanz, 1993), 13–16, Syme, *ZPE* loc. cit. (n. 16).
23 Similarly, Bellemore says that 2.6.8 appears among the Roman *exempla*, not noticing, it seems, that the whole chapter consists of non-Roman items.
24 For Bellemore's further arguments, concerning 2.4.1, 6.1 praef., and the fact that very few *exempla* concern events that occurred after 42 BC, see *Sileno*, 402–4.

3 The Work

The authoritative manuscripts entitle V.'s work *Facta et dicta memorabilia*,[25] and editors (and translators) have followed suit, but it cannot be regarded as certain that this was V.'s own title. The work consists of nearly one thousand[26] short sections, mostly relating deeds and sayings of both Romans and non-Romans, mainly Greeks (labelled *ext(erna)* in editions),[27] though book 2 is concerned with social and political institutions. The work is the only extant instance of a literary genre also known from fragments of works entitled *Exempla* by Cornelius Nepos and C. Iulius Hyginus.[28]

The manuscripts divide the work into nine books, though originally the division may have been into ten.[29] In his preface (lines 4–5) V. describes his potential readers as those *documenta sumere uolentibus* and it has often been thought that his purpose was to provide material for orators and declaimers,[30] but it is preferable to conceive of a wider audience, including those interested in the material for its own sake.

The first five chapters of book 8 (the first is considerably longer than the other four put together) concern trials of various sorts. After a brief chapter on four men hoist by their own petard, chapter 7, the longest in the book, with the non-Roman examples, mainly philosophers, occupying 86% of it, deals with

---

25 A: *capitula librorum* (ed. 1), book 1 *inscriptio* and *subscriptio*, books 4, 9 *subscriptio*; L: book 1 *inscriptio* and *subscriptio*, book 4 *subscriptio*; G: book 1 *inscriptio* and *subscriptio*, books 3, 4, 9 *subscriptio*. The preface of Paris (P; ed. 638) has *Valerii Maximi libros dictorum et factorum memorabilium* ...

26 Bloomer (1) says 967: if this figure represents the total of the *exempla* numbers in each chapter in Kempf's 1888 edition, it should, on my calculations, be 957; if, on the other hand, it includes the lettered sub-divisions of 3.7.1, 5.3.2 and 6.3.1 it should be 971. See further p. 29 n. 101.

27 See p. 29.

28 Cf. *FRHist* i. 398, 480–1. For exemplarity in historiography, emphasized in recent years, see particularly J. D. Chaplin, *Livy's Exemplary History* (Oxford, 2000); cf. Oakley iii. 440–3, C. Damon, *Gnomon* 89 (2017), 71–3, reviewing A. Vasaly, *Livy's Political Philosophy* (Cambridge, 2015); for the importance of *exempla* in oratory cf. J. Martin, *Antike Rhetorik* (Munich, 1974), 119–24, Oakley loc. cit.

29 See p. 21, 1 amb. 2 n., for the subdivisions in modern editions pp. 28–9.

30 Bloomer (11–14; cf. 259, where, without naming him, he wrongly implies that Varro was not a senator (cf. *FRHist* i. 413) and that no non-senator had previously written history: possible candidates are Cassius Hemina, Coelius Antipater, Sempronius Asellio, Claudius Quadrigarius, and Valerius Antias; cf. *FRHist* i. 220, 256, 275, 288, 294) argues that it was primarily designed both for declaimers and for Italian and provincial 'imperial supporters and beneficiaries' (13); Skidmore (p. xvii, expanded in ch. 7) thinks that V.'s purpose was to provide 'moral exhortation and guidance'.

study and hard work; its opposite, leisure, is the subject of the short eighth chapter. Chapters 9 and 10 deal with the power of oratory and the importance of delivery and body-language. The following three chapters concern skills, mainly those of sculptors and painters. Chapter 13 presents examples of longevity, some of them impossible, chapter 14 concerns the desire for glory, while the book concludes with examples of great honours accorded to individuals.

4 Valerius' Sources

Bibliography.[31] F. Zschech, *De Cicerone et Liuio Valerii Maximi fontibus* (Berlin, 1865). M. Kranz, *Beiträge zur Quellenkritik des Valerius Maximus* (Posen, 1876), B. Krieger, *Quibus fontibus Valerius Maximus usus sit in eis exemplis enarrandis quae ad priora rerum Romanarum tempora petinent* (Berlin, 1888). S. Maire, *De Diodoro Siculo Valeri Maximi auctore* (Schoenberg, 1899). A. Klotz, *Hermes* 44 (1909), 198–214. C. Bosch, *Die Quellen des Valerius Maximus. Ein Beitrag zur Erforschung der Literatur der historischen Exempla* (Stuttgart, 1929). R. Helm, *Hermes* 74 (1939), 130–54, *RhM* 89 (1940), 241–75. A. Klotz, *SBAW* 1942, 5. R. Helm, *RE* viiiA (1955), 102–14. M. Fleck, *Untersuchungen zu den Exempla des Valerius Maximus* (Marburg, 1974). R. Guerrini, *RAL* 113 (1979), 152–66, *Studi su Valerio Massimo* (Pisa, 1981), 29–60. G. Maslakov, *ANRW* II. 32, 457–82. Bloomer, 59–146.

Students of V. have devoted more time and space to source criticism than to anything else except textual criticism. In the heyday of *Quellenkritik*, Klotz and Bosch expressed the view that Valerius's source was an earlier collection (two in the view of Bosch, one used by Cicero, the other the *exempla* of Hyginus, already suggested by Klotz) and that he never used Cicero and Livy directly (most implausible, in view of the frequent verbal correspondences, sometimes, to the point of plagiarism). That view was effectively demolished by Helm; the alternative was to search for the source of individual *exempla* (a starting point must be the passages of other authors, especially those earlier than Valerius, who relate the same matters); Helm denied that Valerius made direct use of Greek authors.[32]

---

31 I list here, in chronological order, works known to me which discuss V.'s sources (I exclude the brief discussions in Faranda (18–22), Wardle (15–18), and Themann-Steinke (42–3)). I do not engage with them in detail in what follows. Their views are reported and discussed by Bloomer, whose chapter on sources, not easy to use but generally convincing, constitutes almost a third of his book; see also Briscoe, *Bibliography*, Sources.
32 See p. 9.

4 Valerius' Sources — 7

In the commentary I indicate, whenever possible and normally in the introductory note to each *exemplum*, V.'s immediate source. When it cannot be determined, he will, for the most part, have used lost works (or lost parts of otherwise extant works): candidates include Varro, particularly the *antiquitates rerum humanarum* and the *de uita populi Romani*, Pomponius Rufus, whose *Collecta* are cited by V. at 4.4 praef., Hyginus (see above), and the lost books of Livy. There may also have been occasions when V. was not dependent on a written source: that applies particularly to events during his own lifetime, when he could have been present himself or have learnt about them from acquaintances; the latter could also have been the case with events a little before his own time. And for earlier periods there were, no doubt, people with a good historical knowledge from whom V. could have acquired information; if V. attended declamations, he could have heard or talked to some of them.

When V.'s source is an extant work, it is possible to see the ways in which V. has adapted it, recasting, adding, and omitting (as we have seen, V. often takes over his source's language).

In what follows, I bring together in summary form what I say, *exemplum* by *exemplum*, in the commentary about V.'s source; for notes concerning V.'s use of his source see Index, p. 253.

1. absol. 1. Livy 1.24–6.
1. absol. 2. Cic. *Brut.* 89–90.
1. absol. 3–12. uncertain.
1. absol. 13. Cic. *S. Rosc.* 64–5.
1. damn. 1. Livy 38.55.6.
1. damn. 2. Cic. *Rab. Perd.* 24
1. damn, 3. Cic. *Rab, perd.* 24–5
1. damn. 4. ? Livy 19.
1. damn. 5–6. uncertain.
1. damn. 7. ? Livy 60.
1. damn. 8. Varro.
1. amb. 1–2. uncertain.
2.1. Cic. *off.* 3.66.
2.2 uncertain.
2.3. uncertain.
2.4. ? oral source.
3.1. oral source.
3.2. oral source.
3.3. ? Livy 120.
4.1–3. ? Hyginus.
5.1. Cic. *Font.* 23.

5.2. Cicero (see n. ad loc.).
5.3. Cic. *Font.* 24.
5.4. Cic. *Corn.*
5.5. ? oral source, Livy 103.
5.6. ? Livy.
6.1. uncertain.
6.2. ? Livy 69, 77.
6.3. Livy 7.16.9.
6.4. ? Livy 73–4.
7.1. Livy 48–9.
7.2. Cic. *fin.* 3.7.
7.3. ? oral source.
7.4. uncertain.
7.5. ? V.'s own knowledge.
7.6–7. uncertain.
7. ext. 1. Cic. *de orat.* 1.260–1.
7. ext. 2. Cic. *fin.* 5.87, *Tusc.* 5.7 (among others).
7. ext. 3. Cic. *fin.* 5.87.
7. ext. 4. Cic. *fin.* 5.87, *Tusc.* 5.104 (among others).

7. ext. 5. uncertain.
7. ext. 6. uncertain.
7. ext. 7. Livy 24.34.8–11, 25.31.9–10.
7. ext. 8. ? Cic. *Cato* 26.
7. ext. 9. Cic. *Cato* 13; ? oral source.
7. ext. 10–11. uncertain.
7. ext. 12. uncertain; perhaps own knowledge.
7. ext. 13. uncertain.
7. ext. 14. Cic. *Cato* 26; uncertain.
7. ext. 15. Cic. *Cato* 21; Nep. *Them.* 10.1.
7. ext. 16. uncertain.
8.1. Cic. *de orat.* 2.22.
8.2. Cic. *de orat.* 2.217.
8. ext. 1–2. uncertain.
9.1. Cic. *Brut.* 54.
9.2. ? Livy 80.
9.3. uncertain.
9. ext. 1. uncertain.
9. ext. 2. Cic. *de orat.* 3.138; uncertain.
9 ext. 3. Cic. *Tusc.* 1.83.
10.1. Cic. *de orat.* 3.225.
10.2. uncertain.
10.3. Cic. *Brut.* 277–8.
10. ext. 1. Cic. *de orat.* 3.213.
11.1–2. uncertain.
11. ext. 1. Cic. *rep.* 1.25.
11. ext. 2. Cic. *fam.* 5.12.7.
11. ext. 3. Cic. *nat. deor.* 1.83.
11. ext. 4. uncertain; Livy 41.13.2.
11. ext. 5. uncertain.
11. ext. 6. Cic. *orat.* 74.
11. ext. 7. uncertain.
12.1. Cic. *Balb.* 45.
12. ext. 1. uncertain.
12. ext. 2. Cic. *de orat.* 1.62.
12. ext. 3. uncertain.
13. See p. 193; the references that follow are to be understood as additional to the common source of V. and Pliny.
13.1. Cic. *Cato* 60.
13.2. Cic. *Cato* 30.
13.3. Livy 30.26.7; own addition.
13.4–6. common source of V. and Pliny.
13. ext. 1. Livy 24.4.4; Cic. *Cato* 34, Livy 50.
13.2–3. common source of V. and Pliny.
13.4. Cic. *Cato* 69; Pollio (*FRHist* 56F1).
13.5–7. common source of V. and Pliny.
14.1. Cic. *Arch.* 22.
14.2. Cic. *Arch.* 27.
14.3. Cic. *Arch.* 24.
14.4. uncertain.
14.5. ? oral source.
14.6. uncertain.
14. ext. 1. uncertain; Cic. *Arch.* 20.
14.2. uncertain.
14.3–5. uncertain.
15.1–2. uncertain.
15.3. Livy 29.10.4–11.8, 14.5–14.
15.4. uncertain.
15.5. Livy 7.26.
15.6–8. uncertain.
15.9. Cic. *Manil.* 59.
15.10. uncertain.
15.11. Livy 25.37.5–6.
15.12. ? Varro.
15. ext. 1. Cic. *nat. deor.* 1.10; uncertain.
15. ext. 2. Cic. *de orat.* 1.103, 3.129, *fin.* 2.1.
15. ext. 3. Cic. *diu.* 1.88.
15. ext. 4. uncertain.

The book consists of 133 *exempla*; at 7. ext. 14–15, 9. ext. 2, 11. ext. 4, and 15. ext. 1 the second indication refers to a separate part of the *exemplum*. The list, therefore, contains 138 items. 'uncertain' occurs on 57 occasions, 'oral source' (with or without a question mark) on seven, and 'own knowledge' twice (by 'own knowledge' I mean something that V. had known for some time and for which he did not need a specific source; it may, of course, have come originally from either a written or an oral one). The specific sources I have listed, with two exceptions (Nepos at 7. ext. 15, Pollio at 13. ext. 4), consist entirely of Cicero and Livy.

In the *exempla externa* I indicate that V.'s source is uncertain on twenty-three occasions, eight of which are in ch. 7. There is no reason to question the view of Helm and Bloomer that V. did not use Greek authors directly (or, at least, that it can never be shown that he did) and that for historical matters Pompeius Trogus was a principal source.[33] In ch. 7. ext., however, four of the *exempla* concern philosophers, three literary figures, and it seems necessary to posit an otherwise unattested source, probably writing in Latin.

5 Language and Style

V. writes in a highly rhetorical and often overblown style, and many of those who have talked about his style have said little more than that, sometimes berating him for it.[34] Until recently the only work providing extensive detail was Lundberg's dissertation, written at the beginning of the twentieth century.[35] It consists mainly of lists of nouns, adjectives, adverbs, and verbs that occur first or only in Valerius, are used (or not used) by Livy or Velleius, taken from poets, used by Cicero or Caesar with different meanings or constructions, or the same ones but only rarely.[36]

Bloomer[37] devoted most of the final chapter of his book to the subject, not aiming to provide a full analysis, but making some sensible remarks about vocabulary, word order, colon division, and prose rhythm, as well as seeking to

---

[33] Themann-Steinke (86) wrongly attributes to me the view that V. had read Greek writers; on p. xxviii, to which she refers, I am talking only about occasional Greek words in the text. Carter is similarly misrepresented.
[34] E.g. Carter, 48.
[35] E. Lundberg, *De elocutione Valeri Maximi* (Falun, 1906). The preface mentions some earlier works which discuss the subject.
[36] Bloomer comments (233) that it is 'not an analysis but a collection of categories and instances', which is true but somewhat unfair, given the date at which it was written.
[37] 233–54. Faranda (29–31) merely mentions a number of linguistic innovations.

explain why V. wrote as he did. An important contribution has been made by Themann-Steinke: her commentary on book 2 devotes a great deal of attention to matters of language and style, and in the introduction she lists items of interest under the headings of morphology, syntax, lexicology, and stylistic devices; there follows an extended analysis of what results.[38] Similarly, I list here, under a number of headings, the linguistic and stylistic phenomena discussed at various places in the commentary. The coverage provided by *TLL* (now publishing fascicles of the volumes containing N and R), the PHI database, and Otón Sobrino's lexicon to V. mean that studies of this kind now have a much firmer evidential base.

Almost all Latin writers are linguistically or stylistically innovative to a greater or lesser extent and my purpose is to define that extent as far as possible. I list here, under a number of headings, the phenomena discussed at various places in the commentary (references are to chapters and lines).

(i) Innovations. These are words, forms of words, words used in a certain sense or with a certain construction, phrases, expressions, which do not occur in earlier writers. I include phenomena found also in Velleius Paterculus, since the two were contemporaries and priority cannot be determined. 'unique' indicates items found only in V., 'hapax' those found only this once.

(ii) Words or usages found in Cicero and/or Livy, but rarely or never in other writers before V. In some cases Cicero or Livy is V.'s source and the word has simply been taken over by him. But since Cicero and Livy were his two main identifiable sources (see p. 9), it is quite likely that he was acquainted with their work as a whole and influenced by it.

(iii) Words or usages found before V. but not in Cicero or Livy.

(i) Innovations

1.4. *alter ... alter* with the first referring to an individual, the second to a collective noun. Apparently unique.
1.6. *fortis* 'severe'.
1.31. *iniuria* to describe a person. Perhaps unique. Cf. 1.122.
1.50. *deformiter*. Not found before V.
1.51. *subnectere*. In sense of 'add' not found before V. In sense of 'bind underneath' it occurs in Virgil and Ovid.

---

[38] Unfortunately, some of the items in the first two categories are not matters of morphology or syntax; her use of 'classical' to refer only to writers of the late Republic and her talk of 'golden' and 'silver' Latin is strangely old-fashioned. Some of her categories (e.g. military language (58)) contain items which are in no way remarkable.

1.56–7. *uictoriamque in ipsa uictoria perdidit*. The expression appears to be unique.
1.50. *ualere* + dative of the gerundive. Innovation if the paradosis is correct.
1.88. *fragor*. If the paradosis is correct, unique metaphorical use ('fanfare of glory' SB) of the word.
1.122–3. *iactura* to describe a person. Unique.
1.126. *incursus*. Metaphorical use ('onslaught of a conviction' SB). V. uses it thus on eight occasions.
1.135. *in cenam fieri* (missed by *TLL*).
1.150. *relegare* 'transfer a matter to another body'.
1.151. *consideranter*. Unique before late antiquity.
1.155. If paradosis is correct, unique use of genitive of the gerund.
2.7. (also book 1 praef.) *inclutus* not meaning 'of ancient fame'. Motivated innovation.
(2.12–26. There are an unusually large number of points of linguistic note in this *exemplum* (see also pp. 101–4 below): perhaps V. was seeking to reemphasize the unusual, indeed extraordinary, nature of the case of Otacilia and Visellius).
2.14. *commercium libidinis* as euphemism for a sexual relationship.
2.19. *destrictus* adjective.
2.39. *acceptum ferri*. Influenced by use of *ferre* in accounting.
3.10. *latratus* of persons. Only instance before late antiquity.
3.17–18, 9.44. *repraesentare* 'revive'.
3.21. (?) *sequi* 'attain'.
5.15. *stipendium* used metaphorically. Unique in this sense.
5.21. *umbo* used metaphorically. Unique.
6.3. *equidem* introducing a co-ordinate part of a sentence. If the paradosis is correct, perhaps unique.
6.6. *heredem tollere*. Unique.
6.19. *perrogare*. In the sense of carry a law only in Paris (1.2. ext. 4) and schol. Bob. Cic. p. 149 St.
7.3–4. *cumulus* 'peak'. Also at 3.1. praef., 6.8.7, and 7.1.1.
7.4. *duramentum*. Also at 2.7.10.
7.26. *interpellere ne*. Unique.
7.48–9. *consummatio*. First in V. and Velleius.
7.51. *expresse* 'distinctly'. Elsewhere only in the grammarian Consentius.
7.62. *actus* 'performance'. Unique (*TLL* wrong).
7.67–8. *exactissimae*. Superlative of *exactus* (participle used adjectivally first in Augustan writers).
7.102. *miles* used metaphorically with genitive.
7.141. *citerior* = *propior, anterior*.

(also 13.63) *uiuacitas* 'longevity'.
8.10. *lectitare* 'collect'. elsewhere only in Arnobius (cf. on 7.24).
10.12. *referre* 'transfer'. Innovation if paradosis is correct.
11.12. *coniectare* 'predict'.
12.8. *professor*.
12.12. *professio* 'profession'. First in V. and Velleius.
12.18. *ansula*.
13.14–15. *consulare imperium* = *consulatus*. Unique.
13.63. *neruosus* 'vigorous'.
13.76. *parum benigne acceptus*. Negative formulation unique.
14.51. *insatiabilis* + gen.
14.76. *disicere* 'spread abroad'. Unique.
15.29. *candidatus* + gen. of name of office.

(ii) Words or usages found in Cicero and/or Livy, but rarely or never in other writers before V.

1. praef. 2. *pro* causal (if reading is right). Once in Cicero.
1.23, 8.9, 9.7. *namque* in second position. Once in Varro and frequently in Livy.
1.25. *fomentum*. Twice in Cicero. Medical term.
1.81. *impugnare* 'accuse'. Twice in Cicero.
1.83. *confodere* used metaphorically. Once in Livy.
1.125. *deuerticulum* of a digression in a work of literature. The sense is present in Livy.
1.130. *concidere* used metaphorically. Frequent in Cicero.
1.151. *sustinere* + infinitive 'to endure (doing something)'. Once in Livy.
2.9. *praedictum* 'instruction'. Once in Livy.
2.20. *inuerecundus*. Once each in Plautus, fragment of tragedy, Cicero, Sallust, Horace.
2.40. *manare* + ablative. Once in Cicero; the transmitted reading has been challenged in both places.
2.43. *excessus*. Cicero.
5.32. *cuias*. Plautus, Ennius, Accius, once each in Cicero and Livy.
6.5. *uicissitudo*. Common in Cicero, otherwise only once each in Terence and Livy.
6.23. *constringere* used metaphorically. Cicero, Livy, Manilius.
7.29. *actor* 'pleader of cases'. Cicero and Caelasius.
7.70. *sorbere* used metaphorically. Once in Cicero.
7.126. *imperium* 'order'. Ennius, Plautus, Publilius Syrus, Livy.

7.127. *liniamentum* 'geometrical line'. Cicero, twice (in one the reading is uncertain). Cf. on 11.56–7.
7.131. *peruicax*. Terence, Accius, Horace, Livy; only here in V.
8.9. *umbilicus* 'pebble'. Cicero (V.'s source).
8.14. *calculus* 'gaming pieces'. Cicero, Ovid (word of gaming register; see also on 8.20 below).
8.19. *filiolus*. Plautus, Cicero (coupling with *paruolus* once in Plautus).
9.9. *consternatio*. Livy.
9.23. *peregrinari*. *rhet. Her.*, Cicero, Caelius, Sallust.
9.45–6. *ingenerare*. Cicero, Catullus.
10.11. *temperamentum*. Once in Cicero.
11.19. *securitas*. Cicero, Velleius.
11.38. *lineamentum* 'outlines', of works of art. Once in Cicero.
12.1. *disputator*. Once in Cicero; no other examples before late antiquity.
12.4. *praediatorius*, Once in Cicero.
12.5. *consultor* 'seeker of advice'. Cicero three times, Horace.
12.13. *armamentarium*. Cicero, Varro, Livy.
13.32. *strictim* 'briefly'. Cicero, Varro.
13.43. *durare* 'hold out'. Plautus, Lucretius, Ovid, Livy.
14.66. *innotescere*. Ovid, Livy; only here in V.
15.5. *beneficentissimus* twice in Cicero (*beneficissimus* in Cato); only instance in V. *honoratissimus*. Once each in Plautus and Cicero, five times in Livy.
15.13. *hodieque*. Once in Livy, Vitruvius, and Velleius.

(iii) Words or usages found before V. but not in Cicero or Livy

1.38. *nubes* used metaphorically. Once in Ovid.
1.135. *omasum*. Naevius, Horace (word of culinary register).
2.13. *corripere* of disease. Lucretius, Virgil, Manilius.
2.19. *feneratrix*. Title of play of Plautus (there were not many female moneylenders).
5.9. *proscindere*. In prose, only Varro.
7.2. *uiuax*. Afranius, Augustan poetry.
7.96. *ex facili*. Ovid.
7.148. *extrahere* of drawing water. Plautus, *bell. Alex.*
8.14. *alueus* 'gaming board'. Varro, Vitruvius.
12.15. *institutio* 'arrangement'. Varro, Vitruvius.
15.58. *auspicari* 'embark on'. Inscription of AD 11, Velleius.
15.99. *instituere* + acc. and inf. Virgil, Velleius.

We thus see that of the eighty-three items listed, forty are innovations by V., thirty-three words or usages found before V. in Cicero and/or Livy but never or rarely in other writers, and ten words or usages found before V. in other writers but avoided by both Cicero and Livy. These lists, of course, concern only book 8 and the figures for the whole work will be very much higher, though in some cases phenomena in book 8 also occur in other books. We may conclude that in matters of lexicology (only a few items concern syntax and phraseology) V. was extremely innovative and that to a considerable extent he was influenced, consciously or not, by Cicero and Livy.

I append two lists referring to notes dealing with other matters of lexicological, syntactical, and stylistic interest.

(iv) Other lexicological matters

1.5. *immaturus*. Only twice in V.
1.6–7. *consanguineus*. Never in Cicero's speeches.
1.26. *truci uoltu*. Anticipation of Tacitus; perhaps used of Tiberius in his lifetime.
1.31. *si quidem* 'since'. 35 instances in V.
1.36. *causae dictio*. Seven times in V.
2.27. *animosus*. V. is very fond of it (16 instances), but relatively rare before him.
2.42. *hoc/eo/quodam loci*. V. very fond of it.
2.43. *minutus*. Avoided by Caesar and Livy, only instance in V.
15.5. *beneficus*. Only instance in V.

(iv) Other linguistic or stylistic matters

alliteration 2.16
antithesis 1.31–2, 35–6
dubitatio comparatiua 1.31 (V. very fond of it)
dum + perfect indicative (three times in book 8, if paradosis is correct) 1.56
indicative retained in *oratio obliqua* 9.36
participial construction 7.121
word order 1.24, 26, 9.26
zeugma 5.19–20

6 Text

6a The Direct Tradition

There are over six hundred manuscripts of V. (over eight hundred if one includes the epitomators (see below pp. 21–23), translations, and commentaries (see Schullian, *CTC*)), more than of any other Latin prose author except Priscian.[39] The vast majority, of course, were written in the 14th and 15th centuries, but thirty predate 1200.[40] Of these, only the three oldest, Berne, Burgerbibliothek 366 (A), Florence, Biblioteca Medicea Laurenziana, Ashburnham 1899 (L) (both written in northern France in the ninth century[41]), and Brussels, Bibliothèque Royale 5336 (G) (11th century) possess authority; the remainder are either descended from A (some before, some after it had been corrected from Paris; see below), or are manuscripts related to G but contaminated from the tradition of A.[42]

Kempf, in his first edition,[43] recognized that A was the oldest known manuscript of V.; of the other five manuscripts he used (Berlin, Staatsbibliothek, lat. F. 46 (D), 48 (C), Wolfenbüttel, Herzog August Bibliothek, Gud. lat. 39 (F), 61 (E), 166 (Γ)), all but the last (twelfth/thirteenth century[44]) belong to the renaissance. Some thirty years later he undertook a new edition for Teubner (Kempf's first edition was published by Reimer in Berlin) and was about to send it to the

---

[39] For a complete list see D. M. Schullian in E. Cecchini, A. Gattucci, P. Parroni, P. Peruzzi (eds.), *Miscellanea Augusto Campana* (Padua, 1981), 695–728. Dorothy Schullian devoted herself to the transmission and reception of V. for nearly fifty years, her work culminating in the articles in *CTC* v. 251–5, 287–403.
[40] See B. Munk Olsen, *L'étude des auteurs classiques latins aux xie et xiie siècles*, ii Paris (1985), 659–68.
[41] Munk Olsen, op. cit., 662–3.
[42] For claims that two later manuscripts, Rome, Biblioteca Corsiniana 43 D 37 and Trapani, Biblioteca Comunale V.b, 6, possess authority cf. ed. pp. xvi–xvii.
[43] Kempf (1854), 78–80. It had previously been used, sporadically and inaccurately, by Coler (cf. p. 25, Kempf (1854), 73).
[44] Munk Olsen, op. cit., 668.

Note: This section is a revised English version of the Preface to my edition. The only detailed study of the manuscripts is that of C. J. Carter, *The Manuscript Tradition of Valerius Maximus*, a Ph.D. thesis submitted to the University of Cambridge in 1968; it is detailed and painstaking but difficult both to access and use. It was supervised by A. H. McDonald and based on the latter's methodologically dubious system of selective intensive collation (cf. McDonald, *OCD*^{2} 1049; in the third edition the article was replaced by a much better one by M. D. Reeve). Cf. P. K. Marshall *Texts and Transmission*, 428–30, a generally reliable survey, though Marshall makes the absurd claim that because Carter had demonstrated the unreliability of Kempf's 1888 edition (see below), much of the subsequent work based on it could safely be ignored.

publisher when he learnt that another old manuscript of V. was among those recently acquired by the Medicean Library in Florence from the library of Lord Ashburnham in Battle (Sussex); the Medicean catalogue dated it to the eighth century, but Kempf was advised by F. Rühl, who had seen the manuscript on a number of occasions, that it in fact belonged to the ninth. He did not, however, collate it himself but used a collation made for him by the young Bruno Keil.[45] That collation, inevitably, contained a number of inaccuracies, many, but doubtless far from all, of which are corrected in my edition.

Kempf showed with little difficulty that L and A were almost certainly twins.[46] Nearly fifty years later Schullian[47] discovered G, the third oldest manuscript. It was written in the eleventh century, probably at Gembloux, to whose monastery it later belonged[48] (hence its siglum). Schullian argued, in my view rightly, that G did not derive from the source of AL but possessed authority equal to that of their source. Marshall,[49] however, thought that G's immediate source was a third copy of the source of AL (in view of its date, and because there are a number of manuscripts related to G but not, it seems, derived from it, it is unlikely that G was copied directly from the common source of all three manuscripts).

I argued in my edition, and continue to believe, that Schullian was right. There are a considerable number of passages where G alone has, certainly or probably, the correct reading. Many of them could have been conjectures, of G or his immediate source, but in some cases that seems unlikely; they were rather transmitted readings which had been corrupted in the source of AL. On p. viii of my preface I produced a list of nine such passages: 1.5.6, 2.7.15, 8.5, 3.6.1, 4.4.5, 6.3.1a, 5.3, 7.2.6, 6.5. Winterbottom, reviewing the edition,[50] found the list unimpressive, referring in particular to 1.5.6, where Kempf (1854) correctly restored Κατωβασίλεια: G has ΚΑΤΩΒΑCΙΛΕΑ, AL ΚΑΤΩbasilea. Winterbottom argued that though Carolingian scribes may not have known Greek, they were conversant with the Greek alphabet (*sc.* G or his source would have been capable of emending the hybrid form which appears in AL): to expand what I said on p. xxviii of my preface, when V. wrote Greek, the majuscule forms that appear in all three manuscripts make it clear that neither their scribes nor those of their sources were fully conversant with the Greek alphabet and either were

---

[45] See Kempf, pp. xx–xxiii, T. Stangl, *Philologus* 45 (1886), 201–36.
[46] Kempf, pp. xxiii–xxvii.
[47] *CPh* 32 (1937), 349–59.
[48] f. 1ʳ has *cenobium Gemblacense me habet*. It is almost certainly Pighius' *codex Gemblacensis* (Kempf (1854, 72) realised its quality, but wrongly thought it inferior to his Γ, to which it is related).
[49] op. cit. (General note on p. 15.)
[50] *SCI* 18 (1999), 191–4.

unable to copy Greek letters correctly or, if their exemplar was already corrupt, to correct it. If the transmitted text had been what appears in AL, it would be surprising if G would have succeeded in transliterating the Latin letters.[51] At 4.1 ext. 7, where G, wrongly, has ΦΙΛΟΣΟΦΙΑ, AL the correct ΣΟΦΙΑ, the former may have been a variant in α, taken up by G but not by the source of AL.

None of the passages I listed comes from book 8. Here I have counted 86 places where G's reading differs from that shared by AL, but in ten of which G is certainly correct, possibly so in a further nine. In seven of these, so it seems to me, G may have preserved a transmitted reading. Four of these, however, are proper names, which can legitimately be used for the present purpose, though not as evidence for shared errors; for detailed discussion of all cases except 7.136, 13.49, and 9.27 see nn. ad locc.

1.129. *Aquillio* G : *Aquilio* AL.
3.4. *motusque* G : *partesque* A^c : *mortuusque* L.
7.80. *Socratem* AL^{c}P : *Socraten* G
7.136, 13.49. *Isocratis* G : *His-* AL (in the former G^c corrected the ending to *-es*). It seems unlikely that G would have heard of Isocrates or that if *Is-* had been transmitted, A and L would have independently corrupted it to *His-*.
7.171. *Xerxen* G : *Xerxem* AL
9.27. *Solon* G : *Solo* AL. See 7 line 227 n.
15.2–3. *operum* G : *honerum* A : *onerum* L

There are, moreover a very large number of places where AL are corrupt and G shares a true, or probably true, reading with the correctors of the former (sometimes only one of them; occasionally, of course, such a reading is, certainly or probably, incorrect): in book 8 the indications 'A^{c}L^{c}G' or 'A^{c}G' or 'L^{c}G' appear in my apparatus no fewer than 172 times (on thirteen occasions G's reading is also found in P, in eight of them as well as in A^c (five), L^c (one), or both (two).

Many of the corrections are obvious, and even when they are less so, if they were made independently in A and/or L, there is no reason why G should not have arrived at the same conclusion. Nevertheless, since the agreement in error of AL shows that the corruption stood in their source, if G was also derived from that source, it would be surprising that G or its immediate source succeeded so often in arriving at the truth before or during the copying process.

There is, however, an obstacle to believing that G is a twin of the source of AL. There are eighteen passages where L has what is indubitably the truth,

---

51 On western knowledge of Greek in the Carolingian period cf. L. D. Reynolds and N. G. Wilson, *Scribes and Scholars*, 3rd edn. (Oxford, 1991), 118–19.

while A and G share a corruption. The most remarkable is 4.3 praef., where in A and G there is a manifest lacuna between *flagrat* and *contrarios*, filled in various ways, first by A^c, before the discovery of L (which had no known descendants), which reads *flagrat uis habitat bella gignuntur fauentibus igitur linguis*. It cannot be doubted (and no one ever has) that this is what V. wrote: this metaphorical use of *habitare*, with an abstract noun as subject, occurs five times elsewhere in V. (1 damn. 1, 9. ext. 2, 5.5.2, 6.9. ext. 1, 9.5. ext. 2), before him only three times in Cicero and once in Manilius (*TLL* vi. 3.2477.82 ff.). Moreover, as Michael Reeve observed to me some twenty years ago, a scribe seeking to fill the lacuna would have done so merely with *fauentibus* (as Kempf (1854, 332) wrongly thought that Andreas Schottus had reported from a manuscript which, as Kempf later saw (p. xxv n. 1), was in fact L. The number of such passages, however, is far too small to allow the conclusion that it is A and G who are twins, with L a twin of their immediate source. The explanation of 4.3. praef. must rather be that the words (perhaps the content of two lines) were originally omitted in the common source of ALG, which I call α, but subsequently added in the margin, to be picked up by L but ignored by both A and the source of G. The same will have been the case at 1.1.16 where L's *tensa*, with *templo* in AG, is guaranteed by both Paris and Nepotianus, and perhaps 4.5.2 (*Varro* L : om. *AG*), though here the scribe may have remembered 3.4.4, and 7.8.7 (*Balbum* LP : *bellum* A : *bello* G). At 4.5.3 *C.* could easily have been independently omitted by A and G before *Cicereium*. All the other instances could have been conjectures by L. I do not include 1.1.1 *ciuitatem accepisset nomine*, 1.5.3 *obuenisset*, 4.3.7 om. *uasa* (easily done before *uidisse*), 7 ext. 2 om. *in*, where I do not regard L's reading as correct.

This, therefore, is the stemma:

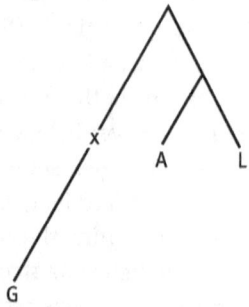

I adopted the following practice in my apparatus: if AG agree against L or LG against A in an indubitably true reading, I did not cite L or A respectively; if, however, AL so agreed against G, I cited the latter, except when the error was corrected by G himself (see p. 20). In the commentary, while, of course, my stemma influences my approach, I allow, explicitly or tacitly, for the possibility that my stemma is wrong and that a reading of G differing from AL does not possess potential authority.

Schnetz,[52] on the basis of errors in transcribing individual letters, thought that A and L were copied from an insular manuscript, perhaps at Fulda, and that the latter's exemplar was a manuscript written in majuscule.

A, Lupus, and Paris

In 1828 Cardinal Angelo Mai, the Prefect of the Vatican Library, published, from Vat. Lat. 4029, ff. 79^v–148 (P)[53] the text of Iulius Paris' epitome of V.[54] and Kempf[55] realised that many of the variant readings, both interlinear and marginal, in A were taken from Paris, often indicated as such by *u.* (= *uetustus*, once thus in full), *I* or *I.P.* (= *Iulius* or *Iulius Paris*), *ADB* or *BR.* or *br.* (= *(ad)breuiator*) or *C.T.* (= *C. Titius*; once *C. Titus*; see p. 21 below).

In A, L and G 1.1. ext.[56] 4 *comperit* is followed by 1.4. ext. 2 *Deiotaro uero*. In A a later hand (A³ in my apparatus) added *eam Delphis portandam*, with the last word corrected to *perferendam*, and all Kempf's later manuscripts have *eam Delphos perferendam*. In 1471 the edition published at Mainz filled the lacuna with the text of twenty-four *exempla* taken from Paris' epitome;[57] its source, however, was not the Vatican manuscript but a manuscript of V. himself, descending from A: the corrector of A had copied these *exempla* from Paris and placed them before the text of V.; they are now reduced to fragments, containing parts of 1.1. ext. 4–8, 2 tit., 1, 3, 5, 3.2–4.

As Ludwig Traube, the best palaeographer of his generation, who died at the age of 46, saw and Joseph Schnetz, Traube's pupil, demonstrated in detail, that corrector was one of the outstanding scholars of the Carolingian age, Servatus Lupus, of Ferrières (near Montargis, in the Département de Loiret).[58] Schnetz

---

52 1904, 4–9; Billanovich (*Aevum* 30 (1956), 322–3) agreed, but Carter dissented.
53 For manuscripts derived from it see Schullian, *CTC*, 253.
54 *Scriptorum ueterum noua collectio* iii (Rome, 1828), part 3, 1–89 ; the *fragmentum de praenominibus* (cf. p. 21) is on pp. 90–2.
55 1854, 78–9, 1888, pp. xiv–xv.
56 At ed. p. xii I omitted 'ext.'.
57 For their presence in other early editions see ed. p. xii n. 19; cf. p. 206 n. 106. Kempf (1854) was the first to add the version of Nepotianus (see p. 21).
58 L. Traube, *Vorlesungen und Abhandlungen* iii (Munich, 1920), 3–6, J. Schnetz, *Ein Kritiker des Valerius Maximus im 9. Jahrhundert* (Nauburg, 1901).

showed that Lupus corrected A twice, once before, once after he had obtained a manuscript of Paris. In the first period, between 859 and 862, he dictated excerpts from V. to his pupil Heiric of Auxerre: those excerpts survive in nine manuscripts (cf. Schullian, *MAAR* 12 (1935), 153–84) and they show no trace of readings taken from Paris. Soon afterwards, using Paris, he corrected A again. P was corrected by Heiric,[59] and Billanovich[60] thought that Lupus used a manuscript lent to him by Heiric, which he had obtained from Irish monks at Laon. What is certain is that Lupus' corrections were not taken from P: otherwise he would not, before the *exempla* taken from Paris, have called the manuscript *uetustus* or attributed some of his corrections to '*u.*'.[61] Moreover, on some occasions Lupus' correction is not identical with what stands in P; a notable case is 7.2.1, where Lupus reports a *titulus* absent from P. It is, in fact, totally inapplicable to what follows in V. and it must be that the scribe of P omitted it. I prefer to think that Lupus used the source of P, and that Heiric had the latter copied after the death of Lupus at the end of 862.

There is no doubt that the majority of the corrections in A, both before and after he had obtained a copy of Paris, are by Lupus. Some of the former, however, are by the original scribe and on a number of occasions it is not possible to be sure about their authorship; I therefore cited all of them as 'A^c' and do so again now.

L

Apart from having lost one quaternion between 9.5. ext. 2 *inpudentius* (sic; V. wrote *imprudentius*) and 9.13.2 *neque relationi*, L is less problematic. In the thirteenth century the manuscript belonged to the Benedictine abbey of Stavelot (Belgium).

Some of the corrections are by the original scribe, but the majority are in a second, but not much later, hand. As with A, I refer to them all as 'L^c'.

G

Many mistakes, particularly omissions and transpositions, were corrected, as far as I can judge, by the original scribe. There were also two other correctors, both much later and one in the age of print.[62] If the conjecture is certainly by

---

[59] Billanovich, *Aevum* 30 (1956), 319–53.
[60] op. cit. 331; cf. 328.
[61] Cf. ed. p. xiv n. 27.
[62] At f. 34^u he wrote *haec non habentur in nouis impressionibus*; Carter thought he was Pighius.

the original scribe or if it is uncertain whether it is or not I cite it as 'G^c', if it is certainly by one of the later correctors as 'G^x'.

6b Transmission: The Indirect Tradition

Paris and the *fragmentum de praenominibus*

P, at the end of the list of chapter headings which precedes the epitome itself, has *libro decimo de praenominibus de nominibus de cognominibus de agnominibus de appellationibus de uerbis*, at the end of book 9 *C· Titi Probi finit epitoma historiarum diuersarum exemplorumque Romanorum feliciter emendaui descriptum Rabennae Rusticius Helpidius Domnulus VC*.[63] At the beginning of the work Paris writes *decem Valerii Maximi libros dictorum et factorum memorabilium ad unum uolumen epitomae coegi*.

Schmidt[64] argued, and I cannot improve on his argument, that Paris used a manuscript of V. which divided the *Facta et dicta memorabilia* into ten books. He did not himself indicate book division, but said that V. wrote ten books. A later reader compared his text of Paris with a manuscript of V. which divided the work into nine books and himself added the index and book division. Puzzled by Paris' reference to ten books, he came to the conclusion that a grammatical treatise, assigned to Titius Probus, which perhaps already followed the epitome in his manuscript, was the tenth book. Subsequently all but the section on *praenomina*, which seemed to have some connection with the matters related by V., were detached, but Probus' name, to whom the epitome had already been assigned, and the index to the whole of the grammatical work survived.

Rusticius Helpidius Domnulus is almost certainly identical with the sixth century author of Christian poems and recipient of letters from Theoderic.[65]

---

63 Lupus copied the text of the *fragmentum de praenominibus* at the end of A, but only part survives; it was first published in the Mainz edition of 1471.
64 *RE*.
65 Cf. Kempf (1854), 59–60, J. Sundwall, *Abhandlungen zur Geschichte des ausgehenden Römertums* (Helsinki, 1919), 126–7 (I ought not to have written 'tamen' at ed. p. xxi n. 52: Sundwall calls the identification 'ziemlich plausibel').

Note: Both Paris and Nepotianus clearly belong to late antiquity, but neither can be assigned a precise date (for a possible *terminus post quem* for Paris cf. 1 line 83 n.); cf. Schullian, cit. n. 33, 251, 253, Schmidt, *Handbuch* (see following note), 193, 195.
Note: I lack the expertise to discuss the content of the fragment, the sources of the author, or his name. Cf. P. L. Schmidt, *RE* Supp. xv. 645–52 and in R. Herzog (ed.), *Handbuch der lateinischen Literatur der Antike*, v (Munich, 1989), 121–2 (cited hereafter as '*RE*', '*Handbuch*').

Nepotianus

The full text of Nepotianus' epitome survives only as far as 3.2.7, in Vat. Lat. 1321, ff. 147ʳ–154ʳ, written in the mid fourteenth century. Labbé[66] published the preface in 1657, Mai the full text in 1828.[67] For the rest we depend on two sources, representing an indirect tradition for an indirect tradition. In the tenth century Landolfus Sagax wrote a work entitled *Historia miscella*. The oldest manuscript, Vat. Pal. Lat. 909, was written *c.* 1000 in Beneventan script, perhaps at Naples.[68] Landolfus' principal source was Orosius, but as Droysen[69] first saw, he also took material from Nepotianus. This is the case in the following passages of book 8:[70]

Valerius	Landolfus[71]
1 absol. 5	254.5–9
7.6	260.25–6
7. ext. 16	278.46–279.2

Nepotianus was also used by the author of the so-called J² recension of the *Historia de preliis Alexandri Magni*. The only passage in book 8 is 14. ext. 2 (i. 134.38–40 Hilka–Bergmeister–Grossman).[72]

The Text of Paris and Nepotianus

The early editors (Mai, Kempf, Halm) and critics (Eberhard, Novák, Gertz) of the texts of the epitomators tried to make their authors conform to the Latinity of V., not to say of Cicero, and sometimes corrected or supplemented them from V. himself. The publication of Kempf's second edition led a number of scholars

---

66 *Nouae bibliothecae manuscript. librorum tomus primus* (Paris, 1657), 669.
67 op. cit. n. 56, 93–115.
68 H. Droysen, *MHG, AA* ii. 226. The text follows on pp. 227–376. Other editions are those of V. Fiorini and G. Rossi (Città di Castello, 1900, Bologna, 1919) and A. Crivellucci (Rome, 1912). Droysen thought that Landolfus himself either wrote or corrected the text, Crivellucci that he dictated it, E. A. Loew (*The Beneventan Script*, 2ⁿᵈ edn., Rome, 1980, i. 9; cf. i. 55, 74, ii. 167) that Landolfus and the scribe were contemporaries.
69 *Hermes* 12 (1877), 390, 13 (1878), 122–32.
70 For a complete list see ed. pp. xxii–xxiv.
71 References are to the pages and lines of Droysen's edition.
72 A. Hilka–H. J. Bergmeister–R. Grossman, *Historia Alexandri Magni (historia de preliis) Rezension J² (Orosius-Rezension)* (Meisenheim am Glan, 1976–7). The references in the table at ed. i. p. xxv are to the edition of O. von Zingerle (Breslau, 1885), though I cite Hilka–Bergmeister–Grossman in n. 62.

to realise that such a procedure was flawed.[73] Lacking confidence in my ability to edit a text of late antiquity, I decided that, unless an emendation seemed to me certain, I would print the manuscript reading, never obelizing. The expected ridicule did not materialize.

The Epitomators and the Editing of Valerius
Since Paris and Nepotianus preserve the *exempla* in book 1 missing from the direct tradition,[74] it follows that they were using a manuscript (not necessarily the same one) of V. which occupies a higher place in the stemma than α.

There is no doubt that Paris is of great use to an editor of V., but he must be used with caution: Paris abbreviates what V. says about deeds, sayings, and institutions, omitting his moralizing and commonplaces. It must also be remembered that P is our only authoritative witness and it cannot be taken for granted that he always represents what Paris wrote; in what follows and in the commentary, therefore, unless there is a particular reason to refer to Paris himself, I say 'P'.

I proceed on the following principles. (i) If P omits a word or series of words found in α, it by no means follows that they are an interpolation in the direct tradition; but (ii) if P has something omitted in α, it is of greater significance (if I print them, I do so without any typographical indication of their status: they are not the equivalent of editorial supplements; cf. 15 line 57 n.); (iii) P often repeats V.'s language without alteration: if, therefore, the two agree except for one word, the matter must be given particularly careful consideration. (iv) Paris certainly drew on sources other than V., including some used by V. himself;[75] so if V.'s sources agree with P against α, it could be that Paris corrected an error made by V. (v) If the readings of α and P are evenly balanced, the former should be followed.

In my apparatus I cited far fewer readings of P than Kempf, who included many which could not conceivably stem from V. himself. I now cite P only, but not always, if I did so previously.

Nepotianus is of less use. He both omits and adds (sometimes whole *exempla*, (labelled 'nou.(a)' in my edition) more than Paris, and for the most part does not take over V.'s language. Occasionally, but not in book 8, he has a contribution to make.

---

73 Cf. C. F. W. Müller, *NJPhP* 141 (1890), 713, M. Petschenig, *Philologus* 50 (1891), 192, Heraeus (1893), 632, Ihm, 248, T. Stangl, *Philologus* 53 (1894), 572 (for Stangl's application of his principles see also op. cit. cit. ed. p. xl).
74 See p. 19
75 Cf. Kempf (1854), 52–3.

7 Editions of Valerius Maximus

The *editio princeps* of V. was published at Strasbourg in, probably, 1470. It was followed by twenty-four other incunables, thirteen of them published at Venice, at least six more than of Livy.[76] In 1502 the first of four Aldines appeared (the others were published in 1508,[77] 1514, and 1534[78]) and the 1783 Zweibrücken edition[79] calls the period from 1502 to 1566 the *aetas ii. Aldina* (the 1806 edition omits *Aldina*); it lists a total of sixty-four editions between 1501 (Leipzig, edited by Martin of Würzburg) and 1566 (Lyon), which was followed by that of Pighius, published at Antwerp in 1567.[80]

Pighius[81] was the first editor to make a major advance in establishing V.'s text and his text long remained the vulgate (the Zweibrücken edition calls the period from 1567 to 1671 the a*etas Pighiana*). He used nine manuscripts; most, of course, were copied in the Renaissance, but his *codex Gemblacensis*, as we have seen, was almost certainly identical with G.[82] His work on the *Fasti*[83] enabled him to restore the correct forms of Roman proper names, just as it did his contemporary Sigonius in his editions of Livy.[84]

As far as book 8 is concerned, the commentary mentions Pighius on 29 occasions, three of which refer merely to his citation of manuscript readings (1 lines 144–5, 7 lines 78–9, 11 line 30). Of the rest, nine concern places where

---

[76] Cf. *Incunabula Short Title Catalogue* (*ISTC*), published online by the British Library, *Liviana*, 2 n. 3.

[77] On the Milan edition of that year cf. p. 206 n. 106.

[78] The John Rylands Library possesses all four.

[79] The Zweibrücken edition of 1783 contained a list of previous editions (18–26; pp. xvii–xxxii in the revised edition published at Strasbourg in 1806 (with both omissions and additions, including Nuremberg 1784 and Stadtamhof 1799; for the latter cf. Schullian, *CTC* v. 308)).

[80] In *Bibliography* (Editions, Introduction) I said that at least sixty-six editions, in addition to the *editio princeps*, appeared before that of Pighius and that this was about the same number as of Livy: the figure for V. was derived from the British Library printed catalogue, but I wrongly included multiple copies of the same edition; I should have said 'fifty-four' (at the time of writing I did not have access to the Zweibrücken edition and was unaware that it had been reprinted in 1806); that for Livy was based on the list in Drakenborch's variorum edition (vii (Amsterdam–Leiden, 1746), 328–38).

[81] Stephan Wynants (1520–1604, born in Kampen (Netherlands)). Pökel (209 n.) says that Wynants was his father's name, which he Latinized as Vinandus, Pighe his mother's (A. W. Lintott, *The Constitution of the Roman Republic* (Oxford, 1999), 246 has 'Wynkens or Wynants'; at ed. p. xxxix I wrongly said 'S. V. Wynants').

[82] Cf. n. 48.

[83] Cf. Lintott, op cit. (n. 81), 246–7.

[84] Cf. *Liviana*, 4, FRHist i. 653.

Pighius emended on historical grounds: seven of them involve proper names, six Roman (1 lines 13, 43, 98–9, 3 lines 18–19, 9 line 21, 13 line 33) and one Greek (7 line 158); only at 1 line 43 and 13 line 33 did I not print Pighius' reading, though at the former he may have been right, at the latter he has been followed by all editors except myself and Shackleton Bailey. At 13 lines 9–10 he adopts the reading of a late manuscript, not realising that Cicero was omitting the dictator years, while at 15 lines 8–11 he absolves V. from a historical error by means of a violent transposition. As far as passages not involving historical issues are concerned, I accepted Pighius' reading at 4 line 7 (following Paris), 6 lines 16–17, 13 line 106 (where he restored the Greek, albeit making two words out of one), 15 lines 16–17, 35, 100 (*bis*), gave it a *fort. recte* at 10 line 13, and rejected it at 1 line 29, 6 lines 5–6, 8 line 7, 10 line 15, 14 line 25, 15 lines 17, 90. Finally, two matters which do not involve what V. himself wrote: in ch. 1 Pighius, helpfully, attached the label *ambustae* to the final two *exempla* and, mistakenly, omitted the heading before 11. ext. 5.

Between them, the 1783 Zweibrücken and 1806 Strasbourg editions list forty editions published between Pighius in 1567 and J. Vorst in 1672 (Berlin), including several which are revisions of Pighius' edition or profess to be based on it. That of C. Coler (Frankfurt, 1601, Hanover, 1614), though unremarkable in itself, deserves notice because he made use, albeit limited and inaccurate, of A.[85]

The list in the Zweibrücken edition labelled the period from Vorst's edition to that of J. Kapp in 1782 (Leipzig) *aetas Vorstio-Torreniana*, rightly regarding Vorst and A. Torrenius (variorum edition, Leiden, 1726; he was Oudendorp's son-in-law) as the two editors who made the greatest contribution to the study of V. in that period. Vorst made use of two manuscripts, Kempf's C and D (the latter, when it was at Utrecht, had been used by Lipsius for the notes he added to Pighius' second edition (1585)),[86] Torrenius of no fewer than forty, but in a sporadic and imprecise way.[87]

1783 was, as it turned out, a good time to publish a list of previous editions of V., since (to the best of my knowledge) apart from the 1806 revision of the Zweibrücken edition, only four more were published before Kempf's 1854 edition, three of them in 1819 (Hase in the *Bibliotheca classica Latina*, Cantel in the Delphin series, and Carey (London)), the fourth at Leipzig in 1830. By contrast, and in reversal of the earlier pattern, at least 35[88] new editions (excluding

---

85 Cf. n. 43.
86 Cf. Kempf (1854), 73.
87 Cf. Kempf (1854), 74.
88 The figure is derived from a combination of the lists in Engelmann–Preuss and the British Library pre-1975 printed catalogue; I say 'at least' because there are almost certainly editions in other libraries which were missed by Engelmann–Preuss.

those of individual books but including those planned to cover all that survives but never completed) of Livy were published between 1783 and Weissenborn's Teubner (1850–1) and the first volumes of his edition with commentary (1854). Since 1830 only six editions of V. have appeared, one of them not progressing beyond book 6.

Kempf's edition was a pioneering work which marks the beginning of the modern study of V. An introduction of nearly 100 pages discusses (i) the author and the date of his work, (ii) his sources, (iii) his reliability, (iv) his style, (v) the reception of his work from the elder Pliny to the Renaissance, (vi) Paris, Nepotianus, and later epitomes, (vii) the manuscripts (the longest section, occupying a quarter of the introduction). Unusually at that time, the apparatus appears underneath the text, as do the notes, which are restricted to textual discussions and lists of other sources for the matters related by V. He includes the *fragmentum de praenominibus*,[89] but not the full texts of Paris and Nepotianus (their summaries of the *exempla* in book 1 missing in the direct tradition[90] appear in parallel columns).

Eleven years later Karl Halm published the first Teubner edition of Valerius, based on a fresh collation of A (which he called B); the preface criticizes Kempf for erroneous reports (Kempf responded in kind in his second edition). Halm's rare reports of other manuscripts are taken from Kempf's apparatus. The text of Paris is printed underneath that of V., Nepotianus at the end.

At the end of the nineteenth century a considerable number of new Teubner editions were commissioned, in order to provide reliable texts for the authors of articles in the *Thesaurus linguae Latinae*, the first fascicle of which appeared in 1900. Among them was Kempf's second edition of V., published in 1888. As we saw,[91] it was only at the last moment that he became aware of L and was able to base his text on twin manuscripts; his citations of renaissance manuscripts are now rare. For its time, the apparatus is technically advanced, with copious citation of conjectures. The introduction, of course, is now concerned only with the manuscripts and there is no commentary (nor are other sources listed: the earliest Teubner in which I recall having encountered them is Jan–Mayhoff's elder Pliny (1906)). The text of V. himself is followed by those of Paris, including the *fragmentum de praenominibus*, and Nepotianus.[92] There are a considerable number of errors in Kempf's reports of A and L (the latter doubt-

---

[89] Cf. p. 21.
[90] Cf. p. 19.
[91] P. 16.
[92] Kempf used the reference system of V. himself for Paris, but provided his own for Nepotianus, giving the former in the margin.

less mostly deriving from Bruno Keil's collation⁹³), but no edition is free from error (*experto crede*) and Marshall's statement that 'much of the published work on Valerius (of necessity dependent on Kempf) may safely be ignored'[94] is absurd: Kempf's edition provided the impetus for a number of important articles discussing individual passages where the readings of A and L are correctly reported or, even if they are not, the discussion is still of value.[95]

There were no further editions of V. for eighty-three years and the one that appeared in 1971, by Rino Faranda in the UTET series (with facing Italian translation), scarcely deserves the label, since the text is that of Kempf (1888). The *nota critica* (pp. 45–52; pp. 52–8 contains brief notes on forty-eight passages) is derived entirely from Kempf's editions and was out of date when it appeared, since Faranda had not read Schullian's article on G. He made a number of additions to Kempf's list of sources, but in many cases the reference he gives is wrong, while in others the passage cited is of no relevance to the *exemplum* concerned.

I shall say nothing for good or ill about my own edition and merely record two matters concerning the epitomators; (i) in the text of Nepotianus I used the reference system for V. himself; (ii) I moved 1.1. ext. 9 in Halm and Kempf (1888) to follow 1.1.18 (thus Kempf (1854)), calling it 1.1.18a, while suggesting that it should be omitted entirely (i.e. that it does not represent anything that V. wrote).

In the final footnote to the Preface of my edition I said that my typescript was almost complete when R. Combès's Budé edition of books 1–3 (Paris, 1995) came into my hands, but that as the editor cited, apart from one in Montpellier (his own University), only the manuscripts used by Kempf and ignored G, I had refrained from examining the work in detail; when books 4–6 were published (1997; the work has not been completed), my edition was in course of production. I reviewed both volumes in *CR* 49 (1999), 76–9 and shall say no more about them here (Combès responded to my footnote in *RÉL* 77 (1999), 26–9 (it is not a formal review)).

Earlier, Shackleton Bailey had been commissioned by Harvard University Press to undertake a Loeb edition of V.[96] SB (as he called himself), with his

---

[93] Cf. p. 16.
[94] *Texts and Transmission*, 428 n. 1. Bengt Löfstedt (*AClass* 34 (1991), 154 described it as an arrogant exaggeration.
[95] I here repeat what I wrote at *Sileno*, 396–7.
[96] In April 1993, during a visit to Harvard (it was on this occasion that I delivered the original version of my article in *Sileno*), I was asked by Zeph Stewart, Executive Trustee of the Loeb Classical Library, whether I would be interested in doing a Loeb of V. (I believe that the suggestion had come from Ernst Badian). I said that I was not averse in principle, but that I could

customary speed, was able to take full account of my edition and produced his in the year 2000. In most cases Loebs cannot be regarded as critical editions in the full sense of the term: their citations of manuscript evidence and conjectures are, deliberately, very selective and few editors are qualified textual critics. The latter is certainly not true of SB, one of the greatest textual critics of the twentieth century,[97] and his judgement must always be taken seriously. It should, though, be remembered that some of his decisions are affected by his reluctance to regard G as possessing authority equipollent to AL. He had earlier published a number of conjectures on V.,[98] but in the Loeb he prints thirty new conjectures, which he justified in *HSPh* 101 (2003), 473–81.

8 Methods of Citation

Chapter, *exempla*, and line numbers

The accepted reference system, used by *TLL*, is that of Kempf's second edition and it would not have been helpful if I had departed from it. Chapter divisions, included in the *editio princeps*, are fundamentally those of the *capitula librorum* (thus A, LG have *capitula* (*cap.* L) *libri*) which in the manuscripts precede the text and are repeated at the beginning of each chapter (they are not authorial[99]). In the former they are numbered consecutively for the whole work, with the numbers of each individual book appearing only in A (apart from book nine) and L^c; in the latter I omitted the chapter numbers preceding the heading, as they appear in the margin. In the text they appear as headings, without numbers in A, with only the consecutive numbers in L and G (in L a later hand added the numbers for each book).

The Venice edition of 1471 divided the exempla in each chapter into Roman and *externa*, but the numbering of *exempla* was introduced by Pighius, who was also responsible for the subdivisions in book 8 ch. 1 and book 9 ch. 7.

The system, however, is not entirely logical. Thus, e.g., in the part of book 1 missing in the direct tradition ch. 4 has the heading *de auspicio*, which appears in Paris after *exemplum* 1, but the *praefatio*, from Nepotianus, is in fact an *exem-*

---

not contemplate beginning work on it until my Teubner edition had been completed, which would take several years, and that in any case the Harvard Press would have to obtain, and pay for, permission from Teubner to use my text. The matter was not pursued further.
[97] I was, therefore, and despite our disagreement about G, much flattered by what he said about my edition (i. 5).
[98] *HSPh* 85 (1981), 158–67 ('678' at ed. p. xl is a misprint), *RFIC* 124 (1996), 175–84.
[99] Cf. Helm, *RE* viiiA. 97–8, 13 line 3 n.; for their syntactical form cf. 11 tit. n.

plum; had I been starting from scratch, I would have made the *praefatio* the first *exemplum* and renumbered *exempla* 1–7 as 2–8. 1.6. ext. 1 lines 177–82 is a preface to the *exempla externa*, not part of the first one; similarly 3.3. ext. 1 lines 53–58 is a preface to *exempla* 2–5. Book 2 chapter 6 consists entirely of *exempla externa*, but 'ext.' does not appear.[100] At book 3 chapter 2 the heading *de fortitudine* appears in the middle of the *praefatio*. 4.4 praef. is a preface and *exemplum* combined. In book 8, 1 lines 105–6 form part of damn. 1, but are in reality an introduction to damn. 1–4; 7. ext. lines 46–7 form part of ext. 1, but are in reality an introduction to all the *exempla externa*; at 11. ext. 5 there is no new chapter after the heading *quaedam nulla arte effici posse* (though a new line sequence begins in my edition; see below); 14 lines 62–7 are a transition to the two *exempla* which follow and would have better been made part of ext. 4.

The conventional way (thus *TLL*) of giving a reference to an *exemplum externum* is, e.g. '8.13. ext. 7'. When copy editing my commentary on Livy books 38–40, however, Leofranc Holford-Stevens altered such references to, e.g. '8.13 ext. 7'; I followed suit in my commentary on books 41–45 but now revert to the conventional system. When I delivered the typescript of my edition to the late lamented firm of B. G. Teubner in Stuttgart, I was told that they would number the lines consecutively through each chapter and the apparatus would refer to these numbers. Some *exempla* are long[101] and a reference, whether in the apparatus or elsewhere, to the *exemplum* alone can be time-consuming; line numbers are much more convenient. The typesetters, however, began a new numerical series after a heading, even when there was not a new chapter (see above).

The text which follows also has line numbers but, obviously, they are not identical with those of my edition. In the commentary I give references to other passages of book 8 (and my notes on them), without book number, by chapter and line (to avoid confusion with numerals I say 'line(s)' rather than 'l(l)'), but to passages of other books by chapter and *exemplum*. Entries in the *apparatus criticus* are restricted to passages discussed in the commentary and give only

---

100 Cf. p. 4 n. 23.
101 3.7.1, 5.3.2 and 6.3.1 were sub-divided by Kempf (cf. n. 26), but not 5.3. ext. 3 (Shackleton Bailey did so, as he did with a number of other sections referring to different people, episodes, or customs: 1.6. ext. 1, 8.1, 12, 2.1.5, 2.1, 4, 9, 6.7, 7.15, 9.6, 10.2, 3.1.2, 2.6, 23, 5.1, 7.1, 7. ext. 1, 4.1.6, 10, 3.5, 6, 14, 3. ext. 3, 4, 7. ext. 2, 5.1.1, 1. ext. 1, 2, 3, 2.1, 3.2, 3. ext. 3, 6.3.1, 3, 4.1, 2, 5.1, 7.2.6, 2. ext. 1, 2, 11, 3.4, 6.1); I followed Kempf in order not to interfere with the reference system (cf. ed. p. xxvii). The sections in Livy (introduced by Drakenborch) are much shorter and cause fewer problems; the old OCTs (up to and including Ogilvie's new edition of books 1–5) used only section numbers in the apparatus, as I did in my Teubner editions. Current OUP practice, however, is to use line (and page when necessary) numbers.

the names of authors of conjectures; more detailed information, and conjectures not mentioned here, can be found in my edition.

The numerals following the names of individual Romans in the commentary are those of the articles, arranged by *gens*, on the person in question in *RE*. For all but the most famous figures, both Roman and foreign, I give a brief summary of their career. For Alexander, Hannibal, the elder Cato, Cicero, the younger Cato, or Augustus, that would be absurd and the introductory note on the *exemplum* in question deals only with the episode related.[102]

Grid references to the Barrington Atlas are given in brackets following the names of places and peoples.

Testimonia

My edition, as was frequently the case with Teubners,[103] contained, above the *apparatus criticus* on each page, a *testimonia* apparatus, indicating the other sources for each matter related by V., whether or not they were, certainly, probably, or possibly, those used by V. himself. In most cases I included all those known to me, but sometimes the number was such that it would have been impractical to cite them all, and instead I merely referred to a work (usually *RE* or *MRR*) where a list could be found. In a commentary the same constraints do not apply, but there are still a few instances where the number of *testimonia* was so large that it seemed preferable to refer readers to a place where all can be found.

I said in my edition (p. xxx) that the business of collecting *testimonia* was never ending and that has continued to be the case. Kempf (1854) was the first to do so, but as they did not feature in nineteenth century Teubners, there was no opportunity for Halm or, in his second edition, Kempf himself, to make additions. Many passages appear for the first time in Faranda's UTET edition, but, as we have seen,[104] the references are frequently erroneous and in other cases his citations are irrelevant. I have taken references from many places, particularly the *RE* articles on the persons mentioned by V., the *testimonia* listed in the Teubner editons of Plutarch, both the *Lives* and *moralia*, and, when V.'s source is Cicero, the commentaries of Pease on *de diuinatione* and *de natura deorum* and of Powell on *Cato*.

---

102 Cf. *FRHist* i. 11, though there the choice was between a brief summary and a full treatment.
103 See p. 26.
104 See p. 27.

Text

SIGLA

Valerius Maximus
α   agreement of ALG
    A   Berne, Burgerbibliothek 366   833–866
    L   Florence, Biblioteca Medicea Laurenziana,
        Ashburnham 1899   850–900
    G   Brussels, Bibliothèque royale 5336   1000–1050
dett. other manuscripts cited[105]

Julius Paris
    P   Vatican City, Biblioteca apostolica Vaticana
        Lat. 4929   *c.* 850

Landolfus Sagax
Land. Vatican City, Biblioteca apostolica Vaticana
        Pal. Lat. 909

---

105 As in my edition, I say 'dett.' even if the reading is known from only one manuscript.

VALERI MAXIMI
FACTORVM ET DICTORVM MEMORABILIVM
LIBER OCTAVVS

INFAMES REI QVIBVS DE CAVSIS ABSOLVTI AVT DAMNATI SINT 1

Nunc, quo aequiore animo ancipites iudiciorum motus tolerentur, recordemur   praef.
inuidia laborantes pro quibus causis aut absoluti sint aut damnati.
    M. Horatius, interfectae sororis crimine a Tullo rege damnatus, ad populum   absol. 1
prouocato iudicio absolutus est. quorum alterum atrocitas necis mouit, alterum
causa flexit, quia immaturum uirginis amorem seuere magis quam impie puni-
tum existimabat. itaque forti punitione liberata fratris dextera tantum consanguineo quantum hostili cruore gloriae haurire potuit.
    Acrem se tunc pudicitiae custodem populus Romanus, postea plus iusto   2
placidum iudicem praestitit. cum a Libone tribuno plebis Ser. Galba pro rostris
uehementer increparetur, quod Lusitanorum magnam manum interposita fide
praetor in Hispania interemisset, actionique tribuniciae M. Cato ultimae senectutis oratione sua, quam in Origines rettulit, subscriberet, reus pro se iam nihil
recusans paruolos liberos suos et Gali sanguine sibi coniunctum filium flens
commendare coepit, eoque facto mitigata contione qui omnium consensu peri-
turus erat paene nullum triste suffragium habuit. misericordia ergo illam quaestionem, non aequitas rexit, quoniam quae innocentiae tribui nequierat absolu-
tio, respectui puerorum data est.
    Consentaneum quod sequitur. A. Gabinius in maximo infamiae suae ardore   3
suffragiis populi C. Memmio accusatore subiectus, abruptae esse spei uideba-
tur, quoniam et accusatio partes suas plene exhibebat, et defensionis praesidia
inualida fide nitebantur, et qui iudicabant ira praecipiti poenam hominis cupide
expetebant. igitur uiator et carcer ante oculos obuersabantur, cum interim omnia ista propitiae fortunae interuentu dispulsa sunt: filius namque Gabini Sisenna consternationis impulsu ad pedes se Memmi supplex prostrauit, inde aliquod fomentum procellae petens, unde totus impetus tempestatis eruperat.

---

1. tit. sint *A* : sunt *LG*   **1** quo *det.* : quoque α : quoque ut A^cL^c **2** pro ... causis *G* : pro ... de causis L^c : per ... de causis *L* : quibus de causis A^c **3** M. α *P* : P. *Liu.* 1.26.7, 9   Tullo PA^c : Tullio α   **6** forti α : forti<s> *Kraffert* : f<e>roci *Gertz* : forti<s facti> *Shackleton Bailey*   liberata α : librata *Lipsius*   **9** Seruius α : Sergius *P*   **13** Gali *scripsi* : Galli α   **14** con(m)mendare α : populo commendare *P* : populo *ante* paruolos *Kempf*   **19** C. PA^c : om. α   **21** praecipiti A^cL^c : percipiti *AL* : perciti *dett., fort. recte*   cupide A^cG : cupidius *A* : cupidine *L* : cupide <omnes> *Damsté*   **22** uiator *AL* : uiras.tor *G* : uiator <ei> *Gertz* quem truci uultu a se uictor insolens repulsum, excusso e manu anulo, humi iacere aliquamdiu passus est. quod spectaculum fecit ut Laelius tribunus plebis adprobantibus cunctis Gabinium dimitti iuberet, ac documentum daretur neque secundarum rerum prouentu insolenter abuti neque aduersis <prae>propere debilitari oportere: idque proximo exemplo aeque patet.

4   Ap. Claudius, nescio religionis maior an patriae iniuria, si quidem illius uetustissimum morem neglexit, huius pulcherrimam classem amisit, infesto populo obiectus, cum effugere debitam poenam nullo modo posse crederetur, subito coorti imbris beneficio tutus fuit a damnatione: discussa enim quaestione aliam uelut dis interpellantibus de integro instaurari non placuit. ita cui maritima tempestas causae dictionem contraxerat, caelestis salutem attulit.

5   Eodem auxilii genere Tucciae uirginis Vestalis incesti criminis reae castitas infamiae nube obscurata emersit. quae conscientia certa sinceritatis suae spem salutis ancipiti argumento ausa petere est: arrepto enim cribro 'Vesta' inquit, 'si sacris tuis castas semper admoui manus, effice ut hoc hauriam e Tiberi aquam et in aedem tuam perferam.' audaciter et temere iactis uotis sacerdotis rerum ipsa natura cessit.

6   Item L. Piso a C. Claudio Pulchro accusatus, quod graues et intolerabiles iniurias sociis intulisset, haud dubiae ruinae metum fortuito auxilio uitauit: namque per id ipsum tempus quo tristes de eo sententiae ferebantur, repentina uis nimbi incidit, cumque prostratus humi pedes iudicum oscularetur, os suum caeno repleuit. quod conspectum totam quaestionem a seueritate ad clementiam et mansuetudinem transtulit, quia satis iam graues eum poenas sociis dedisse arbitrati sunt, huc deductum necessitatis ut abicere se tam suppliciter aut attollere tam deformiter cogeretur.

7   Subnectam duos accusatorum suorum culpa absolutos. Q. Flauius a C. Valerio aedile apud populum reus actus, cum quattuordecim tribuum suffragiis damnatus esset, proclamauit se innocentem opprimi. cui Valerius aeque clara uoce respondit nihil sua interesse nocensne an innoxius periret, dummodo periret. qua uiolentia dicti reliquas tribus aduersario donauit. abiecerat inimicum, eundem, dum pro certo pessum datum credidit, erexit, uictoriamque in ipsa uictoria perdidit.

---

29 aduersis α : aduersis <quemquam> *Pighius* <prae>propere *Halm* : propere A^c : propriae *L* : proprie *G* **31** App(ius) α *P* : P. *Pighius* **37** criminis α : crimine *Gertz* **38** conscientia *LG* : conscia A^c certa *Perizonius* : certae α **40** hoc *dett.* : hanc α; *sic etiam Land., sed om.* hauriam **43** C. *scripsi* : L. *AG* P^c (*om. praenomine et nomine P*) **47** a (ab *Halm*) seueritate A^cL^cG : ad seueritatem *AL* **49** aut : et *Foertsch* : *del. Madvig* **51** Q. α : M. *Liu.* 8.22.2 **52** aedile *AL P* : aedili *G* P^c **54** nocensne an innoxius α : nocens an innocens PA^c **56** credidit α : credit *dett.*

C. etiam Cosconium Seruilia lege reum, propter plurima et euidentissima 8
facinora sine ulla dubitatione nocentem, Valeri Valentini accusatoris eius recitatum in iudicio carmen, quo puerum praetextatum et ingenuam uirginem a se
corruptam poetico ioco significauerat, erexit, si quidem iudices iniquum rati
sunt eum uictorem dimittere qui palmam non ex alio ferre, sed de se dare merebatur. magis uero Valerius in Cosconi absolutione damnatus quam Cosconius
in sua causa liberatus est.

Attingam eos quoque quorum salus propriis obruta criminibus proximorum 9
claritati donata est. A. Atilium Calatinum, Soranorum oppidi proditione reum
admodum infamem, imminentis damnationis periculo pauca uerba Q. Maximi
soceri subtraxerunt, quibus adfirmauit si in eo crimine sontem illum ipse comperisset, diremturum se fuisse adfinitatem: continuo enim populus paene iam
exploratam sententiam suam unius iudicio concessit, indignum ratus eius testimonio non credere cui difficillimis rei publicae temporibus bene se exercitus
credidisse meminerat.

M. quoque Aemilius Scaurus, repetundarum reus, adeo perditam et conplo- 10
ratam defensionem in iudicium attulit ut, cum accusator diceret lege sibi centum atque uiginti hominibus denuntiare testimonium licere, seque non recusare
quominus absolueretur, si totidem nominasset quibus in prouincia nihil abstulisset, tam bona condicione uti non potuerit. tamen propter uetustissimam nobilitatem et recentem memoriam patris absolutus est.

Sed quem ad modum splendor amplissimorum uirorum in protegendis reis 11
plurimum ualuit, ita in opprimendis non sane multum potuit: quin etiam euidenter noxiis, dum eos acrius impugnat, profuit. P. Scipio Aemilianus Cottam
apud populum accusauit. cuius causa, quamquam grauissimis criminibus erat
confessa, septiens ampliata et ad ultimum octauo iudicio absoluta est, quia
homines uerebantur ne praecipuae accusatoris amplitudini damnatio eius donata existimaretur. quos haec secum locutos crediderim: 'nolumus caput alterius petentem in iudicium triumphos et tropaea spoliaque et deuictarum naui-
um rostra deferre: terribilis sit is aduersus hostem, ciuis uero salutem tanto
fragore gloriae subnixus ne insequatur'.

Tam uehementes iudices aduersus excellentissimum accusatorem quam mi- 12
tes in longe inferioris fortunae reo. Calidius Bononiensis in cubiculo mariti noc-

---

59 Valentini α : Valens PA^c **60** quo α : in quo P   **61** erexit A^c : correxit α : protexit Torr.
66 Calatinum α P : fort. Caiatinum   **68–69** con(m)perisset α : deprendisset P : conprendisset
Kellerbauer   **74–75** diceret ... seque α : doceret si ... se A^c **80** in (opprimendis) A^c : om. α,
fort. recte   **86** et deuictarum L^{c}G : aedeuictarum A : edeuictarum L : ac deuictarum A^c **87** is
α : <h>is Gertz   **88** fragore α : fulgore dett.   **90** Calidius P : Callidius AG : Callius L   **90–
91** noctu AL P : nocte G

tu deprehensus, cum ob id causam adulterii diceret, inter maximos et grauissimos infamiae fluctus emersit, tamquam fragmentum naufragii leue admodum genus defensionis amplexus: adfirmauit enim se ob amorem pueri serui eo esse perductum. suspectus erat locus, suspectum tempus, suspecta matris familiae persona, suspecta etiam adulescentia ipsius, sed crimen libidinis confessio intemperantiae liberauit.

13 Remissioris hoc, illud aliquanto grauioris materiae exemplum. cum parricidii causam fratres C<l>oelii dicerent splendido Tarracinae loco nati, quorum pater T. C<l>oelius in cubiculo quiescens, filiis altero cubantibus lecto, erat interemptus, neque aut seruus quisquam aut liber inueniretur ad quem suspicio caedis pertineret, hoc uno nomine absoluti sunt, quia iudicibus planum factum est illos aperto ostio inuentos esse dormientes. somnus, innoxiae securitatis certissimus index, miseris opem tulit: iudicatum est enim rerum naturam non recipere ut occiso patre supra uolnera et cruorem eius quietem capere potuerint.

damn. 1 Percurremus nunc eos quibus in causae dictione magis quae extra quaestionem erant nocuerunt quam sua innocentia opem tulit. L. Scipio post speciosissimum triumphum de rege Antiocho ductum, perinde ac pecuniam ab eo accepisset, damnatus est. non, puto, quod pretio corruptus fuerat ut illum totius Asiae dominum et iam Europae uictrices manus inicientem ultra Taurum montem submoueret. sed alioqui uir sincerissimae uitae et ab hac suspicione procul remotus, inuidiae, quae tunc in duorum fratrum inclutis cognominibus habitabat, resistere non potuit.

2 Ac Scipioni quidem maximus fortunae fulgor, C. autem Deciano spectatae integritatis uiro uox sua exitium attulit: nam cum P. Furium inquinatissimae uitae pro rostris accusaret, quia quadam in parte actionis de morte L. Saturnini queri ausus fuerat, nec reum damnauit et insuper ei poenas addictas pependit.

3 Sex. quoque Titium similis casus prostrauit. erat innocens, erat agraria lege lata gratiosus apud populum: tamen, quod Saturnini imaginem domi habuerat, suffragiis eum tota contio oppressit.

4 Adiciatur his Claudia, quam insontem crimine quo accusabatur uotum impium subuertit, quia cum a ludis domum rediens turba elideretur, optauerat ut frater suus, maritimarum uirium nostrarum praecipua iactura, reuiuesceret,

---

92 naufragii *AL* : nauigii *G*   **93** pueri serui α : pueri eius *P* : pueri *Damsté* : *fort.* serui eius *uel* pueruli   **95** crimen α : crim<i>ine <eum> *Kempf*   **98** fratres α : duo *PA*ᶜ   **98–99** C<l>oelii ... C<l>loelius *Pighius* : Caelii ... Coelius *AL P* : Caelii ... Caelius *G*   **99** altero α : in altero *P*   **108** non ... quod α : *del.* quod *Gelbcke* : *del.* non *Kempf* : non ... quod<am> *Gertz* : nou<um> ... quod *Watt*   ut α : <c>um *Foertsch*   **110** sed α : sed <et> *Madvig*   **111** habitabat α : latitabat *Kraffert*   **113** maximus fortunae *A*ᶜ*LG* : maxima efortunae *A* : maximae fortunae *Halm*   **118** domi α : domi suae *P*   **119** suffragiis α : suffragiis <suis> *Kempf*

saepiusque consul factus infelici ductu nimis magnam urbis frequentiam minueret.

Possumus et ad illos breui deuerticulo transgredi quos leues ob causas 5 damnationis incursus abripuit. M. Muluius, Cn. Lollius, L. Sextilius triumuiri, quod ad incendium in sacra uia ortum exstinguendum tardius uenerant, a tribunis plebis die dicta apud populum damnati sunt.

Item P. Villius triumuir nocturnus a P. Aquilio tribuno plebis accusatus po- 6 puli iudicio concidit, quia uigilias neglegentius circumierat.

Admodum seuerae notae et illud populi iudicium, cum M. Aemilium Porci- 7 nam a L. Cassio accusatum crimine nimis sublime exstructae uillae in Alsiensi agro graui multa adfecit.

Non supprimenda illius quoque damnatio qui pueruli sui nimio amore cor- 8 reptus, rogatus ab eo ruri ut omasum in cenam fieri iuberet, cum bubulae carnis in propinquo emendae nulla facultas esset, domito boue occiso desiderium eius expleuit, eoque nomine publica quaestione adflictus est, innocens, nisi tam prisco saeculo natus esset.

Atque ut eos quoque referamus qui in discrimen capitis adducti neque dam- amb. 1. nati neque absoluti sunt, apud M. Popillium Laenatem praetorem quaedam, quod matrem fuste percussam interemerat, causam dixit. de qua neutram in partem latae sententiae sunt, quia abunde constabat eandem ueneno necatorum liberorum dolore commotam, quos auia filiae infensa sustulerat, parricidium ultam esse parricidio. quorum alterum †ultione, alterum absolutione non dignum† iudicatum est.

Eadem haesitatione P. quoque Dolabellae, proconsulari imperio Asiam obti- 2 nentis animus fluctuatus est. mater familiae Zmyrnaea uirum et filium interemit, cum ab his optimae indolis iuuenem, quem ex priore uiro enixa fuerat, occisum comperisset. quam rem Dollabella ad se delatam Athenas ad Areopagi cognitionem relegauit, quia ipse neque liberare duabus caedibus contaminatam neque punire eam iusto dolore impulsam sustinebat. consideranter et mansuete populi Romani magistratus, sed Areopagitae quoque non minus sapienter, qui

---

125 ob A^cL^c : ob has G : ob han L **126** Muluius α : Mundius PA^c Sextilius α : Sextius PA^c **129** nocturnus G : om. P : ras. A : no tunus L^c Aquillio G : Aquilio AL : Acilio PA^c **131** cum α : quo<d> Kempf : quo Heraeus **134** pueruli α : pueri P **134–135** correptus P : corruptus α **141** fuste A^cL^cG : festem A : fustem, ut uid., L **144–145** †ultione ... non dignum†: ultione dignum alterum ... non dignum dett. : ultione, alterum absolutione dignum Halm : ultione, alterum <uero> non dignum Gertz : <dignum> ultione, alterum ... non dignum Kempf **147** Zmyrnaea P : Zmirnea ALG^c : ras.a G : Smyrnaea P^c **149** Areopagi A^c : Arei pagi AL, fort. recte : Ario pagi G : Areopagitarum P : Ario pagitarum A^c **151** eam α : tam Torr., fort. recte **152** magistratus LG (sic etiam fort. A) : om. A^c Areopagitae AL : Ariopagitae G

inspecta causa et accusatorem et ream post centum annos ad se reuerti iusserunt, eodem affectu moti quo Dolabella. sed ille transferendo quaestionem, hi differendo damnandi atque absoluendi inexplicabilem cunctationem uitabant. 155

2 DE PRIVATIS IVDICIIS INSIGNIBVS

praef. Publicis iudiciis adiciam priuata, quorum magis aequitas quaestionum delectare quam immoderata turba offendere lectorem poterit.
1   Claudius Centumalus ab auguribus iussus altitudinem domus suae, quam in Caelio monte habebat, submittere, quia his ex arce augurium capientibus officiebat, uendidit eam Calpurnio Lanario nec indicauit quod imperatum a collegio augurum erat. a quibus Calpurnius demoliri domum coactus M. Catonem incluti Catonis patrem arbitrum cum Claudio adduxit, quidquid sibi dare facere oporteret ex fide bona. Cato, ut est edoctus de industria Claudium praedictum sacerdotum suppressisse, continuo illum Calpurnio damnauit, summa quidem cum aequitate, quia bonae fidei uenditorem nec comodorum spem augere nec 10 incommodorum cognitionem obscurare oportet.
2   Notum suis temporibus iudicium commemoraui, sed ne quod relaturus quidem sum oblitteratum silentio. C. Visellius Varro, graui morbo correptus, trecenta milia nummum ab Otacilia Laterensis, cum qua commercium libidinis habuerat, expensa ferri sibi passus est, eo consilio ut si decessisset, ab heredibus 15 eam summam peteret, quam legati genus esse uoluit, libidinosam liberalitatem debiti nomine colorando. euasit deinde ex illa tempestate aduersus uota Otaciliae. quae offensa, quod spem praedae suae morte non maturasset, ex amica obsequenti subito destrictam feneratricem agere coepit, nummos petendo, quos ut fronte inuerecunda ita inani stipulatione captauerat. de qua re C. Aquillius, 20 uir magnae auctoritatis et scientia iuris ciuilis excellens, iudex adductus, adhibitis in consilium principibus ciuitatis, prudentia et religione sua mulierem reppulit. quod si eadem formula Varro et damnari et aduersariae absolui potuisset,

---

155 uitabant *Guyet* : *sic, sed* iudicationem *Wensky*, cogitationem *Shackleton Bailey* : mutabant α : *sic, sed* conditionem *Foertsch* : nutabant A^c : notabant *Kellerbauer* : tutabant<ur> *Gertz*
1 aequitas quaestionum α : aequitas *Gertz* : ex<i>guitas quaestionum *Damsté*   7 cum Claudio adduxit A^cLG : *sic, sed* Cladio *A* : cum Claudio sumpsit *P* : Claudio addixit *Guyet*   quidquid *Novák* : formulam quid(c)quid α : ut formulam daret quicquid (dare *infra deleto*) A^c : et formulam quidquid *dett.* : in formula (formulam *Shackleton Bailey*) quidquid *Halm* : formula quidquid *Gertz* : formulam sibi dare quidquid *Damsté*   23 Varro et damnari et aduersariae absolui *A* : *sic, sed* etsi *LG*, aduersarie *L* : et Varro damnari et aduersaria *Perizonius* : Varro damnari et absolui *Torr.* : *sic, sed* et damnari *Kempf* : Varro et damnari et <ab> aduersaria absolui *Foertsch/Madvig*

eius quoque non dubito quin turpem et inconcessum amorem libenter castiga-
turus fuerit: nunc priuatae actionis calumniam ipse compescuit, adulterii crimen publicae quaestioni uindicandum reliquit.

   Multo animosius et ut militari spiritu dignum erat se in consimili genere 3
iudicii C. Marius gessit: nam cum C. Titinius Minturnensis Fanniam uxorem,
quam impudicam de industria duxerat, eo crimine repudiatam dote spoliare
conaretur, sumptus inter eos iudex, in conspectu habita quaestione, seductum
Titinium monuit ut incepto desisteret ac mulieri dotem redderet. quod cum sae-
pius frustra fecisset, coactus ab eo sententiam pronuntiare, mulierem impudici-
tiae sestertio nummo, Titinium summa totius dotis damnauit, praefatus idcirco
se hunc iudicandi modum secutum, cum liqueret sibi Titinium patrimonio Fan-
niae insidias struentem impudicae coniugium expetisse. Fannia autem haec est
quae postea Marium hostem a senatu iudicatum caenoque paludis, qua extrac-
tus erat, oblitum, et iam in domum suam custodiendum Minturnis deductum,
ope quantacumque potuit adiuuit, memor quod inpudica iudicata esset suis
moribus, quod dotem seruasset illius religioni acceptum ferri debere.

   Multus sermo eo etiam iudicio manauit in quo quidam furti damnatus est, 4
qui equo, cuius usus illi Ariciam commodatus fuerat, ulteriore eius municipii
cliuo uectus esset. quid aliud hoc loci quam uerecundiam illius saeculi laude-
mus in quo tam minuti a pudore excessus puniebantur?

QVAE MVLIERES APVD MAGISTRATVS PRO SE AVT PRO ALIIS CAVSAS EGERVNT 3

Ne de his quidem feminis tacendum est, quas condicio naturae et uerecundia praef.
stolae ut in foro et iudiciis tacerent cohibere non ualuit.

   Maesia Sentinas rea causam suam, L. Titio praetore iudicium cogente, maxi- 1
mo populi concursu egit, motusque omnes ac numeros defensionis non solum
diligenter sed etiam fortiter exsecuta, et prima actione et paene cunctis senten-
tiis liberata est. quam, quia sub specie feminae uirilem animum gerebat, Androgynem appellabant.

---

24 amorem *Halm* : errorem α : <f>eruorem *Madvig* : ardorem *Gertz*   **28** Titinius *A P* : Titinnius *L* : Ticinius *G*; *infra* Titinium *ter A* : Titinnium 31 *et* 33 *A^c* : Titinnium, Ticinium, Tittinium *L* : Ticinium *ter G*   Fanniam *A^c* (Fannia *P*) : Anniam α   **37** et iam *Kempf* : etiam α   **39** ferri α : <re>ferri *Schulze*   **40** eo α : <de> *uel* <ex> eo *Halm*   **41** qui *AL P* : quia *G*   illi α : illi usque *PA^c*   **43** minuti *dett.* : muniti *AL* : minimo *G*
3 Maesia *Halm* : Amaesia *LG* : Amesia *A* : Maesta *P* : Mesta *A^c*   Sentinas *P* : sententia α : Sententinas *A^c*   **4** motusque *G* : partesque *A^c* : mortuusque *L* : modosque *Halm*, *fort. recte*   **6–7** Androgynem *AL* : Androgenem *G^c* (*om.* quam ... appelabant *G, add. G^c*) : Androgynen *Kempf*

2   Carfania uero, Licini Bucconis senatoris uxor, prompta ad lites contrahendas, pro se semper apud praetorem uerba fecit, non quod aduocatis deficiebatur, sed quod impudentia abundabat. itaque inusitatis foro latratibus adsidue tribunalia exercendo muliebris calumniae notissimum exemplum euasit, adeo ut pro crimine improbis feminarum moribus Carfaniae nomen obiciatur. prorogauit autem spiritum suum ad C. Caesarem iterum <P.> Seruilium consules: tale enim monstrum magis quo tempore exstinctum quam quo sit ortum memoriae tradendum est.

3   Hortensia uero Q. Hortensi filia, cum ordo matronarum graui tributo a triumuiris esset oneratus nec quisquam uirorum patrocinium eis accommodare auderet, causam feminarum apud triumuiros et constanter et feliciter egit: repraesentata enim patris facundia impetrauit ut maior pars imperatae pecuniae iis remitteretur. reuixit tum muliebri stirpe Q. Hortensius uerbisque filiae aspirauit, cuius si uirilis sexus posteri uim sequi uoluissent, Hortensianae eloquentiae tanta hereditas una feminae actione abscisa non esset.

4 DE QVAESTIONIBVS

praef. Atque ut omnes iudiciorum numeros exsequamur, quaestiones quibus aut creditum non est aut temere habita fides est referamus.

1   M. Agri argentarii seruus Alexander A. Fanni seruum occidisse insimulatus est, eoque nomine tortus a domino admisisse id facinus constantissime adseuerauit. itaque Fannio deditus supplicio est adfectus. paruolo deinde tempore interiecto, ille cuius de nece creditum erat domum rediit.

2   Contra P. Atini seruus Alexander, cum in suspicionem C. Flaui equitis Romani occisi uenisset, sexiens tortus pernegauit ei se culpae adfinem fuisse, sed perinde atque confessus et a iudicibus damnatus et a L. Calpurnio triumuiro in crucem actus est.

3   Item Fuluio Flacco causam dicente, Philippus seruus eius, in quo tota quaestio nitebatur, octiens tortus nullum omnino uerbum quo dominus perstringere-

---

8 Carfania *scripsi* : C. Afrania α *P^c* : C. Afrinia *P* : Cafrania *Shackleton Bailey; sic etiam infra, nisi* C. Afraniae *P*   **17** nec *A^cL^cG* : *om. AL*   **21** posteri uim *AL^cG* : posterium *L* : posteri ui<a>m *Novák, fort. recte*   **22** abscisa *G* : abscissa *AL, fort. recte*
4. tit. de quaestionibus *A^cLG* : de seruilibus *PA^c* : *fort.* de quaestionibus seruilibus   **3** Alexander A. Fanni *PA^c* : Alexandri Rafani α   **5** est ad(f)fectus *LG* : adfectus est *A*   **7** P. Atinii *P* : Rafani *LG* : Putinii *A^c*   Alexander α *P* : *delendum aut corruptum esse iudicauit Shackleton Bailey*   in *P* : in hanc α : in <i>nane<m> *Heraeus*   **8** fuisse α : esse *Halm*   **9** et (a iudicibus) α : e<sse>t *Kempf* : *del. Novák*

tur emisit, et tamen reus damnatus est, cum certius argumentum innocentiae unus octies tortus exhiberet quam octo semel torti praebuissent.

DE TESTIBVS

Sequitur ut ad testes pertinentia exempla commemorem. Cn. et Q. Seruiliis Caepionibus, iisdem parentibus natis et per omnes honorum gradus ad summam amplitudinem prouectis, item fratribus Metellis Quinto et Lucio consularibus et censoriis, altero etiam triumphali, in Q. Pompeium A. f. repetunda-
5 rum reum acerrime dicentibus testimonium non abrogata fides absoluto Pompeio, sed ne potentia inimicum oppressisse uiderentur occursum est.

M. etiam Aemilius Scaurus, princeps senatus, C. Memmium repetundarum reum destricto testimonio insecutus est, item C. Flauium eadem lege accusatum testis proscidit: iam C. Norbanum maiestatis crimine publicae quaestioni sub-
10 iectum ex professo opprimere conatus est. nec tamen aut auctoritate, qua plurimum pollebat, aut religione, de qua nemo dubitabat, quemquam eorum adfligere potuit.

L. quoque Crassus, tantus apud iudices quantus apud patres conscriptos Aemilius Scaurus – namque eorum suffragia robustissimis et felicissimis elo-
15 quentiae stipendiis regebat eratque sic fori ut ille curiae princeps –, cum uehementissimum testimonii fulmen in M. Marcellum reum iniecisset, impetu grauis exitu uanus apparuit.

Age, Q. Metellus Pius, L. et M. Luculli, Q. Hortensius, M'. Lepidus C. Corneli maiestatis rei quam non onerarunt tantum modo testes salutem, sed etiam, ne-
20 gantes illo incolumi stare rem publicam posse, depoposcerunt! quae decora ciuitatis, pudet referre, umbone iudiciali repulsa sunt.

Quid? M. Cicero, forensi militia summos honores amplissimumque dignitatis locum adeptus, nonne in ipsis eloquentiae suae castris testis abiectus est, dum P. Clodium Romae apud se fuisse iurauit, illo sacrilegum flagitium uno
25 argumento absentiae tuente? si quidem iudices Clodium incesti crimine quam Ciceronem infamia periurii liberare maluerunt.

Tot eleuatis testibus, unum cuius noua ratione iudicium ingressa auctoritas confirmata est referam. P. Seruilius consularis censorius triumphalis, qui maiorum suorum titulis Isaurici cognomen adiecit, cum forum praeteriens testes in

---

2 Caepionibus *P* : Ceptonibus *AL* : Scaepotonibus *A^c* : Scipionibus *G*   **6** potentia α : potentia <sua> *Kempf*   **9** iam α : i<t>em *Kempf*   **13** tantus α : tantus <testis> *Georges*   **18** L. et *PA^c* : L. α : *sic, sed* Lucullus, *om.* M., *Halm* M'. *Sigonius* : M. α   **24** iurauit α : iurat *Kellerbauer* flagitium *G* : meflagitium *AL* : et flagitium *A^c* : ne<fariu>m<que> flagitium *Rossbach* : me<hercule> flagitium *Krohn*

reum dari uidisset, loco testis constitit ac summam inter patronorum pariter et
accusatorum admirationem sic orsus est: 'hunc ego, iudices, qui causam dicit,
cuias sit aut quam uitam egerit quamque merito uel iniuria accusetur ignoro:
illud tantum scio, cum occurrisset mihi Laurentina uia iter facienti admodum
angusto loco, equo descendere noluisse. quod an aliquid ad religionem uestram
pertineat ipsi aestimabitis: ego id supprimendum non putaui'. iudices reum, uix
auditis ceteris testibus, damnarunt: ualuit enim apud eos cum amplitudo uiri
tum grauis neglectae dignitatis eius indignatio, eumque qui uenerari principes
nesciret in quodlibet facinus procursurum crediderunt.

6 QVI QVAE IN ALIIS VINDICARANT IPSI COMMISERVNT

praef. Ne illos quidem latere patiamur, qui quae in aliis uindicarant ipsi commiserunt.
1   C. Licinius, cognomine Hoplomachus, a praetore postulauit ut patri suo bonis tamquam ea dissipanti interdiceretur, equidem quod petierat impetrauit; sed ipse paruo post tempore mortuo sene amplam ab eo relictam pecuniam festinanter consumpsit. a uicissitudine poenae afuit, quoniam hereditatem absumere quam heredem maluit tollere.
2   C. autem Marius, cum magnum et salutarem rei publicae ciuem in L. Saturnino opprimendo egisset, a quo in modum uexilli pilleum seruituti ad arma capienda ostentatum erat, L. Sulla cum exercitu in urbem inrumpente ad auxilium seruorum pilleo sublato confugit. itaque, dum facinus quod punierat imitatur, alterum Marium, a quo adfligeretur, inuenit.
3   C. uero Licinius Stolo, cuius beneficio plebi petendi consulatus potestas facta est, cum lege sanxisset ne quis amplius quingenta agri iugera possideret, ipse mille comparauit, dissimulandique criminis gratia dimidiam partem filio emancipauit. quam ob causam a M. Popilio Laenate accusatus, primus sua lege cecidit, ac docuit nihil aliud praecipi debere nisi quod prius quisque sibi imperau<er>it.

---

32 cuias sit P^c : cuius sit α : cui adsit P uitam PA^c : uiam α   **34** noluisse α : noluit P **36** auditis P : additis α   damnarunt α : damnauerunt P
2 Hoplomachus P : Hoplomacus α   **3** equidem α P : et quidem *ed. Ven. 1471*   **4-5** pecuniam PA^c : facundiam LG **5** a α : dignus hac A^c; *u. Foertsch infra*   afuit *Halm* : fuit α : affuit *dett.* : a<t> uicissitudine<m> effu<g>it *Foertsch*   hereditatem α : <populus heredem> hereditatem *Krafft*   **6** tollere α : (dignus hac) ... alere *Pighius*   **12** plebi *dett.* : plebis α : plebei A^c **14** dissimulandique P : simulandique α   **16** aliud α : aliis *Eberhard, fort recte*   praecipi $A^c L^c$: praecipue L : praecipere G **16-17** imperau<er>it *Pighius* : imperauit α, *fort. recte*

Q. autem Varius, propter obscurum ius ciuitatis Hybrida cognominatus, 4
tribunus plebis legem aduersus intercessionem collegarum perrogauit, quae
iubebat quaeri quorum dolo malo socii ad arma ire coacti essent, magna cum
clade rei publicae: sociale enim prius deinde ciuile bellum excitauit. sed dum
ante pestiferum tribunum plebis quam certum ciuem agit, sua lex eum domesticis laqueis constrictum absumpsit.

DE STVDIO ET INDVSTRIA 7

Quid cesso uires industriae commemorare, cuius alacri spiritu militiae stipendia praef.
roborantur, forensis gloria accenditur, fido sinu cuncta studia recepta nutriuntur, quidquid animo quidquid manu quidquid lingua admirabile est, ad cumulum laudis perducitur? quae cum sit perfectissima uirtus, duramento sui confirmatur.

Cato sextum et octogesimum annum agens, dum in re publica tuenda iuue- 1
nili animo perstat, ab inimicis capitali crimine accusatus causam suam egit,
neque aut memoriam eius quisquam tardiorem aut firmitatem lateris ulla ex
parte quassatam aut os haesitatione impeditum animaduertit, quia omnia ista
in suo statu aequali ac perpetua industria continebat. quin etiam in ipso diutissime actae uitae fine disertissimi oratoris Galbae accusationi defensionem suam
pro Hispania opposuit. idem Graecis litteris erudiri concupiuit – quam sero,
inde aestimemus quod etiam Latinas paene iam senex didicit –, cumque eloquentia magnam gloriam partam haberet, id egit ut iuris ciuilis quoque esset
peritissimus.

Cuius mirifica proles, propior aetati nostrae Cato, ita doctrinae cupiditate 2
flagrauit ut ne in curia quidem, dum senatus cogitur, temperaret sibi quo minus
Graecos libros lectitaret. qua quidem industria ostendit aliis tempora deesse,
alios superesse temporibus.

---

19 perrogauit *AL* : prorogauit *A^cG*
3–4 cumulum α : culmen *Halm* **4–5** quae ... confirmatur α : *sic, sed* confirmat *dett.* : quae fit ... cum duramento sui confirmatur *uel* quae ut sit ... confirmatur *Foertsch* : quae, quo sit ... confirmat *Madvig* : quae<cumque enim> sit ... confirmatur (*sic, sed* fit ... confirmata *Bohme*) *uel* consummatur *pro* confirmatur *Kempf* : quae cum sit per <se per>fectissima ... confirmatur *Damsté* : qua ... confirmatur *Shackleton Bailey* **11** accusationi defensionem α : defensioni accusationem *Gertz* **17** flagrauit *A^cG P* : fraglauit *AL* **19** alios superesse temporibus α : alios temporibus *Gertz* : aliis superesse *Kempf* : superesse tempora, deesse alios temporibus *Damsté*

3   Terentius autem Varro humanae uitae †exemplo et† spatio non annis, qui- 20
bus saeculi tempus aequauit, quam stilo uiuacior fuit: in eodem enim lectulo et
spiritus eius et egregiorum operum cursus exstinctus est.

4   Consimilis perseuerantiae Liuius Drusus, qui aetatis uiribus et acie oculorum defectus ius ciuile populo benignissime interpretatus est, utilissimaque di-
scere id cupientibus monumenta conposuit: nam ut senem illum natura, cae- 25
cum fortuna facere potuit, ita neutra interpellare ualuit ne non animo et uideret
et uigeret.

5   Publilius uero senator et Lupus Pontius eques Romanus, suis temporibus
celebres causarum actores, luminibus capti eadem industria forensia stipendia
exsecuti sunt. itaque frequentius etiam audiebantur, concurrentibus aliis quia 30
ingenio eorum delectabantur, aliis quia constantiam admirabantur: †namque
alii† incommodo perculsi secessum petunt, duplicant tenebras fortuitis uolun-
taria<s> adicientes.

6   Iam P. Crassus, cum in Asiam ad Aristonicum regem debellandum consul
uenisset, tanta cura Graecae linguae notitiam animo comprehendit ut eam in 35
quinque diuisam genera per omnes partes ac numeros penitus cognosceret.
quae res maximum ei sociorum amorem conciliauit, qua quis eorum lingua
apud tribunal illius postulauerat, eadem decreta reddenti.

7   Ne Roscius quidem subtrahatur, scaenicae industriae notissimum exemplum, qui nullum unquam spectante populo gestum, nisi quem domi meditatus 40
fuerat, ponere ausus est. quapropter non ludicra ars Roscium sed Roscius ludi-
cram artem commendauit, nec uolgi tantum fauorem uerum etiam principum
familiaritates amplexus est. haec sunt attenti et anxii et nunquam cessantis studii praemia, propter quae tantorum uirorum laudibus non impudenter se persona histrionis inseruit. 45

ext. 1   Graeca quoque industria, quoniam nostrae multum profuit, quem meretur
fructum Latina lingua recipiat.

Demosthenes, cuius commemorato nomine maximae eloquentiae consummatio audientis animo oboritur, cum inter initia iuuentae artis quam adfectabat
primam litteram dicere non posset, oris sui uitium tanto studio expugnauit ut 50
ea a nullo expressius referretur. deinde propter nimiam exilitatem acerbam au-

---

20 †exemplo et† *AL* : exemplum aetatis *G* : exemplum et *Foertsch/Madvig* : Varro <raro> ... exemplo et *anon.* : expleto *Wensky* : exemplo <eximius> et *Damsté*   **23** qui aetatis *G* : qui et aetatis *A^c* : quia e(ae *L^c*)tatis *L*   **28** Publilius *P* : P. α   **31** eorum *AL* : *om. G*   **31-32** †namque alii† α : nam alii qui *uel* namque alii <tali> *Perizonius* : namque alii <qui tali> *Kempf* : nam qui tali *Halm*   **32** incommodo *L^c* : commodo α   **32-33** uoluntaria<s> *Coler* : uoluntaria α   **34** P. α : C. *PA^c*   **41** ponere α : p<r>omere *Schulze*   **45** inserit *G* : inseruit *ALG^c*, *fort. recte*

ditu uocem suam exercitatione continua ad maturum et gratum auribus sonum perduxit. lateris etiam firmitate defectus, quas corporis habitus uires negauerat, a labore mutuatus est: multos enim uersus uno impetu spiritus complectebatur,
55 eosque aduersa loca celeri gradu scandens pronuntiabat, ac uadosis litoribus insistens declamationes fluctuum fragoribus obluctantibus edebat, ut ad fremitus concitatarum contionum patientia duratis auribus uteretur. fertur quoque ori insertis calculis multum ac diu loqui solitus, quo uacuum promptius esset et solutius. proeliatus est cum rerum natura equidem uictor abiit, malignitatem
60 eius pertinacissimo animi robore superando. itaque alterum Demosthenen mater alterum industria enixa est.

    Atque ut ad uetustiorem industriae actum transgrediar, Pythagoras, perfec- 2 tissimum opus sapientiae †a iuuenta pariter et omnis honestatis percipiendae cupiditate ingressus† – nihil enim, quod ad ultimum sui peruenturum est finem,
65 non et mature et celeriter incipit –, Aegyptum petiit, ubi litteris gentis eius adsuefactus, praeteriti aeui sacerdotum commentarios scrutatus, innumerabilium saeculorum obseruationes cognouit. inde ad Persas profectus, magorum exactissimae prudentiae se formandum tradidit, a quibus siderum motus cursusque stellarum et unius cuiusque uim proprietatem effectum benignissime
70 demonstratum docili animo sorpsit. Cretam deinde et Lacedaemona nauigauit, quarum legibus ac moribus inspectis ad Olympicum certamen descendit, cumque multiplicis scientiae maximam inter totius Graeciae admirationem specimen exhibuisset, quo cognomine censeretur interrogatus, non se sapientem – iam enim illud septem excellentes uiri occupauerant – sed amatorem sapienti-
75 ae, id est Graece philosophon, edidit. in Italiae etiam partem, quae tunc maior Graecia appellabatur, perrexit, in qua plurimis et opulentissimis urbibus effectus studiorum suorum adprobauit. cuius ardentem rogum plenis uenerationis oculis Metapontus aspexit oppidum, Pythagorae quam suorum cinerum nobilius clariusque monumentum.

---

54 uno impetu spiritus A^cLG : uno spiritu P conplectebatur PA^c : conplebatur L : complebat G
57 auribus (uel auribus in actionibus) A^c : actionibus LG **59** natura equidem A^cL^cG : naturae quidem AL : natura et quidem *dett.* **63–64** †a iuuenta ... cupiditate ingressus† AL : *sic, sed* cupiditatem G, incensus *Halm, del. et Foertsch,* <scientiae> pariter *Shackleton Bailey* : iuuentam ... cupiditatem ingressus *Wensky* **70** sorpsit A^cL : sorsit A : sorbsit G : hausit *Pighius* : <in>scr<i>psit *Perizonius* **72** multiplicis A^cG : multiplici AL scientiae maximam ... admirationem α : scientia maxima ... admiratione A^c inter totius LG : interrogatus A : inter omnes totius A^c : inter omnis *Halm* **75** philosophon A^cLG; *sic Cic. Tusc.* 5.7 : philosophone A : φιλόσοφον *Ald.* edidit *dett.* : didicit A : edidicit LG : edixit A^c partem α : <eam> partem *Kempf* **77** plenis PA^c : plenum α **79** monumentum α : monumento *dett.*

3   Platon autem patriam Athenas praeceptorem Socratem sortitus, et locum et hominem doctrinae fertilissimum, ingenii quoque diuina instructus abundantia, cum omnium iam mortalium sapientissimus haberetur, eo quidem usque ut si ipse Iuppiter caelo descendisset, nec elegantiore nec beatiore facundia usurus uideretur, Aegyptum peragrauit, dum a sacerdotibus eius gentis geometriae multiplices numeros et caelestium obseruationum rationem percipit. quoque tempore a studiosis iuuenibus certatim Athenae Platonem doctorem quaerentibus petebantur, ipse Nili fluminis inexplicabiles ripas uastissimosque campos, effusam †barbariam† et flexuosos fossarum ambitus Aegyptiorum senum discipulus lustrabat. quo minus miror in Italiam transgressum, ut ab Archyta Tarenti, a Timaeo et Arione et Echecrate Locris Pythagorae praecepta et instituta acciperet: tanta enim uis tanta copia litterarum undique colligenda erat ut inuicem per totum terrarum orbem dispergi et dilatari posset. altero etiam et octogesimo anno decedens sub capite Sophronis mimos habuisse fertur. sic ne extrema quidem eius hora agitatione studii uacua fuit.

4   At Democritus, cum diuitiis censeri posset, quae tantae fuerunt ut pater eius Xerxis exercitui epulum dare ex facili potuerit, quo magis uacuo animo studiis litterarum esset operatus, parua admodum summa retenta patrimonium suum patriae donauit. Athenis autem compluribus annis moratus, omnia temporum momenta ad percipiendam et exercendam doctrinam conferens, ignotus illi urbi uixit, quod ipse quodam uolumine testatur. stupet mens admiratione tantae industriae et iam transit alio.

5   Carneades, laboriosus et diuturnus sapientiae miles, si quidem nonaginta expletis annis idem illi uiuendi ac philosophandi finis fuit, ita se mirificum doctrinae operibus addixerat ut cum cibi capiendi causa recubuisset, cogitationibus inhaerens manum ad mensam porrigere obliuisceretur. sed †eum Melissa, quam uxoris loco habebat, temperato inter studia non interpellandi et inediae succurrendi officio dextera sua† necessariis usibus aptabat. ergo animo tantum modo uita fruebatur, corpore uero quasi alieno et superuacuo circumdatus erat. idem

---

80 Socratem $AL^c P$: Sacratem L : Socraten G, *fort. recte*   **84** dum A^cLG : ubi *det.*   **85** et P : om. α, *fort. recte*   obseruationum rationem PA^c : obseruatione rationum LG percipit α : percepit A^c **88** †barbariam † LG : barbariem A : Mareoti<d>em *Madvig* : et fusam Maream *Gertz* : <et> effusam Mariam *Kempf* : *del.* effusam barbariam *Novák* : effusam per mariam *Achelis* : effusum borborem *Morel*   **89–90** Tarenti a Timeo A : Tarentiat inmeo L : Tarenti atinmeo L^c : Tarenti a Thimeo G : Tarentino Timaeo P **90** Echecrate Locris PA^c : et Chete Lociris (Locris L^c) L : ceteris loci G **96** Xerxis (Xerxes L, *corr.* L^c) ... potuerit α : Xerxi et exercitui (*add.* eius A^c) epulum daret PA^c **103** mirificum α : mirifice A^c **105–107** †eum ... dextera suat LG : *sic*, *sed* dexteram suam A : et ... dexteram suam *Perizonius* : eam ... dextera sua *Torr.* : tum ... *Gertz*   **106** inter α : *del. Madvig* : uiri *uel* rite *uel* scite *Gertz*

cum Chrysippo disputaturus elleboro se ante purgabat, ad expromendum ingenium suum attentius et illius refellendum acrius. quas potiones industria solidae laudis cupidis adpetendas effecit!

Quali porro studio Anaxagoran flagrasse credimus? qui cum e diutina peregrinatione patriam repetisset, possessionesque desertas uidisset, 'non essem' inquit 'ego saluus, nisi istae perissent'. uocem petitae sapientiae compotem! nam si praediorum potius quam ingenii culturae uacasset, dominus rei familiaris intra penates mansisset, non tantus Anaxagoras ad eos redisset. 6

Archimedis quoque fructuosam industriam fuisse dicerem, nisi eadem illi et dedisset uitam et abstulisset: captis enim Syracusis Marcellus machinationibus eius multum ac diu uictoriam suam inhibitam senserat, eximia tamen hominis prudentia delectatus ut capiti illius parceretur edixit, paene tantum gloriae in Archimede seruato quantum in oppressis Syracusis reponens. at is, dum animo et oculis in terra defixis formas describit, militi, qui praedandi gratia domum inruperat strictoque super caput gladio quisnam esset interrogabat, propter nimiam cupiditatem inuestigandi quod requirebat nomen suum indicare non potuit, sed protecto manibus puluere 'noli' inquit, 'obsecro, istum disturbare', ac perinde quasi neglegens imperii uictoris obtruncatus sanguine suo artis suae lineamenta confudit. quo accidit ut propter idem studium modo donaretur uita modo spoliaretur. 7

Socraten etiam constat aetate prouectum fidibus tractandis operam dare coepisse, satius iudicantem eius artis usum sero quam nunquam percipere. et quantula Socrati accessio illa futura scientia erat! sed peruicax hominis industria tantis doctrinae suae diuitiis etiam musicae rationis uilissimum elementum accedere uoluit. ergo dum ad discendum semper se pauperem credidit, ad docendum fecit locupletissimum. 8

Atque ut longae et felicis industriae quasi in unum aceruum exempla redigamus, Isocrates nobilissimum librum, qui Παναθηναϊκός inscribitur, quartum et nonagesimum annum agens, ita ut ipse significat, composuit, opus ardentis 9

---

109 expromendum *P* : exprimendum α   **110** illius α : <ad> illius *Wensky*   **111** effecit α : efficit *Watt*   **112** e *LG* : *om. A* : post *A^c*   **112–113** diutina peregrinatione *L^cG* : diuina peregrinatione *AL* : diuinam peregrinationem *A^c*   **115** dominus α : <et> dominus *Gertz*   **116** tantus α : *del. Gertz*   eos α : deos *A^c*   **118–119** machinationibus α : <etsi> machinationibus *Gertz*   **121** Syracusis *A^c* : Syracusis his α : Syracusis hostis *A^c*   **122–123** domum α : <in> domum *Kempf*   **123** quisnam α : quinam *P*   **125** protecto *ed. Lips. 1830* : protracto α : proiecto *P*   **126** imperii uictoris α : imperium uictoris interrogantis *P*   **130** sero α : uel sero *P*   **132** uilissimum α : u<t>ilissimum *Glar.*   **133** credidit α : credit *Kempf*   **134** fecit α : fecit se *dett.* : se fecit *Kempf*   **136** Isocrates *G^cP* : Isocratis *G* : Hisocratis *AL* : hic Socrates *L^c*   ΠΑΝΑΘΗΝΑΙΚΟΣ *LG* : ΠΑΝΕΓΗΡΙΚΟΠΗΝΑΚΟΣ *A^c*

spiritus plenum. ex quo apparet senescentibus membris eruditorum intus animos industriae beneficio florem iuuentae retinere. neque hoc stilo terminos uitae suae clausit: namque admirationis eius fructum quinquennio percepit. 140

10 Citerioris aetatis metas, sed non parui tamen spatii, Chrysippi uiuacitas flexit: nam octogesimo anno coeptum undequadragesimum Λογικῶν exactissimae subtilitatis uolumen reliquit. cuius studium in tradendis ingenii sui monumentis tantum operae laborisque sustinuit ut ad ea quae scripsit penitus cognoscenda longa uita sit opus. 145

11 Te quoque, Cleanthe, tam laboriose haurientem et tam pertinaciter tradentem sapientiam numen ipsius Industriae suspexit, cum adulescentem quaestu extrahendae aquae nocturno tempore inopiam tuam sustentantem, diurno Chrysippi praeceptis percipiendis uacantem, eundemque ad undecentesimum annum attenta cura erudientem auditores tuos uideret: duplici enim labore uni- 150 us saeculi spatium occupasti, incertum reddendo discipulusne an praeceptor esses laudabilior.

12 Sophocles quoque gloriosum cum rerum natura certamen habuit, tam benigne mirifica illi opera sua exhibendo quam illa operibus eius tempora liberaliter subministrando: prope enim centesimum annum attigit, sub ipsum transi- 155 tum ad mortem Oedipode ἐπὶ Κολωνῷ scripto, qua sola fabula omnium eiusdem studi poetarum praeripere gloriam potuit. idque ignotum esse posteris filius Sophoclis Iophon noluit, sepulcro patris quae rettuli insculpendo.

13 Simonides uero poeta octogesimo anno et docuisse se carmina et in eorum certamen descendisse ipse gloriatur. nec fuit iniquum illum uoluptatem ex inge- 160 nio suo diu percipere, cum eam omni aeuo fruendam traditurus esset.

14 Nam Solon quanta industria flagrauerit et uersibus complexus est, quibus significat se cotidie aliquid addiscentem senescere, et supremo uitae die confirmauit, quod, adsidentibus amicis et quadam de re sermonem inter se conferentibus, fatis iam pressum caput erexit, interrogatusque quapropter id fecisset 165 respondit 'ut, cum istud, quidquid est, de quo disputatis, percepero, moriar'. migrasset profecto ex hominibus inertia, si eo animo uitam ingrederentur quo eam Solon egressus est.

15 Quam porro industrius Themistocles, qui maximarum rerum cura districtus omnium tamen ciuium suorum nomina memoria comprehendit, per summam- 170

---

148 extrahendae aquae *L* : extrahenda ea quae *AG* : extrahentem ea que *A^c* tuam α : suam *Halm* **150** tuos *dett.* : suos α **154** illi *dett.* : illa α : ille *dett.* **156** Κολωνῷ *Kempf* : ΚΟΛΟ-ΝΟΝ α **157** praeripere *A^cG* : proripere *AL* **158** Iophon *Pighius* : Sophum *A* : Sophom *A^cL* : Sophon *L^cG* **159** se *AL* : *om. G* **160** inicum *A* : inimicum α **161** eam *A^cG* : tam *A* : tam̅ *L* : <tan>tam *Kempf* **162** Solon α : Solo *PA^c* **163** addiscentem α : discentem *P* **164** quod α : quo *L^c* **169** districtus *A* : destrictus *LG P*

que iniquitatem patria pulsus et ad Xerxem, quem paulo ante deuicerat, confugere coactus, prius quam in conspectu eius ueniret, Persico sermone se adsuefecit, ut labore parta commendatione regiis auribus familiarem et adsuetum sonum uocis adhiberet.

175 Cuius utriusque industriae laudem duo reges partiti sunt, Cyrus omnium 16 militum suorum nomina, Mithridates duarum et uiginti gentium, quae sub regno eius erant, linguas ediscendo, ille ut sine monitore exercitum salutaret, hic ut eos quibus imperabat sine interprete adloqui posset.

DE OTIO 8

Otium, quod industriae et studio maxime contrarium uidetur, praecipue sub- praef. necti debet, non quo euanescit uirtus, sed quo recreatur: alterum enim etiam inertibus uitandum, alterum strenuis quoque interdum adpetendum est, illis ne †proprie† uitam inertem exigant, his ut tempestiua laboris intermissione ad
5 laborandum fiant uegetiores.

Par uerae amicitiae clarissimum Scipio et Laelius, cum amoris uinculo tum 1 etiam omnium uirtutum inter se iunctum societate, ut actuosae uitae iter aequali gradu exsequebantur, ita animi quoque remissioni communiter adquiescebant: constat namque eos Caietae et Laurenti uagos litoribus conchulas et um-
10 bilicos lectitasse, idque se P. Crassus ex socero suo Scaeuola, qui gener Laeli fuit, audisse saepe numero praedicauit.

Scaeuola autem, quietae remissionis eorum certissimus testis, optime pila 2 lusisse traditur, quia uidelicet ad hoc deuerticulum animum suum forensibus ministeriis fatigatum transferre solebat. alueo quoque et calculis interdum ua-
15 casse dicitur, cum bene ac diu iura ciuium caerimonias deorum ordinasset: ut

---

171 Xerxem *AL* : Xerxen *G, fort. recte*   **172** conspectu α : conspectum *dett., fort. recte*   **173** labore α : <hoc> labore *Kempf*   **176** duarum et xx α : *sic, sed* biginti *Land.* : uiginti duarum *P*   **177** linguas ediscendo A^c : linguae sediscendo *AL* : linguas discendo *G*
1 quod A^c : quod praecipu(a)e α   **4** †proprie† *LG* : propriae *A* : propriãe A^c : propriam *Madvig* : prorsus *Foertsch* : propriam e uita *Thenn* : pro pi<g>ra uita *Thormeyer* : perpetuo *uel* pro re publica *Damsté* :<morti> propiore<m> *uel* perpetua<m> *Watt*   inertem (*uel* eneruem) A^c : inermem *AG* : inermen *L* : *del. Watt*   **7** iunctum α : iuncti *Pighius*   **8** remissioni A^cL^cG : remissionis *AL* : remissioribus *P* : animis ... remissionibus *Halm* : *fort.* remissione   **9** uagos *AL* : uagas A^cL^cG **9–10** umbilicos *P*; *sic Cic. de orat.* 2. 22 : obulicos *A* : obbilicos A^c : obuilicos *LG*   **12** quietae *G* : quiestis, *ut uid., A* : *del.* A^c : quiete *L* : quieť L^c : qui ante *uel* qui et *Perizonius* : pr<aed>ictae *Kempf* : qui erat *Halm* : quietis e<t> *Gertz*   **14** et A^c : et ad α   **15** ciuium α : <et> ciuium *edd. Ven. Mog. 1471*

enim in rebus seriis Scaeuolam, ita in †scaelus† lusibus hominem agebat, quem rerum natura continui laboris patientem esse non sinit.

ext. 1   Idque uidit, cui nulla pars sapientiae obscura fuit, Socrates, ideoque non erubuit tunc cum interposita harundine cruribus suis cum paruolis filiolis ludens ab Alcibiade uisus est.

2   Homerus quoque, ingenii caelestis uates, non aliud sensit uehementissimis Achillis manibus canoras fides aptando, ut earum militare robur leni pacis studio relaxaret.

9 QVANTA VIS SIT ELOQVENTIAE

praef.   Potentiam uero eloquentiae, etsi plurimum ualere animaduertimus, tamen sub propriis exemplis, quo scilicet uires eius testatiores fiant, recognosci conuenit.

1   Regibus exactis, plebs dissidens a patribus iuxta ripam fluminis Anienis in colle qui sacer appellatur armata consedit, eratque non solum deformis sed etiam miserrimus rei publicae status, a capite eius cetera parte corporis pestifera seditione diuisa. ac ni Valeri subuenisset eloquentia, spes tanti imperii in ipso paene ortu suo corruisset: is namque populum noua et insolita libertate temere gaudentem oratione ad meliora et saniora consilia reuocatum senatui subiecit, id est urbem urbi iunxit. uerbis ergo facundis ira consternatio arma cesserunt.

2   Quae etiam Marianos Cinnanosque mucrones ciuilis profundendi sanguinis cupiditate furentes inhibuerunt: missi enim a saeuissimis ducibus milites ad M. Antonium obtruncandum, sermone eius obstupefacti destrictos iam et uibrantes gladios cruore uacuos uaginis reddiderunt. quibus digressis P. Annius – is enim solus in aditu expers Antonianae eloquentiae steterat – crudele imperium truculento ministerio peregit. quam disertum igitur eum fuisse putemus quem ne hostium quidem quisquam occidere sustinuit, qui modo uocem eius ad aures suas uoluit admittere?

3   Diuus quoque Iulius, quam caelestis numinis tam etiam humani ingenii perfectissimum columen, uim facundiae proprie expressit dicendo in accusatio-

---

16 †scaelus† *A(fort. scelus)L(ut uid.)* : scaeuis A^c : scae L^c : scaenicis *G*: *del. Vahlen* : serenis *Eberhard* : <in>tentus *Foertsch* : lasciui<ii>s *Novák*   **20** uisus PA^c : risus *(ras. ante G)* αP^c
9. tit. quanta (quinta *A*) ... eloquentiae α : quanta uis eloquentiae et pronuntiatioñ *P*   **1** animaduertimus α : <iam> animaduertimus *Gertz*   **6** Valeri(i) α : Meneni *Halm* (a Maenenio Agrippa reuocata est *P*; Menenii Agrippae *Par. Lat. 9688mg*)   **8** oratione A^cL^cG : orationem *AL* : oratione <sua> *Gertz*   **14** Annius PA^c : Antonius α   **15** in aditu *Foertsch* : in ambitu α : suauitatis, *om.* eloquentiae, *Madvig*

ne Cn. Dolabellae, quem reum egit, extorqueri sibi causam optimam C. Cottae patrocinio, si quidem maxima tunc †eloquentiae† questa est. cuius facta mentione, quoniam domesticum nullum maius adiecerim exemplum, peregrinandum est.

Pisistratus dicendo tantum ualuisse traditus est ut ei Athenienses regium imperium oratione capti permitterent, cum praesertim e contraria parte amantissimus patriae Solon niteretur. sed alterius salubriores erant contiones alterius disertiores. quo euenit ut alioqui prudentissima ciuitas libertati seruitutem praeferret.

Pericles autem, felicissimis naturae incrementis sub Anaxagora praeceptore summo studio perpolitis instructus, liberis Athenarum ceruicibus iugum seruitutis inposuit: egit enim illam urbem et uersauit arbitrio suo, cumque aduersus uoluntatem populi loqueretur, iucunda nihilo minus et popularis eius uox erat. itaque ueteris comoediae maledica lingua, quamuis potentiam uiri perstringere cupiebat, tamen in labris hominis melle dulciorem leporem fatebatur habitare, inque animis eorum qui illum audierant quasi aculeos quosdam relinqui praedicabat. fertur quidam, cum admodum senex primae contioni Periclis adulescentuli interesset idemque iuuenis Pisistratum decrepitum iam contionantem audisset, non temperasse sibi quo minus exclamaret cauere illum ciuem oportere, quod Pisistrati orationi simillima eius esset oratio. nec hominem aut aestimatio eloquii aut morum augurium fefellit. quid enim inter Pisistratum et Periclen interfuit, nisi quod ille armatus hic sine armis tyrannidem gessit?

Quantum eloquentia ualuisse Hegesian Cyrenaicum philosophum arbitramur? qui sic mala uitae repraesentabat ut eorum miseranda imagine audientium pectoribus inserta multis uoluntariae mortis oppetendae cupiditatem ingeneraret: ideoque a rege Ptolomaeo ulterius hac de re disserere prohibitus est.

QVANTVM MOMENTVM SIT IN PRONVNTIATIONE ET APTO MOTV CORPORIS

Eloquentiae autem ornamenta in pronuntiatione apta et conuenienti motum corporis consistunt. quibus cum se instruxit, tribus modis homines adgreditur,

---

21 C. *Pighius* : L. α   **22** †eloquentiae† questa α : eloquentia questa A^c : ei maxima eloquentiae laus quaesita *uel* uis eloquentiae questa *uel* maxima tunc eloquentiae (ei) laus quaesita *uel* maxima tunc eloquentia questa *dett.* : eloquentiae ei laus questa *Chalc., Ald.* : tum maxima eloquentiae laus quaesita *Perizonius* : <eloquentia de ui> eloquentiae questa *Kempf*   **27** contiones $A^c L^c$: contentiones α   **28** disertiores $A^c L^c G$: dissertiores AL   quo $A^c L^c G$: quod AL   alioqui *dett.* : aliqua α   **30** felicissimis $A^c G$: felicissimus AL : felicissimis us<us> *Halm*   **35** hominis α : omni *Shackleton Bailey*   **39** cauere illum L^c (cauere ... hunc P) : cauerillum A^c : cadauere illum L : cadauer illum G : caueri illum *dett.*
1 conuenienti $A^c G$: conueniente AL, *fort. recte*

animos eorum ipsa inuadendo, horum alteri aures alteri oculos permulcendos tradendo.

1 Sed ut propositi fides in personis inlustribus exhibeatur, C. Gracchus, eloquentiae quam propositi felicioris adulescens, quoniam flagrantissimo ingenio, cum optime rem publicam tueri posset, perturbare impie maluit, quotiens apud populum contionatus est, seruum post se musicae artis peritum habuit, qui occulte eburnea fistula pronuntiationis eius modos formabat, aut nimis remissos excitando aut plus iusto concitatos reuocando, quia ipsum calor atque impetus actionis attentum huiusce temperamenti aestimatorem esse non patiebatur.

2 Q. autem Hortensius, plurimum in corporis decoro motu repositum credens, paene plus studii in eodem laborando quam in ipsa eloquentia adfectanda impendit. itaque nescires utrum cupidius ad audiendum eum an ad spectandum concurreretur: sic uerbis oratoris aspectus et rursus aspectui uerba seruiebant. constat Aesopum Rosciumque ludicrae artis peritissimos illo causas agente in corona frequenter adstitisse, ut foro petitos gestus in scaenam referrent.

3 Nam M. Cicero quantum in utraque re de qua loquimur momenti sit oratione quam pro Gallio habuit significauit, M. Calidio accusatori exprobrando quod praeparatum sibi a reo uenenum testibus chirographis quaestionibus probaturum adfirmans, remisso uoltu et languida uoce et soluto genere orationis usus esset, pariterque et oratoris uitium detexit et causae periclitantis argumentum adiecit totum hunc locum ita claudendo: 'tu istud, M. Calidi, nisi fingeres, sic ageres?'

ext. 1 Consentaneum huic Demosthenis iudicium. cuidam, cum interrogaretur quidnam esset in dicendo efficacissimum, respondit 'ἡ ὑπόκρισις'. iterum deinde et tertio interpellatus idem dixit, paene totum se illi debere confitendo. recte itaque Aeschines, cum propter iudicialem ignominiam relictis Athenis Rhodum petisset, atque ibi rogatu ciuitatis suam prius in Ctesiphontem, deinde Demosthenis pro eodem orationem clarissima et suauissima uoce recitasset, admirantibus cunctis utriusque uoluminis eloquentiam, sed aliquanto magis Demo-

---

5–6 propositi ... propositi α : *prius* propositi *corruptum iud. Gertz* : propositi ... consilii *Damsté* **7–8** apud ... est α : contionaretur *P*; cum contionaretur *Cic. de orat.* 3.225 **8** post se $A^c L^c G$: posse *AL* : prope se *P*; qui staret ... post ipsum *Cic. ibid.* **13** eodem α : eo *P* laborando α *P* : <e>laborando *Pighius, fort. recte* **15** oratoris α : oratoriis *dett.* **16** causas α : causam *P* **17** gestus A^c (*om.* petitos ... 18 quantum *A*)$L^c G$ scaenam α : scaena *Kempf* referrent α : deferrent *Stangl* **19** Gallio PA^c : Gallo α **23** tu *A*; *sic Cic. Brut.* 278: tum *LG* : tunc A^c istud α P^c; istuc *Cic. ibid.* : his iûd *P* **23–24** fingeres ... ageres PA^c; *sic Cic. ibid.* : fingere ... agere α **25** cuidam *G* : quidam *AL* : qui *dett., fort. recte* : <qui> quidem *Foertsch* **26** respondit *hic* α : *post* hypocrisim $P^c A^c$ (*sic, sed* rei spondit *P*) H *A* : IT *LG* ΥΠΟΚΡΙCΙC A^c : ΥΠΟΚΡΙC α : hypocrisim *P* : H (*sic*) ΥΠΟΚΡΙCΙΜ A^c **29** Ctesiphontem *dett.* : Thesipontem *A* : Thesiphontem $PA^c G$: Thespontem *L*

sthenis, 'quid, si' inquit 'ipsum audissetis?' tantus orator et modo tam infestus aduersarius sic inimici uim ardoremque dicendi suspexit ut se scriptorum eius parum idoneum lectorem esse praedicaret, expertus acerrimum uigorem oculo-
35 rum, terribile uoltus pondus, accommodatum singulis uerbis sonum uocis, efficacissimos corporis motus. ergo etsi operi illius adici nihil potest, tamen in Demosthene magna pars Demosthenis abest, quod legitur potius quam auditur.

QVAM MAGNI EFFECTVS ARTIUM SINT 11

Effectus etiam artium †recognosci posse aliquid adferret† uoluptatis, protinus- praef. que et quam utiliter excogitatae sint patebit, et memoratu dignae res lucido in loco reponentur, et labor in iis edendis suo fructu non carebit.

Sulpici Gali maximum in omni genere litterarum recipiendo studium pluri- 1
5 mum rei publicae profuit: nam cum L. Paulli bellum aduersum regem Persen gerentis legatus esset, ac serena nocte subito luna defecisset, eoque uelut diro quodam monstro per<ter>ritus exercitus noster manus cum hoste conserendi fiduciam amisisset, de caeli ratione et siderum natura peritissime disputando alacrem eum in aciem misit. itaque inclutae illi Paullianae uictoriae liberales
10 artes Gali aditum dederunt, quia, nisi ille metum nostrorum militum uicisset, imperator uincere hostes non potuisset.

Spurinnae quoque in coniectandis deorum monitis efficacior scientia appa- 2 ruit quam urbs Romana uoluit. praedixerat C. Caesari ut proximos triginta dies quasi fatales caueret, quorum ultimus erat idus Martiae. eo cum forte mane
15 uterque in domum Caluini Domiti ad officium conuenissent, Caesar Spurinnae 'ecquid scis idus iam Martias uenisse?' et is 'ecquid scis illas nondum praeteris-

---

34 praedicaret G^c : praediceret α   37 quod ... auditur α : del. Damsté
11. tit. quam ... sint α : de effectu artium P   **1** †recognosci posse ... adferret† AL : sic, sed adfert G : recogniti possunt ... A^c : recognosci potest ... Perizonius : recognoscendi possunt ... Halm : recognoscenti possunt ... Kellerbauer : recognosci per se ... adferet Wensky : recognosse aliquid ... adferet (uel adferat) Kempf : recognosse potest ... Böhme : recognosc<ere sc>i<o> ... Gertz: sic, sed recogno<sse> sci<o> Heraeus : recognosse possit ... Thormeyer : recognosci <oportet, quia uidebatur> posse Novák : recognosci posse titulo adiungit Damsté : fort. recognoscere posse ... adfert   **2** patebit G : patebunt AL   **4** Gali scripsi (Galus P, Gallus P^c) : Galli ALG^c (om. Sulpici ... omni G)   recipiendo α : recipiendi A^c **6** serena α : sera P   **7** perterritus A^cL^cG : perritus A : peritus L : territus P   **8** amisisset A^cL^cG : misisset AL   **9** misit α : dimisit P   **10** Gali L^c : Galli A^cG : Gall L   **12** coniectandis Halm : consectantis AL : consectandis L^cG **14** eo α : eo die P : quo die Land.   **15** Caluini Domiti(i) α : Domiti(i) Caluini PA^c conuenissent α : conuenisset P   **16** ecquid (utroque loco) P^c : et quid α P   scis (idus) α : scis inquit P : inquit 'scis Damsté   et α : at P, fort. recte

se?' abiecerat alter timorem tamquam exacto tempore suspecto, alter ne extremam quidem eius partem periculo uacuam esse arbitratus est. utinam haruspicem potius augurium quam patriae parentem securitas fefellisset.

ext. 1 Sed ut alienigena scrutemur, cum obscurato repente sole inusitatis perfusae tenebris Athenae sollicitudine angerentur, interitum sibi caelesti denuntiatione portendi credentes, Pericles processit in medium, et quae a praeceptore suo Anaxagora pertinentia ad solis et lunae cursum acceperat disseruit, nec ulterius trepidare ciues suos uano metu passus est.

2 Quantum porro dignitatis a rege Alexandro tributum arti existimamus, qui se et pingi ab uno Apelle et fingi a Lysippo tantummodo uoluit?

3 Tenet uisentes Athenis Volcanus Alcamenis manibus fabricatus: praeter cetera enim perfectissimae artis in eo †praecurrentia† indicia etiam illud mirantur, quod stat dissimulatae claudicationis sub ueste leuiter uestigium repraesentans, ut non exprobratum tamquam uitium, ita tamquam certam propriamque dei notam decore significans.

4 Cuius coniugem Praxiteles in marmore quasi spirantem in templo Cnidiorum conlocauit, propter pulchritudinem operis a libidinoso cuiusdam complexu parum tutam. quo excusabilior est error equi, qui uisa pictura equae hinnitum edere coactus est, et canum latratus aspectu picti canis incitatus, taurusque ad amorem et concubitum aeneae uaccae Syrasusis nimiae similitudinis inritamento compulsus: quid enim uacua rationis animalia arte decepta miremur, cum hominis sacrilegam cupiditatem muti lapidis lineamentis excitatam uideamus?

QVAEDAM NVLLA ARTE EFFICI POSSE

5 Ceterum natura, quem ad modum saepe numero aemulam uirium suarum artem esse patitur, ita aliquando inritam fesso labore dimittit. quod summi artificis Euphranoris manus senserunt: nam cum Athenis duodecim deos pingeret, Ne-

---

17 tamquam α : tamquam <iam> *Damsté*   ne A^cL^cG : nae L **21** sollicitudine A^cG : solitudine AL angerentur P : agerentur α   **28** †praecurrentia† α : occurrentia (*fort. recte*) uel procurrentia *Gertz*   mirantur *dett.* : miratur α   **29–30** stat ... repraesentans α : stans ... repraesentat A^c **30** exprobratum LG : exprobrans tanquam *uel* tanquam exprobrans A^c tamquam A^c ; tamen quam AL : tamen tanquam G : *del. Vahlen* : tamen *Halm*   **31** dei notam A^c : dein tam L : deitatem G significans α : significa<ta>m *Kempf*   **32** Praxiteles PA^c : Praxitelis A : Praxiteus AG **34** est LG : esset A^c error A^cL^cG (error ... canis *in ras.* A^c, aerrore qui L) : feruor *Halm*   **35** picti α (pictum P) : pictae *dett.*   **37** animalia A^cG : ania AL **38** muti A^cG : multis AL uideamus A^cG : uideas AL

tit. quaedam ... posse (possae L. *corr.* L^c) α ; quae ... possunt P : *fort. sic, sed* possint : *del. Pighius*   **2** in(r)ritam fesso α : inrito fessam *Cornelissen* : inritam fessam *Kempf*

ptuni imaginem quam poterat excellentissimis maiestatis coloribus complexus
est, perinde ac Iouis aliquanto augustiorem repraesentaturus. sed omni impetu
cogitationis in superiore opere absumpto posteriores eius conatus adsurgere
quo tendebant nequiuerunt.

   Quid? ille alter aeque nobilis pictor, luctuosum immolatae Iphigeniae sacri- 6
ficium referens, cum Calchantem tristem, maestum Vlixen, lamentantem Menelaum circa aram statuisset, caput Agamemnonis inuoluendo nonne summi mae-
roris acerbitatem arte non posse exprimi confessus est? itaque pictura eius
haruspicis et amici et fratris lacrimis madet, patris fletum spectantis adfectu
aestumandum reliquit.

   Atque ut eiusdem studii adiciam exemplum, praecipuae artis pictor equum 7
ab exercitatione uenientem modo non uiuum labore industriae suae comprehenderat. cuius naribus spumas adicere cupiens tantus artifex in tam paruula
materia multum ac diu frustra terebatur. indignatione deinde accensus spon-
geam omnibus inbutam coloribus forte iuxta se positam adprehendit et ueluti
corrupturus opus suum tabulae inlisit. quam fortuna ad ipsas equi nares direc-
tam desiderium pictoris coegit explere. itaque quod ars adumbrare non ualuit
casus imitatus est.

SVAE QVEMQVE ARTIS OPTIMVM ET AVCTOREM ET DISPVTATOREM ESSE   12

Suae autem artis unum quemque et auctorem et disputatorem optimum esse ne praef.
dubitemus, paucis exemplis admoneamur.

   Q. Scaeuola, legum clarissimus et certissimus uates, quotienscumque de 1
iure praediatorio consulebatur, ad Furium et Cascellium, quia huic scientiae
dediti erant, consultores reiciebat. quo quidem facto moderationem magis suam
commendabat quam auctoritatem minuebat, ab iis id negotium aptius explicari
posse confitendo qui cotidiano usu eius callebant. sapientissimi igitur artis suae
professores sunt a quibus et propria studia uerecunde et aliena callide aesti-
mantur.

---

9 lamentantem *Kempf* : clamantem Aiacem lamentantem α   **12** spectantis α : spectanti *Wensky*   ad(f)fectu α : affectui *dett.*   **14** pictor equum *L^c* : pictorem cum α : pictor cum equum (... uidisset) *P* : sic, sed om. pictor *A^c*   **18** et ueluti *G PA^c* : eueluti *AL* : eam ueluti *L^c*   **20** explere *PA^c* : exemplare *LG*
12 tit. suae ... disputatorem (actorem *A*, esse *ante* et, *fort. recte, AL*) α : *om. P*   **2** admoneamur *A^{c}G* : admoneamus *AL, fort. recte*   **4** quia *A^{c}LG P* : qui *Perizonius*   **6** minuebat *dett.* : muniebatur *AL* : minuebatur *L^c* : muniebat *L^{c}G*   **8** callide α : can<d>ide *Cornelissen, fort. recte*

ext. 1   Platonis quoque eruditissimum pectus haec cogitatio attigit, qui conductores sacrae arae de modo et forma eius secum sermonem conferre conatos, ad Eucliden geometren ire iussit, scientiae eius cedens, immo professioni.

2   Gloriantur Athenae armamentario suo, nec sine causa: est enim illud opus et impensa et elegantia uisendum. cuius architectum Philonem ita facunde rationem institutionis suae in theatro reddidisse constat ut disertissimus populus non minorem laudem eloquentiae eius quam arti tribueret.

3   Mirifice et ille artifex, qui in opere suo moneri se a sutore de crepida et ansulis passus, de crure etiam disputare incipientem supra plantam ascendere uetuit.

13 DE SENECTVTE

praef.   Senectus quoque ad ultimum sui finem prouecta in hoc eodem opere inter exempla industriae in aliquot claris uiris conspecta est. separatum tamen et proprium titulum habeat, ne cui deorum immortalium praecipua indulgentia adfuit, nostra ornata mentio defuisse existimetur, et simul spei diuturnioris uitae quasi adminicula quaedam dentur, quibus insistens alacriorem se respectu uetustae felicitatis facere possit, tranquillitatemque saeculi nostri, qua nulla unquam beatior fuit, subinde fiducia confirmet, salutaris principis incolumitatem ad longissimos humanae condicionis terminos prorogando.

1   M. Valerius Coruinus centesimum annum compleuit. cuius inter primum et sextum consulatum quadraginta et sex anni intercesserunt, suffecitque integris uiribus corporis non solum speciosissimis publicis ministeriis, sed etiam exactissimae agrorum suorum culturae, et ciuis et patris familiae optabile exemplum.

2   Cuius uitae spatium aequauit Metellus, quartoque anno post consularia imperia senex admodum pontifex maximus creatus tutelam caerimoniarum per duo et uiginti annos neque ore in uotis nuncupandis haesitante neque in sacrificiis faciendis tremula manu gessit.

---

11 sacrae area *LG* : uiae sacrae *PA^c* : area *Kempf*   **12** geometren α : geometram *P*   **17** moneri ... sutore *dett.* : moneri ... sutore suo *L^{c}G* : muneris eas ut ore suo *AL*   **18** crure *L^{c}G* : cruce *AL* : sura *P*   plantam α : plantas *P*

1 prouecta *A^{c}G* : prouectam *A* : prouectum *L*   **3** necui *unum uerbum A^{c}G* : nec ui *L^c*   **4** ornata *A^{c}G* : onata *AL* : <ho>norata *Halm, fort. recte*   **7** fiducia *dett.* : fiduc(t)iam α   **10** xl et vi (xlvi *P*) α; *sic Cic. Cato* 60, *Plin. nat.* 7.157 : πέντε καὶ τεσσαράκοντα *Plut. Mar.* 28.9   **11** publicis *G* : rei publicae *A^c* : solis publicis *L*   **14** quartoque α : quarto qui *Perizonius*

Q. autem Fabius Maximus duobus et sexaginta annis auguratus sacerdo- 3
tium sustinuit, robusta iam aetate id adeptus. quae utraque tempora si in unum
conferantur, facile saeculi modum expleuerint.

Iam de M. Perperna quid loquar? qui omnibus quos in senatum consul uo- 4
cauerat, superstes fuit, septemque tantummodo quos censor, collega L. Philippi, legerat e patribus conscriptis reliquos uidit, toto ordine amplissimo diutur-
nior.

Appi uero aeuum clade metirer, quia infinitum numerum annorum orbatus 5
luminibus exegit, nisi quattuor filios, quinque filias, plurimas clientelas, rem
denique publicam hoc casu grauatus fortissime rexisset. quin etiam fessus iam
uiuendo lectica se in curiam deferri iussit, ut cum Pyrrho deformem pacem fieri
prohiberet. hunc caecum aliquis nominet, a quo patria quod honestum erat per
se parum cernens coacta est peruidere?

Muliebris etiam uitae spatium non minus longum in compluribus apparau- 6
it, quarum aliquas strictim rettulisse me satis erit: nam et Liuia Rutili septimum
et nonagesimum, et Terentia Ciceronis tertium et centesimum, et Clodia Ofili
quindecim filiis ante amissis quintum decimum et centesimum expleuit annum.

Iungam his duos reges, quorum diuturnitas populo Romano fuit utilissima. ext. 1
Siciliae rector Hiero ad nonagesimum annum peruenit. Masinissa Numidiae rex
hunc modum excessit, regni spatium sexaginta annis emensus, uel ante omnes
homines robore senectae admirabilis. constat eum, quem ad modum Cicero re-
fert libro quem de senectute scripsit, nullo unquam imbri nullo frigore ut caput
suum ueste tegeret adduci potuisse. eundem ferunt aliquot horis in eodem uestigio perstare solitum, non ante moto pede quam consimili labore iuuenes fatigasset, ac si quid agi a sedente oporteret, toto die saepe numero nullam in
partem conuerso corpore in solio durasse. ille uero etiam exercitus equo insi-
dens noctem diei plerumque iungendo duxit, nihilque omnino ex his operibus
quae adulescens sustinere adsueuerat, quo mollius senectutem ageret, omisit.
ueneris etiam usu ita semper uiguit ut post sextum et octogesimum annum filium generaret, cui Methymno nomen fuit. terram quoque, quam uastam et de-
sertam acceperat, perpetuo culturae studio frugiferam reliquit.

---

18 duobus *dett.* : duo *AL P* (duo ... annos *Mai*) : ii *G*   **21–22** consul uocauerat *PA^c* : conuocauerat α   **23** reliquos uidit α : reliquit uiuos *Wensky*   **25** Appii *A^cG* : Appio *AL*   **33** Ofili *scripsi*;
sic Plin. nat. 7.158 : Aulifi *A* : Auli f. *LG* : Auli filia *PA^c* : Aufili *Pighius*   **34** ante amissis *L* : antea
missis *A* : amissis *G*   **39** imbri α : imbre *P*   **42** ac α : at *A^c*   a sedente *L^cG* : ad sedentem *AL* :
assidentem *A^c* : ab sedente *Halm*   **45** quo mollius senectutem *C. F. W. Müller* : quo millius
senectutem *A* : quom (cum *A^c*) illius senectutem *A^cL* : quo minus in senectute *G* : *sic, sed om.*
in *dett.* : quo mitius senectutem *Cornelissen*

2 Gorgias etiam Leontinus, Isocratis et complurium magni ingenii uirorum praeceptor, sua sententia felicissimus: nam cum centesimum et septimum age- 50 ret annum, interrogatus quapropter tam diu uellet in uita remanere, 'quia nihil' inquit 'habeo quod senectutem meam accusem'. quid isto tractu aetatis aut longius aut beatius? iam alterum saeculum ingressus neque in hoc querellam ullam inuenit neque in illo reliquit.

3 Biennio minor Xenophilus Chalcidensis Pythagoricus, sed felicitate non in- 55 ferior, si quidem, ut ait Aristoxenus musicus, omnis humani incommodi expers in summo perfectissimae doctrinae splendore exstinctus est.

4 Arganthonius autem Gaditanus tam diu regnauit quam diu etiam ad satietatem uixisse abunde foret: octoginta enim annis patriam suam rexit, cum ad imperium quadraginta annos natus accessisset. cuius rei certi sunt auctores. 60 Asinius etiam Pollio, non minima pars Romani stili, in tertio historiarum suarum libro centum illum et triginta annos explesse commemorat, et ipse neruosae uiuacitatis haud paruum exemplum.

5 Huius regis consummationem annorum minus admirabilem faciunt Aethiopes, quos Herodotus scribit centesimum et uicesimum annum transgredi, et 65 Indi, de quibus Ctesias idem tradit, et Epimenides Cnosius, quem Theopompus dicit septem et quinquaginta et centum annos uixisse.

6 Hellanicus uero ait quosdam ex gente Epiorum, quae pars Aetoliae est, ducenos explere annos, eique suscribit Damastes, hoc amplius adfirmans, Litorium quendam ex his maximarum uirium staturaeque praecipuae trecentesi- 70 mum annum cumulasse.

7 Alexander uero, in eo uolumine quod de Illyrico tractu composuit, adfirmat Dandonem quendam ad quingentesimum usque annum nulla ex parte senescentem processisse. sed multo liberalius Xenophon, cuius περίπλους legitur: insulae enim Latmiorum regem octingentis uitae annis donauit. ac ne pater eius 75 parum benigne acceptus uideretur, ei quoque sescentos adsignauit annos.

14 DE CVPIDITATE GLORIAE

praef. Gloria uero aut unde oriatur aut cuius sit habitus aut qua ratione debeat comparari et an melius a uirtute uelut non necessaria neglegatur uiderint ii quorum

---

49 Isocratis *G* : Hisocratis *AL* **50** sua α : sua <senex> *Gertz* **55** Xenophilus α : Xeno philosophus *PA^c* **58–59** ad satietatem uixisse α : uixisse ad satietatem *Gertz* : uixisse *Damsté* **65** xx(mum) α : xxx(mum) *A^c* : xx *LG* : xxx annos *P* **66** Ctesias *Ald.* : et Eseias α idem *ed. Mediol. 1508* : quidem α Cnosius *A P* : Gnosius *A^cG, fort. recte* : Onosius *L* **68–69** ducenos *AL* : ducentenos *G* : ccc *P* : ducentos *dett.* **74** περίπλους (*ut duo uerba*) *Pighius* : ΠΕΡΙΠΛΟC α : periplus *PA^c* **75** Latmiorum α : Lamiorum *P* : Lutmiorum *MSS. Plin. nat.* 7.154

in contemplandis eius modi rebus cura teritur, quibusque quae prudenter animaduerterunt facunde contigit eloqui. ego in hoc opere factis auctores et
5 auctoribus facta sua reddere contentus, quanta cupiditas eius esse soleat propriis exemplis demonstrare conabor.

Superior Africanus Enni poetae effigiem in monumentis Corneliae gentis 1 conlocari uoluit, quod ingenio eius opera sua inlustrata iudicaret, non quidem ignarus quam diu Romanum imperium floreret, et Africa Italiae pedibus esset
10 subiecta, totiusque terrarum orbis summum columen arx Capitolina possideret, eorum exstingui memoriam non posse, si tamen litterarum quoque illis lumen accessisset, magni aestimans, uir Homerico quam rudi atque impolito praeconio dignior.

Similiter honoratus animus erga poetam Accium D. Bruti suis temporibus 2
15 clari ducis exstitit, cuius familiari cultu et prompta laudatione delectatus uersibus templorum aditus, quae ex manubiis consecrauerat, adornauit.

Ne Pompeius quidem Magnus ab hoc adfectu gloriae auersus, qui Theo- 3 phanen Mitylenaeum scriptorem rerum suarum in contione militum ciuitate donauit, beneficium per se amplum accurata etiam et testata oratione prosecu-
20 tus. quo effectum est ut ne quis dubitaret quin referret potius gratiam quam incoharet.

L. autem Sulla, etsi ad neminem scriptorem animum derexit, tamen Iugur- 4 thae a Boccho rege ad Marium perducti totam sibi laudem tam cupide adseruit ut anulo quo signatorio utebatur insculptam illam traditionem haberet. et quan-
25 tus<quantus> postea, ne minimum quidem gloriae uestigium contempsit.

Atque ut imperatoribus militis gloriosum spiritum subnectam, Scipionem, 5 dona militaria iis qui strenuam operam ediderant diuidentem, T. Labienus ut forti equiti aureas armillas tribueret admonuit, eoque se negante id facturum, ne castrensis honos in eo qui paulo ante seruisset uiolaretur, ipse ex praeda
30 Gallica aurum equiti largitus est. nec tacite id Scipio tulit: namque equiti 'habebis' inquit 'donum uiri diuitis'. quod ubi ille accepit, proiecto ante pedes Labieni auro uoltum demisit. idem, ut audiit Scipionem dicentem 'imperator te argen-

---

4 animaduerterunt A^c : anim aduerteruntur (aduer teruntur L) AL : animaduerterent G **11–12** si ... accessiset AL : sed ... accessisse A^c : se ... accessisse G **15–16** uersibus α : eius uersibus A^c : uersibus eius *dett*. **22–23** Iugurthae ... perducti *dett*. : Iugurthae ... perducto AL : Iugurtha ... perducto G : Iugrthae Boccho ... perducto A^c **23** tam A^c : om. α : <adeo> *ante* adseruit *Heraeus* **24–25** et quantus<quantus> postea *Perizonius* : et quantus postea α : en quantus postea *Halm* : et quantus postea! (*sic distinxit Pighius*) <ita> *uel* qui tantus postea *Gertz* : et quantus<cumque> postea *Kempf* : et quantus postea <euasit>! <tunc> *Novák* **32** demisit A^c : dimisit α

teis armillis donat', alacer gaudio abiit. nulla est ergo tanta humilitas quae dulcedine gloriae non tangatur.

6   Illa uero etiam a claris uiris interdum ex humillimis rebus petita est: nam quid sibi uoluit C. Fabius nobilissimus ciuis, qui cum in aede Salutis, quam C. Iunius Bubulcus dedicauerat, parietes pinxisset, nomen his suum inscripsit? id enim demum ornamenti familiae consulatibus et sacerdotiis et triumphis celeberrimae deerat. ceterum sordido studio deditum ingenium qualemcumque illum laborem suum silentio oblitterari noluit, uidelicet Phidiae secutus exemplum, qui clipeo Mineruae effigiem suam inclusit, qua conuolsa tota operis conligatio solueretur.

ext. 1   Sed melius aliquanto, si aliena imitatione capiebatur, Themistoclis ardorem esset aemulatus, quem ferunt, stimulis uirtutum agitatum et ob id noctes inquietas exigentem, quaerentibus quid ita eo tempore in publico uersaretur respondisse 'quia me tropaea Miltiadis de somno excitant '. Marathon nimirum animum eius ad Artemisium et Salamina, naualis gloriae fertilia nomina, inlustranda tacitis facibus incitabat. idem theatrum petens cum interrogaretur cuius uox auditu illi futura esset gratissima, dixit 'eius, a quo uirtutes meae optime canentur'. dulcedinem gloriae, paene adieci gloriosam!

2   Nam Alexandri pectus insatiabile laudis, qui Anaxarcho comiti suo ex auctoritate Democriti praeceptoris innumerabiles mundos esse referenti 'heu me' inquit 'miserum, quod ne uno quidem adhuc sum potitus!' angusta homini possessio †gloriae† fuit, quae deorum omnium domicilio sufficit.

3   Regis et iuuenis flagrantissimae cupiditati similem Aristotelis in capessenda laude sitim subnectam: is namque Theodecti discipulo oratoriae artis libros quos pro suis ederet donauerat, molesteque postea ferens titulum eorum sic alii cessisse, proprio uolumine quibusdam rebus insistens, planius sibi de his in Theodectis libris dictum esse adiecit. nisi me tantae et tam late patentis scientiae uerecundia teneret, dicerem dignum philosophum cuius stabiliendi mores altioris animi philosopho traderentur.

---

33 donat α : donat ⟨accepto dono⟩ *Gertz*   gaudio abiit *AL*^{c}(habiit *L*)*G* : gaudium excepit *P*   **35** a claris *A*^{c} : alacris α   **37** inscripsit *A*^{c}*L*^{c}*G* : inscribit *AL* : inscribsit *L*^{c} : scribsit *P* : scripsit *P*^{c} **38** consulatibus et sacerdotiis *dett.* : consularibus et sacerdotibus α; *fort.* consulibus et sacerdotibus   **38–39** celeberrimae *A*^{c} : celeberrimum α   **39** deerat *dett.* : dederat α   **44** uirtutum α : uirtutis *P*   **46** de somno excitant α : exagitant *P*   **47–48** ad ... incitabat *Perizonius* : et ... incitabant α : *sic, sed* illum inlustrando, *ut uid.*, *A*^{c} **49** uirtutes *P*; *sic Cic. Arch.* 20 : artes *AL*^{c}*G* α : artis *L* : res *Novák*   **50** canentur α : referrentur *P*   **53** ne *det.* : nec α, *fort. recte*   **54** †gloriae† (*ante* possessio *G*) α : *del. Perizonius* : gloriae *ante* cupiditati (55) *Kempf*   **56** Theodecti *LG P*^{c} : Theodenti *A* : Theodectae *PA*^{c} **57** pro suis *P* : *om.* α   **58** planius α : plenius *Shackleton Bailey*

Ceterum gloria ne ab iis quidem qui contemptum eius introducere conantur neglegitur, quoniam quidem ipsis uoluminibus nomina sua diligenter adiciunt, ut quod professione eleuant usurpatione memoriae adsequantur. sed qualiscumque horum dissimulatio proposito illorum longe tolerabilior qui, dum aeternam memoriam adsequerentur, etiam sceleribus innotescere non dubitarunt.

Quorum e numero nescio an in primis Pausanias debeat referri: nam cum 4 Hermoclen percontatus esset quonam modo subito clarus posset euadere, atque is respondisset, si aliquem inlustrem uirum occidisset, futurum ut gloria eius ad ipsum redundaret, continuo Philippum interemit, et quidem quod petierat adsecutus est: tam enim se parricidio quam Philippus uirtute notum posteris reddidit.

Illa uero gloriae cupiditas sacrilega: inuentus est enim qui Dianae Ephesiae 5 templum incendere uellet, ut opere pulcherrimo consumpto nomen eius per totum terrarum orbem disiceretur; quem quidem mentis furorem eculeo impositus detexit. ac bene consuluerant Ephesii decreto memoriam taeterrimi hominis abolendo, nisi Theopompi magnae facundiae ingenium historiis eum suis comprehendisset.

QVAE CVIQVE MAGNIFICA CONTIGERVNT 15

Candidis autem animis uoluptatem praebuerint in conspicuo posita quae cui- praef. que magnifica merito contigerint, quia aeque praemiorum uirtutis atque operum contemplatio iudicanda est, ipsa natura nobis alacritatem subministrante, cum honorem industrie appeti et exsolui grate uidemus. uerum etsi mens hoc loco protinus ad Augustam domum, benificentissimum et honoratissimum templum, omni impetu fertur, melius cohibebitur, quoniam cui ascensus in caelum patet, quamuis maxima, debito tamen minora sunt quae in terris tribuuntur.

---

63 ipsis α : <iis> ipsis *Shackleton Bailey* **69** si ... occidisset *AL* : *om. G* **71** tam enim A^c : tamen α : tam L^c uirtute L^cG : uirtutem *AL* : uirtute fuerat A^c **75** dissiceretur α : diffunderetur *det*. **77** abolendo *G* : in abolendo *AL* : in <aeternum> abolendo *Kempf* : in *ante* historiis *Damsté*

15. tit. contigerunt α : contigerint *P* **2–3** aeque α : aequa *Perizonius* : uirtutis L^cG : uirtutes *AL* : uirtus A^c : operum *Madvig / Foertsch* : honerum α : overum honorum *G*   iucunda *Badius* : iudicanda α : honorum <adpetitus> iudicanda *Blaum* : <iucunda> iudicanda *Gertz* **4** cum α : <et> cum *Gertz*   industrie *dett.* : industria A^c : industriae *LG*   appeti L^cG : *ras.*aepeti *A* : peti A^c : atpeti *L*   grate *dett.* : gratiae α **6** cui A^c : cuius α

1   Superiori Africano consulatus citerior legitimo tempore datus est, quod fieri oportere exercitus senatum litteris admonuit. ita nescias utrum illi plus decoris patrum conscriptorum auctoritas an militum consilium adiecerit: toga enim Scipionem ducem aduersus Poenos creauit, arma poposcerunt. cui quae in uita praecipua adsignata sint et longum est referre, quia multa, et non necessarium, quia maiore ex parte iam relata sunt. itaque quod hodieque eximium capit adiciam. imaginem in cella Iouis Optimi Maximi positam habet, quae, quotienscumque funus aliquod Corneliae gentis celebrandum est, inde petitur, unique
2 illi instar atrii Capitolium est: tam hercule quam curia superioris Catonis effigies †illius ad cuius† generis officia expromitur. gratum ordinem, qui utilissimum rei publicae senatorem tantum non semper secum habitare uoluit, omnibus numeris uirtutis diuitem magisque suo merito quam fortunae beneficio magnum, cuius prius consilio quam Scipionis imperio deleta Carthago est.
3   Rarum specimen honoris in Scipione quoque Nasica oboritur: eius namque manibus et penatibus nondum quaestorii senatus Pythii Apollinis monitu Pessinunte accersitam deam excipi uoluit, quia eodem oraculo praeceptum erat ut haec ministeria Matri deum a sanctissimo uiro praestarentur. explica totos fastos, constitue omnes currus triumphales, nihil tamen morum principatu speciosius reperies.
4   Tradunt subinde nobis ornamenta sua Scipiones commemoranda: Aemilianum enim populus ex candidato aedilitatis consulem fecit. eundem, cum quaestoriis comitiis suffragator Q. Fabi Maximi, fratris filii, in campum descendisset, consulem iterum reduxit. eidem senatus bis sine sorte prouinciam, prius Africam deinde Hispaniam dedit, atque haec †neque ciui ambitioso senatori†, quem ad modum non solum uitae eius seuerissimus cursus, sed etiam mors clandestinis inlata insidiis declarauit.

8–11 quod poposcerunt *hic* α : *post* 29 fecit *Pighius*   **15** funus *Pighius* : munus α   **16** curia α : <e> curia *Eberhard*   **17** †illius ad cuius† α : illius ad eius *uel* effigiei: (*sic distinxit Vorst*) unde ad eius *dett.* : superiori Catoni <unde> effigies illius ad eius<dem> *Pighius* : effigiei, <quae> illinc ad huius (*uel* eius) *Kempf* : ad illius *Eberhard* : unius ad huius *Madvig* : cuius effigies illi<nc> ad <hu>ius *Halm* : superiori s<oli> Catoni: <inde enim> effigies illius ad huius *Gertz* : superiori Catoni (*uel ut* α) <e qua> effigies illius ad huius *Kempf* : superiori Catoni cuius <inde> effigies ad huius *Novák* : effigies illius *post* officia *Damsté* : ad huius *Faranda* : cuius effigies ad illius *Shackleton Bailey*   **21** in A^c : om. α : a *det.*   **22** quaestorii *scripsi* : quaestori α : quaestoris A^c **23** deam α :<matrem I>d<a>eam *Kellerbauer*   **28** aedilitatis α : aedilicio P^c **31** †neque ... senatori† α : neque ciui neque ambitioso senatori *uel* necuiquam ambitioso senatori A^c : neque cuiquam bioso L^c : neque ciui ambitioso neque <apud populum gratioso> senatori *Kempf* : sic, sed sine apud populum *Halm* : neque ciui<li> neque ambitioso senatori *Foertsch* : ut *Halm*, sed <contigerunt> *post* ambitioso *Gertz*

M. quoque Valerium duabus rebus insignibus di pariter atque ciues specio- 5
sum reddiderunt, illi cum quodam Gallo comminus pugnanti coruum propugnatorem subicientes, hi tertium et uicesimum annum ingresso consulatum largiti.
quorum alterum decus uetustae originis optimi nominis gens, Coruini amplexa
cognomen usurpat, alterum summo subiungit ornamento, tam celeritate quam
principio consulatus gloriando.

Ac ne Q. quidem Scaeuolae, quem L. Crassus in consulatu collegam habuit, 6
gloria parum inlustris, qui Asiam tam sancte et tam fortiter obtinuit ut senatus
deinceps in eam prouinciam ituris magistratibus exemplum atque formam officii Scaeuolam decreto suo proponeret.

Inhaerent illi uoci posterioris Africani septem C. Mari consulatus ac duo 7
amplissimi triumphi: ad rogum enim usque gaudio exsultauit quod cum apud
Numantiam sub eo duce equestria stipendia mereret et forte inter cenam quidam Scipionem interrogasset, si quid illi accidisset, quemnam res publica aeque
magnum habitura esset imperatorem, respiciens se supra ipsum cubantem 'uel
hunc' dixerit. quo augurio perfectissima uirtus maximam orientem uirtutem
uideritne certius an efficacius accenderit perpendi uix potest: illa nimirum cena
militaris speciosissimas tota in urbe Mario futuras cenas ominata est: postquam
enim Cimbros ab eo deletos initio noctis nuntius peruenit, nemo fuit qui non
illi tamquam dis immortalibus apud sacra mensae suae libauerit.

Iam quae in Cn. Pompeium et ampla et noua congesta sunt, hinc adsensio- 8
ne fauoris, illinc fremitu inuidiae litterarum monumentis obstrepuntur. eques
Romanus pro consule in Hispaniam aduersus Sertorium pari imperio cum Pio
Metello principe ciuitatis missus est. nondum ullum honorem auspicatus bis
triumphauit. initia magistratuum a summo imperio cepit. tertium consulatum
decreto senatus solus gessit. de Mithridate et Tigrane, de multis praeterea regibus plurimisque ciuitatibus et gentibus et praedonibus unum duxit triumphum.

Q. etiam Catulum populus Romanus uoce sua tantum non ad sidera usque 9
euexit: nam cum ab eo pro rostris interrogaretur, si in uno Pompeio Magno
omnia reponere perseuerasset, absumpto illo subiti casus incursu in quo spem
esset habiturus, summo consensu acclamauit 'in te'. uim ho<no>rati iudicii admirabilem, si quidem magnum Pompeium cum omnibus ornamentis quae rettuli, duarum syllabarum spatio inclusum Catulo aequauit.

---

37 nominis *Perizonius* : hominis α   **38** subiungit *Perizonius* : subiungitur α   **40** Crassus *G* : Crassius *AL*   consulatu *L^cG* : consulatum *AL*   **41** gloria *A^cL^cG* : gloriam *AL*   qui Asiam *A^cG* : quia suam *A* : quia si iam *L* : *sic, sed* quia *L^c*   **44** illi α : uni *Kempf*   **47** illi α : ipsi *Halm*   **50** accenderit *dett.* : acciderit α : acuerit *Torr.*   **55** litterarum α : <in> litterarum *Torr.*   obstrepuntur α : obstrepunt *Madvig*   **57** honorem α : honore curulem *P, fort. recte*   **62** in uno *A^c*; *sic Cic. Manil.* 59 : uno *AL* : uiuo *G*

10   Potest et M. Catonis ex Cypro cum regia pecunia reuertentis adpulsus ad ripam Tiberis memorabilis uideri, cui naue egredienti consules et ceteri magistratus et uniuersus senatus populusque Romanus officii gratia praesto fuit, non quod magnum pondus auri et argenti, sed quod M. Catonem classis illa incolumem aduexerat laetatus.

11   Sed nescio an praecipuum L. Marci inusitati decoris exemplum, quem equitem Romanum duo exercitus P. et Cn. Scipionum interitu uictoriaque Hannibalis lacerati ducem legerunt, quo tempore salus eorum in ultimas angustias deducta nullum ambitioni locum relinquebat.

12   Merito uirorum commemorationi Sulpicia Ser. Paterculi filia, Q. Fului Flacci uxor, adicitur. quae, cum senatus libris Sibyllinis per decemuiros inspectis censuisset ut Veneris Verticordiae simulacrum consecraretur, quo facilius uirginum mulierumque mens a libidine ad pudicitiam conuerteretur, et ex omnibus matronis centum, ex centum autem decem sorte ductae de sanctissima femina iudicium facerent, cunctis castitate praelata est.

ext. 1   Ceterum quia sine ulla deminutione Romanae maiestatis extera quoque insignia respici possunt, ad ea transgrediemur. Pythagorae tanta ueneratio ab auditoribus tributa est ut quae ab eo acceperant in disputationem deducere nefas existimarent. quin etiam interpellati ad reddendam causam hoc solum respondebant, ipsum dixisse. magnus honos, sed schola tenus: illa urbium suffragiis tributa. enixo Crotoniatae studio ab eo petierunt ut senatum ipsorum, qui mille hominum numero constabat, consiliis suis uti pateretur, opulentissimaque ciuitas †tam frequentem† uenerati post mortem domum Cereris sacrarium fecerunt, †quaque† illa urbs uiguit, et dea in hominis memoria et homo in deae religione cultus est.

2   Gorgiae uero Leontino studiis litterarum aetatis suae cunctos praestanti, adeo ut primus in conuentu poscere qua de re quisque audire uellet ausus sit, uniuersa Graecia in templo Delphici Apollinis statuam solido ex auro posuit, cum ceterorum ad id tempus auratas conlocasset.

---

68 Tiberis *dett.* : urbis α   **72** praecipuum α : praecipuum sit A^c Marci α : Marci<us> *Gertz*   **82** deminutione A^c : dimunitione α   **83** transgrediemur α : transgrediamur *dett.*   **84–85** deducere nefas existimarent $A^c L^c G$: deducerent fas existimarent *AL* : non adducerent *P*   **87** ipsorum *AL* : eorum *G*   **89** †tam frequentem† α : tam frequenter *dett.* : Metapontini *Madvig* : <Metapontini> iam praesentem ... domum <eius> *Gertz* : <Metapontini uiuum> iam frequenter domum <eius> *Novák* : <unum uirum magis quam coetum> tam frequentem *Morel*   **90** †quaque† α : qua<ntum>que *Pighius* : qua<mdiu>que *Vorst* : quu<m>que *Perizonius* : qu<o>a<d>que *Kempf* : : quaque ... uiguit <aetate> *Novák*   **92** Leontino G^c *P* : Leontini *AL* (praestantis *infra* A^c) : Fleontini, *ut uid.*, *G*   **93** in $A^c G$: ei in *AL*   **94–96** posuit ... gens *AL P* (*sed* inauratas) : *om. G, spat. minore relicto*

Eadem gens summo consensu ad Amphiaraum decorandum incubuit, locum quo humatus est in formam condicionemque templi redigendo atque inde oracula capi instituendo. cuius cineres idem honoris possident, quod Pythicae cortinae, quod aheno Dodonae, quod Hammonis fonti datur.

Berenices quoque non uolgaris honos, cui soli omnium feminarum gymnico spectaculo interesse permissum est, cum ad Olympia filium Euclea certamen ingressurum adduxisset, Olympionice patre genita, fratribus eandem palmam adsecutis latera eius cingentibus.

---

99 aheno *Ald.* (*fort.* aen(e)o *scribendum*) : Athenae α   Dodonae α : Dodonae<o> *Morel* (*u. p.* 242)   fonti *Pighius* : fronti α   **101** ad Olympia (Olimpia *L*, Limpia *L^c*) α : Olympiae *P*   **102** ingressurum *PA^c* : ingressu α

Commentary

1 cap. sint: A; LG have *sunt*, but *quibus* makes it clear that the clause is an indirect question with the main verb understood. *sint*, moreover, occurs in all three manuscripts in the list of chapters preceding the whole work (ed. 4) and in AL (it is absent from G) in the *inscriptio* to this book. The agreement of LG suggests that α had *sunt*, corrected by A from the *inscriptio*.

In this chapter I give references, by trial number, to the entries in Alexander.

praef. 1 quo: *det.* (Kempf (1854) implies Γ). α has *quoque*, with *ut* added by the correctors of A and L because of the following subjunctive. *quoque* has no reference and probably arose from a corrupted dittography of *quo*. The comparative following *quo* is, of course, regular in final clauses. (cf. K–St ii. 233).

ancipites iudiciorum motus: 'unpredictable emotions of the courts' (SB's 'uncertain operations of trials' is unhelpful). V. writes *iudiciorum* rather than *iudicum* because the decision of the court represents the sum of those of the individual jurors.

2. pro quibus: G. L has *per* (corrected to *pro*) *quibus de*; the corrected reading of A is *quibus de* (the dots in my apparatus should be deleted), preceded by an erasure. *per* is probably an idiosyncratic error, whether of L alone or the source of AL, with *pro quibus de* being the reading of α, the omission of *de* a conjecture of G, that of *pro* an emendation in A to cohere with the title above. It is not impossible, though, that the latter is right, the title being derived from the original reading: *pro* could have been caused by *pronuntiatione* in the *inscriptio*. Causal *pro* is very rare before V.; cf. *TLL* x/2.1434.7 ff., citing Plaut. *Truc.* 230, Cic. *Verr.* 2.2.23, and Prop. 3.7.24; from V. they cite only 9.13. ext. 1: there, however, it means 'on behalf of' and is followed by a causal clause; in the passages listed by Otón Sobrino, iii. 1628 under '*por* (idea casual)' *pro* means 'in return for'.

absol. 1. *Horatius.* At 6.3.6 V. narrated the story of Horatius, after the combat of three Horatii with three Curiatii, the result of which was to determine the outcome of the war between Rome and Alba Longa, killing his sister because she was weeping at the death of one of them, her fiancé; there he mentions only the trial before the people, when Horatius was defended by his father.

The episode is narrated at length by Livy 1.24–26, who was almost certainly V.'s main source, and Dionysius of Halicarnassus 3.13–18; the earliest source is Cic. *inu.* 2.78–9, *Mil.* 7; for later sources, deriving only from Livy and Dionysius, see Münzer, *RE* viii. 2324.

Livy's account has provoked a great deal of discussion, largely concerning the fetial formula, the charge of *perduellio*, and *prouocatio*. It is most unlikely that *prouocatio* and *iudicia populi* existed in the regal period. See Münzer, op. cit., 2322–7, Ogilvie, 109–17. V. simplifies by making the original condemnation the decision of the king alone and having no mention of the trial for *perduellio* before the *duumuiri*.

In my testimonia apparatus delete stop after *ad*.

3. M.: thus also Cicero, *Mil.* 7 (not *diu.* 2.78–9, as claimed by Ogilvie, 116) and Dionysius in later references to Horatius (3.27.1, 30.4, 31.1;). Livy (1.26.7, 9, of both father and son) calls him Publius, while Zonaras 7.6.3 calls all three brothers Πουπλιοράτιοι. It is unclear whether V. took the *praenomen* from another source or it was altered later by someone who had read Dionysius; corruption in Livy seems unlikely. I ought to have indicated the possibility that V. wrote *P.*

Tullo: PA^c. α has *Tullio*, an easy error by a scribe thinking of Cicero (though it does not occur in the MSS of Livy 1.22.1–32.1).

3–4. ad populum prouocato iudicio: Livy 1.26.8 'prouoco' inquit. itaque prouocatione certatum ad populum est. For *prouocatio* I do no more than refer to Oakley, iv. 120–34.

4. alterum ... alterum: the first *alterum* refers to an individual, the second to the collective noun *populus*. The usage appears to be unique (*TLL* i. 1740.50 ff. do not cite the passage).

5. immaturum: 'untimely' (SB's 'precocious' (cf. Otón Sobrino, iii. 1027 'precoz, apasionado') gives the wrong sense). V. took the phrase from Livy 1.26.4, where it is put into the mouth of Horatius as he kills his sister. The only other occurrence of *immaturus* in V. is 5.1.7, of military service undertaken (by a Numidian) at too young an age.

impie: V. *impius, impie*, and *impietas* occur a total of eighteen times in V; he chooses *impie* here because it conveys the sense both of an offence against close relatives (cf. *TLL* vii/1.621.1 ff.) and of the religious offence of *parricidium*.

6. forti: the coupling of *fortis* with *punitio* has puzzled a number of critics: Kraffert proposed *fortis*, agreeing with *dextera*, Gertz *feroci*, Shackleton Bailey *fortis facti* (a scribe's eye would have moved from the first *ti* to the second). In fact, *fortis* here has the sense of 'severe' found at Quint. *decl.* 286, Plin. *epist.* 5.16.10, Tac. *ann.* 1.29.3, all cited by *OLD s.u.* 5b., and constitutes the first occurrence of the usage. V. has in mind the *lex horrendi carminis* cited at Livy 1.26.6. Kempf (1854) wrongly took *forti punitione* to refer to the murder of Horatia, so that the phrase means 'the blame incurred by the severe punishment'.

liberata: Lipsius proposed *librata*, apparently meaning 'poised (*sc.* to strike a blow)', so that the *fortis punitio* is the murder of Horatia. V. may sometimes write obscurely, but obscurity should not be introduced by conjecture; it is, though, not an objection that *librare* is not found elsewhere in V.

6–7. consanguineo ... cruore: the blood he had spilt was related to his own. *consanguineus* occurs also at 5.5.3; it is found from Plautus onwards, though never in Cicero's speches (cf. *TLL* iv. 359.14 ff.).

7. haurire: syntactically with *tantum ... quantum ... gloriae*, but it is the verb regularly used of drawing blood.

absol. 2. *Ser. Sulpicius Galba* (Alexander 1). See also 7.1, 9.6.2. V.'s source is Cic. *Brut.* 89–90, but he portrays the episode as if it were a trial before a *iudicium populi* (though in line 14 he talks of a *contio*; cf. damn. 3 n.). In fact L. Scribonius Libo, plebeian tribune in 149, proposed that a special court should be established to try Ser. Sulpicius Galba (58), praetor in 151 (and subsequently consul in 144), who, as propraetor in Further Spain in 150, had murdered or sold into slavery a large number of surrendered Lusitanians (for full citation of sources see Münzer, *RE* ivA. 762–3; cf. *MRR*, i. 456–7, 459); Cato's speech and Galba's histrionics took place at the debate on Libo's *rogatio*, not at a trial. The same version is found at Livy 39.40.12, but not at *per.* 49, and in a number of other sources (see my note on Livy loc. cit., failing to mention V.). In V.'s time, of course, controversial tribunician legislation and trials before the people were things of the past and V. neither understood nor cared about the details. Contrast his apparent knowledge about matters of private law, evidenced in ch. 2. On the episode cf. Astin, *SA* 58–60, *Cato*, 112–13.

8. pudicitiae: Horatia's expression of her grief is portrayed as if it were itself a sexual act.

8–9. pudicitiae ... populus ... postea plus ... placidum ... praestitit: the alliteration is probably not deliberate; cf. Goodyear, i. 339 n. 1.

9. Libone: L. Scribonius Libo (18). V.'s early readers will have been reminded of M. Scribonius Libo Drusus, who in AD 16 was accused of conspiracy against Tiberius and committed suicide (Tac. *ann.* 2.27–32, cf. p. 4); he was not necessarily a direct descendant of the tribune of 149 (for his immediate ancestry see Münzer, *RE* iiA. 885–6, Syme, *AA 256*–8).

Ser.: α has *Seruius*, Paris *Sergius*. The likelihood is that Paris was using a manuscript which had the abbreviation and he expanded it wrongly; but it could be that it was corrupted in the transmission of Paris. Cf. *Liviana*, 151.

10–11. Lusitanorum ... interemisset: he had promised to give them land, divided them into three, ordered them to stay on the land and then attacked each group in turn. He later claimed that he had acted to forestall an attack on his army; see 9.6.2, Cic. *Brut.* 89, Livy *per.* 49, App. *Ib.* 60.249–54, Oros. 4.21.10.

10. interposita fide: Cic. loc. cit. *contra interpositam, ut existimabatur, fidem*.

11–12. M. Cato ... rettulit: *FRHist* 5T13, F106–7. Cic. loc. cit. *M. Cato ... quam orationem in Origines suas rettulit, paucis ante quam mortuus est diebus an mensibus*. Cato also inserted his speech on the Rhodians (*FRHist* 5F87–93) into the *Origines*; he may have done the same with the *de consulatu suo* (cf. vol. ii. 64–5, *FRHist* iii. 152–3).

ultimae senectutis oratione sua: 'in his speech, belonging to extreme old age'; one would expect *suae ultimae senectutis oratione* (SB translates 'in a speech of his extreme old age'), but V. has allowed the possessive adjective to be attracted into agreement with *oratione*; I have played with the idea that V. wrote *ultima senectutis suae oratione*. It is unlikely that V. meant *ultimae senectutis* to be taken with *M. Cato*, with an ellipse of *uir*; for such genitives with *uir* cf., e.g., Livy 3.58.2, 40.54.4.

12. Origines: on the title of Cato's historical work see *FRHist* i. 98–105. α has *origine* but Cic. *Brut*. 89 says *quam orationem in Origines suas rettulit* and *rettulit* clearly requires the accusative plural (citations of the work are normally in the form *originum* (*libro*) + numeral, although Aulus Gellius has *origine* + numeral at *FRHist* 5F27, 41, 77b, 78, 97, 103). For *referre* cf. *TLL* xi/2.612.35 ff.

12–14. pro se ... coepit: Cic. *Brut*. 90 *tum igitur <nihil> recusans Galba pro sese ... cum suos pueros tum C. Gali etiam filium flens commendabat, ...*

13. Gali ... filium: C. Sulpicius Galus (66) was one of the *patroni* chosen by the Spanish communities to present their case against Roman governors in 171 (Livy 43 ch. 2) and praetor in 169. He served under L. Aemilius Paullus in Macedonia in 168 and 167, and reached the consulship in 166; he was an ambassador in Greece and Asia Minor in 164. His exact relationship to Galba is uncertain.

α has *Galli*. The evidence of the *Fasti*, as well as M, the oldest MS, at Cic. *fam*. 4.6.1 and the unanimous *Gaios* at *Lael*. 21, demonstrates that the *cognomen* of this branch of the Sulpicii was *Galus*, though most scribes, unsurprisingly, wrote *Gallus* (cf. Münzer, *RE* ivA. 808). Thus the Vienna MS of Livy 41–45, apart from 44.27.6; Heraeus (*JAW* 1894, 138) corrected 44.37.5, 8, and I followed suit in the other passages where Livy gives the *cognomen*. See further 11 line 4 n.

Halm, on the basis of Cicero (loc. cit.) added *C.* before the *cognomen*; the omission is easy, but in view of V.'s other departures from his source, the supplememt is unjustified.

14. com(n)mendare: α. P has *populo commendare*, but this is probably an addition by Paris, thinking it necessary to explain to whom the commendation was addressed; Kempf placed *populo* before *paruolos*, which would explain the omission, a scribe moving from the first *p* to the third, but places undue emphasis on *populo*, relegating the pathetic *paruolos* to second place, and weakens the antithesis between *pro se* and *paruolos liberos suos*.

15. triste: for *tristis* of a vote for condemnation cf. *OLD s.u.* 5c. Livy uses *triste responsum* of a hostile reply to a plea; cf. Oakley, i. 542.

misericordia ... data est: chiastic order, *aequitas* going with *innocentiae tribui nequiuerat*, *misericordia* with *respectui puerorum data est*.

absol. 3. *A. Gabinius* (Alexander 303). Gabinius (11), as consul in 58, had acquiesced in Clodius' exiling of Cicero and had been rewarded with the governorship of Syria; in 55, in defiance of a *senatus consultum*, he had restored Ptolemy XII (Auletes) to the Egyptian throne. On his return to Rome in 54 he was prosecuted for *maiestas* but acquitted; there followed a trial for *repetundae*, the accusation being that Gabinius had been bribed by Ptolemy. Cicero, obliged after the conference of Luca to support the friends of the triumvirs, defended him, albeit lukewarmly, but he was convicted and went into exile (he was recalled by Caesar in 49; for exile following conviction for *repetundae* cf. A. N. Sherwin-White, *PBSR* 17 (1949), 5–14). As in absol. 2, V. is confused about the procedure, and is under the misapprehension that Gabinius was acquitted. The episode must in fact belong to a *contio* on *a.d. vi kal. Oct.*, two days before a hearing (*diuinatio*) to determine which of three contenders, C. Memmius, the eventual winner, Ti. Claudius Nero, and C. Antonius should be allowed to act as prosecutor (see Cic. *Qfr.* 3.2.1). Memmius, who was a tribune of the plebs, will have summoned the *contio* and ordered Gabinius to appear.

For the extensive sources on the trials of Gabinius see Vonder Mühll, *RE* vii. 429–30, *MRR* ii. 218, 223. V.'s source is uncertain.

18. consentaneum: *consentaneus*, a favourite word of Cicero, occurs before him in Plautus and *rhet. Her.* V. uses it on fourteen occasions, in eight (including our passage; the others are 10. ext. 1, 1.5.8, 2.1.7, 4.3.6, 5.3.2a, 3.4, and 9.1. ext. 6) of which it serves to link a new *exemplum* to the preceding one.

maximo ... ardore: V. is probably alluding to the popular belief that the floods of the Tiber were the result of divine anger at Gabinius' acquittal in his first trial; see Cic. *ad Q. fr.* 3.5.8, Dio 39.61 (confused).

19. C. Memmio: (9). Not known apart from his tribunate. He is not to be confused with C. Memmius (8), tribune in 66, praetor in 58 and a candidate for the consulship of 53; in 52 the latter was convicted of *ambitus* and exiled.

P has the *praenomen*, omitted in α (and restored in A by Lupus). V. would not have omitted it on the first occasion he mentions him. If he had done so, it would have been conceivable that Paris added it from 6.1.13 (where C. Memmius may be the praetor of 58).

abruptae: a true participle: Gabinius' hopes of acquittal had been destroyed.

20. partes ... exhibebat: 'played its role to the full'.

20–21. defensionis ... nitebantur: 'the support on which the defence counted was untrustworthy'; thus SB, adding in a footnote that the reference is to Pompey. If so, V. means that people did not trust Pompey, not that Pompey could not be relied on to give his support to Gabinius; Vonder Mühll's statement (*RE* vii. 429) that Pompey addressed the people on Gabinius' behalf appears to derive only from our passage. But V. may be referring to Cicero, whose defence of Gabinius he had mentioned at 4.2.4.

21. praecipiti: A^{c}L^{c}G. AL have *percipiti*, a *uox nihili*. Some later manuscripts have *perc(t)iti* and this, read by Kempf, could be right: *ira percitus*, for which see Kraus's note on Livy 6.38.8, occurs at 5.11.1.

cupide: A^{c}G. A has *cupidius*, L *cupidine*. If my stemma is right (cf. pp. 18–19), *cupide* could be the transmitted reading, corrupted in the source of AL and emended by one or the other. Damsté's addition of *omnes*, designed to account for L's reading, may be ignored.

22. uiator ... obuersabantur: it is unclear what V. has in mind. At first sight, *carcer* might seem to refer to the Tullianum as a place of execution, but even if, in some cases at least, Caesar's law of 59 had made *repetundae* a capital offence, the death penalty could be avoided by exile (cf. Walbank, i. 682–3 and line 77 n.), and it is unlikely that V. thought that execution followed conviction for *repetundae* in the reign of Tiberius; cf. Sherwin-White, op. cit. (absol. 3 n.). Perhaps he was thinking of temporary imprisonment of someone who had been unable to pay a fine or provide sureties; cf. Livy 38.60. Or maybe he was writing rhetorically without thinking at all about what was involved.

Gertz proposed adding *ei* after *uiator*: that is totally unnecessary, even though the omission would be readily explicable, a scribe's eye moving from *e(i)* to *e(t)*.

cum interim: *cum inuersum*, in a peripateia, frequent in Livy; cf. Oakley i. 593–4.

23. interuentu: elsewhere in V. only at 4.6.2.

23–24. filius namque ... Gabini Sisenna: the *cognomen* is otherwise attested only in the Cornelii (perhaps not a patrician branch; see *FRHist* i. 306), first for the praetor of 183 (Livy 39.45.2) and most famously for the historian (*FRHist* 26), praetor in 78; Dio (39.56.5), also calling him a son of Gabinius, says that the latter left him in charge of Syria while he was himself fighting Aristobulus II of Judaea, while Josephus (*AJ* 14.92) says that Sisenna was one of three leaders sent by Gabinius against Aristobulus, but makes no mention of his relationship to Gabinius. Münzer (*RE* iv. 1510–11) suggested that Sisenna was a son of the historian adopted by Gabinius: since the historian served under Pompey against the pirates (App. *Mith.* 95.435, Dio 36.18.1, 19.1 = *FRHist* 26T21–22) and Pompey owed his command to a law passed by Gabinius (cf. *MRR* ii. 144–5), that is indeed very likely; if so, the adoption may have been testamentary. Sisenna will have retained his original *cognomen*.

V. frequently has *namque* in second position (also at 8 line 9 and 9 line 17); before him it occurs in Varro ap. Gell. 3.10.2 and Livy (*TLL* ix/1.37.50 ff.).

24. ad pedes se Memmi supplex prostrauit: for falling at someone's feet in supplication cf. Naiden, 50.

The unemphatic pronoun *se* splits *pedes* and *Memmi*, indicating that *ad pedes ... prostrauit* constitutes a colon; *filius ... Sisenna* can be regarded as a 'weighted subject' (see my note on Livy 39.11.2 *iurgantes ... seruis*), with *consternationis impulsu* a separate *articulus*.

25. fomentum: 'poultice'. The metaphorical use of the word occurs before this passage twice in each of Cicero, Horace, and Ovid; used literally, it is found twice in Horace and frequently in Celsus. See *TLL* vi/1.1018.67 ff.

procellae ... tempestatis: there is no essential difference in meaning between *procella* and *tempestas* and it would have been more logical if V. had written *unde totus impetus eius eruperat*.

26. truci uoltu: the expression is used by Tacitus *ann.* 4.34.2, of Tiberius at the trial of Cremutius Cordus (Tacitus was fond of the adjective, using it on 23 occasions; for its application to physical features cf. *OLD s.u.* 1b).

a se uictor insolens repulsum: one would expect the subject to follow *quem*, but V. allows it to split *a se repulsum*.

27. Laelius tribunus plebis: (6). D. Laelius, son of D. Laelius (5) who was killed in 77 or 76 while serving under Pompey in Spain (*MRR* ii. 95, iii. 116–17), and probably grandson of D. Laelius (4) mentioned at Lucilius 593M = 594 Krenkel. Their relationship to C. Laelius, consul in 140 and close friend of Scipio Aemilianus (see 8.1 nn.) is uncertain. Our Laelius was probably a quaestor in Sicily before or after his tribunate (Münzer, *RE* xii. 411–12; not in *MRR*). He was an envoy of Pompey in 49 and a prefect of part of his fleet in 49 and 48. His action now is consistent with his Pompeian connections.

28. Gabinium dimitti iuberet: Laelius uses his *ius auxilii* against his colleague.

29. prouentu: 'harvest' (thus SB).; see my note on Livy 45.41.6, where I ought to have drawn attention to *TLL*'s extraordinary claim (x/2.2113.29) that *sum* is there to be understood with *secutus*. V. uses *prouentus* similarly at 3.2. ext. 5, 5.1. ext. 3, and 5.10.2; at 3.5.4 and 6.9.5 it means 'supply'. Before V. the word is found only in Caesar, Virgil, Ovid, and Livy.

aduersis: Pighius added *quemquam*, unnecessarily since the subject of *abuti* and *debilitari* is easily understood; and if V. had wanted to express it, he would naturally have placed it in the preceding clause (there is no palaeographical reason for its omission here).

<prae>propere: Halm's emendation of *propere*, itself a correction in A of a word now illegible but almost certainly the *propri(a)e* of LG. The sense of 'prematurely' is clearly required, V. uses the adjective at 4.1.2 and 6.3.6, and the corruption, whether it occurred before or after that of *-propere*, is easy, a scribe's eye moving from the first *p* to the second. The adverb is a (certainly correct) conjecture of Maurenbrecher at Sallust *hist.* fr. inc. 1 (= 20 Ramsey) and occurs four times in Livy.

absol. 4. *P. Claudius Pulcher.* Claudius (304; son of Ap. Claudius Caecus), consul in 249, attacked the Carthaginian fleet at Drepanum and suffered a major defeat, losing 95 out of 123 ships. Later sources (but not Polybius) claimed that Claudius was punished for his contempt of the auspices: when the sacred chickens refused to eat, he ordered them to be thrown into the sea, saying 'then let them drink'. Cf. Oakley iii. 360, D. Miano, *Fortuna: Deity and Concept in Archaic and Republican Italy* (Oxford, 2018), 26.

For full citation of sources see *MRR* i. 214; V. told the story at 1.4.3 (this is in the section missing in α and we have only the summaries of Paris and Nepotianus; V., no doubt, recounted it at some length) and refers to it at *damn.* 4 below. His source is uncertain. V.'s version of Claudius' trial is found elsewhere, but with more detail, only at schol. Cic. Bob. p. 90.3–8 Stangl (on Cicero's lost *in Clodium et Curionem*), an account which gives the impression of deriving from a good source (Stangl suggests Asconius or an epitome of Livy: *per.* 19 has nothing about a trial). He says that the trial was for *perduellio* and that the accusers were the tribunes Pullius and Fundanius. The storm arose when the centuries were just about to vote and this was a *uitium* (i.e. the trial did not continue). Subsequently (*sc.* the other) tribunes used their veto to prevent a retrial for *perduellio* with the same accusers. The latter, however, proceeded on a different charge and Claudius was condemned and fined 120,000 (*sc. asses*) of *aes graue*.

This account enables us to make sense of Polybius' vague διὸ καὶ μετὰ ταῦτα μεγάλαις ζημίαις καὶ κινδύνοις κριθεὶς περιέπεσεν (1.52.3). It also shows that Walbank (i. 115) and I (*OCD*[4] 328) ought not to have said that Claudius was acquitted of *perduellio*.

31. Ap.: thus both α (*Appius*) and P (*App.*); Pighius restored the truth (the apparatus of ed. wrongly attributes *C.* to Torrenius). Both Paris and Nepotianus have *P.* at 1.4.3, but the likelihood is that V. wrote carelessly here.

maior ... iniuria: for the idiom see C. L. Whitton, *CQ* 61 (2011), 267–77, calling it *dubitatio comparatiua*; V. is extremely fond of it (cf. Whitton, op. cit.,

273 n. 39); there are further instances at 7. ext. 11, 10.2, and 15.7; cf. vol. iv 58, 192.

Claudius himself is portrayed as an *iniuria*. Cf. *TLL* vii/1.1675.56 ff.; the only parallels they cite are Sall. *hist*. 3.20 (= 15 Ramsey) and Claudian 18.475, indicating that in neither case is the text certain (it is perhaps surprising that no one has ever suggested reading *maiore* here; there is, of course, no doubt that the transmitted *iniuriam* is to be corrected to *iniuria*). In the Sallust passage Ramsey translates *uostrarum rerum ultro iniuria<e> debere* 'to feel spontaneous gratitude for the misuse of your own property'. Cf. lines 172–3 n.

si quidem: V. is extremely fond (35 instances) of this use of *si quidem* + indicative, found first in Cicero, to mean merely 'since', without any true conditional sense; cf. K–St ii. 427–8. Editors often print it as a single word (it is listed in *OLD* under *siquidem*).

31–32. illius ... amisit: exact antithesis (*illius/huius, uetustissimum/pulcherrimam, morem/classem, neglexit/amisit*).

34. subito: it is perhaps an unreal question to ask whether V. intended this as an adverb with *coorti* or an adjective with *beneficio*, though the former is more likely.

35. aliam ... non placuit: *uelut dis interpellantibus* goes with *non placuit*, not *aliam ... de integro instaurari*: 'as if the gods had interrupted the trial, they decided not to begin another one all over again'. A *iudicium populi* took place over four separate days (cf. my note on Livy 38.51.5) and it would, presumably, have been possible to repeat just the final day (interruption of trial by the weather cannot have been a rare occurrence). The view taken, no doubt at the instance of friends of Claudius, must have been that the gods disapproved of the trial for *perduellio* as a whole.

35–36. maritima ... caelestis: a forced antithesis: both storms came from the sky, but only the first affected the sea.

36. causae dictionem: *causae dictio* occurs in Cicero, Caesar, Livy, and seven times in V. (also at line 148).

absol. 5. *Tuccia*. The complex evidence for this episode is discussed in detail by Münzer (*RE* viiA. 768–70). Livy *per*. 20 reports the condemnation of a Vestal whose name appears as *Lucia* or *Luccia* in the manuscripts; Sigonius printed *Tuccia*, which he had found in a manuscript, and Jal, in the Budé edition of the *periochae*, says that it is the reading of Vat. Ottob. Lat. 2089. Tuccia is the name of the Vestal both here and at Pliny *nat*. 28.12, while the MSS at D.H. 2.69 have Τυγκία. Corruption of *Tuccia* to *Luccia* is extremely easy and there is no case whatsoever for the view of Cichorius (*RS* 20–1) that the correct reading is *Lucilia*, *Luc(c)eia*, *Luscia*, or *Lucretia*.

The report in Livy *per.* 20 comes between those relating the repression of a revolt in Sardinia and Corsica in 231 and the declaration of war against the Illyrians, i.e. in 230–229; in Pliny, however, the year is given as *a.u.c. DCVIII* = 145 BC; Münzer plausibly proposed emendation to *DXXIIII* = 230. Cichorius, in accordance with his view about *per.* 20, accepted Pliny's date for the acquittal of Tuccia.

But if we are dealing with only one episode, was Tuccia convicted or acquitted, and how are the rival versions to be explained? The likelihood is that she was condemned and that the acquittal, with the story related by V., is a subsequent invention. Münzer thought that Livy had both versions and that the epitomator omitted the latter; he compared 28.11.6–7, where Livy reports the whipping of a Vestal for allowing the sacred flame to be extinguished and adds a comment, omitted by the epitomator, about the expiation that followed. That, however, is entirely different from the omission of a totally contradictory variant. It is more likely that Livy, whether or not he knew the story related by V., did not include it. V.'s source, therefore, cannot be determined.

37. eodem auxilii genere: divine intervention.

criminis: a manuscript cited by Torrenius has *crimine* and Gertz gave his support to the reading, adducing line 3 *interfectae sororis crimine ... damnatus*: *reus*, however, is constructed with both genitive and ablative of the charge (cf. K–St i. 447–8; for the ablative cf. line 66) and there is no reason to think that the three successive genitives, the first depending on the second, the second on the third, would have worried V. (there is no ambiguity). Nor is it likely that *incesti* would have caused *crimine* to be corrupted to *criminis*.

38. infamiae nube: V. uses *nubes* in a metaphorical sense (he never does so literally) also at 1.8 praef. and 5.7. ext. 1. Before him the usage occurs only at Ovid *trist.* 5.5.22 (for *nubes, nubecula* of the brow cf. Nisbet's note on Cic. *Pis.* 20). Livy uses *nubes* on only nine occasions, none of them in the first decade.

38–39. conscientia ... ausa: the triple alliteration (*conscientia certa, sinceritatis suae spe salutis, ancipiti argumento ausa*) is clearly deliberate.

38. conscientia certa: the paradosis is *conscientia* (LG) *certae* (α); *conscia* in A is a correction which has obscured the original reading, no doubt also *conscientia*: the correction was caused by the apparent illogicality of *conscientia certae sinceritatis* (one could not fail to be conscious of something which was certain), but it is far more convincingly dealt with by Perizonius' change of *certae* to *certa*: the former resulted from anticipation of the following genitives.

39. cribro: 'sieve'. Before or contemporaneously with V. the word is found three times in Plautus, seven in Cato *agr.*, Lucilius, Cic. *diu.*, Varro *Men.*, and the *moretum*. Most writers, of course, had no occasion to talk of sieves, but the word must have been common in the spoken language.

40. hoc: a correction in D (Kempf, 1854, 82; in 1888 he says '*dett. pauci*') of the transmitted *hanc* (also in Landolfus Sagax (see p. 22), but with *hauriam* omitted, probably accidentally). *hanc* is clearly impossible: Tuccia did not have the water with her at the time of her prayer (though she is presumably to be envisaged as standing on the bank of the Tiber).

41. temere: because the chances of her being successful seemed very slight.

41–42. rerum ... natura: for the (extremely frequent) phrase see *TLL* ix/ 1.179.12 ff., 181.27 ff. It occurs in V. also at absol. 13, 7. ext. 1, 12, 8.2, 1.8. ext. 18, 3.2.23, 3. ext. 2, 5.3.2d, 10. ext. 3, 4.7, 4. ext. 5, 9.2. ext. 11.

absol. 6. *L. Calpurnius Piso* (Alexander 48). The identity of both prosecutor and defendant in this trial, and hence the date of the episode, are disputed. A and G have *L.* as the *praenomen* of Claudius, L the impossible *B.* (no *praenomen* begins with that letter); P omits both *praenomen* and *nomen*, which were added, the former as *L.*, by Heiric of Auxerre, probably from A rather than the exemplar (see p. 20). The patrician Claudii avoided Lucius, since it had been held by two members of the *gens* who had been convicted, respectively, of brigandage and murder (see Suet. *Tib.* 1.2; *L.* at Cic. *har. resp.* 12 (cf. *dom.* 127) is probably corrupt) and Pighius read *P.*, presumably intending P. Clodius; Münzer (*RE* iii. 1387) stated as a fact that L. Calpurnius Piso, the consul of 58, was prosecuted by Clodius in 59: that is unlikely, since Caesar sanctioned Clodius' *transitio ad plebem* in March (Cic. *Att.* 1.19.5) and his marriage to Piso's daughter Calpurnia must have occurred around the same time; and, as Gruen (*Athenaeum* 49 (1971), 55–6; cf. *LGRR* 525) argued, had Piso been prosecuted by Clodius for *repetundae*, one would expect Cicero to have mentioned it). There is a lot to be said for the suggestion of Syme (*RP* i. 303) that the defendant was in fact the consul of 112, the grandfather of the consul of 58, whose trial for extortion is mentioned at Cic. *de orat.* 2.265, 285; cf. *MRR* iii. 46–7) and the prosecutor C. Claudius Pulcher, consul in 92; Gruen objected that since Piso was supported by L. Crassus and M. Aemilius Scaurus, he would not have needed to humiliate himself in the way described by V. (Gruen strangely says 'he would not likely have felt the need to embrace jurors' knees'): but V. says that he did so when the voting was taking place and going against him (the voting was secret but the jurors' intentions will often have been clear). I therefore printed *C.*, which, unlike *P.*, could easily have been corrupted to *L*. I added that V. himself may have made a mistake, but it is unlikely that someone who addressed and wrote about Tiberius as he did would not have known of the ban and the reasons for it. Gruen himself suggested that the defendant was L. Calpurnius Piso Frugi, praetor in 74, and the prosecutor C. Claudius Pulcher, praetor in 56.

The consul of 112 (88) was killed in Gaul when serving as a *legatus* of L. Cassius Longinus (Caes. *Gall.* 1.12.7, saying that he was the grandfather of his (Caesar's) father-in-law, App. *Celt.* 1.8, Oros. 5.15.24). C. Claudius Pulcher (302) was curule aedile in 99 and praetor in 95; for his *elogium* see *I.I.* xiii/3.70b. Cf. *MRR* iii. 57–8.

V.'s source is uncertain.

45. tristes: cf. line 15 n.

47. caeno: 'mud'. At *Pis.* 13 Cicero addresses the consul of 58 as *caenum*, but one could hardly use that as an argument in favour of the latter being the Piso of our passage. Cicero also uses *caenum* as a term of abuse at *dom.* 47, *Sest.* 20, 26, *Phil.* 5.16, but only at *Pis.* 13 is it a vocative; elsewhere it is found in this sense only at Plautus *Persa* 407 (at *Most.* 41 it forms part of a conjecture by Leo) and Pliny *epist.* 7.29.3. Cf. *TLL* iii. 99.47 ff.

a seueritate: thus the correctors of A and L, together with G. AL have *ad seueritatem*, the result of anticipation of the following *ad clementiam et mansuetudienm*. Halm read *ab seueritate*, presumably thinking that *ab* was first corrupted to *ad* and then the ablative changed to the accusative. If my stemma is correct, *a* will be the transmitted reading: but even if it is wrong, the posited process of corruption is less plausible. Moreover, V., unlike Livy, normally writes *ab* only before vowels and the aspirate; cf. 13 line 42 n. If I am not mistaken, Otón Sobrino lists three passages where *ab* precedes *s*: at 1.6.13 AL have *ab*, A^{c}G *a* and at 2.2.6 *ab* is a misprint for *ad*, leaving 5.1.4 as the only passage where ALG all have *ab*.

49. aut: illogical, since Piso was compelled both to throw himself to the ground in supplication and to pick himself up with his mouth full of mud; hence Foertsch proposed *et* and Madvig the deletion of *aut*. V. means, however, that whether they thought about the former or the latter, Piso had paid sufficient penalty; for similar usages of *aut* cf. K–St i. 102–3.

50. deformiter: the adverb does not occur before V., who uses it again (also with *tam*) at 9.5. ext. 2; it is then found in Quintilian, Suetonius, and Apuleius; cf. *TLL* v/1.369.46 ff. V. was, of course, motivated by the desire to provide an antithesis with assonance to *suppliciter*, which occurs before him in Cicero, Caesar, Virgil, Livy, Ovid, and Germanicus.

absol. 7. *Q. Flavius.* The trial must be that related at Livy 8.22.3 ... (sc. *populus*) *eum die dicta ab aedilibus crimine stupratae matrisfamiliae absoluisset* ('he had been prosecuted (*sc.* before the people) on a charge of having had sexual relations with a married woman and acquitted'). See Oakley ii. 625–7.

The two accounts differ in a number of ways: (i) Flavius' *praenomen* is Marcus in Livy, Quintus in V.; (ii) V. does not indicate the charge; (iii) Livy says just *ab aedilibus*, V. gives the name of the prosecutor; (iv) Livy merely says that Flavius was acquitted, with nothing corresponding to Flavius' protest of innocence and Valerius' reply, both coming after fourteen tribes had voted for condemnation. It is more likely that Livy and V. were drawing on different sources than that, as Oakley thinks, the former 'omitted some of the sensational detail which the annalistic tradition provided' (and while it should not be assumed that any favourable reference to the Valerii comes from Valerius Antias (cf. *FRHist* i. 302, 323 n. 20), it would be surprising if Valerius Antias had related a story so much to the discredit of a Valerius). As to Flavius' *praenomen*, in Livy the *uisceratio* (see below) leads to Flavius' election to the tribunate; at 8.37.8 Livy again refers to a tribune M. Flavius (the transmitted reading is *Fabius*, but the truth is scarcely in doubt; cf. Oakley ii. 756), as does V., reporting the same episode, at 9.10.1. If, as is generally assumed (cf. Münzer, *RE* vi. 2528–9, *MRR* i. 146, 149) Flavius (19) held the tribunate twice, we must conclude either that V. made a mistake here or that *Q.* is corrupt. It is not impossible, though, that the two tribunes are not identical, in which case it may be that *M.* at Livy 8.22.2 is a mistake or a corruption; cf. Oakley ii. 627.

Livy relates the trial under 328, but in connection with the belief of some people that Flavius gave a *uisceratio* for the people on the occasion of his mother's funeral as reward for his acquittal; in fact, if a Valerius (see below) was indeed the prosecutor, it will have been in the previous year, since patricians and plebeians held the curule aedileship in alternate years and a Fabius was aedile in 331 (see Oakley ii. 33, 626).

51. subnectam: before V. *subnectere* occurs only in Virgil and Ovid, in the sense of 'bind underneath'; V. is the first to do so in the sense of 'add' and he does so on twelve other occasions (8 praef., 14.5. ext. 3, 1.8. ext. 8, 2.6.15, 8.6, 3.3.2, 3.7. praef., 4.8. ext. 2, 5.6.2, 6.1. ext. 1, 7.6.6), all in similar passages of transition and, with the exception of 8. praef. (*subnecti debet*) and 1.8. ext. 8 (*subnecto*), all with *subnectam* (to be taken as future indicative, not present subjunctive).

51–52. C. Valerio: Broughton (*MRR* i. 144) tentatively identifies him with C. Valerius Potitus (306), consul and perhaps *magister equitum* in 331: there is no certain case of a curule aedile holding the office after the consulship.

52. aedile: for prosecutions by aediles on sexual charges see Oakley ii. 627.

A, L, and P have *aedile*, G and the corrector of P *aedili*; both forms are found (cf. *TLL* i. 928.44 ff.; cf. *FRHist* 21F6 and commentary ad loc.) and in these circumstances it is impossible to determine which represents the paradosis; for a similar situation cf. Livy 31.50.10, where B, V, and α have *aedile*, φ, N, L, and Voss. (the latter being one of the α group) *aedili*.

quattuordecim tribuum suffragiis: V. must mean that the first fourteen tribes to vote had done so for condemnation and thus that the vote of one further tribe would be decisive. That presupposes that the total number of tribes was 29, which was the case only between 332, when the Maecia and Scaptia were created (Livy 8.17.11) and 318, when the Ufentina and Falerna became the thirtieth and thirty-first tribes (Livy 9.20.6); that may be an indication that the detail is authentic (cf. Oakley ii. 626, though one may doubt his assertion that otherwise 'one would have to postulate that an annalist had taken extraordinary care to get the number of tribes correct in his reconstruction').

53. opprimi: for *opprimere* of condemnation cf. damn. 3, 5.7, 1.5.2, 3.8. ext. 4, 6.5.6, 9.10.

clara: 'loud'; both Flavius and Valerius were shouting.

54. nocensne an innoxius: α. P has *nocens an innocens*, clearly merely variation (Paris may have thought that *innoxius* was obscure, though *innocens* could be a corruption caused by perseveration from *nocens* and not evidence for what V. wrote).

54–55. periret: for *perire* of any kind of judicial penalty cf. *TLL* x/1.1333.24 ff.; there is no suggestion of a capital penalty, since such cases would be heard in the centuriate, not the tribal assembly (cf. Plaut. *Pseud.* 1232, Cic. *rep.* 2.61, *leg.* 3.11, Mommsen, *StR* iii. 357); in any case, death could be avoided by exile (cf. line 22 n.).

55. qua uiolentia dicti: 'by this violence of language': one would have expected *cuius* ('by the violence of these words'); perhaps V. wanted to make it clear that *uiolentia* is not the subject of *donauit*.

56. credidit: α. A later manuscript, cited by Torrenius, has *credit*, which could be a haplography of *-di-* rather than an emendation to accord with the normal use of the present with *dum* to refer to something which continued during the time in which the action designated by the main verb occurred. For instances of the perfect rather than the present see K–St ii. 376; it occurs also at 5.5 and 7. ext. 8, both of which have been emended (see nn. ad locc.), but it is unlikely that the same corruption would have occurred three times in book 8 and nowhere else. V. may have been attracted by *credidit ... perdidit*, and having once written the perfect with *dum*, twice did so again.

erexit: cf. line 61 n.

56–57. uictoriam ... perdidit: the opposite of 'snatching victory from the jaws of defeat'. (I have a recollection that 'snatching defeat from the jaws of victory' was applied by someone to the Labour Party's failure to win the British General Election of 1992, as it had been expected to do.)

absol. 8. *C. Cosconius* (Alexander 356). V.'s source cannot be determined. The date of this trial depends on V.'s statement that it took place under the *lex Seruilia*. There were two *leges Seruiliae* dealing with *repetundae*, the *lex Seruilia*

Caepionis, passed by Q. Servilius Caepio, the consul of 106, which restored the *repetundae* court to senatorial juries, and the *lex Seruilia Glauciae*, which reinstated equestrian control and also provided that a Latin who brought a successful prosecution was to be given Roman citizenship (Cic. *Balb.* 54); the latter is to be dated to 101, not, as Mommsen held, to before 111; see *MRR* i. 571, 573 n. 2. Valerius' *cognomen* (see below) must mean that he came from Vibo Valentia, a Latin colony founded in 192 (Livy 35.40.5; cf. my note on 31.3.3) and he was presumably hoping to obtain Roman citizenship; moreover, equestrian jurors were perhaps more likely than senators to believe that Valerius' poem was autobiographical. The trial must be earlier than 81, when the *lex Seruilia* was superseded by Sulla's legislation.

Valerius is known also from Festus 496L, who says that in a poem he mentioned a fictitious *lex Tappula*, which was referred to by Lucilius (1307M = 1323 Krenkel) in a line which, it seems, mentioned L. Opimius, the consul of 121 and murderer of Gaius Gracchus; see Buecheler, *Kleine Schriften* ii (Leipzig–Berlin, 1927), 190–5. There is, of course, no difficulty in Valerius both knowing Opimius, who was exiled in 110, and undertaking a prosecution after 101.

The identity of Cosconius is problematic. The *terminus ante quem* of 81 excludes the man who governed Illyria c. 78–76 (cf. *MRR* ii. 86–7, 88 n. 4; Münzer (*RE* iv. 1668) initially thought that only the age of Valerius precluded the possibility, but cf. *RE* Supp. 3.262); he was a *legatus* in the Social War in 89 (*MRR* ii. 36), but that is unlikely to have led to a *repetundae* trial (Buecheler, op. cit., 191, dated it *c*. 87). Krenkel (on Lucilius, loc. cit.) had the strange idea that he was the elder brother of M. Cosconius, praetor of 135, who had the filiation *C.f.* (*IGRR* iv. 134).

See Volkmann, *RE* viiiA. 236–7.

59. Valentini: see above. P (and Lupus in A) have *Valentis*; if this is what Paris wrote, it was presumably because he had the Emperor Valens in mind; if so, it provides a *terminus post quem* for Paris.

59–60. recitatum: by the defence, presumably.

60. quo: α. Paris has *in quo*, but for the plain ablative in references to a work of literature cf. K–St i. 354; in any case, it is much more likely that Paris (or a later scribe) added *in* than that it was omitted in the course of the transmission of V.

60–61. puerum ... poetico ioco significauerat: like Catullus (16.5–6), Valerius believed that a poet should be chaste, but his poetry need not be.

61. erexit: a correction in A for the transmitted *correxit*. It is guaranteed by line 56 above, though there it continues the metaphor of *abiecerat*; Torrenius proposed *protexit*, in any case less likely to be corrupted to *correxit*.

si quidem: cf. line 31 n.

absol. 9. *A. Atilius.* This episode is almost certainly connected with the Samnite capture of Sora in 306 recorded at Livy 9.43.1 and D.H. 20.80.1. The MSS of Livy associate the latter with the capture of Calatia, while those of D.H. have ἀτ(τ)ίαν; Mommsen (*CIL* x, p. 444) plausibly emended both to refer to Caiatia; the same corruption occurs at Livy 22.13.6 and 23.14.13; see Oakley iii. 557 n. 2, 561–2. The MSS of V. give Atilius the *praenomen* A., but P has *M.*, while both have *Calatinum* as his *cognomen*. He is probably the father of A. Atilius, consul in 258 and 254 (thus Münzer, *RA* 57; cf. Oakley iv. 576), whose *cognomen* appears as Caiatinus in the *fasti Capitolini*, but as Calatinus in the literary evidence and I suggested in my apparatus that we should read *Caiatinum* here. As to the *praenomen*, Oakley (iv. 351 n. 1, 576–7) suggests that if V. wrote *M.*, he could be identical with M. Atilius Regulus, consul in 294, who would have had *Caiatinus* as an additional *cognomen*. However that may be, there is no need to believe that the Atilii originated from or owned land at Cai(l)atia; the *cognomen* could have arisen from some other connection with the city. And it is pure coincidence that Atilius was serving at Sora at the time that Caiatia was captured: Sora is c. 85 km north-west of the latter.

V.'s source is uncertain.

66. proditione: cf. line 54 n. It is totally incredible that the son-in-law of Fabius Rullianus (see below) would have betrayed Sora to the Samnites. I do not understand why SB has '(?)' after 'Sora' in his translation.

67. admodum: 'extremely', not 'quite'.

Q. Maximi: (114). Q. Fabius Maximus Rullianus, who held the consulship on five occasions (322, 310, 308, 297, 285); on his extraordinary career cf. Oakley ii. 598–600. The index to ed. (p. 865) wrongly lists this passage under Fabius Verrucosus.

68–69. comperisset: α. P has *deprendisset* and Kellerbauer proposed *conprendisset*. Livy (9.42.6) records that Fabius was a proconsul in 307, but does not mention him under 306. If the words attributed to him are historical, he probably meant that if he had discovered later that Atilius had betrayed Sora to the Samnites, he would have broken off his connection to him; it is not impossible, though, that Livy has failed to mention a further prorogation of Fabius' *imperium* and that he was still in Samnium. There is, though, no reason to think that he held command at Sora and both *deprendisset* and *conprendisset*, implying that Fabius might have caught Atilius red-handed, are out of the question. The former is probably a deliberate alteration by Paris, perhaps thinking that *comperisset* was obscure, not a corruption of what Paris wrote.

70. exploratam: 'certain'; cf. *TLL* v/2.1750.38 ff.; they also cite 7.2.2., where, however, the meaning is rather 'researched'.

71. exercitus: accusative plural: different armies at different times.

absol. 10. *M. Aemilius Scaurus* (Alexander 295). Scaurus (141), son of M. Aemilius Scaurus (140), consul in 115 and subsequently *princeps senatus* (see 5.2), and step-son of Sulla, who married Scaurus' mother, Caecilia Metella, after his father's death. He was praetor in 56 and governor of Sardinia in 55. In the following year he was accused of *repetundae*, defended by Cicero (in the *pro Scauro*) and five others and acquitted. He then stood for the consulship of 53, but was accused of *ambitus* and convicted, going into exile. For the sources on his trial for *repetundae* see Klebs, *RE* i. 589 (388–9 in ed. is an error). V.'s source is uncertain.

73–74. perditam et comploratam: 'hopeless and lamentable'; cf. Livy 22.53.4 (of the situation after Cannae) *nequiquam eos perditam spem fouere; desperatam comploratamque rem esse publicam*.

74–75. diceret ... licere: it is not known which *repetundae* law (the trial took place under the provisions of the *lex Iulia* of 59) introduced this provision. For *testimonum denuntiare* 'summon as a witness' cf. *RS* 7.3, Cic. *S. Rosc.* 110, *Verr.* 2.1.51, 2.65, *TLL* v/1.556.3 ff.

AL have *diceret legem ... liceret, seque,* G the same except for *licere*. In A *diceret* was altered to *doceret si, legem* to *lege,* and *seque* to *se*: *lege* is manifestly correct, while the addition of *si* and the deletion of *-que* were designed to take account of *liceret*; the motive for *doceret* is obscure. *liceret* was caused by perseveration from *diceret*, but it is impossible to say whether *licere* was the transmitted reading corrupted in the source of AL or a conjecture in G.

77. uetustissimam nobilitatem: of the Aemilii as a whole; Scaurus belonged to a branch of the *gens* which had fallen on hard times and the three generations preceding the consul of 115 (the first attested Aemilius Scaurus) had not held office; cf. *FRHist* i. 267. The *cognomen* was also used by the Aurelii (the praetor of 186 and the suffect consul of 108).

78. recentem memoriam patris: in fact Scaurus' father was dead by 88 (cf. *FRHist* i. 268), so that the jurors' memory of him (and some will have had none) was not at all fresh.

absol. 11. *L. Aurelius Cotta.* Cotta was consul in 144. For the sources on the trial (Alexander 9) see ed. 501, adding Cic. *Font.* 38 to those listed by Astin, *SA* 258; it took place in 138 (Livy *epit. Oxyrh.* 55) and Cotta was defended by Q. Caecilius Metellus Macedonicus (Cic. *Brut.* 81). V. wrongly portrays it (line 82) as a *iudicium populi*: that would have required a tribune as prosecutor and Cicero (*Mur.* 58) would not have said that *homines sapientissimi* voted for acquittal. The charge must have been one of *repetundae* and heard by a senatorial jury under the *lex Calpurnia* of 149, though we do not know of any provincial command held by Cotta after his consulship; cf. Astin, loc. cit.

V.'s source is uncertain.

80. in opprimendis: *in* was added by the corrector of A. The omission is easy after *ita*, though it is possible that V. intended it to be understood from *in protegendis*.

80–81. euidenter: the adverb occurs first in Livy (6.26.7, 34.54.8) and then, contemporaneously with V., in Celsus.

81. impugnat: in the sense of 'accuse' *impugnare* is found before V. only at Cic. *Quinct.* 8 and *or. frg.* VIII 18, and next at Quint. *inst.* 4.1.14 (*TLL* vii/1.715.2 ff.).

P. Scipio Aemilianus: (Cornelius 335). V. refers to Aemilianus (the natural son of L. Aemilius Paullus, consul in 182 and 168 and victor over Perseus in the Third Macedonian War, adopted by P. Cornelius Scipio, son of Africanus) by name on 22 occasions (in book 8 also at 8.1, 15.4, 7); the list at ed. 862, which omits 8.1, includes pasages which refer to Aemilianus without naming him (at 15.1, 2.4.3 and 5.1.7 he confuses him with the elder Africanus; my list omits the first of these passages and wrongly refers to the two others in different ways); he uses various forms of nomenclature (the others are *posterior Africanus/Africanus posterior, Scipio Aemilianus/Aemilianus Scipio* (at 15.4, following *Scipiones*, just *Aemilianus*), *P. Africanus, Scipio Africanus, Scipio*), but this is the only instance of *P. Scipio Aemilianus*.

On all matters concerning Aemilianus see Astin, *SA*. To summarize his career, he was a military tribune in Spain in 151, a *legatus* in Africa in 150, military tribune in Africa in 149 and 148, consul in 147, with command prorogued in 146, when he captured and destroyed Carthage. He was censor in 142, a *legatus* in the East in 140 and 139, consul again in 134, with command prorogued in 133 and 132, when he brought the Numantine War to an end. He was an augur from an unknown date until his death in 129.

83. confossa: before late antiquity the metaphorical use of *confodere* is found elsewhere only at Livy 5.11.12, Sen. *dial.* 7.27.6, and Quint. *decl.* 351 (*TLL* iv. 246.18 ff.).

septiens ampliata ... octauo iudicio: *ampliatio* was the procedure by which if a third of the jurors said *non liquet*, the presiding magistrate said *amplius* and a further hearing was held. If our passage is historical (it is accepted by Astin, *SA* 129, 178), it shows that the procedure, attested at *RS* 1 lines 47–8, was provided for in the *lex Calpurnia*; seven occurrences in the same case must have been highly unusual, if not unique. Cf. vol. iv. 392, *RS* i. 105–6, A. W. Lintott, *Judicial Reform and Land Reform in the Roman Republic* (Cambridge, 1992), 133, 167.

84. homines: 'people'; cf. *TLL* vi/3.2880.65 ff. Cicero (*Mur.* 58) has *noluerunt sapientissimi homines qui tum rem illam iudicabant ita quemque cadere in iudicio ut nimiis aduersarii uiribus abiectus uideretur*, and in 1854 Kempf, denying that *homines* alone was possible, indicated a lacuna after it and suggested adding *sapientissimi illam rem iudicantes* after *homines* (perhaps thinking that a scribe's eye had moved from the first *-es* to the second); in 1888 he preferred either *sapientissimi* or *illam rem tum iudicantes*: in Cicero *sapientissimi homines qui tum rem illam iudicabant* follows *noluerunt*, from which V. takes *nolumus* in line 120, writing *uerebantur* after *homines*. Foertsch, presumably accepting Kempf's premise, proposed *omnes* for *homines*, while Damsté added *uerecundi* (the omission would result from a scribe moving from one *uer-* to another).

85. crediderim: for other authorial statements with the potential perfect subjunctive see 3.6.1, 4.6.1, 6.6. ext. 1, 9.12. ext. 7; in none of them, however, is V., as here, speculating about what people said or thought.

85–88. nolumus ... insequatur: V.'s rhetorical elaboration of *ita quemque ... abiectus uideretur* in Cicero (see above).

86. et deuictarum: L^cG. A has *aedeuictarum*, L. *edeuictarum*, and A^c *ac deuictarum*. The latter is possible palaeographically, but there are no secure examples of – *et* – *ac* (*-que* joins only *tropaea* and *spolia*) – before the elder Pliny; see H–S 516.

87. is: taking up *petentem*; Gertz' *his* is misconceived and in any case one would expect it to come at the beginning of the sentence.

88. fragore gloriae: *fragor* means 'crashing noise' and is used literally by V. at 7. ext. 1, 1.7. ext. 1, and 3.1.1. The metaphorical usage here is quite unlike any of the others listed at *TLL* vi/1.1235.82 ff.; many of them, however, occur in military contexts and V. was probably continuing the image conveyed by *terribiliis sit is aduersus hostem*. It is possible, though, that some later manuscripts (Torrenius says ten of his) were right to read *fulgore*, a word used by V. on eight occasions.

absol. 12–13. The line numbers in my testimonia apparatus are incorrect and should read '**136–147**', i.e. Cic. *Rosc. Am.* (I should have said *S. Rosc*, the *TLL* abbreviation) 64–65 (the reference should also be corrected) concerns the episode related in absol. 13. There are no other sources concerning Calidius (see below).

absol. 12. Nothing else is known of Calidius of Bononia (not in *RE*). Until the legislation of Augustus adultery was normally dealt with within the family, though there are instances of aedilician prosecutions before a *iudicium populi* (cf. S. M. Treggiari, *Roman Marriage* (Oxford, 1991), 275–7). Bononia (mod. Bologna) was a Latin colony founded in 189 (Livy 37.57.7) and it is possible that the trial took place under local law. In view of the absence of any other reference to it (see above), however, it could be that it was conducted under the provisions of the *lex Iulia* and that V.'s knowledge of it did not derive from a literary source. See also 2 lines 25–6 n.

90. Calidius: P; AG have *Callidius*, L, the scribe's eye moving from the first -*i*- to the second, *Callius*: a number of Calidii are known (*RE* iii. 1353–4; in V. at 10.3 and 5.2.7), but no Callidius.

90–91. noctu: the agreement of P with AL eliminates G's *nocte*. In any case, V. writes *noctu* on four other occasions, but never uses *nocte* to mean 'by night'.

92. fluctus ... fragmentum naufragii: V. thus continues the maritime metaphor.

92–93. tamquam ... defensionis: *tamquam fragmentum naufragii* and *leue admodum defensionis genus* are of identical metrical length. *leue* takes up *fragmentum* (no one, of course, could have imagined that it goes with the latter rather than *genus*).

naufragii: AL; G has *nauigii*, but the context clearly requires a reference to a shipwreck, not just a ship.

93. pueri serui: α; P has *pueri eius* (i.e. the husband). Damsté's *pueri* is impossible: 'love of a boy' without further specification would be intolerably obscure. I suggested either *serui eius* or *pueruli*: the latter, also with *amore*, occurs at damn. 8 below, but is open to the same objection as Damsté's conjecture; the former would presuppose that *pueri* was added by someone who thought it necessary that the age of the slave should be specified, and that from *pueri serui eius* α omitted *eius*, Paris *serui*. It is more likely that *eius* is merely variation by Paris.

94–96. suspectus ... liberauit: fourfold polyptoton, leading to the paradoxical conclusion. V. is apparently saying that in comparison with adultery, homosexual desire for a young slave was merely a matter of lack of self-control (a view with which many Romans would no doubt have agreed). Before V., when *intemperantia* is used in a sexual context, it has no such connotation; see *rhet. Her.* 4.23, Cic. *p. red. in sen.* 11, and, particularly *off.* 1.23 *libidinum intemperantia* (*TLL* vii/1.2106.81 ff.): V. however, uses it, as here, of permitted sex at 2.1, 3, 5, 3.5.3, and 4.3.2.

95. crimen: for *liberare* with the accusative of the burden removed rather than the accusative of the person and ablative of the burden cf. my note on Livy 36.25.6; Kempf wrongly suggested *crimine eum*.

absol. 13. *Cloelii* (Alexander 367, confusing Tarracina and Tarraco). This *exemplum* is taken from Cicero *S. Rosc.* 64–5 (see above).

97. remissioris ... materiae: V. means that the previous *exemplum* was amusing, this one serious. According to Cicero (*S. Rosc.* 71) those found guilty of *parricidium* were tied in a sack and thrown in a river. Modestinus (*dig.* 48.9.9 pr.) says that *more maiorum* a dog, a cock, a viper, and a monkey were also placed in the sack, and that it was thrown into the sea, or to the beasts if the sea was not close by, Justinian (*inst.* 4.18.6) that this (though he says 'sea or river') was a provision of the *lex Pompeia de parricidiis*); Marcian (*dig.* 48.9.1), however, says that the *lex Pompeia* made the punishment the same as that of the *lex Cornelia de sicariis*. The probability is that the latter is correct and that in the time of Cicero the sack contained only the parricide. See further Hitzig, *RE* iv. 1747–8, J. D. Cloud, *ZSS* 68 (1971), 166, Dyck, *Sex. Rosc.* 1. In any case, parricide was regarded as a particularly heinous crime and it follows that *aliquanto* must mean 'considerably', not 'somewhat'; *seuerioris*, moreover, is a true comparative, but *remissioris* means 'rather light-hearted'.

97–98. cum ... dicerent: Dyck (*Sex. Rosc.* 131), apparently misunderstanding this, makes the extraordinary statement that V. 'adds the detail that the victim's brothers conducted the prosecution' (and falsely implies that Münzer (*RE* iii. 1256) said the same).

98–99. fratres C<l>oelii ... C<l>oelius: Pighius. α and P have *Caelii*, AL and P *Coelius*, with *Caelius* in G. The authoritative MSS of Cicero have *Cloelium*, which editors have altered to *Caelium*. Wiseman (*CR* n.s. 17 (1967), 263–4), unaware of Pighius' conjecture, observed that a C. Cloilius is attested at Tarracina (*ILLRP* 991) and identified the father and his elder son with, respectively, the *monetalis* and quaestor of *RRC* nos. 260 and 332, dated by Crawford to 128 and 98 respectively, and thought the latter was identical with or related to the Marian commander mentioned by Plut. *Pomp.* 7.1; had that been the case, Cicero would not have talked of the victim as *quendam Tarracinensem, hominem non obscurum* (see next note).

98. splendido Tarracinae loco: he was probably of equestrian status; V. exaggerates and there is no reason to think that he had any additional information. For *locus* of social rank cf. *TLL* vii/2.1588.38 ff. On Tarracina (mod. Terracina), Volscian Anxur, see Oakley ii. 620–1. It was a Roman colony, founded in 329, and there is thus no difficulty in principle about the Cloelii holding office at Rome.

99. altero cubantibus lecto: in the same room, as Cicero (*in idem conclaue cum duobus adulescentibus filiis isset*) makes explicit. P has *in altero*, *in* being almost certainly an addition by Paris.

102. securitatis: cf. 11 line 19 n.

103. rerum naturam: cf. lines 41–42 n.

103–104. rerum naturam non recipere ut ... potuerint: cf. Sen. *epist.* 82.17, Quint. *decl.* 271 (*OLD* s.u. *recipere* 9b). K–St ii. 225 classify the subordinate clause in our passage as final, but (ii. 242) that of Seneca as consecutive. The perfect subjunctive here is not decisive, since it could have been determined by the present infinitive rather than *iudicatum est*.

damn. 1–4. As V. says in lines 105–106, which, though they appear in editions as part of *damn*. 1, are in reality an introduction to damn. 1–4, these four *exempla* concern innocent defendants who were convicted because of factors irrelevant to the case against them. Apart from L. Scipio (damn. 1), V. cannot have had any good evidence for their innocence (see lines 160, 165–6, 169 nn.); rather he is at pains to stress their innocence in order to emphasize the extraneous factors.

damn. 1. *L. Scipio.* I discussed the trials of the Scipios at length in vol. iii. 170–9 and have no wish to repeat or add to that discussion, except to say that John Rich's treatment, mentioned on p. 171, will be found at *FRHist* iii. 352–6.

V. here follows the version given by Livy at 38.55.6, derived from Valerius Antias, that Lucius Scipio was convicted of having been bribed by Antiochus III in order to secure a more favourable peace following the Roman victory at the battle of Magnesia in 190. That version is manifestly false; see vol. iii. 174 and lines 108–10 n.

105. causae dictione: cf. line 36 n.

105–106. quae ... erant: in the case of L. Scipio *inuidia* of both himself and Africanus (lines 111–12).

106. L. Scipio: (337). L. Cornelius Scipio Asiagenes; for a summary of his career see my note on Livy 34.54.2.

106–107. speciosissimum ... ductum: in 189, on the last day of the intercalary month (Livy 37.59.2, saying that as a spectacle it was greater than the triumph of Africanus).

108–110. non ... quod ... ut ... summoueret: V. means that Scipio was not condemned because the terms imposed on Antiochus were the result of a bribe (but because of *inuidia*). Gelbcke's deletion of *quod*, Kempf's of *non*, Gertz' *quodam*, and Watt's *nouum* ('a novelty'; in my apparatus add '(1995)' after 'Watt') are all instances of trying to improve what V. actually wrote. Similarly with attempts to emend *ut* (*cum* Foertsch) and *summoueret* (-*erat* Krafffert).

The argument is the same as that attributed to P. Cornelius Scipio Nasica by Livy at 38.59.1–2: the terms imposed on Antiochus were such that nobody could possibly believe that they were the result of a bribe. The same argument shows that Lucius was not in fact accused of taking a bribe; see vol. iii. 174.

109. ultra Taurum montem: the Roman demand for Antiochus to withdraw beyond the Taurus is first mentioned in the reply to Antiochus' envoy Heraclides of Byzantium at Livy 37.35.10, included by Africanus in the terms laid down after the battle of Magnesia (Livy 37.45.14), and confirmed in the Peace of Apamea (Livy 38.38.4; there is a lacuna at this point in Pol. 21.43.6). For the meaning of the Taurus boundary see vol. iii. 133–4.

110. sed: Madvig, without argument, proposed adding *et*; again, V. could have written thus, but did not.

111. inuidiae: cf. Livy 38.53.7 *Petilii ... aliena inuidia uoluissent*.

111–112. habitabat: V. conceives of *inuidia* as residing in the names *Africanus* and *Asiagenes*, rather than deriving from them, a striking image. For V.'s metaphorical use of *habitare* with an abstract noun as subject see p. 18. Kraffert's *latitabat* can be ignored.

damn. 2. *C. Appuleius Decianus* (Alexander 79). V. takes this *exemplum* from Cicero (*Rab. perd.* 24) and is, therefore, unaware that Decianus' *nomen* was Appuleius (21; schol. Bob. Cic. p. 95St) and that he was in some way related to Saturninus. Decianus was tribune in 98, Furius (19) in 99 (the index in my edition (p. 867) wrongly repeats '4.7.6; 9.13.3' from the previous entry but one instead of referring to our passage). Decianus will have been convicted in 97; according to Schol. Bob., loc cit., he went into exile in Pontus and joined Mithridates. Cicero, however, (*Flacc.* 77) says only *non potuerit priuatus in ciuitate consistere*. This sounds like a euphemism and it may be that there was a rumour that Decianus had joined Mithridates but that Cicero chose not to refer to it.

Appian (*b.c.* 1.33.148) says that Furius was accused by C. Canuleius and lynched by a mob before the speeches were delivered (in Dio fr. 95.3 he is killed at an assembly); this probably refers to a later trial; cf. Gabba on App. loc. cit., Alexander 41–2 n. 5.

113. maximus fortunae: A^{c}LG. A has *maxima efortunae*, but Halm's *maximae* is eliminated by the agreement of LG (of whose existence Halm, of course, was unaware).

113–114. spectatae integritatis uiro: Cicero says only that Decianus accused Furius *summo studio bonorum omnium*.

114–115. iniquinatissimae uitae: Cicero has *hominem omnibus insignem notis turpitudinis*.

115–116. L. Saturnini morte: L. Appuleius Saturninus (29). After Marius, with whom he broke in 100, the leading *popularis* politician of the end of the second century BC. He was tribune in 103 and 100; re-elected for 99, he was, together with Glaucia and his fellow-tribune L. Equitius, murdered on his first day in office.

116. insuper ... pependit: Cicero says just *condemnatus est*. It is unclear what V., who cannot have had any additional information, means by his expression, perhaps just that the conviction of Decianus was itself the assigned penalty paid by him to Furius (Gertz' *addictus* is out of the question: V. cannot have said that Decianus was bound over to Furius). Decianus could not have stood trial while still in office and the conviction must belong to 97 (Cicero would not have felt the need to make this explicit).

damn. 3. *Sex. Titius* (Alexander 80). Titius (23) was tribune in 99, when he carried a *lex agraria*. Opposed by the consul M. Antonius, its passage was said to have been accompanied by bad omens and it was annulled by the remainder of the tribunician college. His trial, conviction, and exile followed in 98. See Cic. *Rab. perd.* 24–5, *de orat.* 2.48, *leg.* 2.14, 31, Obs. 46. Cicero (*Rab. perd.* 24) says that the jury at his trial was equestrian, from which it follows that he was accused of *maiestas* (ironically, under the law of Saturninus passed in 103). V. wrongly imagines that it was a *iudicium populi* (for his use of *contio* cf. absol. 2 n.): hence his assertion that though his agrarian law made him popular with the people, the vote was swayed by his having an image of Saturninus in his house. That is not to deny that there were those who, like Marius, were in favour of agrarian legislation but hostile to the methods of Glaucia and Saturninus.

117. prostrauit: for *prosternere* of condemnation cf. 4.2.7, 5.4.1, TLL x/2.2231.57 ff.

innocens: since V. is unaware that the charge was one of *maiestas*, he cannot have known whether or not Titius was innocent.

118. gratiosus: 'enjoyed favour'; see my note on Livy 39.32.8.

domi: Paris has *domi suae*, otherwise reproducing the clause as it stands in α: there is no paleographical reason for *suae* being omitted and it should be regarded as an addition by Paris.

119. suffragiis: Kempf suggested adding *suis*, which is palaeographically plausible (a scribe would have moved from the first -*is* to the second), but totally unnecessary.

oppressit: cf. line 53 n.

damn. 4. *Claudia.* The other sources for this episode are Livy *per.* 19 (the original was perhaps V.'s source, despite the discrepancy noted below), Suet. *Tib.* 2.3, and Gell. 10.6; for the sources on P. Claudius Pulcher see absol. 4 n. The discussion of J. Suolahti, *Arctos* 11 (1977), 133–51, is vitiated by misconceptions (admittedly widely shared at the time) about *iudicia populi* and an uncritical acceptance of the views of Münzer, Schur, and Scullard on the nature of Roman politics in the third century BC.

V. assimilates the episode to the three preceding ones by claiming that Claudia was *insons* and that she was convicted because of what she had said when she was being jostled by the crowd, the implication being that the conviction was for a different offence. The *periocha* of Livy, however, says that she was fined because of her remarks; so too Aulus Gellius, citing the Augustan jurist Ateius Capito, in his *commentarius de iudiciis publicis*, who said that in 246 she was fined 25,000 *asses* of *aes graue* by the aediles C. Fundanius and Ti. Sempronius. It follows that Claudia was prosecuted by the aediles before a *iudicium populi*. Capito was not born before 36 BC (cf. Klebs, *RE* ii. 1904), so Livy cannot have used him when he was writing book 19, but the details could well have stood in one of his annalistic sources. Suetonius also talks of a *iudicium populi*, though without mentioning a fine, but anachronistically says that she was accused of *maiestas*, an offence which did not exist at the time.

The story forms part of the picture of the arrogance of the Claudii, on which see Oakley iii. 358, 363.

122 frater ... reuiuesceret: the episode indicates that Claudius was dead by 246. Münzer (*RE* iii. 2858) reports, without being specific, the view of some modern scholars that Claudius, like his colleague, L. Iunius Pullus (see 1.4.4 and testimonia ad loc.), committed suicide: had that been the case, it is most unlikely that it would not have been recorded in our sources.

iactura: V. describes Claudius himself as a *iactura*, just as in line 31 he had called him an *iniuria* (see n. ad loc.); this appears to be the only instance of *iactura* used in this way (cf. *TLL* vii/1.65.93 ff.): recalling the earlier passage, V. was perhaps attracted to the idea of using a linguistically similar abstract noun in the same way.

damn. 5–8. These four *exempla* concern defendants condemned for what V. regards as trivial reasons (line 125 *leues ob causas*), though two of them concern minor magistrates who had failed to fulfil their duties. He describes the connection with the preceding *exempla* as a *breue deuerticulum*, but there is in fact a considerable difference between conviction for reasons unconnected with the case and conviction for minor crimes.

damn. 5. *M. Mulvius, Cn. Lollius, L. Sextilius.* The episode may belong to 241; cf. Livy *per.* 19, Oros. 4.11.5–9, *MRR* i. 220 ('120' in ed. is an error).

125. deuerticulo: see Oakley iii. 207. V. uses the word on four other occasions. At 8.2 and 2.6.9, as here, it means 'digression', a sense present at Livy 9.17.1. At 4.3.2 it has the literal sense of 'retreat', while at 9.1.3 it is pejorative ('deviation' SB). The correct orthography is *de-* ('turning aside'), but *di-* is often found in manuscripts (thus G here). Cf. 8 line 13 n.

ob: thus the correctors of A and L. L has *ob han*, G *ob has* and A presumably had one or the other. *has* is clearly inappropriate but the origin of the corruption is obscure: perhaps α had *han*, a miscopying of *cau-*, the scribe then writing the correct reading without deleting the error; *has* would be a correction in G.

126. incursus: the metaphorical use of *incursus* does not occur before V., who is particularly fond of it (15.9, 3.4.1, 4.1. ext. 2, 4 praef., 8. ext. 2, 6.2.3, 7.2. ext. 2); cf. *TLL* vii/1.1093.45 ff.

M. Muluius Cn. Lollius L. Sextilius: (3), (5), (8) respectively; none of them is otherwise known. α has *Muluius*, P (and Lupus in A) *Mundius* (Halm proposed *Mundicius*). Mulvii are attested elsewhere and one of them must have built the *pons Muluius*, the bridge by whch the via Flaminia crossed the Tiber (cf. Groag, *RE* xvi. 516), but not Mundii or Mundicii. P (and Lupus) has *Sextius*, clearly the result of a scribe moving from the first *-i-* to the second.

triumuiri: the *triumuiri nocturni*, as V. specifies in damn. 6; it is possible that he in fact wrote *triumuiri nocturni* here, a scribe's eye moving from the first *-i* to the second. They are not necessarily identical with the *triumuiri capitales*; cf. vol. iii. 270.

127. sacra uia: see vol. iv. 440.

damn. 6. *P. Villius.*There is no other evidence for this episode and neither Aquillius (not in *RE*) nor Villius (3) is otherwise known. Broughton (*MRR* i. 273, 276; cf. iii. 221), without giving reasons, tentatively assigns it to 211; G. Niccolini, *I fasti dei tribuni della plebe* (Milan, 1934), 398, thought that 'la relativa tenuità' of the offence pointed to an early date. Gundel (*RE* viiiA. 2161–2) has the strange idea (he was perhaps under the impression that V. did not write *nocturnus*; see below) that Villius was a member of one of the two colleges of *iiiuiri* appointed in 212 to levy troops (Livy 25.5.5–9).

129. nocturnus: a concatenation of phenomena has occurred here. *nocturnus* is the reading of G, while P omits the word. There is an erasure in A, equivalent in length to *nocturnus*. L has *no tunus*: Kempf reports that *c* was erased, but I was unable to confirm this. The likelihood is that Paris omitted *nocturnus* because V. had done so in damn. 5 (or because he was using a text of V. which did so; see above), and Lupus therefore erased the word in A. I am unable to explain what appears in L.

Aquillio: G. AL have *Aquilio*, P (and Lupus) the clearly incorrect *Acilio*. *Aquillius* is the form found in older inscriptions, including the *Fasti Capitolini* (cf. *TLL* i. 375.5 ff.) and corruption from a double to a single *l* is much more likely than the reverse.

130. concidit: for *concidere* used metaphorically cf. 7.6.1, *TLL* iv. 32.23 ff. It is frequent in Cicero, but found elsewhere before V. only at Nep. *Phoc.* 2.4 and *culex* 226.

damn. 7. *M. Aemilius Porcina* (Alexander 12). This is apparently a variant version of the episode reported by Velleius 2.10.1. The latter says that Aemilius Lepidus the augur was summoned to appear before them by the censors Cassius Longinus and Caepio (i.e. L. Cassius Longinus Ravilla, consul in 127, and Cn. Servilius Caepio, consul in 141, who held the office together in 125), because he had rented a house for 6,000 *sestertii* (HS is a supplement). Cassius was tribune in 137, the year of Porcina's consulship, and there is no case of a tribune prosecuting, or attempting to prosecute, a consul in office before a *iudicium populi* (for cases involving other magistrates cf. vol. iv. 443). It is, therefore, virtually certain that Velleius' version is correct and that, as at absol. 2, 3, 11, damn. 3 (see nn. ad locc.), V. has wrongly converted the proceedings into a *iudicium populi* (it is possible that both V. and Velleius used Livy 60). It is impossible to say whether Velleius was also right about the nature of Porcina's offence; perhaps he both built an excessively tall house at Alsium and rented an excessively expensive one in Rome.

Cassius and Porcina had clashed in 137, when the latter opposed the former's *lex tabellaria*, introducing secret ballots in all *iudicia populi* except those for *perduellio* (cf. *MRR* i. 485; Broughton (*MRR* i. 510) strangely describes Porcina as 'Caepio's old enemy').

131. cum: 'at the time when'; alteration to *quod* (Kempf) or *quo* (Heraeus) is quite unjustified.

131–132. M. Aemilium Porcinam: (83). M. Aemilius Lepidus Porcina. See above. His praetorship may have been in 143 (see *MRR* i. 473 n. 1). The date of his election to the augurate is unknown (cf. *MRR* i. 496).

132. L. Cassio: (72). L. Cassius Longinus Ravilla. For his tribunate and consulship see above. In 113 he was elected as a special judge ('special prosecutor' at *MRR* i. 537 is misleading: he alone delivered the verdicts) in the case of the Vestal Virgins accused of having had sexual relations with men (cf. *MRR* i. 536–7). He was famed for his severity (cf., e.g., Cic. *Brut.* 97) and his standard question in cases of murder: *cui bono?* (cf. Cic. *S. Rosc.* 84, *Mil.* 32, Ascon. p. 45C)

sublime: my apparatus entry was unnecessary, since Paris used a different construction, writing *quod nimis sublimem uillam suam extruxerat*, and it is not a question of a variant reading.

132–133. Alsiensi agro: Alsium (Barrington Atlas 44B2; mod. Palo, near Ladispoli) is on the coast, about half-way between Ostia and Centumcellae (mod. Civitavecchia); cf. Hülsen, *RE* i. 1639–40.

damn. 8. In this *exemplum*, as in the two following, the defendant is anonymous.

The only *testimonium* I cited was Plin. *nat.* 8.180, no doubt because at the time I was unaware of Münzer's discussion (*Plinius*, 256). In fact both Varro *rust.* 2.5.4 and Columella 6 praef. 7 say that in earlier times (*antiqui* Varro, *apud antiquos* Columella) killing an ox was a capital offence, but do not refer to the present instance. Their language is reflected in V. (lines 192–3 *publica quaestione adflictus est* and Pliny (*apud priores*), who says that the culprit was *damnatus a populo Romano* and exiled. As Münzer argued, both V. and Pliny, who talks of the case being *inter exempla*, probably derive from another passage of Varro (perhaps in the *de uita populi Romani*), which mentioned both the general rule and our instance (Pliny cannot derive from V., since the former does not include him in his index of sources for book 8 and the latter does not mention the rule). Münzer suggests that Varro's source was a collection of excerpts from early jurists, which also contained the ban on women drinking wine (cf. 6.3.9, B. Riposati, *M. Terenti Varronis de uita populi Romani* (Milan, 1939), 290–1, fr. 38, *FRHist* iii. 41).

134–135. qui ... iuberet: for an accusation of a far more heinous crime being committed to gratify a lover cf. Livy 39.42.8–43.4, concerning L. Quinctius Flamininus (with versions differing on the gender of the lover), vol. iii. 358–9.

pueruli sui: Pliny has *concubino procaci*; which, if either, is closer to what Varro wrote is a matter of guesswork.

P has *pueri*, clearly a banalisation of the diminutive, whether by Paris himself or in the course of transmission. V. uses *puerulus* also at 1.6.1 and 6.9. ext. 6; before him it is found in a fragment of comedy, Cicero, Varro, and Nepos. In a sexual context it occurs also in a poem (perhaps by Apuleius; cf. Holford-Strevens, *Aulus Gellius*, 23) cited by Gell. 19.11.4 and *hist. Aug. Heliog.* 26.4. See *TLL* x/2.2530.44 ff.

correptus: P, clearly preserving what V. wrote, while α has *corruptus*.

135. omasum: 'ox tripe'; the word occurs elsewhere only at Naev. *com.* 65, Hor. *sat.* 2.5.40, *epist.* 1.15.34, Plin. *nat.* loc. cit., 28.161, 189, and *hist. Aug. Pert.* 12.6. See *TLL* ix/2.573; they gloss it with '*species carnis bubulae* (*uilioris, ut uid.*)', but this episode indicates that some people regarded it as a delicacy.

in cenam fieri: 'to be prepared for dinner'. Columella 4.15.2 and Quint. *inst.* 10.5.11 are the only examples of *facere in* cited by *TLL* vi/1.443.2 ff. (the article treats *facere* and *fieri* together). Paris, perhaps puzzled by the construction, wrote *in cena*.

137. innocens: equivalent to an apodosis 'though he would have been judged innocent'.

amb. There is no manuscript authority for attaching the heading *amb(ust.)* to these two *exempla*. To the best of my knowedge, the first edition in which it occurs (as *ambustae*, since in both *exempla* those accused are women; see below) is that of Pighius (see p. 24); it has become part of the reference system and I therefore followed suit in my edition. The word was taken from Livy 22.35.3; see *Liuiana*, 68–9 (this note largely repeats what I said there). *TLL* i. 1878.13 ff. ('*rubrica* ambust(i)') and Münzer (*RE* xiii. 893) wrongly claim that V.'s *qui in discrimen capitis adducti neque damnati neque absoluti sunt* is a definition of *ambusti*. V. uses the masculine because the category in principle includes both men and women and the clause corresponds to *aut absoluti sint aut damnati* in line 2. In neither *exemplum* is the defendant named. On the reception of these two *exempla*, including their influence on the jurisprudence of the sixteenth and seventeenth centuries, cf. Holford-Strevens, *IJCT* 7 (2000–2001), 489–514.

amb. 1. *Anonymous woman* (Alexander 4). There are no other references to this episode.

140. M. Popillium Laenatem praetorem: five M. Popillii Laenates are attested, the consuls of 359, 356, ?354, 350, and 348 (20), 316 (21), 173 (24), and 139 (22), and a *legatus pro praetore* mentioned in an inscription from Cos (23; Münzer, *Klio* 24 (1931), 333–4 n. 1); cf. 6 line 15 n. Broughton identifies the praetor with the consul of 139 (*MRR* i. 475; the question mark relates to the year of Popillius' praetorship, which cannot have been later than 142, not the identification with our praetor, as Brennan, 311 n. 102 thinks; Volkmann (*RE* xxii. 60; not Münzer, as stated by Brennan, loc. cit.) says that the matter cannot be decided). Equally possible is the consul of 173, who was praetor in 176. He was assigned Sardinia, but successfully argued that Ti. Sempronius Gracchus, consul in 177 (and father of the Gracchi) and T. Aebutius Parrus, praetor in 178, should remain in Sardinia (Livy 41.15.6–8). No alternative province is mentioned, but it is possible that he was assigned judicial duties in Rome. As Brennan (148) observes, praetors assigned Sardinia spent all or part of their year dealing with judicial matters in Rome in 184 (Livy 39.41.5), 180 (Livy 40.37.4, 43.2–3), 177 (Livy 45.9.10), and 167 (Livy 45.16.4).

141. fuste: A^cL^cG. A has *festem*, a *uox nihili*, while the original reading of L appears to have been *fustem*; the accusative results from assimilation to the preceding and following words.

142. latae sententiae sunt: presumably by members of Popillius' *consilium* (Brennan, loc. cit.).

144–145. alterum †ultione ... dignum†: the transmitted text is impossible (the sentence, as often with conclusions of this sort, was ignored by Paris): *parri-*

cidium is the murder of the children by their grandmother, *parricidio* that of the latter by her daughter. The decision to neither convict nor acquit was, presumably, given on the grounds that the murder of the children deserved to be avenged but that the mother ought not to have done so by murdering her own mother, but the paradosis makes V. say that the murder of the children did not deserve to be avenged.

None of the solutions proposed, however, is satisfactory, and I cannot think of one that is. Later MSS (cited by Pighius) added *dignum* after *ultione* and this became the vulgate: it is hard to see, though, how *dignum* in this position came to be omitted; Kempf suggested adding it before *ultione*, which is not open to the same objection (a scribe's eye would have moved from one *-um* to another), but one would not expect chiastic order with a positive followed by a negative in this way. Halm deleted *non*, but this makes V. says that it was decided that the defendant deserved to be acquitted, not that she should be neither convicted nor acquitted. Gertz added *uero* after *alterum*, otherwise accepting the paradosis; according to Kempf (I should have added '(K)'; Gertz' conjectures were communicated to the former, but not published elsewhere), he thought that there was a '*leue zeugma*' and that *dignum* could be understood from *non dignum* (and presumably this is what Kempf himself intended by retaining the paradosis), a strange notion.

amb. 2. *The woman of Smyrna.* On this *exemplum* see Holford-Strevens, *Aulus Gellius*, 79–80, D. Campanile, *RAL*, 9ª serie (2004), 155–75.

The story is repeated by Gellius 12.7, who concludes his account with *scripta haec historiast in libro Valeri Maximi factorum et dictorum memorabilium nono.* The last is probably an indication that Gellius was using a text of V. which divided the work into ten books (see p. 5), not a mistake, as Holford-Strevens seems to think. It is found also at Ammianus 29.2.19, derived from Gellius (for John of Salisbury and Rabelais see Holford-Strevens, loc. cit.). Holford-Strevens argues convincingly that the differences between Gellius and V. are deliberate changes by the former, not the result of the use of another source.

146. P. ... Dolabellae: P. Cornelius Dolabella, suffect consul after the assassination of Caesar and son-in-law of Cicero. The MSS of Gellius have *Cn.*, to be regarded as an error of Gellius himself (cf. Holford-Strevens, loc. cit.), not a corruption (not that anyone has ever proposed emending the text of Gellius).

146–147. proconsulari imperio Asiam obtinentis: Dolabella was allotted Syria (for sources see *MRR* ii. 317), but early in 43, passing through Asia, he captured Smyrna, held by Trebonius, and expelled the governor of Asia, P. Cornelius Lentulus Spinther (for sources see *MRR* ii. 344); the present episode would have to belong to that period (Dolabella, besieged by Cassius at Laodicea, committed suicide later in the year) and *Asiam obtinentis*, therefore, describes the *de facto* rather than the *de iure* position. Its historicity, however, is open to grave doubt: it seems unlikely that in the pressing circumstances and with Brutus in control of Greece, Dolabella would have taken such a step.

Holford-Strevens describes *proconsulari imperio* (also used by V. at 6.9.7) as an 'anachronistic term', saying (n. 55) that it was 'invented under Tiberius'; he refers to K.M. Girardet, in A. Giovannini (ed.), *La revolution romaine après Ronald Syme, bilans et perspectives* (Entretiens Fondation Hardt, 46; Geneva, 2000), 167–227, who (176 n. 30) cites, in addition to the two passages of V., Tacitus *ann*. 1.14.3, 76.2, 3.58.2, 12.41.1, 59.1, 13.21. 3 (*proconsulare ius*), 52, 1. Gell. 5.14.17 (but not, oddly, 12.7.1). The *imperium* of ex-consuls had been prorogued *pro consule* since, almost certainly, 327 (cf. Oakley ii. 558–61) and occasionally *priuati* had such *imperium* conferred on them (first the future Scipio Africanus in 210); the proper term is *pro consule*, not *proconsul*, but it is likely that Cicero, once, and Livy, on several occasions, were willing to regard *proconsul* as a declinable noun (cf. vol. iii. 574); Polybius and inscriptions use ἀνθύπατος. *proconsulare imperium* is indeed not found before V., but it occurs at Livy *per*. 91 and it is possible that this reproduces Livy's own language; he writes *proconsularis imago* at 5.2.9. In any case, once Augustus had been granted, in 23, *imperium* greater than that of the governors of consular provinces (Dio 53.32.5; I am totally unconvinced by Girardet's rejection of this evidence (op. cit., 200–16)), it is quite likely that it was referred to, if not officially, as *imperium proconsulare maius*.

147. Zmyrnaea: P; the MSS of V. differ only in having -*i*- for -*y*- and -*e*- for -*ae*-, common confusions, found, e.g., frequently in the Puteaneus of Livy's third decade. On Smyrna (mod. İzmir), normally spelt *Z*- in Latin MSS, see vol. i. 321.

147–149. interemit ... occisum: Gellius (12.7.2) says that she poisoned them and that her older son had been *exceptum insidiis*.

149–150. Athenas ad Areopagi cognitionem: the council of the Areopagus dealt with cases of murder at Athens, most famously in the trial of Orestes in Aeschylus' *Eumenides*.

In Greek the regular form of the name is Ἄρειος πάγος, with Ἀρειόπαγος occurring only at *IG* ii–iii² 1722, though Ἀρεοπαγίτης is used by fourth century writers. ει is transliterated in Latin as *e* or *i* (but not *ei*); possible Latin forms, therefore, are *Areus pagus*, *Arius pagus*, *Areopagus*, and *Ariopagus*. Here A and L have *Arei pagi*, G *Ario pagi*, and the first corrector of A *Areopagi*; P has *Areopagitarum* (*Aero-* in my apparatus is an error), with Lupus writing *Ario pagitarum* in A (which may, therefore, have been the reading of the exemplar of P; see

p. 20): Paris, while not reproducing the rest of *consideranter ... sapienter* (lines 213–215) moved the reference to the Areopagites into the previous sentence, which he then joined to what follows with *qui*. I printed *Areopagi*, thinking that G's -*o* probably preserved the paradosis, but gave *Arei pagi* a fort. recte.

150. relegauit: this is the first instance of the rare use of *relegare* to mean 'transfer a matter to another body' (cf. *OLD s.u.* 3a). Paris, no doubt puzzled by the word, replaced it with *remisit*.

151. eam: one would expect the pronoun to follow *liberare* rather than *punire*, and Torrenius' *tam* could be right (not so Stangl's *tamen*); without *eam* the reference is general ('a woman').

sustinebat: *sustinere* + infinitive 'to endure doing something' occurs before V. only in Livy (23.9.7) and Ovid; cf. *OLD s.u.* 6.

consideranter: the only occurrence of the adverb before late antiquity (*TLL* iv. 432.15 ff.).

152. magistratus: LG. A has an erasure, doubtless (my '*sic etiam fort. A*' is too hesitant) of the same word), caused by the unfortunate idea that *pr.* was an abbreviation of *praetor* rather than *populi Romani*.

Areopagitae: AL. G has *Ario-*, no doubt for consistency with *Ario pagi* above: the Greek form (see lines 149–50 n.) guarantees *Areo-*.

155. damnandi ... cunctationem uitabant: α has *cunctationem mutabant*, which is impossible without an indication of what the hesitation was exchanged for. Guyet's *uitabant* makes excellent sense and the corruption of *ui-* to *mu-* is extremely easy. *nutabant*, a correction in A, introduces an intransitive verb, by *notabant* Kellerbauer presumably meant 'indicate', which is very weak, while Gertz' *tutabantur* ('guard against'; cf. *OLD s.u.* 3) involves two alterations. There remains, however, the problem that *damnandi atque absoluendi cunctationem* must mean 'hesitation between condemning and acquitting': one expects *inter damnandum et absoluendum* and there is no parallel for genitives being used in this way. Hence Wensky proposed *iudicationem*, Shackleton Bailey *cogitationem*, which he printed in his Loeb edition. In neither case is the posited corruption at all plausible, and we should probably simply accept that V. here used the genitive of the gerund in an unusual way. But perhaps it would have been better to obelize.

2 praef. 1–2. aequitas quaestionum ... immoderata turba: my apparatus records two conjectures, Gertz' deletion of *quaestionum* and Damsté's *exiguitas* for *aequitas*.

One might imagine that the former was based on the fact that at first sight *iudiciis* and *quaestionum* appear to have the same meaning: Kempf's note, however, reads '*quaestionum non sine causa delend. uid. Gertzio: nulla enim in quaestionibus sed in iudiciis aequitas*', which presumably represents Gertz' own argument. One could argue that V. (as Livy often does) has combined two different forms of expression, *quorum magis aequitas* and *in quibus magis aequitas quaestionum*: in fact *quaestio* here has the sense of 'argument' (see *OLD s.u.* 5b; SB's 'conduct' is misleading; cf. 1 line 1 n.) and *aequitas quaestionum* ('the arguments based on equity') makes perfect sense. In any case, *quaestionum* would be a very strange interpolation.

Damsté's conjecture was also designed to deal with Gertz' claim: it is hard to see why the reader should take pleasure in insubstantial arguments. Without reading what he wrote (*Mnemosyne* 42 (1914), 264), one might imagine that he was puzzled by *immoderata turba*, since V. provides only four *exempla* of *iudicia priuata*, and that by *exiguitas* he intended 'small number'. That is a genuine difficulty, but perhaps when V. wrote the preface he intended to provide a larger number of *exempla*, but subsequently changed his mind, nevertheless leaving this sentence as it stood.

1. *Claudius Centumalus and Calpurnius Lanarius.* This *exemplum* is derived from Cicero *off.* 3.66; see Dyck, 576–8.

3. Claudius Centumalus: (107). Not otherwise known. Cicero gives his *praenomen* as Titus (for the possibility that we should read *Ti.* see Dyck, 576 n. 60). The *cognomen* is otherwise attested only among the Fulvii (cf. *TLL* onom. C 324.62 ff.): perhaps he had been adopted by the Claudii from the Fulvii.

3–5. auguribus ... officiebat: the augurs took the auspices from the *auguraculum* on the *arx* (according to Paulus Festus 17L *auguraculum* was once the name of the *arx*), which commanded a wide view across the city; cf. Linderski, *ANRW* ii. 16.3, 2257–79, Coarelli, *LTUR* i. 142–3, Dyck, 577, Oakley, iv. 108. Festus 466–8L says that Marius built his temple of *Honos* and *Virtus* lower than others (Coarelli wrongly says lower than planned) lest the augurs order him to demolish it (cf. Linderski, op. cit. 2258).

4. in Caelio monte: for the Caelian hill, south of the Oppian and east of the Palatine, see Giannelli, *LTUR* i. 208–11.

5. Calpurnio Lanario: (49); Cicero gives his *praenomen* as Publius. In 81 he killed L. Livius Salinator (Plut. *Sert.* 7.3 has Julius, but the *cognomen* is otherwise restricted to the Livii and the error, or corruption, is easy), who was a member of Sertorius' army in Spain; see Sall. *hist.* 1.95–6M = 83–4 Ramsey, Plut. loc. cit. (Ramsey says that Plutarch wrongly makes Lanarius 'a traitor among the blockading Sertorian forces': δολοφονήσας means just 'murder' (cf. L–S–J *s.u.*).

6. a quibus ... coactus: Paris rewrites as *sed iussus Calpurnius domum demoliri*; my apparatus misleadingly cites only *iussus*.

6–7. M. Catonem ... adduxit: the distinction between a single *iudex* and an *arbiter* in civil cases is not clear; cf. Crook, 78, H. F. Jolowicz and B. Nicholas, *Historical Introduction to the Study of Roman Law*, 3rd edn (Cambridge, 1972), 178.

Cicero has *arbitrum illum adegit 'quidquid sibi dare facere oporteret ex fide bona'*. *adigere* is used of compelling someone to appear before a court (cf. *TLL* i. 677.24 ff.), but it is hard to see how this ('he summoned the former owner before a court of equity to decide ...' W. Miller (Loeb) or 'he compelled him to go before the arbitrator as to ... ' E. M. Atkins in eadem and M. T. Griffin, *Cicero on Duties* (Cambridge, 1991), 'er zwang ihn (*sc.* Claudius) zur Einsetzung des Cato als *arbiter* mit folgendem Streitprogramm' G. Broggini, *Iudex arbiterve. Prolegomena zum Officium des römischen Privatrichters* (Cologne–Graz, 1957), 227) can be got out of the Latin: either *adegit* means 'brought to the case' and *illum* is the *arbiter* or we should read <ad> *arbitrum* (a scribe's eye moving from one *a-* to another). Maybe V. too was puzzled by Cicero's formulation, but his own is equally problematic: *adducere* too is regularly used of bringing someone to court (cf. *TLL* i. 594.71 ff., 595.80 ff., *OLD s.u.* 4) and *iudex adductus* occurs in the following *exemplum* (line 21), but there is no parallel for *adducere arbitrum cum* with the ablative of the defendant; perhaps Paris found *adduxit* strange and therefore replaced it with *sumpsit* (cf. line 30 n.). Guyet's *Claudio addixit* ('assigned to Claudius', presumably) is out of the question.

M. Porcius Cato (12), as V. says, was the father of Cato Uticensis (16). He was a plebeian tribune in 99 and died while a candidate for the praetorship (Gell. 13.20.14). That must have been in or after 96, since Uticensis was born in 95, and before 91, the year of the murder of M. Livius Drusus, his brother-in-law, with whom Uticensis lived after his father's death (Plut. *Cato min*.1.1; Dyck, 576, confuses Drusus with his father, the consul of 112). 96–91, therefore, is the *terminus ante quem* for the present episode.

7. incluti: on *inclu(i)tus* see vol. iv. 629–30. V. uses it on twenty-one occasions, in nineteen of which it refers to a person or event in the remote past, with its regular sense of 'of ancient fame'. The exceptions are this passage and the preface to the whole work (1 praef. line 22), the *incluta claritas* of Caesar and Augustus (the epithet is used in the titulature of later emperors; cf. *TLL* vii/1.960.59 ff.): in both cases the fame is such that, though Cato, Caesar, and, particularly, Augustus, belonged to recent history, their fame made them comparable to the great heroes of the past. V. mentions Cato on sixteen occasions (see ed. 879, unfortunately omitting our passage), but nowhere else does he refer to him in this way. For the idealization of Cato in the early Principate see, e.g., Nisbet and Hubbard, i. 156: it was his good fortune to have committed suicide before the Ides of March.

quidquid: α has *formulam quid(c)quid*, which has no syntax. A *formula* constitutes the instructions, given by the praetor, after consultation with the parties, to the *iudex/arbiter* who is to hear the case (cf., e.g., Crook, 76–7); the correction in A *ut formulam daret quidquid*, with the following *dare* deleted, wrongly implies that it is Cato who is to lay down the formula; so too *et formulam quidquid* in CΓ, strangely making *formulam* the object of *adduxit*, and Damsté's *formulam sibi dare quidquid* (the syntax of *dare* is inexplicable). *in formula* (Halm; Gertz' omission of *in* would be preferable) is possible. In Cicero, however, *adegit* is followed immediately by *quidquid sibi dare facere oporteret ex fide bona* and I believe that Novák was right to delete *formulam* (though he did not convince Shackleton Bailey, who prints <*in*> *formulam*): it will have arisen as a gloss by someone who thought that the connection of *quidquid sibi dare facere oporteret ex fide bona* with what precedes was obscure. It is not likely that V. himself thought it necessary to say that *quidquid sibi dare facere oporteret ex fide bona* was a formula; he would have expected his readers to be conversant with the basic principles of Roman legal procedure.

9. praedictum: 'instruction'; cf. Livy 23.19.5, the only other instance of the usage before late antiquity (*TLL* x/1.570.11 ff.; for Livy 33.6.8 cf, vol. 1, 257). *edictum* in DEΓ, which is not used of an order to an individual except in legal texts concerning a summons to appear in court (cf. *TLL* v/2.69.63 ff.), no doubt resulted from puzzlement at the usage.

2. *Visellius and Otacilia.* There is no other evidence for this episode, though three of the four persons involved can be identified. It will be as well to paraphrase V.'s narrative in lines 20–30, which may appear somewhat obscure.

Otacilia, married to Laterensis, was having an affair with C. Visellius Varro. The latter, seriously ill, allowed Otacilia to record a (*sc.* fictitious) loan to him of 300,000 HS, on the understanding that if he died she should demand repayment from his heirs. To Otacilia's dismay he recovered, and she proceeded to demand payment from Visellius.

The text is discussed by W. A. J. Watson, *The Law of Obligations in the Later Roman Republic* (Oxford, 1965), 32–6, which I do not fully understand. His view, following U. von Lübtow, *Eranion in honorem Georgii S. Maridakis* i (Athens, 1963), 197 (he discusses the case as a whole on pp. 196–200) that *expensa sibi ferri passus est* (line 15) and *inani stipulatione* (line 20) stood in the judgement of Aquillius is over-optimistic.

13. oblitteratum: *sc. est.*

13–14. C. Visellius Varro ... Otacilia Laterensis: Visellius (3), a cousin of Cicero (Cic. *Brut.* 264), was a military tribune in 80–79, perhaps tribune of the plebs in 69 (cf. *MRR* ii. 136 n. 6) and perhaps curule aedile in 59 (cf. *MRR* ii. 193 n. 4). The only known Laterensis in this period is M. Iuventius (16), quaestor *c.* 62, praetor in 51, and a *legatus* under Lepidus in 43, when he committed suicide and was honoured by the senate with a public funeral and a statue (Dio 46.5.4). Münzer (*RE* x. 1366, xviii. 1.1866) thought that he was the son of Otacilia, but there seems no reason why he should not have been her husband: he is normally referred to by *cognomen* alone (cf. Münzer, *RE* x. 1365) and while he is clearly younger than Visellius, the gap may be no more than 11 years, if Visellius was quaestor before 73 (cf. *MRR* ii. 114–15) and Laterensis *c.* 62 (cf. *MRR* ii. 175).

The Iuventii, apart from one claimed to have been the first plebeian to hold the curule aedileship (Cic. *Planc.* 58), first appear in the historical record in the early second century and were ennobled by the consul of 163. The Otacilii held three consulships in the mid third century (M'. Otacilius Crassus in 263 and 246 and his brother Titus in 261), while T. Otacilius Crassus, praetor in 217 and 214, and married to the niece of Fabius Verrucosus, commanded the fleet off Sicily from 216 until his death in 211. A dubious plebeian aedile in 491 apart (cf. *MRR* i. 17), no other Visellius is known to have held office in the Republic.

13. graui morbo correptus: *corripere* of a disease is found before V. only at Lucr. 6.822, Virg. *georg.* 3.472, and Manil. 1.881; V. also uses it at 1.7.4 and 5.1.3 (*TLL* iv. 1043.35 ff.).

14. commercium libidinis: this euphemism for a sexual relationship occurs otherwise only at 6.1.10 and Suet. *Cal.* 36 (*TLL* iii. 1876.50 ff.). (Ronald Syme talks somewhere of the 'commerce of the sexes'.)

15. expensa ferri: 'to be entered (*sc.* in her accounts) as paid'. For *expensum ferre* as an accounting term see *TLL* i. 314.38 ff., v/2.1643.57 ff. (cf. 1644.66 ff.), *OLD* s.u. *fero* 24b. See also lines 38–9 n.

15–17. ab heredibus ... colorando: he could not leave Otacilia a legacy without disclosing his affair, with the risk of its validity being challenged, while the *heredes*, so he hoped, would discharge any debts owed at the time of his death.

16. libidinosam liberalitatem: deliberate alliteration.

libidinosus is frequent in Cicero (though in a sexual context only at *Verr.* 2.3.77, *Cael.* 70, and *Tusc.* 4.71), but otherwise occurs before V. only in two passages of Nepos, though both Sallust (*Cat.* 51.30) and Livy (3.36.7) use the adverb, non-sexually. V. employs it on five other occasions (11. ext. 4, 4.3. ext. 1, 6.1.11, 9.2. ext. 3, 5, all but the penultimate in a sexual context). See *TLL* vii/2.1328.72 ff.

17. colorando: for the metaphorical use of *colorare*, here with the sense of 'conceal', cf. *TLL* iii. 1724.21 ff.

tempestate: for *tempestas* of a disease cf. *OLD* s.u. 5b (not citing our passage). Paris paraphrased *liberatus deinde ex illa ualetudine.*

19. destrictam: 'inexorable' ('uncompromising' SB). As an adjective *destrictus* does not occur before V., who uses it also at 5.2 and 2.9.6, and again before late Latin only at Tac. *ann.* 4.36.3, though *destricte* is found in the epigraphically preserved speech of Claudius on the admission of Gauls to the senate (*ILS* 212, 2.31), Quint. *decl.* 342, and Pliny *epist.* 9.21.4. See *TLL* v/1.771.6 ff. (Ronald Syme once suggested to me, in conversation, that *distincte* at Livy 34.58.1 should be emended to *destricte*; I did not cite the conjecture in my apparatus.)

feneratricem: *feneratrix* occurs elsewhere only as the title of a lost play of Plautus (Varr. *ling.* 7.96, Fest. 512L). Most moneylenders, of course, were male. The implication is that Otacilia was demanding repayment with interest.

20. fronte ... stipulatione: for *frons* as an indication of shame or lack of it cf. *TLL* vi/1.1357.83 ff.

Before V. *inuerecundus* occurs only at Plaut. *Rud.* 652, a fragment of tragedy (*trag. inc.* 179), Cic. *Cael.* 69 (Σ, clearly correct against *non uer-* Pπδ; it has been conjectured at *ac.* 2.126), Sall. *hist.* 2.16M = 17 Ramsey, Hor. *epod.* 11.13). (*TLL* vii/2.161.57 ff.)

A *stipulatio* is the demand for a guarantee from a creditor (cf. *OLD s.u.*, Watson, op. cit. (2 n.), ch. 1); *inani* here has the sense of 'lacking legal force' (cf. *TLL* vii/1.826.74 ff., *OLD s.u.* 13b, misclassifying our passage at 11b): Visellius could not guarantee that his heirs would agree to pay Otacilia the money (Watson, op. cit., 35–6, thinks that *inanis* means either that 'the stipulation is devoid of legal content or that it is valid but can be rebutted by an *exceptio*'; in the former case, it is 'void as being *contra bonos mores*', in the latter, which Watson prefers, Aquillius used the *exceptio doli* 'since it amounted to fraud for Otacilia to sue when it was intended that the gift should take effect only if Visellius died').

20–21. C. Aquillius ... excellens: C. Aquillius (23) Gallus was praetor in 66 but did not seek the consulship (cf. Cic. *Att.* 1.1.1). He is said by Pliny (*nat.* 17.2) to have been an *eques Romanus*, though he was probably a descendant of L. Aquillius Gallus, praetor in 176 (cf. Shackleton Bailey on Cic. loc. cit.). He was one of the leading jurists of his generation; cf. Watson, *Law Making in the Late Roman Republic* (Oxford, 1974), 72–5.

21. iudex adductus: cf. lines 6–7 n.

23. quod si: 'but if'; cf. K–St ii. 321–2, H–S 571. V. uses the idiom also at 5.1.10, 3. ext. 3, 9.1, 7.3. ext. 6, 9.1.3.

eadem formula: i.e. if the *formula* laid down by the praetor (cf. line 7 n.) had so allowed.

Varro ... potuisset: the sense must be 'if Aquillius had been able to both condemn Varro for adultery and find against Otacilia'. α had *Varro etsi* (LG, *et*

A) *damnari et aduersariae* (AG, *aduersarie* L; L normally writes the diphthong in full) *absolui*. Most conjectures have followed, reasonably, A in changing *etsi* to *et*: *etsi* will be the result of perseveration from the preceding *si*. A corrector of A altered *aduersariae* to *aduersaria*, though it is unclear whether he intended this as a nominative, which gives the opposite of the required sense, or an ablative, which is unparalleled of a person with *absoluere*, as is *ab aduersaria* (an easy omission, a scribe's eye moving from the first *a* to the second), independently proposed by Foertsch and Madvig. The omission of either *absolui*, with *aduersaria* as a nominative (Perizonius) or *aduersariae* (Torrenius) lacks all plausibility. In these circumstances I obelized, but now believe that Shackleton Bailey was right to retain *aduersariae*; he cites Cic. *Verr*. 2.2.22 *hunc hominem Veneri absoluit, sibi condemnat* and translates 'in respect of his female opponent'; that passage is discussed at H-S 93, who take *Veneri* as a dative of disadvantage, combined with a dative of advantage (*sibi*, i.e. Verres himself); for such datives cf. Pinkster, i. 892-3. For *absoluere* in civil cases, with the meaning 'find in favour of the defendant' cf. *TLL* i. 175.34 ff., citing neither passage. Translate 'to the disadvantage of his opponent'. For *damnare* cf. lines 32-3 n.; here, however, the reference is as much to a criminal trial (see lines 25-6 n.).

24. inconcessum amorem: α has *errorem*, which went unchallenged (and was retained by Kempf) until Halm proposed *amorem*, Madvig *feruorem*, and Gertz *ardorem* (the last printed by Shackleton Bailey, presumably because it was the closest to *errorem*). *errorem* would have to refer to the fictitious loan and the agreement with Otacilia, but *inconcessus* demands a noun which refers explicitly to the sexual relationship (V. uses it on two other occasions, writing *inconcessam uenerem* at 2.1.5 and *inconcessis ac periculosis facibus accensum* (in contrast with *permissa uenere*) at 7.3.10), and *amorem* fulfils this requirement.

25. calumniam: the primary meaning of *calumnia* is 'malicious prosecution' in a criminal case (*TLL* iii. 1863.32 ff.), but it is also frequently used of improperly brought private cases (1888.3 ff.); see also 3 line 11 n. V. uses it of a criminal prosecution at 3.7.1e, of a private suit also at 3.2 and 9.15.4. Otacilia was committing *calumnia* because she had not in fact made a loan to Visellius.

A person convicted of *calumnia* in a criminal prosecution was branded with K (i.e. *kalumniator*) on his forehead; in a civil case the penalty was financial (cf. Gaius *inst*. 4.171-81, Gell. 14.2.8).

See Hitzig, *RE* iii. 1414-21.

compescuit: by finding against Otacilia.

25-26. adulterii ... reliquit: as perhaps in 1. absol. 12 (see n. ad loc.) V. is under the misapprehension that adultery was a criminal offence in the Republic.

3. *Titinius and Fannia.* The story is also told by Plutarch *Marius* 38.3–6 (§§ 7–10 correspond to what V. relates at 1.5.5); V.'s source cannot be determined. Plutarch (§ 4) says that Marius heard the case during his sixth consulship, i.e. 100; there was nothing to prevent a consul from hearing a case himself, but one wonders whether, in the political situation of 100, Marius would have done so: Plutarch could have been misled by a statement in his source that at the time Marius was declared a *hostis* (cf. line 36 n.), he had been consul six times. See further lines 30, 32–3 nn.

V. says (lines 28–9) that Titinius had deliberately married Fannia, who was (sc. though she was) *impudica*, i.e. that he expected her to be unfaithful to him and that he could then divorce her and keep her dowry (in Plutarch the initiative came from Fannia, who demanded the return of her dowry); this is more explicit in lines 34–5. Matters are complicated by Cicero's statement at *Verr.* 2.1.128 that Cn. Fannius (11), an *eques Romanus*, was the *frater germanus* (full brother) of Q. Titinius. Münzer (*RE* vi. 1992) suggested that Fannius was the illegitimate son of Fannia, that is to say, presumably, that he was the result of a relationship between Fannia and Titinius before they were married: in that case, however, one would have expected Titinius, on marrying Fannia, to have adopted their son (an illegitimate child would have had the name of its mother). It is more likely that Fannius was adopted into his mother's family following the divorce.

It will be as well at this point to deal with the tissue of error and confusion in T. F. Carney, *A Biography of C. Marius* (*PACA* Supp. 1 (1961)), 58 n. 258; cf. id. *RhM* 105 (1962), 309. He first claims that Fannia was in Marius' *clientela*, citing V. and Plutarch as evidence: in fact V. says that Fannia helped Marius, regarding the fine he had imposed as being the result of her character, the retention of her dowry of Marius' scrupulousness, while according to Plutarch the magistrates of Minturnae had placed Marius in Fannia's house because they believed her to be hostile to him. She may indeed have concealed her real feelings, but that does not constitute *clientela*. Carney next says that Fannia 'may also have been M.'s kinswomen (*sic*): that her son, in spite of illegitimate birth, could attain a quaestorship ... must surely mean relationship with the *nobilis gens Fannia*, with which M. had become related by his son's marriage'. Had Fannia been a member of a consular family related to Marius, it is most unlikely that she would have been living in Minturnae (unless she had been disowned by them) or that Marius would have wanted to adjudicate the case. As to kinship with Marius, it is very distant: the younger Marius was married to the daughter of L. Licinius Crassus (consul in 95), whose mother-in-law was the sister-in-law of C. Fannius, the consul of 122 (her grandfather was Q. Mucius Scaevola the augur, whom Plutarch (*Mar.* 35.9) wrongly calls her father-in-law). 'illegitimate birth' is taken from Münzer (see above) and the quaestorship appears to be a figment of Carney's imagination.

Marius features in no fewer than twenty-nine *exempla* (see the index to my edition, 873-4). In book 8 he appears again at 6.2, 9.2, 14.4, and 15.7. On V.'s portrayal of him see Carney *RhM* 105, 289-337.

27. multo animosius: 'with much more vigour' (SB). V. is fond of *animosus*, using the adjective on thirteen, the adverb on three occasions. Before him it is relatively rare, occurring in a fragment of Novius, Cicero, Varro, Livy, and Augustan poetry (*TLL* ii. 88.32 ff.).

militari spiritu dignum: reflecting the (largely justified) view that Marius was essentially a military leader, unhappy in domestic politics. Cf. Sall. *Iug.* 63.2, Vell. 2.11.1, Plut. *Mar.* 28, Weynand, *RE* Supp. vi. 1423-5.

28. C. Titinius: a number of other Republican Titinii are known and the form of the name, correct in P and, both here and in lines 31, 33, 34, in A (for variations in L and G see my apparatus; the MSS of Plutarch have Τίννιος, by haplography of τι), is not in doubt.

Minturnensis: Minturnae (Barrington Atlas 44E3), on the border of Latium and Campania, was a citizen colony, founded in 295. Perhaps the case had been referred to Rome by the local magistrates.

Fanniam: thus Lupus, from P's *Fannia*. α has *Anniam* but *Fanniam* in lines 50 and 51; Plutarch has Φα- consistently.

29. impudicam de industria duxerat: see above.

impudicus is regularly used of persons, particularly women, of loose morals; cf. *TLL* vii. 1.711.36 ff. For *de industria* 'deliberately' cf. *TLL* vii/1.1276.31 ff.

30. sumptus inter eos iudex: cf. lines 6-7 n. The phrase suggests that V. did not think that Marius was consul at the time.

in conspectu: 'in public'. The phrase is rare, occurring before V. only at Livy 1.31.2; cf. *TLL* iv. 492.35 ff. The implication is that private cases were normally heard in private.

31. incepto desisteret: cf. 6.5. ext. 2, 9.5.1, Livy 7.5.6, 25.2.7, 38.30.5, 36.8, Vell. 1.10.1, *TLL* v/1.732.51 ff.

32-33. mulierem ... damnauit: if Marius was indeed consul at the time, he could have fined Fannia by virtue of his *imperium*; otherwise, perhaps his decision was in fact that Fannia should retain the whole of her dowry except for HS1. For *damnare* of finding against the defendant in a civil case cf. *TLL* v/1.13.38 ff.; see also line 23 n.

35-36. haec est quae: for this way of indentifying someone who occurs in another context cf. Livy 21.46.1, 24.43.8.

36. hostem a senatu iudicatum: after Sulla's march on Rome in 88; cf. 3.8.5, Cic. *Brut.* 168, Livy *per.* 77, Vell. 2.19, Plut. *Sull.* 10.1, App. *b.c.* 1.60.271.

36-37. caenoque ... oblitum: cf. Plut. *Mar.* 37.12, 38.2.

37. et iam ... deductum: cf. Plut. *Mar.* 38.3. Kempf, in his 1854 edition, first realised that the sense is that Marius, after being dragged from the marsh, had now been taken to Fannia's house, not that he was also taken there, and, therefore, that V. wrote *et iam*, not *etiam*.

37–38. ope ... adiuuit: cf. Plut. *Mar.* 38.6.

38–39. suis moribus ... illius religioni acceptum ferri debere: the datives convey the sense of 'received and to be credited to'; *referre* is normally used in the idiom (cf. *TLL* i. 314.13 ff.), with the sense of 'attribute', and was conjectured here by Schulze, *Philologus* 37 (1877), 572) but *ferre*, no doubt influenced by its use in accounting (cf. line 15 n.), occurs also at Sen. *epist.* 78.3, Plin. *nat.* 2.22, 12.82, 19.37 (*TLL* i. 314.37 ff.).

4. *The man who hired a horse.* There are no other sources for this story. *illius saeculi* indicates that it belongs to a far distant period (cf. 9.1.3, of 195 BC) and the absence of a name perhaps suggests that V. did not take it from a written source.

40. eo: Halm proposed adding *de* or *ex*: the only other instance of *manare* with the plain ablative is Cic. *fat.* 19, where Baiter added *e* (cf. *TLL* viii. 321.49 ff.); there the preposition could easily have been omitted after *naturae*, but there is no similar palaeographical explanation here and the two passages can be allowed to support each other.

41. qui: thus both AL and P, showing that G's *quia* is a conjecture. *qui* is unexceptionable, even though one might have expected *quia* (were the two readings equipollent, one could argue that *qui* is the *lectio difficilior*).

usus illi Ariciam: 'for him to use to get to Aricia', the name of the town without a preposition, as normal. P (and Lupus in A) has *usque* before *Ariciam*, clearly an addition resulting from failure to understand the idiom (and, again, there is no plausible palaeographical explanation for the omission).

On Aricia (Barrington Atlas 43C3; mod. Ariccia), in the Castelli *c.* 27 km south-east of Rome, see Oakley ii. 561–2.

commodatus: *commodare*, used only here by V., can mean both 'lend' and 'hire'; the latter is clearly the sense here: if he had merely been lent the horse, no point of law would have arisen. The participle is made to agree with *usus*, since otherwise V. would have had to write *cui equus, ut Ariciam eo uteretur, commodatus fuerat*; before V. the only example of such a metaphorical use of the verb is Cic. *off.* 2.15; cf. *TLL* iii. 1918.49 ff.

41–42. ulteriore ... cliuo: presumably he had hired the horse in Rome (and the case was heard there); he rode the horse up the slope to the south-east of Aricia, though his contract of hire had provided for him to to do so only as far as Aricia itself.

42. hoc loci: V. is fond of *hoc/eo/eodem/quodam loci*: cf. 2.2.6, 4.5, 3.2. ext. 3, 8.6, 4.1. ext. 4, 4.8, 5.1. ext. 1, 6.3.1a (our passage is omitted by Otón Sobrino ii. 1185). For the idiom see K–St i. 430, H–S 652-3, Nisbet and Hubbard on Hor. *carm.* 1.38.3.

uerecundiam: *uerecundia* is one of V's favourite abstract nouns, used by him on thirty-one occasions, eight of them in book 4 chapter 5, which is devoted to the ideal. Otón Sobrino divides them into fourteen different meanings, with our passage the only one listed under 'respeto, honestidad'; SB translates 'scrupulousness': perhaps 'sense of propriety' would come closer to what V. intended. Cf. ch. 3 line 1 n.

43. minuti: an obvious correction, found in later manuscripts (Kempf implies DEF), of *muniti* in AL. On this occasion G's reading, the totally impossible *minimo*, is clearly a (disastrous) conjecture. The fault was tiny because all he had done was to go a little way uphill after leaving Aricia. This is the only occurrence of the adjective, avoided by Caesar and Livy, in V.

a pudore: from what a sense of shame demanded.

excessus: before V. *excessus* occurs only in Cicero, at *rep.* 2.23, 52, *fin.* 3.61, *Tusc.* 1.27, all with the meaning 'death'; V. uses it on ten occasions, in eight of which (1.8. ext. 10, 3.2.14, 4.3.3, 5.6. ext. 3, 7.2. ext. 1, 9.12 ext. 2, 5, 9.13 praef.) it means 'death', while at 9.9.2 *excessus uiae* are 'detours'. In our passage it coneys the sense of 'deviation from a standard', otherwise found only in Christian writers (cf. *TLL* v/2.1230.10 ff.). Velleius Paterculus employs *excessus* at 1.15.1, with the meaning 'departure'.

3 praef. 1. ne ... quidem: 'neither'.

1–2. uerecundia stolae: 'the modesty of the matron's robe' (SB). The MSS have *uerecundiae stola* and Perizonius realised that the cases had been interchanged: V. could have written chiastically but would scarcely have talked of 'the robe of modesty'. For *uerecundia* cf. 2 line 42 n.

1. *Maesia*. There are no other sources for this episode. It was probably recent (see note on *L. Titio* below) and was well known in V.'s time. V's language indicates that it was a criminal trial before a *quaestio perpetua*.

3. Maesia: (10). L and G have *Amaesia* (which became the vulgate), A *Amesia*, P the ill-omened *Maesta* (*Mesta* Lupus in A). The *gentilicium* Am(a)esius does not exist and Halm saw that the woman's name was Maesia: a number of Maesii are attested in the imperial period, including a father and son at Sentinum (*CIL* xi. 5783). See *RE* xiv. 281-2.

Sentinas: on Sentinum in Umbria (Barrington Atlas 42D2), modern Sassoferrato, cf. Oakley iv. 314. The correct form of the ethnic (cf. Livy 10.27.1, 30.4, 31.12; not in *OLD*) is preserved by P (*sententia* α; *Sententinas* Lupus in A).

L. Titio praetore: apart from a highly dubious tribune of 462 (D.H. 9.69.1), all known Titii lived in the first century BC (see *MRR* ii. 626). Münzer (*RE* viA. 1558; cf. Broughton, *MRR* ii. 466) suggested that he is the father of M. Titius L.f., suffect consul in 31 (cf. *MRR* ii. 420) and that either he or C. Titius Rufus, praetor in 50, is the Titius mentioned by Pliny *nat.* 31.11. *Tito* in P is clearly an anticipation of the *nomen*.

4. motusque: G; L has *mortuusque* and so presumably did A before correction to *partesque* (no one would have altered *motusque*, which is also read by a late corrector of L (L⁴; cf. ed. p. xv) and all Kempf's later manuscripts except D). Halm suggested, but did not print, *modosque* and convinced both Kempf and Shackleton Bailey. I printed *motusque*, but gave *modosque* a *fort. recte*: the matter is indeed very evenly balanced and I could well have chosen to do the reverse.

Whether *motusque* is a conjecture or a transmitted reading, it must have been the origin of *mortuusque*; if, therefore, V. wrote *modosque*, we have a double stage of corruption before the Carolingan age.

modus is often used in rhetoric: see *TLL* viii. 1265.7 ff., under rhe rubric *pertinent ad rationem dicendi*, and is coupled with *numeri* at Cic. *inu.* 1.49 (*TLL* do not cite our passage, though the files were based on Kempf's 1888 edition). *motus* does not occur as a rhetorical term before Quintilian *inst.* 8.5.35 and 9.1.2; see *TLL* viii. 1537.41 ff., where it is the Latin term for τρόπος, In the first passage A has *motus*, B *modos* (A and B have equal authority), but the second passage shows that both could be used and V. may have been acquainted with the use of *motus* (at 8.5.35 Quintilian says that *motus/modus* was used by *clarissimi nostrorum auctores*).

7–8. Androgynem: as is evident from my apparatus, I intended to print *Androgynem*, the reading of AL (G initially omitted *quam ... appellabant*, perhaps because of skipping a number of lines, whether by G himself or his source; he then inserted it, writing *Androgenem* (on the corrections in G see ed., pp. xv–xvi); *Androgynen* is a conjecture by Kempf, to which I gave a *fort. recte*.

Those who invented the nickname could have regarded it as the transliteration of either Ἀνδρογύνης or Ἀνδρογύνη; moreover, the accusative of the former could be represented in Latin by either *Androgynem* or *Androgynen* (see my note on Livy 38.12.6). In these circumstances my preference is to follow the transmitted reading.

2. *Carfania*. The only other author to mention Carfania (on the name see below) is Ulpian *dig.* 3.1.1.5 and since she died in 48 BC (see line 13 n.), it is again likely that V. did not depend on a written source.

Ulpian says that Carfania's activities led to a praetorian edict banning women from making applications on behalf of others (there was no question of any general bar): V., however, talks only of her speaking on her own behalf (line 9 *pro se*).

8. Carfania: α has *C. Afrania*, P *C. Afrinia*, corrected to *C. Afrania* by Heiric of Auxerre (cf. p. 20); so too in line 12, except that P there has *C. Afraniae*: C. Afrania is not a possible female name. Ulpian has Carfania and he may well have been using V. (he says *Carfania improbissima femina, quae inuerecunde postulans et magistratum inquietans*). I therefore read *Carfania* in V.: Münzer (*RE* iii. 1589) thought that her name was indeed Carfania but that V. wrote *C. Afrania*. Shackleton Bailey (1996, 181), however, says 'her name was doubtless Cafrania', and does not mention Ulpian. In his Loeb edition, however, he printed *Carfania* and in a note attributed *Carfania* to Ulpian, *Cafrania* to Schulze; he is referring to the latter's *Zur Geschichte Lateinischer Eigennamen* (Berlin, 1904), 353 n. 1 '*Carfania* Ulpian Dig. 3, 1, 1, 5 heisst bei Valerius Maximus 8, 3, 2 *C. Afrania* di. *Cafrania*'. Both Cafranii and Carfanii are attested in inscriptions (Schulze, op. cit. 137, 353) and *Cafrania* should perhaps be given a *fort. recte*, but since Afranii held office in the republic, reaching the praetorship in 185 and the consulship in 60, I prefer to follow Ulpian and posit a double corruption in the transmission of V.

Licini Buccionis uxor: (39). The husband is not otherwise known. α has *Buccionis*, P *Bucconis*; both *cognomina* are attested elsewhere (cf. Kajanto 225, 268), and either could be right. *bucco* means a garrulous or stupid person (cf. *TLL* ii. 2229) and Münzer (*RE* xiii. 232), apparently under the impression that *Bucconis* was certain, wondered whether the *cognomen* originated as a term of ridicule because of his wife's activities. *prorogauit autem spiritum suum* (lines 12–13) suggests that she was long-lived and Münzer thought that Licinius may have been a senator in the Sullan period (i.e., presumably, that he was one of the 300 *equites* added to the senate by Sulla); thus too Broughton, *MRR* ii. 492.

10. latratibus: this is the only instance before late antiquity of *latratus* (lit. 'barking') being used of persons. In its literal sense it is found before V., who uses it thus at 11 ext. 4 and 9.13. ext. 2, in Varro, Virgil, and Ovid, metaphorically of the noise of the sea at Accius *trag.* 569 (Scaliger proposed *latrans* for metrical reasons) and Sallust. *hist.* 4.27M = 18 Ramsey (see *TLL* vii/2.1011.80 ff.). *latrare* is used both literally and metaphorically, *adlatrare* only metaphorically (see my note on Livy 38.54.2, its first occurrence).

11. calumniae: here in the sense of 'improper use of the law' ('litigiousness' SB); cf. *TLL* iii. 188.3 ff. See also 2 line 25 n.

12–13. prorogauit ... spiritum: for *prorogare* of life cf. 13 praef., 9.2. ext. 11, *TLL* x/2.2151.14 ff., 47 ff.

13. C. Caesarem iterum <P.> Seruilium consules: in 48. Caesar had held his first consulship in 59. P. Servilius Isauricus (67) had been praetor in 54. He was governor of Asia from 46 to 44 and an augur.

α had *iii iterum* (thus LG and a correction in A). It is unclear whether this was a triple repetition of *i-* or an annotation by somebody under the impression that the year was Caesar's third consulship. Servilius' *praenomen* was added by Pighius: V., having written *C. Caesarem*, would scarcely have referred to him by *nomen* alone.

14. enim: explaining why V. has mentioned the date of Carfania's death; cf. *TLL* v/2.582.13 ff.

3. *Hortensia.* This episode, of 43, is narrated at length by Appian *b.c.* 4.32.136–34.146, perhaps deriving from Livy, who may have been V.'s source, and including (32.137–33.144) the speech of Hortensia: according to Quintilian (*inst.* 1.1.6) that speech was extant, but Appian's version is probably his own: it seems unlikely that Livy would have given Hortensia a speech if he knew that the genuine speech existed (cf. vol. ii. 39–40).

V. fails to indicate that the episode took place soon after Antony, Octavian, and Lepidus became *iiiuiri rei publicae constituendae* (in Appian it follows his account of the proscriptions) and that the levy on the women was to be used to fund the forthcoming war against the tyrannicides.

16. Q. Hortensi: (13). Q. Hortensius Hortalus, second only to Cicero among the orators of the late Republic. He was consul in 69 and an augur from some time before 67 until his death in 59.

16–17. ordo ... oneratus: see lines 19–20 n.

17. nec: the reading of G and added in A and L. There is no alternative, though the reason for the omission is obscure.

17–18. repraesentata: 'reviving' (SB). Before V. *repraesentare* occurs in Cicero and Livy and V. uses it on fourteen occasions; it does not, however, occur in the present sense before this passage (cf. *OLD s.u.* 6a; they also cite 9.2.1 and Horace *epist.* 1.19.14, where it means 'portray, 'exhibit' (sense 3a). Cf. 9 line 44 n.

19–20. maior pars ... remitteretur: according to Appian (*b.c.* 4.32.135) only the richest 1,400 women were affected and the amount was to be decided in each case by the triumvirs. They eventually reduced that number to 400 and ordered all men with property worth over 100,000 (*sc. sestertii*, the property qualification for the first class in the *comitia centuriata*) to lend the state 2% of it interest free and contribute a year's income (34.146). V. is not interested in such details.

21-22. cuius si ... non esset: V. is probably thinking of Hortensius' grandson, who, so Tacitus (*ann.* 2.37-8) relates, had been given the senatorial census by Augustus to enable him to marry and have children, *ne clarissima familia exstingueretur*; in AD 16 he appealed to the senate for further subvention; the initial reaction was favourable but the request was opposed by Tiberius, who, however, sensing that a majority of the senate was against him, eventually agreed to give 200 *sestertii* to each of the male great-grandchildren of the orator. The family, however, continued to slide into disgraceful poverty.

See further my note at *ZPE* 95 (1993), 249-50, arguing that the name of the grandson was Marcius Hortalus not, as has usually been thought, M. Hortensius Hortalus and that he was identical with the praetor of AD 25 (so too M. Corbier, *MEFRA* 103 (1991), 655-701); his mother was probably the daughter of the orator and his second wife Marcia, while she herself married a Marcius.

21. uim: Novák may have been right to propose *uiam*, which assorts better with *sequi*: if V. had meant 'attain to', 'emulate' one would expect him to have written *ad(s)sequi* (cf. *OLD s.u.* 2, 3): *sequi*, though, is used for 'attain' in Persius and the younger Seneca (*OLD s.u.* 17) and may have been an innovation by V. For a reverse conjecture see my note on Livy 38.18.9.

22. abscisa: G, to which I gave a *fort. recte*; AL have *abscissa*. If my stemma is right, *abscissa* and *abscisa* are equipollent. In neither case is there a real parallel for the usage here, but the sense must be that Hortensia's speech marked the end of the oratorical tradition of the Hortensii: the ablative, that is to say, is circumstantial (SB translates 'would not have been cut short with a single speech'; *OLD s.u. abscindere* 2c cite only this passage for 'break (a tradition)'.

Otón Sobrino (i. 20) lists eighteen passages under a*bscidere*, only ours for *abscindere*; eleven of the former contain the past participle: in ten of them *abscis-* is either unanimously attested or clearly transmitted. At 2.7.9 (Otón Sobrino wrongly says '2, 7, 8') AL have *abscissis*, G and Paris *abscisis*; both Kempf and I printed the latter (if my stemma is right, *abscissis* is eliminated) and I now follow suit here.

4 tit. DE QVAESTIONIBVS: thus the direct tradition (LG and a pre-Paris correction in A); P has *seruilibus*. All three *exempla* concern the questioning of slaves under torture and *quaestio* must therefore have that limited sense (cf. *OLD s.u.* 2). The likelihood is that the author of the headings wrote *de quaestionibus* and that Paris decided to add *seruilibus*, *quaestionibus* being subsequenty omitted in the course of transmission. I suggested, however, that the original heading may have been *de quaestionibus seruilibus* and that at praef. line 1 *seruiles* should be added after *quaestiones*, in which case it somehow happened that *seruilibus* was omitted at some point in the direct tradition, perhaps as a result of the loss of *seruiles* in the text, *quaestionibus* in that of Paris. It is, of course, inconceivable that Paris himself wrote *de seruilibus*.

None of the three episodes is related by another writer, none can be dated, and only in the third is identification of the Roman citizen(s) involved possible. It is likely that V. took all three from the same source, perhaps Hyginus; cf. pp. 6–7.

On V.'s attitude to the use of torture, with reference also to book 3 ch. 3 and book 6 ch. 8, see S. J. Lawrence, *CQ* 66 (2016), 245–60.

praef. 1. omnes ... numeros: 'every kind' (cf. *OLD s.u.* 12a); cf. 7 line 36, 15 line 19.

1. *Alexander, the slave of M. Agrius.*

3. M. Agri: (3). Seven Agrii are known, none of senatorial rank; cf. *RE* i. 902.
   argentarii: 'banker'.
   Alexander A. Fanni: P (and Lupus in A); the direct tradition has the strange corruption *Alexandri Rafani*.
   4. constantissime: Shackleton Bailey (1996) observed that the word is inappropriate for a slave confessing to murder 'as though the torturers were trying to force him into a denial'; he did not, however, seek to emend but thought that V. had misunderstood his source; in his edition he said 'the facts are evidently garbled': perhaps Alexander confessed under torture and then, once the torturing had stopped, made no attempt to withdraw his confession; Agrius, not wanting to condemn Alexander unjustly (and to lose a slave), hoped that he would do so.
   5. est adfectus: the agreement of LG eliminates A's *adfectus est*.

2. *Alexander, the slave of P. Atinius.*

7. P. Atini: (not in *RE*). P (-*ni*); LG have *Rafani*, by perseveration from the corruption in line 4; presumably that stood in A also, altered by Lupus, no doubt misreading his manuscript of Paris, to *Putinii*.
   Alexander: Shackleton Bailey (1996) wrote 'the slave's name is obviously a reflection of the foregoing. Either it has replaced the real name or he is anony-

mous'; in his edition he deleted the name. It is not at all obvious: many slaves of Greek or Macedonian origin were doubtless called Alexander or Philippus (for an (alleged) Carthaginian Philippus see my note on Livy 39.42.8) and since the slave in the third *exemplum* is Philippus, there is no reason why both the other two should not have been called Alexander.

in: P. α has *in hanc*, but *hanc* has no reference (it was first omitted by Pighius). As Kempf (1854) argued, the interpolation, strange at first sight, was probably caused by the corruption of *P. Atini* to *Rafani* (line 10 n.): a scribe, not having read what followed, had the absurd idea that V. was still talking about the previous case. Heraeus' *inanem*, untypically, lacks all plausibility.

8. fuisse: Halm suggested *esse* (Kempf indicated his agreement, but printed *fuisse*), presumably because guilt is something that is in question at the time of a trial *uel sim*. But what Alexander is portrayed is saying is 'I was not involved in the murder' (*adfinem* indicates that he was accused of being an accessory).

9–10. perinde ... actus est: the *et* after *damnatus* shows that it goes with *actus est*, not with *confessus*. Kempf (I wrongly attributed the conjecture to Halm) altered the *et* before *a iudicibus* to *esset*, while Shackleton Bailey added *esset* before *et* (both are easy corruptions, a scribe's eye moving from the first *e* to, respectively, the second or third); Kempf adduced 1 damn. 1 and 4.7 praef., where *perinde ac* is followed by a verb in the subjunctive (Novák, WS 18 (1896), 268–9, who proposed deleting *et* as an anticipation of *et* before *a L.*, weirdly denied that V. uses *perinde ac* with a finite verb): V. writes *perinde ac* no fewer than twenty-eight times, in a number of which it is followed by an adjective or participle (e.g. 1.8.7, 2.9.4 (adjective), 3.2. ext. 6, 8. ext. 6 (participle); see Otón Sobrino iii. 1517, TLL x/1.1480.28 ff.

9. a iudicibus damnatus: in the previous *exemplum* Alexander was handed over for execution to the owner of the murdered slave. In this case it is likely that Atinius himself was accused of the murder of Flavius (cf. line 8 n.) and that it was left to the *quaestio publica* to determine the guilt of both master and slave. The former, presumably, was exiled, his slave crucified.

10. in crucem actus: in Rome crucifixion was a punishment usually reserved for slaves; cf. M. Hengel, *Crucifixion in the Ancient World and the Folly of the Message of the Cross* (London, 1977), 51–63 (39–45 for the rare instances of crucifixion of citizens).

3. *Philippus, the slave of Fulvius Flaccus.* The slave's refusal to incriminate his master under torture matches that of the slave of the great orator M. Antonius, consul in 99, related at 6.8.1. Antonius was accused of *incestum* and Shackleton Bailey plausibly suggested that the defendant in this *exemplum* was Ser. Fulvius Flaccus, perhaps identical with the consul of 135 (64), who was also accused of *incestum* and was defended by C. Scribonius Curio, praetor in 121 (*rhet. Her.* 2.33, Cic. *inu.* 1.80, *Brut.* 122, Schol. Bob. p. 85St); cf. Münzer, *RE* vii. 248.

12-13. perstringeretur: for *perstringere* meaning 'injure the reputation or prospects of someone' cf. *OLD s.u.* 2b, citing also 7.3. ext. 8 and 9.2.3 (add 9. ext. 2 line 34), together with Cic. *Sull.* 46: *TLL* however, who list examples of the usage at x/1.1756.24 ff., strangely cite our passage under '*usu uario*' at 1757.7 ff.

5 tit. DE TESTIBVS: P has *quibus testibus creditum non sit*, which applies only to the first five *exempla*.

1. *The trial of Q. Pompeius.* Pompeius (12), originally a protégé of Scipio Aemilianus, broke with him as a result of his decision to stand against C. Laelius for the consulship of 141. Pompeius was elected and campaigned in Spain against the Numantines; in 140 his attempts to besiege Numantia failed and he eventually (in 139) concluded a treaty with the Numantines, which was rejected by the senate (for sources see *MRR* i. 477, 480, 482). In 138 (probably) he was prosecuted for *repetundae* and acquitted. The only other evidence for the trial is Cicero *Font.* 23, who is almost certainly V.'s sole source; Cicero does not mention the charge and gives only the *praenomina* and *cognomina* of the four witnessess against Pompeius. Since Fonteius was accused of *repetundae*, it was not difficult for V. to deduce that this was the accusation against Pompeius and lists of magistrates would have given him the information about the relationships of and offices held by the four witnesses, though he is in fact either wrong or misleading about the censorships (see the following notes). Cf. Astin, *SA* 129.

1-3. Cn. et Q. ... prouectis: Gnaeus (46) Servilius Caepio was consul in 141, Quintus (48) in 140. The former reached the censorship in 125, the latter never, so that neither had proceded *per omnes honorum gradus* at the time of the trial.

Paris preserves the *cognomen* correctly: AL have the non-existent *Ceptonibus* (*Scaept*- A^c), G *Scipionibus*, a desperate guess.

3-4. item ... triumphali: Q. Caecilius Metellus Macedonicus (94) was consul in 143, L. Caecilius Metellus Calvus (83) in 142. Quintus was censor in 131, Lucius never: neither was a *censorius* at the time of the trial. Quintus triumphed over the Macedonians and Andriscus in 146 (see *MRR* i. 467). V. mentions Quintus' triumph at 7.1.1: *altero*, therefore, means 'one of the two', not 'the second'; it also demonstrates that *Cn. et Q. ... testimonium* is an ablative absolute and that datives are to be understood with *occursum est*.

6. potentia: Kempf needlessly suggested adding *sua* (much earlier Lupus (presumably) had made *potentia* nominative by altering the transmitted *uiderentur* to the singular).

2. M. Aemilius Scaurus. This *exemplum* relates three unsuccessful attempts by Scaurus to secure convictions by appearing as a witness in criminal cases. All three are taken from Cicero.

V. has mentioned Scaurus (140) on six previous occasions: 1. absol. 10 (as the father of the praetor of 56), 3.2.18, 7.8, 4.4.11, 5.8.4, 6.5.5. He was consul in 115 and was appointed *princeps senatus* (for the position see my note on Livy 38.28.1 and addendum thereto at vol. iv, 773) by the censors of the same year; for the rest of his life he was the dominant figure in Roman politics. A leading opponent of the *populares*, in 104 he nevertheless supported appointing Marius to the command against the Cimbri and in 91 was in favour of the proposals of Livius Drusus. He died between 90 and 88. He wrote an autobiography, an innovation in Latin literature, perhaps covering only the period ending in his consulship. See further *FRHist* i. 267-70.

Cicero is V.'s source for this *exemplum*; he mentions the accusation of Memmius at *Font.* 24, of Flavius at *Font.* 24, 26, and at *Brut.* 168, where he gives the name of the accuser, M. Gratidius, of Norbanus on several occasions in *de oratore* book 2 (89, 107, 109; cf. 164, 200-3) as well as at *off.* 2.49 and *part.* 104-5.

7-9. C. Memmium ... C. Flauium ... proscidit: Memmius (5) was tribune in 111, when he was responsible for the decision to declare war on Jugurtha and accused a number of *nobiles* of taking bribes from the Numidian king (Sall. *Iug.* 27.3, 30.4-34.1). He will have been accused of *repetundae* following his praetorship and Münzer (*RE* xv. 606; cf. Broughton, *MRR* i. 562 n. 4) argued that since both Memmius and C. Flavius Fimbria (87), consul in 104, were accused of *repetundae* and acquitted, with Scaurus appearing as a witness against them, and since Memmius, a candidate for the consulship of 99 (see below) must, under the provisions of the *lex Villia annalis*, have held the praetorship by 102 at the latest, Memmius' praetorship also belonged to 104; while possible, that is not a necessary conclusion. Memmius may have governed Macedonia during and/or after his praetorship and be identical with the Μέμμιος ... ἀνθύπατος of *IG* v/1. 1432.36 (*RE* 3). In 100 he stood for the consulship in opposition to Glaucia, who was supported by Saturninus, and was murdered at their instigation (for sources see Münzer, *RE* xv. 607). Nothing is known of Fimbria's actions as consul (or of a proconsulship).

9. proscidit: *proscindere* is found in verse from Plautus onwards, in prose only in Varro (*rust.*, apart from *ling.* 7.74) before V. Used literally, it is a technical agricultural term; metaphorically ('cut ... to pieces' SB; cf. colloquial English 'make minced meat of') it occurs only at Ovid *Pont.* 4.16.47 before V., who uses it thus also at 5.3.3. (*TLL* x/2.2172.50 ff.).

9-10. iam C. Norbanum ... conatus est: Norbanus (5) was tribune in, almost certainly, 103 (for the date see Broughton, *MRR* i. 565-6 n. 7; accepted by

Badian, *Studies*, 35), when he successfully prosecuted Q. Servilius Capio (49), consul in 106, for the loss of his army at the battle of Arausio in 105 (for sources see *MRR* i. 557, 564). V. mentions the trial at 4.7.3 and 6.9.13: in the former passage he says that Caepio was freed from prison by Norbanus' fellow tribune L. Reginus (the *nomen* is uncertain), in the latter that he died in prison; the former is almost certainly correct.

Norbanus was prosecuted by the young P. Sulpicius Rufus (tribune in 88) in either 95 (Badian, *Studies*, 35–6) or, less probably, 94 (thus Broughton, loc. cit.); cf. Gabba, *Athenaeum* n.s. 31 (1953), 264 n. 4. He was defended by L. Licinius Crassus (consul in 95; see line 18 n.) and M. Antonius (consul in 99) and acquitted (Cicero's references to the trial in *de orat.* 2 are put into the mouths of Crassus and Antonius). On the political significance of the trial see Badian, *Studies*, 49–50.

Norbanus was consul in 83, when he was defeated by Sulla near Capua; in 82 he suffered another defeat, by Q. Caecilius Metellus Pius (see line 18 n.), at Faventia, and fled to Rhodes, where he committed suicide. For sources see *MRR* ii. 62, 70.

9. iam: 'next'. Kempf suggested *item*, ('*ex more Val.*'), but V. is emphasizing that in the trial of Norbanus Scaurus openly set out to destroy him, which was not the case with Memmius and Flavius.

11. religione ... dubitabat: no one doubted that Scaurus believed that the evidence he gave was the truth (despite his openness in the case of Norbanus).

3. *L. Licinius Crassus.* Cicero *Font.* 24 is again the source for this *exemplum* (see 2 n.).

13. L. ... Crassus: L. Licinius Crassus (55), with M. Antonius one of the two leading orators of his age (see 9.2 n.) and teacher of Cicero, who made them the principal speakers in the *de oratore*. He was tribune in 107, consul in 95, and censor in 92. He died in 91, shortly after a famous speech in the senate attacking the consul L. Marcius Philippus over his opposition to the proposals of M. Livius Drusus, particularly to grant Roman citizenship to the Italians. Initially a *popularis*, he supported the bill of Q. Servilius Caepio (consul in 106) to return the extortion court to senators. Thereafter his political position is hard to define: thus he defended Norbanus (see above), but gave evidence against Marcellus, who had served under Marius (see below). Soon afterwards, though, his daughter married the son of Marius. See Badian, *Studies*, 43–4 and *OCD*[4] 852–3.

tantus: Georges' addition of *testis* is absurd: the contrast is between Crassus and Scaurus as orators in the courts and senate respectively, without any reference to Crassus' appearance as a witness in the present case (I probably cited the conjecture only because Kempf had done so).

14–15. eloquentiae stipendiis: 'campaigns of eloquence' (SB). A striking expression; there appears to be no parallel for such a metaphorical use of *stipendium*.

15. curiae princeps: perhaps with particular reference to Scaurus' position as *princeps senatus*; cf. 2 n.

16. fulmen: for *fulmen* of oratory cf. Cic. *orat.* 21, 234, *Att.* 15.1a. 2, *fam.* 9.21.1, Quint. *inst.* 8.6.7, *TLL* vi/1.1527.71 ff. (classifying our passage differently at 1528.27 ff.).

M. Marcellum: M. Claudius Marcellus (226) served under Marius at the battle of Aquae Sextiae in 102 (*MRR* i. 569) and under Sex. Iulius Caesar, consul in 90, in the Social War. He may be the man of praetorian rank who appears in Sherk no. 23 line 6. He must be distinguished from the curule aedile of 91 (227), who was a friend of Crassus (Cic. *de orat.* 1.57). For the date of the trial see Alexander, no. 87.

4. *The trial of C. Cornelius.* C. Cornelius (18) was tribune of the plebs in 67, when, among a number of other bills, most of which were vetoed, he proposed that only the people, not the senate, should have the power to exempt individuals from laws. It was vetoed by a fellow tribune, who forbad the *praeco* to read the bill. Cornelius then did so himself, leading to a riot in which the *fasces* of the consul, C. Calpurnius Piso, were broken. Cornelius subsequently carried a compromise measure, providing that there should be a quorum of 200 when the senate passed a dispensation, that it should be ratified by the people, and that tribunician veto of the ratification should be prohibited.

At the beginning of 66, Cornelius was accused of *maiestas*, the charge being that his actions constituted a diminution of tribunician *maiestas*; on the day fixed for the trial the presiding praetor failed to appear, the accusers, two Cominii, brothers, were threatened with violence and themselves did not appear on the following day, leading to the abandonment of the trial. In 65, following the conviction of Manilius, tribune in 66, for *maiestas*, the charge being that he had been responsible for the violence at the abortive trial of Cornelius, one of the Cominii renewed the accusation (Asconius pp. 60–62C mentions only one: Marshall (22), and Alexander (no. 209) think that both brothers were still involved, but, as Griffin (op. cit. below, 213 n. 169) observed, Cicero *Corn.* 1 fr. 61 Puccioni (cited by Priscian *gramm.* ii. 530, 545) *coeptum igitur per eos qui agi uolebant, desitum per hunc qui decessit* may refer to the change, though the exact meaning of the fragment is obscure). Cornelius was defended by Cicero, who spoke on four successive days; for publication he condensed what he had said into two speeches (Asconius p. 62C).

Asconius' commentary, together with the fragments of the speeches which he preserves (he also had access to the speech of Cominius; pp. 61–2C), is one of the two main sources of information about Cornelius' tribunate: the second is Dio 36.38–40 (for other sources see *MRR* ii. 144). The only detail mentioned by V. is the identity of the witnesses against Cornelius, given by Asconius at pp. 60 and 79C (for the textual problem see next note): since Cicero is V.'s source for the preceding *exempla*, it is likely that he took this information from Cicero.

For full discussion of Cornelius' tribunate and trial see M. T. Griffin, *JRS* 63 (1973), 196–213. Cf. Alexander nos. 203, 209.

18. Q. Metellus ... M'. Lepidus: Asconius p. 60C has *Q. Hortensius, Q. Catulus, Q. Metellus Pius, M. Lucullus, M'. Lepidus*; he mentions the same five men at p. 79C (commenting on *duo reliqui sunt de consularibus*) Thus each has five names, but V. omits Catulus and instead has, apparently, two Luculli; moreover, the order of the names differs in the two writers. Asconius is generally reliable on details, V. not so, and one will naturally prefer the former; the omission of Catulus was probably inadvertent, resulting from V.'s moving, like a scribe, from the second to the third *Q*. (the omission cannot be a corruption, since in V. the names appear in chronological order of their consulates: V. probably used a consular list to arrange the names). Sumner (*JRS* 54 (1964), 41) has the notion that V. omitted Catulus because he had added L. Lucullus (see below), i.e. in order to retain a total of five names: there is no evidence that Cicero (unlike Asconius p. 79C) specified the number. The remaining problems, concerning the Luculli and Lepidus, are discussed at the appropriate point in what follows.

Q. Caecilius Metellus Pius (98) was consul in 80 and commanded against Sertorius in Spain from 79 until the end of the war in 72. He was *pontifex maximus* from 81 until his death in 63.

Asconius lists only M. Lucullus, i.e. M. Terentius Varro Lucullus (Licinius 109), consul in 73. α has *L. Marcus Luculli*, Paris (and Lupus in A) adds *et* (it is impossible to say whether Paris preserves the transmitted text or *et* is his own addition). If V. listed both Marcus and Lucius (104), consul in 74, he must be wrong, but not because Lucius was 'still in the East' in 65 (thus Marshall 226): he had returned the previous year.

If V. wrote *Luculli*, there is no alternative to *et*. Halm, however, read *L. Lucullus*, but *M. Lucullus* would clearly be preferable. One could imagine that *L.* was added in the margin by someone who knew that it was the *praenomen* of the great Lucullus and subsequently placed in the text; another scribe, finding two *praenomina*, changed *Lucullus* to the plural. It would perhaps have been better to obelize *L. Marcus Luculli*.

On Hortensius see 3 line 16 n.

The identification of Lepidus was the subject of an article by G. V. Sumner in *JRS* 54 (1964), 41–49, who argued that he was not, as had always been thought, M'. Aemilius Lepidus, consul in 66, but Mam. Aemilius Lepidus Livianus, consul in 77. He convinced Marshall (227), Broughton (*MRR* iii. 8), Alexander (no. 209 n. 2), and Lewis (266), but not Griffin (op. cit. 213, unfortunately talking of 'Mamercus Aemilius Scaurus, the consul of 78') or myself.

At Asconius p. 60C P has *M.*, SM *L.*; at p. 79C all three manuscripts have *M.*; Paulus Manutius emended to *M'.* in both passages. In V. both the direct tradition and Paris have *M.* (Kempf wrongly reports the latter as *M'*, misleading Sumner (op. cit. 41)); Sigonius emended to *M'.* (the corruption, unsurprisingly, is regular in manuscripts).

Sumner has two principal arguments: (i) that in the abortive trial of 66, M'. Lepidus had been about to act as an *aduocatus* to Cornelius (Asconius p. 60C) and it is therefore unlikely that he would have been a witness against him a year later; (ii) that Lepidus is an 'inconspicuous figure', a 'lightweight', not a man to be ranked among the *principes ciuitatis qui plurimum in senatu poterant* (Asconius loc. cit.). The first argument is dealt with by Griffin: she observed that *Corn.* 1, fr. 16 Puccioni *das enim mihi facultatem eos qui tum adfuerunt Cornelio nominandi* is plausibly seen as an allusion to Lepidus' *volte-face* and argued that it could well have been caused by the repeated violence at trials in 66 and 65.

As to the second argument, it should first be said that even if Sumner is right, if four of the witnesses were indubitably *principes ciuitatis*, Asconius may not have felt precluded from writing as he did if the fifth was not of the same standard; in any case, he may have regarded all *consulares* as *principes ciuitatis* and influential in the senate by definition.

With regard to the consul of 77, Syme (*Ten Studies in Tacitus* (Oxford, 1970), 141) remarked that if Sumner were right it would be 'the last appearance of this elderly person who had not been on prominence since his consulship' (if it be thought that this hardly justifies Griffin's 'Syme is highly sceptical of this solitary late appearance', she knew Syme well and doubtless understood what he meant). In fact, as Griffin herself mentioned, Sumner (op. cit. 47–8) argued that Mamercus was named *princeps senatus* by the censors of 70; that is based on V. 7.7.6, where Mamercus, at the time of his consulship, is described as *principi senatus*. V., though, may here be using *princeps senatus* in the sense, which it had in the Ciceronian period, of 'a leading man in the senate' (cf. Cic. *dom.* 132, *Pis.* 6): no holder of the position is known after Sulla and it is quite likely that he abolished it (thus Mommsen, *StR* iii. 970, denied by Sumner). Sumner, admitting that the title is anachronistic for 77, says that the anachronism is 'typical of this writer's rhetoric': indeed, and if V. meant *princeps senatus* in its original sense, he would have been quite capable of giving the title to someone who had never held it. There is no clear evidence that the consul of 77 was still alive in 65.

19–20. non onerarunt ... salutem ... depoposcerunt: a striking zeugma: the witnesses not only weighed down on Cornelius' survival, but demanded that it be surrendered to them.

21. umbone: another striking expression: *OLD* cite the passage as the only metaphorical use of *umbo* (V. uses it literally at 3.2.3 and 5.1.3).

iudiciali: before V. the adjective occurs once in *rhet. Her.* and frequently in Cicero; V. uses it also at 10. ext. 1 and 6.9.1. (*TLL* vii/2.604.72 ff.)

5. *Cicero and Clodius.* The extensive evidence for what is often referred to as 'The *Bona Dea* scandal' is cited and discussed by Dacre Balsdon, with his customary panache, in *Historia* 15 (1966), 65–73; Cicero's motives for appearing as a witness are discussed by D. F. Epstein, *CPh* 81 (1986), 229–35. V. assumes that his readers are acquainted with the story, merely alluding to the charge with *sacrilegum flagitium* and *incesti crimine*.

It was alleged that in December 62, Clodius, dressed as a woman, had infiltrated the festival of the *Bona Dea*, from which all men were banned, held that year in the *domus publica*, the official residence of Caesar as *pontifex maximus*. After much controversy, a special court was established to try Clodius on a charge of *incestum* ('irreligious behaviour', not 'incest'). Clodius' alibi was that he had been at Interamna (Nahars, mod. Terni) on the night in question: Cicero gave evidence to break the alibi, stating that Clodius had called on him that day. Clodius was acquitted by 31 votes to 25: Cicero consistently claimed that the jury had been bribed (V. does not mention the allegation, but assumes that Clodius was guilty). The evidence Cicero gave was the direct cause of his exile, secured by Clodius as tribune in 58.

V. may not have needed a written source for the episode, though it was related by Livy (cf. *per.* 103).

22–23. Quid? ... nonne: V. is fond of beginning an *exemplum* with *quid*, with *nonne* following (1.8.6, 8. ext. 12, 2.1.7, 3.8.2, 6.9.12, 7.4. ext. 2, 9.3.8). In most places I placed a question mark after *quid*; the exceptions are 7.4. ext. 2, where, probably not deliberately, I followed Kempf (his own practice varies for no apparent reason) in printing *Quid, Hannibal ...* and 9.3.8 *Quid Sulla? ... nonne*: the two passages are parallel in structure, with the proper name immediately following *quid*, and I ought to have printed *Quid Hannibal?* In the present passage, however, the participial clause *forensi militia ... adeptus* goes closely with *M. Cicero* and *Quid M. Cicero? forensi ...* would clearly be wrong. See also 11 *bis* line 8 n.

militia ... castris: the metaphor in *militia* (cf. 7.7.1, Cic. *Mur.* 19, Manil. 3.106, *TLL* viii. 958.56 ff.) is continued in *castris*.

24. dum ... iurauit: cf. 1 line 56 n. Here, though, it is not the case that Cicero was cast down while he was swearing an oath; rather, we have a case of *dum* with the perfect in the sense of *cum* (cf. K–St ii. 376).

flagitium: G. AL have *meflagitium*. Even if *flagitium* is a conjecture and not the transmitted reading corrupted in the source of AL, Rossbach's *nefariumque flagitium* and Krohn's *me hercule flagitium* are misguided: *me* probably originated from a dittography of the preceding -*m*.

25. si quidem: cf. 1 line 31 n. Here the clause can scarcely be tacked on to the long period that precedes and *si quidem* is no more than the equivalent of *nam*.

6. P. Servilius Vatia. Servilius (93) was praetor by 90 and consul in 79. He was proconsul in the newly created province called, misleadingly, Cilicia from 78 until 74; in, probably, 75 he defeated the Isauri (Barrington Atlas 66B/C2-3) and took the *cognomen* Isauricus (also held by his son (67), consul in 48); see D. Magie, *Roman Rule in Asia Minor* (Princeton, NJ, 1950), i. 285–91, *MRR* ii. 87, 90–1, 99; he triumphed in 74 (cf. *MRR* ii. 105). He became censor in 55, aged around 80, and died in 44, sometime after the Ides of March (Cic. *fam.* 16.23.2, *Phil.* 2.12, Dio 45.16.1, Aelian fr. 113 Domingo-Forasté = 110 Hercher = Suda α 3213, Münzer, *RE* iiA. 1816–17.

The present episode is mentioned by Dio 45.16.2 (missed by Kempf (1854), Faranda, and myself; the Loeb mistranslates βαδίζοντι as 'walking'). Perhaps it stood in Livy, as part of an obituary notice. It cannot be dated.

27. eleuatis: 'made light of' (SB); at 14 line 64 it means 'belittle'.

28. triumphalis: in fact Servilius celebrated two triumphs, the first in 88, though over whom is unknown; see *MRR* ii. 43.

maiorum ... adiecit: among the later Servilii (the *gens* disappears from the *fasti* between 342 and 288) he had consular ancestors in P. Servilius Geminus (62), consul in 252 and 248, and M. Servilius Pulex Geminus (78), consul in 202; his mother was a daughter of Q. Caecilius Metellus Macedonicus (94), consul in 143 (cf. Cic. *Verr.* 2.3.211, *p. red. in sen.* 25, 37, *dom.* 123, *Sest.* 130).

30. loco testis: for (*in*) *loco* + gen. in the sense of 'by way of', 'in the capacity of' cf. *TLL* vii/2.1586.1 ff., *OLD s.u.* 18c; for *loco testis* cf. Cic. *Q. Rosc.* 5, Sen. *nat.* 5.18.16, Quint. *inst.* 5.7.5.

31–35. hunc ego ... non putaui: the words put into Servilius' mouth are doubtless an invention by V.

32. cuias sit: 'where he comes from' Heiric's correction of *cui adsit* in P, with *cuius sit* in the direct tradition. *cui(quoi-)as(-atis)* is rare, being found in Plautus, Ennius (*ann.* 81V = 235Sk; the fragment is not cited in *OLD*, no doubt because at Cic. *Balb.* 51, where it is quoted, Peterson, in the OCT, printed Baiter's conjecture *cuius ciuitatis sit*: a spectacular misjudgement), Accius, once each in Cicero (*Tusc.* 5.108) and Livy (27.19.9), Apuleius, and Aulus Gellius (see L–S and *OLD*; the *TLL* article is to appear under *quoias*; see iv.1285.68). It is not surprising that scribes of late antiquity or later did not understand it, though in Livy it survived in the Puteaneus.

uitam: P (and Lupus in A). α has *uiam*, an easy corruption, here assisted by *uia* in line 47.

33. Laurentina uia: the road leading to Lavinium (*Laurentinus* or *Laurens* is the ethnic of Lavinium; there was no such place as Laurentum (except, perhaps, at a very early date); cf. Ogilvie 39, Oakley ii. 506). It left the *uia Ostiensis* about 5 km. south of Rome (Pliny *epist.* 2.17.2 says that his Laurentine villa could be approached from either the *uia Ostiensis* or the *uia Laurentina*); for its route see Radke, *RE* Supp. xiii. 1485–6.

iter facienti: either on horseback or in a carriage (cf. 6 n. above).

34. equo descendere noluisse: there was not room for the two to pass without stopping; presumably Servilius told the man who he was and expected him to show due deference by dismounting (the complaint can scarcely have been that the man failed to recognize him).

P has *noluit*: that is to say, Paris intended *illud scio* and *cum ... noluit* as separate sentences and I ought to have punctuated (ed. 761) with a colon after *scio*. There is, of course, no doubt that the direct tradition preserves what V. wrote, deliberately altered by Paris.

religionem uestram: 'your sense of duty'.

36. auditis: P; *additis* α. Here, unless *auditis* is a conjecture, of Paris himself or made at some point in the transmission of his text, the indirect tradition preserves what V. wrote.

damnarunt: α; P has *damnauerunt*: the former is more likely to be altered to the latter than vice-versa.

6.1. C. Licinius Hoplomachus. Hoplomachus (91) is otherwise unknown and Münzer (*RE* xiii. 371) suggested that like Licinius Bucco (see 3 line 11 n.) and M. Licinius Crassus Agelastus (57; Münzer wrongly says 59), praetor in 127 or 126 and grandfather of the triumvir, the *cognomen* (otherwise unattested) was given to him as a term of ridicule; if so, the nature of the ridicule is obscure. He also wondered (*RE* xiii. 295) whether Hoplomachus was the grandson of the P. Crassus (probably, he thought, P. Licinius Crassus Dives Mucianus (72), consul in 131), said at 6.9.12 to have been the first to be called Dives (cf. Cic. *Tusc.* 1.81, Plin. *nat.* 33.133).

2. Hoplomachus: the correct orthography is preserved in P; α omits the aspirate.

2–3. bonis ... interdiceretur: for *interdictio bonorum*, also used in cases of insanity, see Cic. *Cato* 22 and Powell ad loc., *TLL* vii/1.2174.70 ff. At 3.5.2 V. reports a case where it was used to prevent an heir from dissipating his inheritance.

3. equidem: thus both α and P. *equidem* is normally used with the first person singular (*TLL* v/2.720.62 ff.); for its use with other persons see *TLL* art. cit. 722.72 ff. The present passage is one of only three in pagan Latin where it is attested as introducing a coordinate part of a sentence; the others are Livy 45.39.9 and Statius *silu.* 3 praef. 1. (*TLL* art. cit. 723.69 ff., who fail to cite our passage and wrongly include Sen. *nat.* 2.4.1, where it goes with a single word (*necessaria*)), and in all of them *equidem* has been emended to *et quidem* (the Basle edition of 1531 for Livy, accepted in my edition of books 41–45, and Markland for Statius).

Since *equidem* is the reading of both α and P, the corruption, if there is one, is early: it was altered to *et quidem* in the Venice edition of 1471, accepted by all subsequent editors except myself; I cannot now recall the reasons for my decision and it may have been wrong. *equidem* occurs with the first person singular at 5.5.3 and can be regarded as the paradosis at 7 line 80 (see n. ad loc.). In favour of retaining the transmitted reading, one can point to the agreement of the direct and indirect traditions; moreover, in view of the degree of linguistic innovation to be found in V. (see pp. 10–12), I am reluctant to deny him this example.

4. pecuniam: P; *facundiam* LG (and no doubt A before correction), a strange corruption.

5–6. a uicissitudine poenae ... maluit tollere: i.e. if Hoplomachus had had a son, he might have applied for the same interdict.

uicissitudo, common in Cicero but otherwise found before V. only at Terence *Eun.* 276 and Livy 3.39.8 (cf. Ogilvie ad loc.), is used by him also at 3.7. ext. 7 and 5.1.3.

liberos tollere (Pighius suggested *alere*) is regularly used of a father or other person lifting up a new-born child as a sign of willingness to rear it (*TLL* vii/2.1302.56 ff.); V. varies the idiom with *heredem tollere*, a unique usage (not cited in the list of verbs governing *heredem/-es* at *TLL* vi/3.2651).

α has *a ... fuit* (*a* was corrected in the margin of A to *dignus hac*, which became the vulgate; 'P' in my apparatus is an error: Paris omitted the whole sentence). Halm saw that the addition of *a-* to *fuit* is all that is required (Foertsch's *at uicissitudinem ... effugit* is most unlikely, while Kraffert's insertion of *populus heredem* before *hereditatem*, which he thought gave the natural sense, is absurd: the views of the Roman people are not in question).

2. *Marius*. V. here contrasts Marius' role, as consul, in the suppression of Saturninus and Glaucia in 100 with his own actions in 88 when Sulla, also consul, having been forced to flee to his army in Campania, marched on Rome. There are copious sources for both episodes and in my testimonia apparatus, therefore, I merely gave references to *MRR* i. 574 (I ought to have added 576, on Saturninus) for 100 and ii. 40 for 88. In fact there is no other evidence for Saturninus' offering freedom to slaves who fought for him, while in the case of Marius the appeal to slaves is reported by Plutarch *Mar.* 35.7, Appian *b.c.* 1.57.262, and Orosius 5.19.5, but without mention of the *pilleum* (both Ampelius 26.2, of Opimius' murder of Gaius Gracchus and his supporters in 121, and *uir. ill.* 69.2, of Cinna in 87, say *uocatis ad pilleum seruis*; for the phrase cf. Livy 24.32.19). The source of V.'s information is obscure, but it could have been in Livy.

V. forces the facts to fit his theme: Saturninus' appeal to slaves was not the reason or justification for Marius' action in 100.

See also 2.3 n.

8. uexilli: 'ensign'.

pilleum: the *pilleum* (-*us*; both genders are attested; see *TLL* x/2.2139.65 ff.) was a soft cap worn by slaves on manumission; see my note on Livy 33.23.6, to which add references to 24.16.18, 32.19 (see above), 38.55.2, 45.44.19.

9. ostentatum: on *ostentare* cf. *FRHist* i. 29 n. 86.

L. Sulla: mentioned again at 14.4; for other references to Sulla in V. see the index to my edition (p. 863).

11. alterum Marium: it is unclear whether V. was being deliberately paradoxical in calling Sulla a second Marius.

adfligeretur: unlike Saturninus, Marius was not killed, but declared a *hostis* by the senate (cf. 2. lines 53–4 n.), fleeing to Campania and eventually to Africa. For sources on Marius' flight see Greenidge–Clay–Gray, 165.

3. *C. Licinius Stolo*. The main source for the so-called Licinian–Sextian rogations, carried by Stolo and L. Sextius, tribunes in 367 (V. does not mention Sextius (36), who became consul in the following year), is Livy 6.34–42; for other sources see *MRR* i. 114. For full discussion of the opening of the consulship to plebeians see Oakley i. 652–4, of the agrarian legislation 654–9. Stolo (161) became consul in 364 or 361 (cf. Oakley i. 664).

The prosecution and conviction of Stolo under his own law, in 357, is reported by Livy 7.16.9, who is V.'s source; for other sources and discussion of the authenticity of the story see Oakley ii. 183–4.

12. plebi: an easy correction (Kempf (1854) implies that it is in all his manuscripts except A and F) of the transmitted *plebis*, altered to *plebei* in A (for this form of the dative cf. *TLL* x/1.2379.10 ff., but it is unlikely that V. would have used it). *plebis* resulted from anticipation of the following genitives.

14. dissimulandique criminis: α has *simulandique*, while P omits *criminis*. *simulare* is used of invention, *dissimulare* of concealment (I recall learning at school the mnemonic *quod non est simulo dissimuloque quod est*) and it is most unlikely that anyone would have added *criminis*.

14–15. dimidiam ... emancipauit: V. has either misunderstood or deliberately altered what Livy wrote: he has *emancipandoque filium*, i.e. that he freed his son from *patria potestas*, probably by a form of fictitious sale (see Oakley ii. 184, F. De Zulueta, *The Institutes of Gaius* ii (Oxford, 1953), 42–4). V., on the other hand, talks of the sale of half of the land to his son; *emancipare* is used to mean both 'free' and 'sell'; cf. *TLL* v/2.442.44 ff. (failure to realise this may have led Paris to write *mancipauit*). V. was probably puzzled, as well he might have been, by Livy's *cum filio possideret*, since a son in *patria potestas* could not legally own anything (Livy is sometimes remarkably hazy about Roman law; cf., e.g., my notes on 34.2.11 and 39.9.2, W. A. J. Watson, The *Law of Persons in the Later Roman Republic* (Oxford, 1967), 110), and Livy does not make it clear that Stolo transferred 500 *iugera* to his son once he was no longer in his *potestas*.

15. M. Popillio Laenate: (20). He was curule aedile in 364, and perhaps aedile again when making this accusation, consul in 359, 356, perhaps 354, 350 and 348; see Oakley ii. 153. He is the first, and most distinguished, member of a plebeian family which held consulships in 316 (our man's son), 173 and 172 (two brothers, Marcus and Gaius, who behaved disreputably; see vol. iv, 794, *s. nn.*), 158 (the second consulship of Gaius) and 132; cf. 1 line 140 n.

16. aliud: I gave Eberhard's *aliis* a *fort. recte*: it provides a strong antithesis to *quisque sibi* and *nihil aliud* is so common a phrase that the corruption would be readily intelligible. But *aliud*, going with *nisi quod*, is unobjectionable and the conjecture probably an instance of making an author write what he perhaps should have written, but did not.

praecipi: a correction in both A and L; the latter has *praecipue*, which was doubtless the reading of A also. It is hard to say whether G's *praecipere* is a transmitted corruption, further corrupted by the source of AL, or a conjecture.

16–17. imperau<er>it: α has *imperauit*, corrected to the perfect subjunctive by Pighius and the pluperfect by Kempf. The latter posits an unlikely corruption and V. could have used primary sequence because of the preceding present infinitives (for deviations from the normal sequence of tenses rules cf. K–St ii. 193–5). It cannot be excluded, however, that he retained the indicative in *oratio obliqua* to stress that the clause represents his own view; cf. K–St ii. 542–5.

4. Q. Varius. I here largely repeat the note on the *lex Varia*, for which I was primarily responsible, at *FRHist* i. 317.

For the sources for the law see *MRR* ii. 26–7 (for fragments of Sisenna which probably refer to the passing of the law or trials conducted under it see *FRHist* i. 314), for discussion Gruen, *JRS* 55 (1965), 59–73, Badian *Historia* 18 (1969), 447–91; I largely follow the latter.

In January 90 the tribune Q. Varius carried a law establishing a special court to try Roman citizens accused of aiding and abetting the revolt of the allies against Rome; the existing *quaestiones perpetuae* had been suspended, probably at the beginning of the Social War.

Of those initially prosecuted, L. Calpurnius Bestia, probably the consul of 111, and C. Aurelius Cotta, consul in 75, forestalled a hostile verdict by going into exile. A Mummius, probably a descendant of the consul of 146, was convicted, Q. Pompeius Rufus, consul in 88, acquitted, while the fate of L. Memmius (see commentary on Sisenna *FRHist* 26F31) is unknown. Whether the aged M. Aemilius Scaurus (see 5.2n.) was prosecuted in 90 or 89 is uncertain, but he was acquitted (cf. 3.7.8).

The convictions (there were no doubt others of which we do not know) eventually caused the senate to suspend the court. In 90 the juries were entirely equestrian, as they had been since the passing of the *lex Seruilia Glauciae* in, probably, 101. Early in 89, the *lex Plautia* reformed the composition of the juries, so that they contained senators, *equites*, and members of the *plebs*. The Varian court, if not the others, was reinstated and Varius himself prosecuted and convicted.

18. Q. autem Varius ... cognominatus: Varius (7) is not known apart from his tribunate and subsequent conviction, and no Varii are known before him. This is the only evidence for his being called *Hybrida*: at Asconius p. 22C Scaurus is quoted as calling him *Q. Varius Hispanus*, while at 3.7.8 (where V. conflates his trial under the *lex Varia* with an earlier one for *repetundae*) he is *Q. Varius Seuerus Sucronensis*. Perhaps he claimed descent from one of the original settlers of Italica, founded by Scipio Africanus in 206 (App. *Ib.* 38.153) and Scaurus was implying doubt about the legitimacy of this claim: the status of children born to settlers and Spanish women may well have been obscure. Sucro (Barrington Atlas 27E2), the site of a battle between Pompey and Sertorius in 75, was *c.* 25 km SSW of Valencia (cf. Schulten, *RE* ivA. 561); if Scaurus did call Varius *Sucronensis*, perhaps he deliberately chose the name of a place few of his audience will have heard of. For this sort of abuse in ancient rhetoric cf. Nisbet, 193–4.

Pliny (*nat.* 8.213) says that C. Antonius (19), Cicero's consular colleague in 63, was called *Hibrida*: the reason is obscure, but nobody ever challenged his right to Roman citizenship.

19. aduersus collegarum intercessionem: thus also Appian *b.c.* 1.37.166; we know the names of three, perhaps four, other members of the tribunician college of 90 (*MRR* ii. 26), but none are specifically said to have vetoed Varius' bill. Since 133, of course, the validity of such vetoes had been controversial.

perrogauit: meaning 'carry a law' *perrogare* (*prorogauit* in A^cG is manifestly wrong) is used by Paris 1.2. ext. 4, but otherwise only at schol. Bob. Cic. p. 149 St.

20. quaeri ... essent: cf. Asconius p. 22C *ut quaereretur de iis quorum ope consilioue socii contra populum Romanum arma sumpsissent*. See Badian, op. cit., 447–52, arguing that this was the offence defined by the *lex Varia* and it was not, as Gruen (op. cit.) held, a general *maiestas* law.

21. sociale ... excitauit: having correctly said that the court established by the *lex Varia* was to hear charges of being responsible for the Italian revolt, V. contradicts himself by saying that it was the law which caused the revolt. The latter claim is also found in Appian *b.c.* 1.38.169 (the passage of V. should have been mentioned at *FRHist* i. 317). The origin of this mistaken view cannot be determined. Badian's tentative idea (op. cit. 459) that Sisenna was responsible can be dismissed: he related the outbreak of the war in book 2 of his history, the events of 90, including the *lex Varia*, in book 3 (cf. *FRHist* i. 313–14) and cannot conceivably have said that the law caused the war. Livy, however, cannot be excluded, if only because the *periochae* make no mention of the *lex Varia*.

V.'s statement that the law caused the Civil, as well as the Social, War is at first sight puzzling. It can be seen as part of the view that the Social and Civil Wars were one continuous process (cf. Cic. *fam.* 5.12.2) and that the former was in reality a civil war (cf. Flor. 2.6.1). It might also have been said that the tensions produced by the law and the subsequent trials contributed to the outbreak of civil conflict. Again, it could have been a view expressed by Livy.

'The Social War' is not, as one might be tempted to think, a term invented by modern writers, though before V. the war with the Italians is called *sociale bellum* only at Cic. *Font.* 41 (at Nepos *Chabr.* 3.4, *Iph.* 3.3, Trog. *prol.* 6 it refers to Athens' war with her allies in 357–355 BC); V. uses the phrase also at 1.6.4 and 6.9.6 and he is followed by Pliny *nat.*, Juvenal, and Tacitus. See *TLL* ii. 1851.47 ff.

21–23. dum ... agit ... absumpsit: here V. conforms to the regular usage of *dum* + present indicative, with the perfect indicative in the main clause (cf. 1 line 56, 5 line 22 nn.). Unfortunately, he seems to be unaware that Varius could not be prosecuted until he had left office on 10 December 90 (for the date of the trial see Badian, op. cit., 461).

22. pestiferum: V. uses *pestifer* on fifteen occasions; before him it occurs in Novius, *rhet. Her.*, thirty-three times in Cicero, Virgil, the *dirae*, and Ovid (*TLL* x/1.1921.5 ff.).

22–23. domesticis laqueis constrictum: 'caught on a noose of his own tightening' (SB); a striking and effective expression.

For *domesticus* in the sense of '*suus, proprius*' see *TLL* v/1.1870.14 ff., citing 3.7. ext. 2, 4.3.7, 4.11: at 4.3.7, however, the adjective means 'in his house'. V. uses *laqueus* ('trap', 'snare') metaphorically also at 3.2.12 and 7.4. ext. 2; see *TLL* vii/2.962.63 ff. The metaphorical use of *constringere*, found before V. in Cicero, Livy, and Manilius, occurs also at 2.9.5, 4.6.4, 5.3. ext. 3 (3c SB, line 177 in my edition), 7.2. ext. 14; cf. *TLL* iv. 544.18 ff. (mis-citing the last two passages).

7 praef. V. begins this long chapter with an elaborate period. The main clause (*quid cesso ... commemorare*) is followed by a relative clause beginning *cuius alacri spiritu* and containing four elements, each with its own passive verb (*militia stipendia roborantur, forensis gloria accenditur, fido sinu ... nutriuntur, quidquid ... perducitur*). The first two are of more or less equal length, the third longer, while the fourth is longest of all, its subject being expressed by a secondary relative clause with double anaphora of *quidquid*. For a more extreme example of V.'s technique cf. the eulogy of Sex. Pompeius at 4.7.2.

2. roborantur: *roborare* occurs before V. in Cicero, Lucretius, and Horace. He uses it also at 1.7. ext. 3 (as here, metaphorically) and 2.1.9 (literally).

3. animo ... manu ... lingua: *animo* refers to *studia*, *manu* to *militiae stipendia*, *lingua* to *forensis gloria*.

3–4. cumulum: Halm wondered whether V. wrote *culmen*, to which Kempf rightly replied that he uses *cumulus* in the sense of 'peak' also at 3.1. praef., 6.8.7, and 7.1.1. The usage, though, is not found before V. (cf. *TLL* iv. 1587.25 ff.; *OLD s.u.* 4b mis-classify Cic. *Att.* 16.11.2).

4–5. quae ... confirmatur: this final sentence of the preface has been assailed by no fewer than eight conjectures.

First of all, A and L have *confirmat'*, Kempf (misreporting L as having *confirmatur* in full) implausibly took this to be an indication that *confirmat* was the end of the question which began with *quid cesso* (line 1): the probability is that the scribe or corrector of the source of AL intended *confirmatur*, writing, unusually, the abbreviation as a correction of what had originally been wrongly copied as the active (it is possible, though that what appears after *t* is punctuation). There is no reason to doubt that *confirmatur*, written thus in G, represents what stood in α. *confirmat* is reported by Kempf from C; if this was a deliberate alteration, the scribe will have taken *quae* as accusative, referring to all the subjects of the preceding clauses.

Modern conjectures began with Foertsch, who initially (1864) proposed transposing *cum* to precede *duramento*, with *sit* altered to *fit*, later (1870) merely changing *cum* to *ut*. Madvig altered *cum* to *quo* and adopted *confirmat*. Kempf, in an article published shortly before his second edition (*NJPhP* 133 (1886), 57–8) suggested *quaecumque enim sit* ... (accepted by Böhme (ibid. 798), but preferring *confirmata*), which he presumably intended to mean 'for whatever might be', but in his edition he printed the paradosis, preceded by an obelos (weirdly saying '*ut nos L*' in his apparatus), but wondered whether *confirmatur* should be *consummatur*. Finally (for Damsté see below) Shackleton Bailey read *qua, cum*: *qua* (abl.) refers to *industria* and Shackleton Bailey translates 'By diligence, virtue even at its most perfect is confirmed through a hardening of itself'.

The paradosis is, in fact, unexceptionable. *quae* refers to *industria*, and V. is saying that while hard work is already the most perfect virtue, it is given extra strength by its own hardening (thus Damsté (*Mnemosyne* n.s. 42 (1914), 265, though he added that one might conjecture *per se perfectissima* (a scribe's eye moving from one *per* to the next)).

4. perfectissima: the comparative and superlative of *perfectus* are common, despite the disapproval of grammarians (cf. *TLL* x/1.1373.46 ff.). V. uses the positive on only two occasions (2.10.8, 3.7. ext. 2), the superlative on eight, six of them in book 8 (the others are 7. ext. 2, 9.3, 11. ext. 2, 13. ext. 3, 15.7, 4.3.5, 6.8.7). At 9.3 it is pleonastically coupled with *columen*, which itself connotes perfection (cf. *TLL* x/1.1382.8 ff.).

duramento: the noun does not occur before V., who uses it also at 2.7.10. Subsequently it is found only in the younger Seneca, Columella, Pliny *nat*., Palladius, and *the mulomedicina Chironis* (*TLL* v/1.2287.47 ff.).

1. *The elder Cato.* For Cato's final speech in self-defence (lines 7–13) see Livy 39.40.12, Plut. *Cato mai.* 15.4 (my testimonia apparatus here omits the passage of Livy, that on Livy 39.40–41 omits this passage). V. gives the age of Cato at the time of this speech as 85, as does Livy; the latter says that he was 89 at the time of the speech against Galba, while Plutarch gives the two ages as 86 and 90 respectively. Presumably both V. and Plutarch derive their (false; see below) information from Livy; lines 8–10 *neque ... continebat*, however, are elaboration by V.: Livy (39.40.11) has just *ne senectus quidem, quae soluit omnia, fregerit*, while Plutarch quotes Cato as having said that it is hard for someone who has lived in one generation to defend himself before another, which does not appear in Livy.

For the sources on Galba see 1. absol. 2 n., on Cato's acquisition of a knowledge of Greek literature and his legal knowledge see lines 12–15 nn.

6. sextum et octogesimum: see above. In fact he was only 80 or 81; see my note on Livy 39.40.12.

7. ab inimicis ... accusatus: Livy 39.40.8–9 talks of the large number of occasions on which Cato was prosecuted or himself prosecuted others (Plutarch says there were nearly fifty of the former, Plin. *nat.* 7.100 forty-four). Cf. Astin, *Cato*, 107–9.

capitalis in my edition is a misprint for *capitali*. Livy does not say that the charge was capital (i.e. Cato would have gone into exile if he had been convicted) and V. may be wrong.

10. aequali: 'steady' (SB), not in fits and starts.

10–12. See 1. absol. 2 n.; as in that passage, V. regards Cato as the prosecutor in a trial of Galba.

11. disertissimi oratoris Galbae: at 1. absol. 2 V. did not mention Galba's distinction as an orator, for which see the passages cited at *ORF* 109–10 (the fragments of his speeches are on pp. 111–15).

accusationi defensionem: paradoxical, since Cato is the accuser, Galba the defendant (in V.'s view). Glareanus changed *opposuit* to *apposuit*, so that both the *accusatio* and the *defensio* belong to Cato's speech. More plausibly, Gertz proposed the inversion *defensioni accusationem*. Such a corruption is not impossible, but what V. means is that Galba defended himself by accusing the Spaniards of actions which justified his response, while Cato defended them (that is not, of course, to say that Cato actually argued that the Spaniards had done nothing wrong).

12–13. idem Graecis ... senex didicit: this is one of a number of passages (see Astin, *Cato*, 159 n. 3; in my testimonia apparatus '**16–20**' should read '**16–18**' and there should have been a separate entry (see below) for lines 18–20) saying that Cato learnt *litterae Graecae* in his old age. They refer to the deep study of Greek literature and do not mean that Cato did not learn Greek until old age; see Astin, *Cato*, 159–69, *FRHist* i. 194 (with further bibliography at n. 8). There is no other evidence for V.'s claim about Cato's knowledge of previous Latin (i.e. verse) literature, but it could well be that he did not study it in detail until late in life.

13–15. cumque ... peritissimus: cf. Cic. *de orat.* 1.171 *iuris ciuilis omnium peritissimus*, Nepos *Cato* 3.1 *peritus iuris consultus*, Livy 39.40.6 *si ius consuleres, peritissimus*, Quint. *inst.* 12.3.9 *iuris idem fuit peritissimus*, 11.23 *idem iuris ... peritissimus fuit*. Cicero (*Cato* 38) represents Cato in old age as saying *ius augurium pontificium ciuile tracto* (at the same time as he is working on the seventh (and final) book of the *Origines* (cf. Astin, *Cato*, 185)). It is unlikely that Cato did not seek to acquire a detailed knowledge of the law until he had achieved fame as an orator.

19. partam haberet: for *habere* + perfect participle of a verb indicating acquisition cf. G. V. M. Haverling in *Continuity or Change*, 189.

2. *The younger Cato.* Unsurpisingly, V. mentions Cato the younger (Porcius 16), praetor in 54, on sixteen occasions, usually as the subject of the *exemplum* (the others are 2.1, 15.10, 2.8.1, 10.7–8, 3.1.2, 2.14, 4.6, 6.7, 4.1.14, 3.2, 12, 6.5, 5.1.10, 6.2.5, 7.5.6).

V.'s source is clearly Cic. *fin.* 3.7 *quippe qui ... soleret legere saepe dum senatus cogeretur*, but Cicero does not say that the books were in Greek; so too Plutarch *Cato min.* 19.1, who, however, adds that Cato hid them behind his toga. It is unclear whether V. took the detail from another source or it is his own invention.

16. mirifica proles: cf. 3.4.6 *prorogata familia in qua maximum decus posterior ortus est Cato.* He was the great-grandson of the censor, his grandfather being M. Porcius Cato Salonianus, the son of the censor by his second wife, Salonia. Cf. Astin, *Cato*, 105.

17. flagrauit: V. uses *flagrare* on eight occasions (7. ext. 6, 14, 3.2. ext. 8, 4.3 praef., 5.2. ext. 4, 6.8, 6.5.5; only at 3.2. ext. 8 is the meaning literal), *flagrantissimus* on five (10.1, 14. ext. 3, 3.2.21, 8. ext. 4, 6.9. ext. 4). Here and at 3.2.21, 8. ext. 4, 5.2. ext. 4, 6.8 some of the MSS exhibit forms of *fraglare*, a non-existent verb; for the same corruption in MSS of other authors cf. *TLL* vi/1.846.26 ff. *flagrare*, moreover, is often confused with *fragrare* (art. cit., 30 ff.), which V. does not use, though *fragrantia* occurs at 9.1. ext. 1 (*fraglantia* AL^{c}G, *flagrantia* L).

TLL art. cit., 46 ff. say that *flagrare* is first found in *rhet. Her.* and 'inde uiguit per totam Latinitatem': it is, in fact, absent from Caesar.

dum ... cogitur, temperaret: the normal use of *dum* + present indicative (cf. 1 line 56, 5 line 24, 6 lines 21–3 nn.).

18. lectitaret: the frequentative occurs before V. in Cicero, Varro, and a fragment of Santra. V. uses it again at 8 line 14, but in the sense of 'collect', found otherwise only in Arnobius. See *TLL* vii/2.1089.61 ff.

18–19. aliis ... temporibus: 'some lack time, others are above the times' (an adaptation of SB's translation). The contrast is forced, V. using the plural with *deesse*, when the singular is normal in the sense of 'available time' (Curt. 4.8.4 and Stat. *Achill.* 1.937, cited by *OLD s.u.* 6a, are different), and *temporibus* meaning 'circumstances' (SB says 'is there a play on two senses of *tempora*, time and circumstances?', but I would not put it quite like that).

None of this justifies tampering with the text (Gertz deleted *superesse*, Kempf *temporibus*, with *alios* changed to *aliis*, while Damsté, typically, rearranged the passage to read *aliis superesse tempora, deesse alios temporibus*; none is an improvement and all lack palaeographical plausibility).

For the contrast of *deesse* and *superesse* cf. Cic. *de iur. ciu.* fr. 2 (C. F. W. Mueller, *M. Tullii Ciceronis opera omnia* iv/3 (Leipzig, 1898), 311), cited by *OLD s.u. supersum* 2.

3. Varro. On the life of M. Terentius Varro, the greatest Roman intellectual, see *FRHist* i. 412–15 (Andrew Drummond), for his voluminous literary output *FRHist* 52T1, Jerome's confessedly incomplete catalogue (works with historical content are discussed at *FRHist* i. 415–23). Only the *de re rustica* and books 5–10 of the *de lingua Latina* survive intact; in addition, there are a considerable number of fragments and many attempts have been made to identify unattributed Varronian material in later writers (particularly the elder Pliny).

V. may not have depended on a written source.

20. humanae uitae ... spatio: AL have *exemplo et*, G *exemplum aetatis*; a corrector of L and G then have *spatio*, A *ospitio*, L *ospatio*; Lupus added *nominandus* after *spatio*, a remarkable example of a medieval conjecture with palaeographical plausibility (a scribe's eye would have moved from the *no(minandus)* to *no(n)*), though Lupus may not have realised this. In these circumstances the paradosis cannot be determined. I obelized *exemplo et*, which can be retained only by accepting *nominandus* (thus SB, 'exemplo et *intra cruces Briscoe*').

That is not impossible (for *nominandus* see 1.8.8), though there is no example of a causal ablative (cf. Pinkster 903) with *nominare*, and the genitive has to be taken in different ways with *exemplo* and *spatio* ('for the example he gave of human life and for his length of it' SB). Madvig and Foertsch independently proposed *exemplum et* (i.e. a combination of the readings of G and AL); Madvig retained *spatio*, most implausibly taking it to mean that Varro was also an example because of his longevity, while Foertsch altered it to *specimen*. An anonymous scholar wanted to add *raro* (easily omitted) after *Varro*, to go with both *exemplo* and *spatio*, Wensky read *expleto spatio* (which would mean that Varro became *stilo uiuacior* only after his death), and Damsté added *eximius* after *exemplo* (the omission would be better explained before *exemplo*, but the word order is then awkward). After the publication of my edition Watt (*Eikasmos* 10 (1999), 245) suggested *exemplum et <felicitate> et spatio*. I have wondered about <*ob*> *humanae uitae exemplum et spatium* (the *o* in AL could then be the remnant of *ob*).

20–21. quibus ... aequauit: an exaggeration: according to Jerome, Varro was born in 116 and died in 28 (*FRHist* i. 412, 423).

21. uiuacior: *uiuax* occurs only here in V., before him in Afranius and Augustan poetry. Cf. line 141 n.

4. *Livius Drusus.* This is C. Livius Drusus (15), the son of C. Livius Drusus Aemilianus, the consul of 147, and elder brother of M. Livius Drusus (*cos.* 112), tribune in 122 and opponent of Gaius Gracchus. He is not known to have held any magistracies, probably because he went blind when still young (or even was blind from birth); V., however, appears to think that his blindness belonged only to his old age.

Cicero *Tusc.* 5.112 similarly talks of Drusus giving legal advice, in his house, but says nothing of his writings and there is no similarity of language between Cicero and V.

23. qui aetatis uiribus: G; L, and no doubt A before correction, has *quia e(ae* L^c)*tatis*. *quia etatis* results from a faulty division of *qui aetatis* and whether the latter in G preserves the paradosis or is a conjecture, there is no stemmatic justification for SB's adoption of *qui et aetatis*, a correction in A: V. could, of course, have written thus but there is nothing objectionable about *qui aetatis*.

aetas here means 'youth'; cf. *TLL* i. 1127.23 ff., *OLD s.u.* 3a, but both include passages where *aetas*, though it refers to youth, does not mean it.

23–24. acie oculorum: 'eyesight'; cf. *TLL* i. 400 73 ff., for *acies* alone in this sense 401.18 ff.

24. defectus: 'bereft of'; cf. line 53, 3.1. ext. 1, 5.4. ext. 6, 7.6.2, 5, *TLL* v/1.324.67 ff.

interpretatus est: 'expounded'.

24–25. utilissimaque ... composuit: nothing of them survives. An opinion of Drusus is cited at *dig.* 19.1.38.1.

26. interpellare ... ne non: a unique instance of *interpellare ne* (*TLL* vii/1.2241.58 ff.; Livy 4.43.8 is different); for the pleonastic negative cf. 1.7.6, *TLL* ix/1.318.56 ff., B. Lofstedt, *Acta Classica* 34 (1991), 156.

5. *Publilius and Pontius.* Neither is otherwise known; perhaps they were contemporaries of V., who had heard them in action (but cf. line 28 nn.).

28. Publilius: (1). The Publilii are a plebeian *gens*, first appearing in the historical record with Volero Publilius, plebeian tribune in 472 and 471. Their only consular was Q. Publilius Philo, who held the office on four occasions (339, 327, 320, 315; cf. Oakley ii. 211–12) and the last attested office holder was C. Publilius (6), quaestor in 146. A Publilia (17) was Cicero's second wife. At 6.3.8 the MSS indicate that V. gave Publicia as the name of the woman put to death for murdering her husband L. Postumius Albinus when he was in office as consul in 154, but those of Livy *per.* 48 call her Publilia (16).

The name, corrupted to *P.* in the direct tradition, is preserved by Paris.

Lupus Pontius: the only Pontius kown to have held office in the Republic is L. Pontius Aquila (17), tribune in 45. On the inversion of *nomen* and *cognomen* cf. my notes on Livy 33.30.10, 34.5.9; it occurs also at 11 line 15, 15 lines 56–7, elsewhere in V. only of Pompeius Magnus (5.3.5, 6.2.6, 9.14.1), in whose case the adjectival force of the *cognomen* makes it less striking (particularly with the vocative at 5.3.5). At 3.2.6 (*Aemilianus Scipio*) and 13 (*Scipio Metellus*) two *cognomina* are in the reverse of their normal order.

29. actores: 'pleader of cases'; before V., who employs it only here (at 2.4.4 (twice; the second is a virtually certain supplement) it means 'actor')), the usage is common in Cicero but otherwise found only in Caelius.

31. eorum: AL; it is omitted by G. There is no palaeographical explanation of the omission and if my stemma is correct, an addition by the source of AL is a possibility; *aliis quia ingenuio delectabantur* would exactly balance *aliis qui constantiam admirabantur*. I am, however, unaware of any other passage where there is a reason for thinking that a word or words omitted by G were interpolated by the source of AL and it is unlikely that anyone would have felt the need to insert *eorum*.

31–32. †namque alii†: the transmitted text is impossible, since it makes V. say that everyone except Publilius and Pontius isolated themselves when struck by a disability, while it is clear from *duplicant ... adicientes* that he is talking only about blindness. One may wonder, furthermore, whether V. meant to say that Publilius and Pontius were the only ones who went blind but carried on with their previous activities; and, while one could not argue that V. would not have written *aliis ... aliis ...: alii*, it is not the most elegant of expressions: there is, therefore, a case for thinking that *alii* arose by perseveration from *aliis ... aliis* and that Halm, reading *nam qui tali*, was right to alter it. Perizonius proposed either *nam alii qui* or *namque alii tali*: the former, with the sense 'those others who' deals with the second but not the first and third points, the latter with the first but not the second and third. Halm's conjecture meets all three, but has the disadvantage of altering both *-que* and *alii*. In the circumstances I would continue to obelize but if forced to choose, would print *alii qui tali*.

32. incommodo: L^c, a clearly necessary correction of *commodo*. *incommodum* is a common euphemism for a disease or ailment (*TLL* vii/1.988.24 ff.) and V. naturally uses it of blindness.

secessum: 'withdrawal'.

33. uoluntaria<s>: Coler, in his edition published at Frankfurt in 1601, saw that the adjective must agree with *tenebras*.

6. *P. Licinius Crassus.* Cf. Quint. *inst.* 11.2.50 *qui cum Asiae praeesset quinque Graeci sermonis differentias sic tenuit ut qua quisque apud eum lingua postulasset* *eadem ius sibi redditum ferret*. The similarity of language suggests that V. and Quintilian were drawing on a common source; see Adams, *Bilingualism*, 9–10.

34–35. P. Crassus ... uenisset: P. Licinius (72) Crassus Dives Mucianus was consul in 131, when he went to Asia to fight Aristonicus; in the following year, as proconsul, he was defeated and killed (see 3.2.12, *MRR* i. 503).

Attalus III of Pergamum died in 133, in his will leaving his kingdom to Rome. Aristonicus, an illegitimate son of Eumenes II, led a revolt against Roman annexation, but was eventually defeated and captured by M. Perperna, the consul of 130. He was put to death in Rome in 128. See conveniently Magie, i. 32–3, 147–54 (for sources ii. 1034 n. 2), Sherwin-White, *Roman Foreign Policy*, 84–8.

Crassus' *praenomen*, correctly given in α, has been corrupted to *C.* in P, probably by anticipation of the initial letter of his *cognomen*.

35–36. in quinque diuisam genera: five dialects: Attic, Ionic, Aeolic, Doric, and the *koine*; cf. Adams, *Bilingualism*, 10 n. 29.

36. numeros: cf. 4 line 1 n.

37–38. ei ... reddenti: V. attaches the participle to a pronoun in the unemphatic position; one might have expected *cum qua ... redderet*.

38. eadem: *lingua*, not *decreta*; there is, of course, no ambiguity.

7. *Roscius*. Q. Roscius (26) Gallus, the greatest of Roman actors, came from near Lanuvium and was given equestrian status by Sulla (Macr. *Sat.* 3.14.13). His year of birth is not known, but he was a *senex* when he died shortly before Cicero defended Archias in 62 (*Arch.* 17). See Vonder Mühll, *RE* iA. 1123–5, Richards–Badian, *OCD*[4] 1297. See also 10.2. V.'s source cannot be determined.

41. ponere: α. Schulze (*Philologus* 37 (1877; my apparatus wrongly has 1878), 573) proposed *promere* and this was accepted by Kempf and Shackleton Bailey (and the passage is cited under *promere* by Otón Sobrino; *TLL* x/2.1884.12, *s.u. promere*, say 'e coni. dub.', but do not cite it under *ponere*). Schulze adduced, among other passages, Hor. *ars.* 183 *promes in scaenam* and Quint. *inst.* 1.1.22 *si quis ea quae domi suae recte faceret in publicum promit. ponere* can, however, be defended as belonging with the passages cited at *TLL* x/1.2658.50 ff. under the rubric '*proponendi, exhibendi, praebendi sim.*'; note *s.c. de Pisone* 96 *qui complura modestiae suae posuisset pignora*, from a piece of Latin contemporary with V. One of the passages is Pollio ap. Cic. *fam.* 10.32.3 *ludis praetextam posuit*, on which Shackleton Bailey commented 'this use of *ponere* does not seem to be found elsewhere', but expressed no doubt about the reading: we thus have two passages in which *ponere* is used to mean 'display' in a theatrical context. But perhaps *promere* deserves a *fort. recte*.

41–42. ludicra ... commendauit: another forced antithesis: Roscius brought fame to acting rather than his acting bringing fame to Roscius. On the low repute of actors and the disabilities they suffered see Oakley ii. 69–71; cf. lines 44–5.

42–43. principum familiaritates: known are those with Q. Lutatius Catulus, the consul of 102 (Cic. *nat. deor.* 1.79), Sulla (Plut. *Sull.* 36.2 and see above), and above all Cicero: Roscius' sister was married to P. Quinctius, defended by Cicero in a private suit in 81, and it was Roscius who was responsible for Cicero's getting the brief (*Quinct.* 77); Roscius himself was later defended by Cicero in another private case (*Rosc. com.*); see also *leg.* 1.11, *diu.* 1.79, Plut. *Cic.* 5.3.

44–45. non impudenter ... inserit: see lines 41–2n. On *histrio* cf. 2.4.4, Oakley ii. 59.

G has *inserit*, corrected to *inseruit*, the reading of AL. That perhaps suggests that *inserit* was not the reading of G's exemplar and does not possess authority, though it could be that *inseruit* was an emendation by the corrector. I printed *inserit*, but gave *inseruit* a *fort. recte. inseruit* will refer to the view of Roscius' relations with leading men taken at the time. *inserit* to V.'s putting him on a par with the men who have featured in the preceding six *exempla*. The latter forms the more effective conclusion to the Roman *exempla* of this chapter.

ext. 1. 46–47. This sentence is in reality a preface to the *exempla externa* (cf. p. 29). It is striking that they occupy three times as much space (131 lines against 40, sixteen *exempla* compared with seven) as the Roman *exempla* in this chapter. It is almost as if V. is displaying his own *industria* in collecting them.

Graeca industria and *Latina lingua*, form an antithesis, though, of course, the former is a nominative, the latter an ablative.

Of the seventeen men mentioned (ext. 16 concerns both Cyrus and Mithridates), four are Athenian political figures and/or orators (Demosthenes (1), Isocrates (9), Solon (14), and Themistocles (15)), eight are philosophers (Pythagoras (2), Plato (3), Democritus (4), Carneades (5), Anaxagoras (6), Socrates (8), Chrysippus (10), Cleanthes (11)), one a mathematician and inventor (Archimedes (7)), two literary figures (Sophocles (11), Simonides (13); Solon could also be regarded as belonging to this category), and two members of Asiatic royal families (Cyrus and Mithridates (17)).

It is hard to discern any conscious ordering here. The series of philosophers is interrupted by Archimedes and Isocrates (though V. may have thought of the former as an honorary philosopher), and the three pre-Socratic philosophers (Pythagoras, Democritus, Anaxagoras) are interrupted by Plato and Carneades; one might have expected V. to have placed Socrates before Plato. Chrysippus and Cleanthes are in inverse order, but this is probably caused by V.'s misapprehension that the former was the teacher of the latter (see line 149 n.). Six men (Carneades, Isocrates, Chrysippus, Cleanthes, Sophocles, Simonides) are examples of longevity, though only Isocrates and Sophocles are mentioned in Cicero *Cato* and that is not V.'s source in the case of Sophocles. V. probably had only a hazy idea of the history of Greek philosophy.

48–61. *Demosthenes.* V.'s source is Cicero *de orat.* 1.260–1; see also *fin.* 5.5, *diu.* 2.96, Quint. *inst.* 1.11.5, 10.3.30, 54, Plut. *Dem.* 6.4, 11.1, [Plut.] *mor.* 844E–F, and other sources cited by Pease on Cic. *diu.*, loc. cit.

48–49. consummatio: the word does not occur before V., who uses it, in various senses, also at 13. ext. 5, 3.4.2, and 9.8.3, and Velleius Paterculus. It is very frequent in Christian writers. (*TLL* iv. 594.52 ff.).

49–50. artis ... non posset: i.e. he could not pronounce rho, the first letter of ῥητορική. The most famous modern case of this defect of speech was the British politician and writer Roy Jenkins, Home Secretary and Chancellor of the Exchequer in the Labour Governments of the 1960s and 1970s (in 1981 he was one of the 'gang of four' who left the Labour Party to found the Social Democratic Party), President of the European Commission from 1977 to 1980, and Chancellor of the University of Oxford (he was sometimes refered to as 'the people's Woy'). Cf. J. Campbell, *Roy Jenkins: A Well-rounded Life* (London, 2014), 28.

51. expressius referretur: 'rendered more distinctly'. This use of *expresse* is found elsewhere only at Consentius *gramm.* p. 15 Niedermann (*TLL* v/ 2.1796.39 ff.); for *referre* in the sense of 'render a sound' see *OLD s.u.* 13d, citing Cic. *orat.* 38, *Brut.* 192, *TLL* xi/2.628.34 ff., misclassifying the passages of Cicero at 623.26 ff. and 613.62 ff. respectively.

51–53. deinde ... perduxit: adjectives accompany four of the six nouns in this sentence (*nimiam exilitatem, acerbam ... uocem, exercitatione continua, maturum et gratum ... sonum*).

53. defectus: cf. line 24 n.

54. impetu spiritus complectebatur: α (a correction in A) has *impetu spiritus*, P *spiritu*, probably a deliberate abbreviation by Paris, though a corruption of what he wrote is not impossible. Paris may have been puzzled by the phrase, which occurs elsewhere only at Gell. 5.9.2, though Augustine *anim.* 3.4.5 has *anhelandi impetus* (*TLL* vii/1.604.46 ff.).

By contrast, P preserves the clearly correct *conplectebatur*, corrupted to *conplebatur* in L (and no doubt in A, before correction by Lupus) and *complebat* in G: *uersus complere* has no sense.

55. aduersa: 'uphill'; cf. *TLL* i. 867.2 ff.

56. edebat: P and a correction in A and L; *sedebat* (*sedabat* G) resulted from a dittography of *s*.

57. patientia duratis auribus: it is not easy to translate (hence, no doubt, SB's somewhat misleading 'to harden his ears and enable him to endure the clamour of excited assemblies'): 'his ears hardened by endurance' gives the sense accurately, but the pleonasm is awkward. Faranda has 'per avere gli orecchi ben allenati'. *TLL* x/1.66 classifies it, together with 2.6.1 and 3.3.1, under the rubric '*de statu quo quis tolerat, sustinet*'.

auribus is A^c's correction of the strange corruption *actionibus* (thus LG).

59. rerum natura: cf. 1 lines 41–2 n.

equidem: cf. 6 line 3 n. AL have *naturae quidem*, corrected to *natura equidem*, which is the reading of G. The former is clearly the result of faulty word division and the latter can be taken as the paradosis. It was altered to *natura et quidem* in later manuscripts (Kempf (1854) implies ΕΓΓ), and this became the vulgate, printed by all editors except myself (Shackleton Bailey does not even indicate that it does not have authority). *equidem* does not here introduce a coordinate part of a sentence and the case for retaining it is therefore stronger than at 6 line 3.

ext. 2. *Pythagoras*. This, obviously, is not the place, and I am not the person, to add to what has been written on what is known, or not known, about Pythagoras; see, briefly, F. Graf, *OCD*⁴ 1245–6. The best introduction to the subject is Kirk–Raven 214–38, with a selection of sources; the fullest citation of sources will be found in DK i. 96–104; I added six passages, three of them Latin, in my testimonia apparatus (Diels–Kranz do not include V.). In what follows I attempt to cite the sources for the matters mentioned by V.

62. uetustiorem: the only secure date for Pythagoras is that he left his native Samos during the tyranny of Polycrates (*c.* 535–*c.* 522) (Kirk–Raven, 224). For full discussion of the evidence cf. von Fritz, *RE* xxiv. 179–85.

actum: 'performance' (SB); cf. 3.2 praef., 20 (the latter cited at *OLD s.u.* 10). *TLL* i. 453.3 ff. classify our passage with 3.2. praef., 5.3.4, and 6.5.5 under the rubric '*de singulis factis: opus, factum*, citing Grattius 233 and Manilius 2.140 as the only examples before V.: apart from 3.2. praef., none of these are parallel and the last is totally different.

62–64. perfectissimum ... †a ... ingressus†: AL; G has *cupiditatem*. With the reading of AL and the conjecture of Shackleton Bailey *perfectissimum opus sapientiae* is the object of *ingressus*, with the conjectures of Halm and Wensky (and perhaps this is what G intended; on Foertsch see n. 1) it refers to Pythagoras himelf.

AL's text was retained by Kempf, accepting Gertz' explanation of it as saying that Pythagoras embarked on his *opus* both from the beginning of his youth and with the greatest desire for understanding: it is scarcely credible that V. would have combined temporal and causal indications in this way.

Halm changed *ingressus* to *incensus*, taking, presumably, *a iuuenta pariter* with *perfectissimum opus sapientiae*, and *pariter* to mean 'uniformly', a most unlikely word order. Foertsch (accepting *incensus*; so too Shackleton Bailey (in 1981) but retaining *ingressus*) deleted *et*: *a iuuenta pariter* now goes with what follows, but the double change is undesirable. Wensky adopted *cupiditatem* (cited from later manuscripts by Kempf; in 1854 he implies that it was in all those he used) and changed *a iuuenta* to *iuuentam*, *pariter* now meaning 'simultaneously': the corruption is implausible and the zeugma involved in *ingressus* governing both *iuuentam* and *cupiditatem* not something that should be attributed to V. by conjecture. Lastly, Shackleton Bailey (1996) added *scientiae* before *pariter*: he presumably thought (he is not explicit) that the preceding *-ent-* was responsible for the omission, but that does not convincingly explain the retention of *-a* and the omission of *-iae*.

62–63. perfectissimum: cf. line 4 n.

65. et mature et celeriter: he began both early in life and got on with it rapidly: Gertz' *alacriter* is totally unjustified.

65–67. Aegyptum ... cognouit: Pythagoras' visit to Egypt is mentioned by Isocr. 11.28, Cic. *fin.* 5.87, *Theol. Ar.* p. 40, amd Porph. *VP* 6; for Pythagoras' doctrine of the transmigration of souls see Kirk–Raven, 219–21. If Cicero was V.'s source (cf. next note), *litteris ... cognouit* may be an addition from his own knowledge.

67–70. inde ... sorpsit: Cic. *fin.* 5.87 says that Pythagoras visited the Magi, Porph. *VP* 6 that he learnt mathematics and astronomy from the Chaldaeans, religious rituals and other practices from the Magi: again, V. has added to what he found in Cicero.

67–68. exactissimae: the positive of the perfect participle of *exigo* is used adjectivally by Horace, Ovid, Manilius, Grattius, and Vitruvius, the comparative by Ovid; the superlative does not occur before V., who uses it also at ext. 10, 2.1.8, and 4.3.5, but never employs either positive or comparative. (*TLL* v/2.1467–8.)

69. uim proprietatem effectum: for the asyndeton *trimembre* cf. 10.20–1 n.

70. sorpsit: thus A^{c}L, appearing as *sorsit* in A and *sorbsit* in G. The only other instance of this metaphorical use of *sorbere* is Cic. *ad Q. fr.* 3.7.5. It is inconceivable that it originated from *hausit* (Pighius) or *inscripsit* (Perizonius). It is, moreover, the only instance of *sorpsi* rather than *sorbui* as the perfect of *sorbere* (though *absorpsi* occurs at Lucan 4.100), declared to be vulgar by Velius Longus *gramm.* 7.74 (*cum recens haec declinatio a sordidi sermonis uiris coeperit* (see also Caper *gramm.* 7.94); no one has ever wanted to emend to *sorbuit*); cf. M. Di Napoli, *Velii Longi de orthographia* (*CGrL* 8, Hildesheim, 2011), 145, Adams, *Informal Latin*, 268–9.

Cretam ... Lacedaemona: the visits to Crete and Sparta appear not to be mentioned elsewhere. Admiration for their constitutions began in the fourth century (cf. Walbank, i. 642, 726–8) and it was no doubt at that time that Pythagoras was first said to have visited them.

71. Olympicum certamen descendit: Pythagoras' attendance at the Olympic games is not mentioned elsewhere.

71–72. multiplicis ... admirationem: there is no doubt that this is what V. wrote (P has *multiplicis scientiae specimen*): *multiplicis* is the reading of G; AL have *multiplici*, corrected to *multiplicis* in A. In addition, A has *interrogatus* (an anticipation of the word in line 73, corrected to *inter omnes totius*; *scientia maxima ... admiratione* is part of the same correction, retaining *multiplici*.

73–75. quo cognomine ... edidit: cf. Cic. *Tusc.* 5.9, Quint. *inst.* 12.1.19, D.L. 1.12, Clem. *strom.* 1.61.

73. censeretur: 'registered' (SB). V. uses the language of the Roman census.

74. septem ... uiri: the 'seven wise men'; see DK i. 61–6, Barkowski, *RE* iiA. 2242–63. The sources (the earliest is Plato *Prot.* 343A) differ about the names, and some even make the number greater than seven. Latin writers who mention them (for a full list see Barkowski, op. cit., 2243) include Cicero (*de orat.* 3.137, *rep.* 1.12, *Tusc.* 5.7) and Quintilian (*inst.* 5.11.39).

75. philosophon: thus also Cic. *Tusc.* loc. cit. The Aldine edition of 1502 printed the word in Greek: had V. written thus, he would not have added *Graece*.

edidit: 'declared' (cf. *OLD s.u.* 8a); an obviously correct emendation in later manuscripts (Kempf (1854) implies it is in CDEF) for (*e*)*didicit* in α (*edixit* A^c).

75–79. For Pythagoras' stay in Croton (twenty years, according to Iust. 20.4.17) see DK 102–4, Kirk–Raven, 222–8, for his death in Metapontum Iust. loc. cit., Iamb. *VP* 249, *PHerc* 1788. Cf. 15 line 89 n.

75. partem: Kempf suggested adding *eam* before *partem*: the omission is easy after *etiam*, but by the same token it assorts badly with *etiam*; the emphasis is on *Italiae*: Pythagoras not only travelled in Greece and Egypt, but went to part of Italy too.

maior Graecia: in Cicero the term is always *magna Graecia* (similarly Μεγάλη Ἑλλάς in Greek); he uses it at *de orat.* 2.154, 3.139, *rep.* 3.7, *Tusc.* 1.38, 4.2, 5.10, *Lael.* 13, with the exception of *rep.* 3.7 also in a Pythagorean context (so too at Pol. 2.39.1), and always, as here, with the implication that the term was not in current use. The comparative appears also at Livy 31.7.11, Ovid *fast.* 4.64, and Festus p. 120L, suggesting a change of usage in the Augustan period (similarly, in Britain 'Greater Manchester' is the name of the Metropolitan County which looks to Manchester as its centre). On the origin of the name cf. Walbank i. 222.

77. plenis: P (and Lupus in A); α has *plenum*, by perseveration from *rogum*.

78-79. Metapontus ... monumentum: Metapontum (Barrington Atlas 45E4), *c.* 40 km, as the crow flies, west of Tarentum, was an Achaean colony, perhaps founded from Sybaris *c.* 700. It defected to Hannibal in 212 (Livy 25.15.6; he includes it in his list of defections at 22.61.12, but does not necessarily mean that it occurred in the immediate aftermath of the battle of Cannae). In 207 Hannibal uprooted the population and transported it to Bruttium (Livy 27.51.13). (The account of these events in Mayer, *RE* xv. 1344-5 is a tissue of confusion and false references; the rest of the long article (1326-67) should therefore be treated with caution). The city gradually became a ruin; Pausanias (6.19.11) says that in his time only the city walls and the theatre were standing (cf. Mayer, op. cit., 1345-6, U. Kahrstedt, *Historia* 8 (1959), 204-5, *Die wirtschaftliche Lage Grossgriechenlands in der Kaiserzeit* (Wiesbaden, 1960), 102-7) and SB reasonably suggests that V.'s form of expression is an allusion to that.

Cicero visited the site of Pythagoras' house (not his tomb, as stated by Mayer, op. cit. 1346), probably in the 70s (*fin.* 5.4).

This is the only occurrence of *Metapontus* (also in Paris) rather than *Metapontum* as the name of the city and it is surprising that no one has ever proposed alteration to the latter: -*s* could have arisen from perseveration after the three preceding words. *monumentum* stands in apposition to *oppidum*; a later manuscript, reported by Pighius, for some reason changed it to *monumento*, so that *nobilius clariusque* goes with *oppidum*.

ext. 3. *Plato.* V.'s immediate source is Cic. *fin.* 5.87 (whom I ought to have cited specifically in my testimonia apparatus). D.L. 3.6 (the whole of book 3 is devoted to Plato) refers to Socrates as Plato's teacher and Plato's visits to Egypt and southern Italy (naming Philolaus and Eurytus, but none of the four Pythagoreans listed by Cicero and V.); for the copy of the mimes of Sophron under his pillow see line 93 n. For full citation of the extensive sources see H. Breitenbach-F. Buddenhagen-A. Debrunner-F. Vonder Mühll, *Diogenis Laertii Vita Platonis* (Basle, 1907). I restrict myself, for obvious reasons, to comment on V.'s text and refrain from general remarks about Plato.

80-85. One of V.'s stranger periods: the general statement about Plato's training and abilities is expressed in a series of subordinate clauses, unexpectedly followed by his visit to Egypt as a brief main clause, with a *dum* clause dependent on it.

80. praeceptorem: V. uses *praeceptor* on eight occasions, all in *exempla externa*, six of which are in book 8 (the others are ext. 11, 9. ext. 3, 11. ext. 11, 13. ext. 2, 14. ext. 2, 1.8. ext. 17, 7.3. ext. 4). Before him it occurs in Plautus, *rhet. Her.*, Cicero, and Nepos. It is frequent in Christian writers.

Socratem: thus A, L^c (*Sa-* L) and P. The agreement of ALP would appear to eliminate *-en* in G, but it possible that it preserves the transmitted reading, altered to the normal Latin termination in both the tradition of Paris (perhaps by Paris himself) and the source of AL. Cf. line 171, 3 lines 7–9 nn.

84–89. Plato's travels in Egypt are almost certainly an invention; they are not mentioned in the so-called *Academicorum philosophorum index Herculanensis* papyrus (ed. Mekler, Berlin, 1902), the earliest evidence for his journeys, and appear first at Cic. *rep.* 1.15 and *fin.* 5.87 (cf. Leisegang, *RE* xx. 2350).

84. dum: inverse; one might have expected V. to have written *dum Aegyptum peragrat, a sacerdotibus ... percipiebat*. It was, no doubt, this that led D (followed by Halm) to alter *dum* to *ubi*.

84–85. Cic. *fin.* 5.87 *cur Plato Aegyptum peragrauit ut a sacerdotibus barbaris numeros et caelestia acciperet?*

85. et caelestium obseruationum rationem: P. α omits *et*, while LG (and no doubt A before correction) have *obseruatione rationum*. The latter is clearly wrong: geometry and astronomy are different subjects and *obseruatione rationum* was presumably an alteration to take account of the absence of *et*. The former, however, may be right, *et* being added by Paris (or in transmission) to remove the asyndeton.

percipit: α. The present accords with the normal practice (cf. 1 line 56 n.) and the correction in A (with *percipit* subsequently restored) to *percepit* (followed by Halm) is manifestly erroneous.

87. inexplicabiles: 'labyrinthine' (SB); cf. *OLD s.u.* 1b (*TLL* vii/1.1328.8 misleadingly gloss '*i. longissimas*').

88. effusam †barbariam†: LG (*barbariem* A). There is little doubt that V. is talking about the lake called Μάρεια or Μαρεῶτις, named after a town called Μάρεια (Barrington Atlas 74B/C 2–3; cf. Kees, *RE* xiv. 1676–8), but exactly what V. wrote cannot be determined. Madvig proposed *Mareotidem*, but *Mari(e)am* is much closer to *barbariam* (*et fusam Maream* Gertz, *et effusam Mariam* Kempf, *effusam per Mariam* Achelis (my apparatus is in error in three respects: read 'effusam per Mariam *Achelis* (*CQ 1911, 112*)'). In Latin, however, only *Mareotis* is attested (Curt. 4.7.9, 8.1, Plin. *nat.* 5.39, 62–3); Novák's deletion (in his later years he was given to implausible excisions) and Morel's *effusum borborem* (i.e. βόρβορος; attested in Latin only in Ambrose) may be ignored.

flexuosos fossarum ambitus: 'winding course of dykes' (SB). They took the floodwaters at the time of the summer floods of the Nile (on which see Rehm. *RE* xvii. 571–90; cf. H. G. Lyons, *The Physiography of the River Nile and its Basin* (Cairo, 1906), 350). The completion of the Aswan Dam in 1970 meant the end of the annual floods.

flexuosus occurs before or contemporaneously with V. at Cato *agr.* 33, Cic. *nat. deor.* 2.144, and Celsus 1.2.6, 8.1.6. This is the first time it refers to water. (*TLL* vi/1.907–8).

89. lustrabat: Cic. *fin.* 5.87 (just after the passage cited on lines 84–5 above) *cur ipse Pythagoras et Aegyptum lustrauit?*

89–90. ab Archyta ... Pythagorae: Cic. loc. cit. *cur post Tarentum ad Archytam? cur ad reliquos Pythagoreos, Echecratem, Timaeum, Arionem Locros, ...*

On Archytas, the greatest of all Pythagoreans, see conveniently Nisbet–Hubbard, i. 320, with bibliography (testimonia and fragments in DK i. 421–440). V. mentions Tarentum or its citizens also at 2.2.5, 7.15, 4.1. ext. 1, 3.14, 6.3, 5.1. ext. 3.

Timaeus (DK i. 441) is the principal speaker in the Platonic dialogue named after him. Nothing else is known about his philosophy (the work entitled περὶ φύσεως attributed to him is derived from the dialogue), but the view (cf., e.g., Harder, *RE* viA. 1204, F. M. Cornford, *Plato's Cosmology* (London, 1937), 2–3; neither mentions the passages of Cicero and V.) that he is a figment of Plato's imagination is far from certain. The name, garbled in L and G, is preserved in A (*-meo*), P (though with *Tarenti* altered to *Tarentino*, wrongly emended to the former by Kempf), and the manuscripts of Cicero.

Arion (DK i. 443) is known only from the passages of Cicero and V.

Echecrates (DK loc. cit.), originally of Phlius, is one of the interlocutors in Plato's *Phaedo*. *Echecrate Locris*, correctly preserved in P, is hopelessly garbled in LG (and doubtless in A before correction by Lupus).

92. per totum ... posset: a considerable exaggeration, as often with *orbis terrarum*; see my notes on Livy 35.12.18, 42.12 (vol. ii. 163, 206); add S. Hornblower, *Lycophron*, Alexandra (Oxford, 2015), 437–8).

dispergi: *dispergere*, occurring from Terence onwards, is used by V. on seven other occasions (2.7.15, 4.1. ext. 4, 5.1.1d, 3. ext. 3 (*bis*), 9.2.1, 2. ext. 3).

dilatari: before and contemporaneously with V. *dilatare* is found in Cicero, Sallust, Varro, Livy, Ovid, Vitruvius, and Celsus; V. uses it also at 3.4.2, 5.6. ext. 4, 7.2.6.

92–93. altero ... decedens: the majority of sources agree with V. that Plato died at the age of 81 (see Powell on Cic. *Cato* 13 ('*Proleg. Plat. Phil.* 6.1–7' = *Prolegomena philosophiae Platonicae*, ed. Westerink (Amsterdam, 1962), 2 lines 6–7 (p. 7)); Jacoby (*Apollodors Chronik*, 309) adds Ath. 217B, Suda *s.u.* Πλάτων,

Vita Aristot. Marc. p. 428 Rose, but they talk of Plato living 82 years. The exception is Cic. *Cato* 13, who says that Plato died in his 81st year (Jaboby, loc. cit., wrongly adds Lucian *macr.* 21 and Aug. *ciu.* 8.11; his belief (op. cit. 308) that this was the view of Apollodorus is unjustified). According to D.L. 3.2, from Apollodorus and Hermippus respectively, Plato was born in the 88th Olympiad, i.e no earlier than 428/7 and died in Ol. 108.1 = 348/7: in that case, he cannot have been 81 at the time of his death. Either, then, Cicero was right or Plato was in fact born earlier in 428, in the archonship of Epameinon (429/8); thus D.L. 3.3, perhaps the view of Neanthes (cf. Jacoby, op. cit. 306), Ath. 217E.

93. sub capite Sophronis mimos: there is no real ambiguity, but one would have expected s*ub capite mimos Sophronis*; the idiom by which a genitive does not go with the noun nearest to it (cf. my note on Livy 38.3.11) is different.

Sophron was a Syracusan who lived, it seems, in the second half of the fifth century; for the fragments of his mimes, with commentary, see J. H. Hordern, *Sophron's Mimes* (Oxford, 2004); he wrote in prose (despite his appearance in *Poetae Comici Graeci* i (ed. R. Kassel and C. Austin, Berlin–New York, 2001)). Quint. *inst.* 1, 10.17, 7, D.L. 3.18, Olympiodorus *uit. Plat.* p. 2 lines 26–7 (*ap.* Didot edition of D.L., Paris, 1862) also mention a copy of Sophron's mimes being found under his pillow; for Plato's admiration of Sophron see also Duris *FGrH* 76F72, anon. *uit. Plat.* p. 7 line 10 (ed. cit. above), Choricius 32.14. See further Körte, *RE* iiiA. 1100–4, Hordern, op. cit., 1–34.

94. agitatione studii: for *agitatio* 'pursuit' cf. *TLL* i. 1329.1 ff.; *agitatio studiorum* occurs at Cic. *Cato* 33.

ext. 4. *Democritus.* Cicero *fin.* 5.87 talks of Democritus' neglect of his inheritance, *Tusc.* 5.104 relates his statement that he came to Athens and no one knew him (see also D.L. 9.34, 36, Aelian *u.h.* 4.20), but neither of these passages is V.'s source for the *exemplum* as a whole.

Democritus came from Abdera, on the Thracian coast. He developed the theory of atomism, first propounded by Leucippus. See DK ii. 81–230, Kirk–Raven, 402–33.

95. diuitiis censeri: cf. line 73 n. Here *diuitiis* is the equivalent of *diues* (cf. K–St i. 391).

96. Xerxis ... potuerit: α (L has *Xerxes*, corrected). P's *Xerxi et exercitui* (Lupus added *eius*) *daret* is a piece of re-writing. For the meals which the Greek cities were forced to provide for the Persian army as it marched on Greece see Hdt. 7.119, for Xerxes' friendly relations with Abdera 8.120.

ex facili ('easily') occurs before V. only in Ovid (cf. *TLL* vi/1.59.31 ff.); V. uses it also at 4.3.1, 6.8.6, 7.2. ext. 1.

97. operatus: 'engaged in'; an adjective, with *esset* a copula, not part of a pluperfect subjunctive (Perizonius, not realising this, proposed *operaturus*). In fact, the adjective occurs in verse from Lucilius onwards, verbal forms not before the elder Pliny (cf. *TLL* ix/2.689.73 ff.).

97-98. patrimonium ... donauit: no other source says this: for Cicero see above; D.L. 9.36 says that he spent his inheritance, Aelian *u.h.* 4.20 that he took only as much as he needed for his travels, leaving the rest to his brothers.

99-100. ignotus illi urbi: see above and D.L. 9.36.

100-101. stupet ... alio: *iam transit alio* makes it clear tha *mens* refers to V.'s mind, not, as might at first appear, to the mind of anyone aware of Democritus' habits.

ext. 5. *Carneades.* He was the head of the Academy from some time before 155 until 137/6, and, together with the heads of the Stoa and the Peripatetic school, was a member of the famous embassy from Athens sent to appeal to the Senate against the fine imposed by Sicyonian arbitrators, appointed by the Senate in a dispute between Athens and Oropus; cf. Walbank iii. 531-3, 543-4. It is mentioned a number of times by Cicero, as well as by other authors (see Walbank iii. 543-4; add Cic. *rep.* 3.6 (from Lactantius *inst.* 5.14.3-5), saying that Carneades gave a public lecture in favour of justice, on the following day another lecture arguing the opposite case. According to Plutarch (*Cato mai.* 22.6-7), Carneades created so much enthusiasm among young Romans that Cato urged the senate to come to a decision quickly, so that the ambassadors could return to Athens as soon as possible.

None of the passages of Cicero contains the matters related by V., and his source cannot be determined (Livy probably mentioned the embassy, though there is no reference to it in *per.* 47, but is unlikely to have digressed in this way). Of the passages listed in my *testimonia* apparatus, that of Censorinus says that Carneades lived until his ninetieth year, the others (read '*Plin. nat.* 25.51') refer to his use of hellebore.

102. laboriosus: in the sense of 'active' *laboriosus* occurs before V. in Cicero (*Verr.* 2.3.86, 4.51), Rutilius Lupus, and Nepos (cf. *TLL* vii/2.799.39 ff.).

sapientiae miles: the first instance of *miles* used metaphorically with the genitive; cf. *TLL* viii. 944.39 ff. (the metaphorical use is not mentioned at all by *OLD*).

si quidem: cf. 1 line 31 n.

102-103. nonaginta expletis annis: see above. According to Apollodorus (*FGrH* 244F51 = D.L. 4.65) he died in 129/8 at the age of 85.

103. mirificum: adverbial (cf. K–St i. 234–9); A^c altered it to *mirifice*.

105–107. †eum Melissa ... dextera sua†: the transmitted text (as established by the agreement of LG in respect of *dextera sua*; A's *dexteram suam* became the vulgate) is impossible, since it makes *eum* the object of *aptabat* and 'adapting him with her own right hand' makes no sense, while *studia* has to be taken with *inter* rather than, as one would naturally do, with *interpellandi*.

Perizonius, changing *eum* to *ei* and retaining *dexteram suam*, dealt with the first problem but not the second; so too Torrenius, with *eam* (sc. *manum*) ... *dextera sua* (the latter he took from some of his manuscripts). Madvig, otherwise following Perizonius, did so by deleting *inter* (thus Shackleton Bailey), while Gertz proposed changing it to *uiri* or *rite* or *scite* (*intenta* Damsté); he also, gratuitously, suggested adding *eius* after *necessariis*. It is hard to see why anyone should have added *inter*.

105–106. Melissa ... uxoris loco: perhaps identical with the concubine to whom a pupil of Carneades, Mentor, made advances, as a result of which he was expelled from the School (D.L. 4.63–4, Eus. *PE* 14.8.13 (saying that Carneades came upon the pair *in flagrante delicto*; cf. von Fritz, *RE* xv. 528)).

For *uxoris loco* (*in uxoris loco* occurs at Ter. *Haut.* 104) cf. Livy *per.* 131 (of Antony and Cleopatra), Suet. *Vesp.* 3, *TLL* vii/2.1587.10 ff.

109. Chrysippo: since Carneades was born in 214 (see above) and Chrysippus died between 208 and 204 (see ext. 10 n.), that is a chronological impossibility. Pliny *nat.* 25.51 and Gell. 17.15 say Carneades was preparing to argue against the writings of Zeno, i.e. Zeno of Citium, the founder of the Stoa, and, if the anecdote is historical, they are likely to be right.

elleboro: the name of a number of poisonous plants used for medicinal purposes. Petronius 88.4 says that Chrysippus used it, which perhaps explains V.'s error.

expromendum: P; the direct tradition has *exprimendum*: *expromere* ('reveal') gives the required sense, while none of the meanings of *exprimere* fits *ingenium*.

110. illius: Wensky proposed inserting *ad* before *illius*: *ad* (*expromendum*) clearly goes with both gerundives (*ingenium*, of course, is to be understood with the second).

111. effecit: Watt (*Latomus* 60 (2001), 937) argued that *cupidis* shows that in this concluding sentence V. is generalizing, not talking about Carneades alone, and that this requires *efficit* (he says that at 6.1. ext. 1 '*efficit* has become *effecit*' in the paradosis: there the present is certainly correct, but it is not clear whether *efficit* (A^cG) or *effecit* (AL) represents the paradosis). V., however, is no doubt aware that Carneades was not the only person who took hellebore to sharpen his wits.

ext. 6. *Anaxagoras.* Anaxagoras of Clazomenae lived *c.* 500 to 428. See DK ii. 5–44, Kirk–Raven, 352–84. His neglect of his property is mentioned by Plato *Hipp. mai.* 283A, Cic. *Tusc.* 5.115, and D.L. 2.7, but without specific reference to his travels. He spent a considerable time in Athens, probably before 450 (cf. Kirk–Raven, 354) and Alcidamas ap. Ar. *Rhet.* 1398b15 indicates that he died in Lampsacus, which conflicts with Plut. *Per.* 16.7, implying that he died in poverty in Athens. V.'s source cannot be determined. V. mentions him also at 9. ext. 2, 11. ext. 1, 5.10. ext. 3, 7.2. ext. 12.

112. flagrasse: cf. line 17 n.

112–113. e diutina peregrinatione: thus G. L has *e diuina peregrinatione*; so too A, but omitting *e*, corrected to *post diutinam peregrinationem*. The truth is not in doubt.

114. compotem: 'possessed of' (SB).

115–116. dominus ... mansisset: the first part of the apodosis; Gertz wrongly inserted *et* before *dominus*, converting the clause into a second part of the protasis.

116. tantus Anaxagoras: 'the great Anaxagoras' (SB). Gertz implausibly proposed deleting *tantus*.

eos: A^c altered to *deos*, doubtless a piece of *interpretatio Christiana* by Lupus.

ext. 7. *Archimedes.* The great Syracusan mathematician and engineer, killed in the aftermath of the capture of Syracuse in 212; see, conveniently, R. Netz, *OCD*[4], 141–2.

The device invented by Archimedes to thwart Marcellus' attempt to capture Syracuse by sea is described by Livy 24.34.8–11 (213), his death at 25.31.9–10 (212); both passages derive from Polybius, the former from Pol. 8.5–6. It is likely that Livy is V.'s source, but if so, he has embroidered the account of Archimedes' death with his statement that Marcellus' had given orders that his life was to be spared and the details of his death; see lines 119–21 n. Other sources are listed by Ziegler in his testimonia apparatus on Plut. *Marc.* 19.8–12; Plutarch has three different versions of Archimedes' death, in none of which is there any mention of Marcellus' instruction. See also Cic. *Verr.* 2.4.131, *fin.* 5.50, Plin. *nat.* 7.125, Sil. 14.676, Zon. 9.5.5, Tzetzes *chil.* 2.136–49; only Zonaras and Tzetzes have V,'s version.

117. fructuosam: the only occurrence of the adjective in V.; before and contemporaneously with him it is used frequently by Cicero and Varro, once each by Caesar and Velleius.

118. dedisset uitam: i.e. through Marcellus' order.

Syracusis: the defection of Syracuse, subsequent internal conflicts, and Marcellus' long campaign to recapture it (215–212) occupy a lare part of Livy books 24 and 25.

Marcellus: M. Claudius Marcellus (220), with Fabius Verrucosus and Scipio Africanus one of the three great Roman commanders in the Hannibalic War, was consul in 222, 215 (when he was forced to abdicate), 214, 210, and 208; in the latter year he was killed in an ambush.

118–119. machinationibus: Livy (24.34.2) uses *machinator* of Archimedes, *machinamenta* (24.34.7) of devices employed by Marcellus. On *machinatio* cf. my note on Livy 37.5.6; this is its only occurrence in V.

Kempf followed Gertz in inserting *etsi* before *machinationibus*: there is nothing objectionable in *captis enim ... senserat* and *eximia tamen ... edixit* being in parataxis and there is no palaeographical explanation of the posited omission. V. could have written thus, but did not.

119–121. eximia ... reponens: Livy has nothing of this but says (25.31.10) *aegre id Marcellum tulisse sepulturaeque curam habitam, et propinquis etiam inquisitis honori praesidioque nomen eius fuisse.*

121. Archimede seruato ... Syracusis oppressis: 'saving Archimedes ... crushing Syracuse' (SB): the participial constructions provide a neat alternative to, e.g., *tantum se gloriae quod Archimeden seruasset quantum quod Syracusas oppressisset adeptum esse ratus.*

α has *his* after *Syracusis*, erased in A with *hostis* written in the margin: *his* arose from a dittography of the preceding *-is*.

122–123. domum: Kempf proposed adding *in*, but for *irrumpere* used transitively cf. *TLL* vii/2.444.78 ff. (with *domum* Caes. *ciu.* 3.111.1).

123. quisnam: α. P has *quinam*. The former is the regular form for 'who, tell me', but *quinam* occurs in an indirect question at Caes. *Gall.* 5.44.2: in these circumstances preference should be given to the direct tradition.

123–125. propter ... non potuit; as if anyone could be so engrossed in what they were doing that they could not remember their own name.

125. protecto: α has *protracto*, P *proiecto*, neither of which makes any sense in the context. It is surprising that no one realised the truth (a change of only one letter in P's reading) before the Leipzig edition of 1830.

126. neglegens imperii uictoris: α. P has *neglegens imperium interrogantis*, presumably the result of the misapprehension that *neglegens* is a participle. *imperium* 'order' occurs before V. in Ennius, Plautus, Accius, Publilius Syrus, and Livy; cf. *TLL* vii/1.568.37 ff. The soldier, of course, did not possess *imperium*.

127. lineamenta: in reference to a line in geometry *lini(e)amentum* occurs before V. only at Cic. *de orat.* 1.187 and, if the reading is correct, *ac.* 2.118; cf. *TLL* vii/2.1438.62 ff. Cf. 11 line 38 n.

127–128. quo accidit ... spoliaretur: ring composition, taking up lines 117–18 *nisi eadem ... abstulisset*.

ext. 8. *Socrates.* As in the case of Pythagoras and Plato (see ext. 2, 3 nn.), I say nothing about Socrates in general.

For other references, including a considerable number not mentioned in my testimonia apparatus (though missing Quint. *inst.* 1.10.13; cf. ext. 9 n.), to Socrates' learning the lyre see Powell's note on Cic. *Cato* 26. If the latter is V.'s source, he has elaborated considerably.

130. satius ... sero quam nunquam: 'better late than never'; cf. Livy 4.2.11 (with *potius* instead of *satius*). P has *uel sero*, which is clearly wrong ('better even late than never' is senseless); it is hard to see why Paris should have added *uel*, and it may well be an error of transmission.

131. quantula: V. uses *quantulus* also at 4.4.11; before him it occurs as an adjective in Lucretius and *bell. Afr.*, as a substantivized neuter in Cicero, *rhet. Her.*, and Horace.

peruicax: only here in V. Before him, it is used by Terence, Accius, Horace, and Livy. See my note on Livy 42.7.8, where I make the extraordinary statement that V. was fond of the word (no doubt a careless misunderstanding of the heading at Otón Sobrino iii. 1532); add a reference to *TLL* x/1.1868–9.

132. uilissimum: Glareanus absurdly proposed *utilissimum*: V. means that playing the lyre was the least important part of a knowledge of music. (*uilisimum* in my apparatus is a misprint.)

133–134. ergo ... locupletissimum: V. has been carried away by his own rhetoric: it is nowhere stated that Socrates always regarded himself as a bad learner; and if the midwife analogy in the *Theaetetus* (149A–151D) does not misrepresent the historical Socrates, he claimed that he himself did not possess knowledge, just the ability, like a midwife, to draw out of others what they already knew; at *Symposium* 216D Alcibiades is made to say that Socrates claims to know nothing. Cf., e.g., W. J. Prior, in H. H. Benson (ed.), *A Companion to Plato* (Malden, MA–Oxford–Carlton, Victoria, 2006), 31–5.

133. credidit: α. Kempf, followed by SB, emended to *credit*; cf. 1 line 56 n.

134. fecit: α. Some later MSS (cf. Torrenius) have *fecit se* and Kempf, in 1854, proposed *se fecit* (in 1888 he attributed the conjecture to Halm, adding *non recte*). The omission of *se* before *fe-* would be easy, but it is readily understood from *se pauperem* above.

ext. 9. *Isocrates.* Isocrates ranks as one of the canon of ten Attic orators, though he lacked the voice and confidence to speak in public himself. His twenty-one orations (there are also nine letters) were either written for others to deliver or intended to be read. He was born in 436 and died in 338. V.'s source is evidently Cic. *Cato* 13 (for other references, many omitted in my *testimonia* apparatus, see Powell ad loc.; cf. ext. 8 n.), but the value judgements in lines 136 and 137-9 are an addition, probably from another source, perhaps oral, rather than a result of V.'s own reading of the *Panathenaicus*.

135-136. ut ... redigamus: a somewhat strange expression, presumably meaning that Isocrates epitomizes all the preceding *exempla*.

136. Isocrates: PG^c (G has *Isocratis*; my apparatus fails to report P). AL read *Hisocratis*, corrected in L to *hic Socrates*: the corrector had clearly never heard of Isocrates. At 13 line 70 G has *Isocratis*, AL *Hisocratis*.

136-137. librum ... composuit: Cic. *Cato* 13 *eum librum qui Panathenaicus inscribitur quarto et nonagesimo scripsisse se dicit.*

136. Παναθηναικός: thus, in capitals, LG, and no doubt A before correction to ΠΑΝΕΓΥΡΙΚΟΠΗΝΑΚΟΣ. P has *Pana* (followed by an erasure and a space of about ten letters) *thenaiakas*. Since Lupus used not P, but its exemplar (see p. 20), it must be that Paris, or a predecessor, knowing of Isocrates' *Panegyricus* (written *c.* 380), somehow combined the titles of the two works, and this, written in Greek capitals, and perhaps already corrupted, is what stood in the exemplar of P, to be copied by Lupus and transliterated into the Latin alphabet by P (who never uses Greek), in both cases inaccurately.

137. ita ut ipse significat: Isoc. *Panath.* 3 τοῖς ἔτεσι τοῖς ἐνενήκοντα καὶ τέτταρσιν, ἀγω τυγχάνω γεγονώς.

139-140. terminos ... clausit: a strange expression, apparently a combination of *uitam suam clausit* (cf. 9.12 praef.) and *terminos uitae suae imposuit*.

140. namque ... quinquennio percepit: Cic. *Cato* 13 *uixitque quinquennium postea*. In fact, as Isocrates explains at *Panath.* 267-70, a severe illness forced him to discontinue the work when it was only half completed; three years later, when he was 97, friends persuaded him to complete it.

ext. 10. *Chrysippus*. He was born between 281 and 277 and died between 208 and 204, at the age of 73 (Apollodorus *FGrH* 244F46 = D.L. 7.184). V., like [Lucian] *macr.* 20, who says that he died at 81, is therefore wrong to say that he began the 39th book of the *Logica* in his eightieth year (there is no other evidence on the matter, but it is unlikely that V.'s value judgement is his own). He succeeded Cleanthes (see ext. 11 n.) as head of the Stoa in 232.

141-142. citerioris ... flexit: an extraordinary way of saying that Chrysippus died at a younger age than Isocrates. For *citerior* in the sense of '*propior, anteri-*

or', not found before V., cf. *TLL* iii. 195.32 ff. (with the unhelpful comment on our passage '*fere i.q. humanae*'); at 15.1 *citerior legitimo tempore* it means 'earlier than prescribed by law', at 3.8.1, 8. ext. 1 'more urgent'. For *flectere* 'to round a turning point' cf. Cic. *Att.* 5.9.1, *diu.* 2.94, *TLL* vi/1.895.31 ff; there is no parallel for its referring to death.

141. uiuacitas: 'longevity' (SB). V. is the first writer to use the word and does so again at 13. ext. 4. Cf. line 21 n.

142. Λογικῶν: for the fragments see *SVF* ii. 18–110, for its importance von Arnim, *RE* x. 2506–8.

142–143. exactissimae: cf. line 91 n.

ext. 11. *Cleanthes*. The second head of the Stoa, he lived from *c.* 331 to *c.* 232 and succeeded Zeno *c.* 263. See von Arnim, *RE* xi. 558–74, for the fragments *SVF* i. 103–8; other sources for his age or poverty when young are Sen. *epist.* 44.3, [Lucian] *macr.* 19, Cens. 15.3, D.L. 7.168, Suda *s.u.* V.'s source is uncertain.

146. te ... Cleanthe: V. is fond of authorial apostrophe but this is the only example in book 8. Cf. 1 praef., 6.13, 8.8, 2.2.3, 7.6, 7, 10.3, 4, 3.2 praef., 14, 23, 3. ext. 7, 8.6, 4.6.1, 5, 7.1, 3, 4, 7, 5.1.4, ext. 6, 3.5, 4.7, ext. 2, 3, 6. ext. 2, 6.1 praef., 8.4, 7.2. ext. 1, 6.1, 7.4, 9.11. ext. 4, 13.3. He employs it here for variation.

147. quaestu: 'trade'; cf. my note on Livy 39.8.4.

148. extrahendae aquae: thus L. AG have the nonsensical word division *extrahenda ea quae* (corrected in A to *extrahentem ea que* (meaning, presumably, *eaque*)): this will have resulted from misinterpretation of an uncial manuscript.

The normal verb for drawing water is *haurire*, but V. has just used it in a different sense (line 146) and does not want to repeat it here (though in general Latin writers are not averse to such repetition; cf. vol. ii. 13 and the passages of Livy listed at vol. iii. 10–11). For *extrahere* of drawing water see Plaut. *Rud.* 461, *bell. Alex.* 5.3, *TLL* v/1.2065.24 ff. (missing our passage).

148, 150: tuam ... tuos: α has *tuam ... suos*, *tuos* being the reading of D and Γ. Halm's suggestion that *suos* should be retained and *tuam* altered to *suam* is out of the question: the whole of the rest of the *exemplum* is addressed to Cleanthes and it is inconceivable that V. used the third person for these two pronouns (there is no difficulty in *eundemque* referring to the second person; cf. *TLL* vii/1.193.52 ff.).

149. Chrysippi: a mistake for Zeno: Chrysippus was Cleanthes' successor as head of the Stoa (ext. 10 n.). For a similar error see line 109 n.

151–152. incertum ... laudabilior: cf. 1 line 31 n.

reddendo: the gerund instead of the present participle; cf. Oakley ii. 368.
praeceptor: cf. line 80 n.

ext. 12. *Sophocles.* For other sources see below (my testimonia apparatus wrongly indicates that Macleod does not mention Cic. *Cato* 22). V.'s own source, if there was one, is uncertain.

154. illi opera sua ... illa operibus eius: *illi* and *illa* refer to *rerum natura*, *sua* and *eius* to Sophocles. α, by anticipation, has *illa* twice. CDE have *ille*, grammatically possible, but wrecking the antithesis, other manuscripts (see Torrenius) the correct *illi*.

155. prope enim centesimum annum: Diodorus (13.103.4) says he was 90, the *marmor Parium* (FGrH 239A64) 92, ps.-Lucian (*macr.* 24) 95: the last is not irreconcilable with V.'s expression (cf. Jacoby, *Apollodors Chronik*, 253). Both Diodorus and the *marmor Parium* give the date of his death as 406/5. Ps.-Lucian (loc. cit.) and *uita Soph.* 14 say that Sophocles died from swallowing a grape.

156. Oedipode ἐπὶ Κολωνῷ: the *O.C.* was first produced by Sophocles' homonymous grandson in 402/1 (*O.C.* arg. 2).

α has ΚΟΛΟΝΟΝ, first corrected by Kempf in his 1854 edition.

157. praeripere: 'preempt' (SB); A^cG have the correct prefix, AL *pro-*. Not only did the *O.C.* surpass all previous tragedies, but it was not going to be surpassed by any written in the future.

158. Iophon: V. does not have the (implausible) story, first attested in the grammarian Satyrus (ap. *uita Soph.* 13), who lived, it seems, in the second half of the third century BC (cf. Gudeman, *RE* iiA. 228–9), and among extant sources by Cic. *Cato* 22, that Iophon brought a lawsuit for insanity against his father, to which Sophocles successfully responded by reading out part or the whole of the *O.C.*; for other sources and discussion see Powell ad loc. Since the *Cato* is used by V. elsewhere, he either forgot the story or chose to omit it.

Iophon, the son of Sophocles by Nicostrate (*uita Soph.* 13), was himself a tragedian, winning the first prize in 435 (A. W. Pickard-Cambridge, *The Dramatic Festivals of Athens*, 2nd edn., revised by J. P. A. Gould and D. M. Lewis (Oxford, 1988), 105) and the second in 428 (Eur. *Hipp.* didask.). According to the Suda, *s.n.*, he wrote fifty plays (for the fragments see *TrGF* i². 132–4). Cf. Diehl, *RE* ix. 1898–1900.

The name, corrupted (not surprisingly) to *Sophu(o)m(n)* in the manuscripts, was restored by Pighius.

ext. 13. *Simonides.* He came from the island of Ceos and lived from the middle of the sixth century until some time after the battle of Plataea (479); cf.

Geffcken, *RE* iiiA. 186. He wrote poetry in a variety of different genres (cf., conveniently, Parsons, *OCD*⁴ 1368–9). V.'s source is uncertain.

159-160. octogesimo anno ... gloriatur: V. is referring to Simonides fr. xxviii in Page, *Epigrammata Graeca* (Oxford, 1975).

ἦρχεν Ἀδείμαντος μὲν Ἀθηναίοισ', ὅτ' ἐνίκα
Ἀντιοχὶς φυλὴ δαιδάλεον τρίποδα.
Ξεινοφίλου δέ τις υἱὸς Ἀριστείδης ἐχορήγει
πεντήκοντ' ἀνδρῶν καλὰ μαθόντι χορῷ.
ἀμφὶ διδασκαλίῃ δὲ Σιμωνίδῃ ἕσπετο κῦδος
ὀγδωκονταέτει παιδὶ Λεωπρέπεος.

(I regret that I was unaware of this epigram when preparing my edition; it is cited by Shackleton Bailey, but as 'fr. 147 Diehl': that was the number in Bergk's edition (*Poetae lyrici Graeci*, iii (4th edn., Leipzig, 1882), 496), given in brackets by Diehl, *Anthologia lyrica Graeca*, 2nd edn. (Leipzig, 1942), fr. 77).)

se: AL, omitted in G. Haplography or dittography could easily have occurred after (*docuis*)*se*: ellipse of the pronoun in an accusative + infinitive is frequent (cf. K–St i. 700–1), but it is more likely that V. wrote it, in the unemphatic position, pointing forward to *ipse gloriatur*.

in eorum certamen descendisse: 'attended the competitions' (SB).

160. iniquum: α has *inimicum*, corrected to *inicum* in A and the regular *iniquum* in later manuscripts (Kempf (1854) implies CDEF). V. uses *iniquus* on fifteen occasions, in eleven of which the manuscripts present *iniquu-*: at 3.7.8 AL have *inicum*, corrected to *iniquum*, which is the reading of G; at 4.7.5 *unicam* is unanimously transmitted, corrected to *iniquam* in A and to *inicam* by Gertz; at 6.5.4 A has *iniquum* in an erasure, L *inicum* corrected to *iniquum*, and G *iniquum*. In no case, therefore, is *inicu-* indisputably the transmitted reading. *iniquus* is frequently corrupted to *inimicus* and *inimicum* here does not show that the original reading was *inicum*. It is, in any case, unlikely that V. (or Livy; in books 41–45 the Vienna MS has *inicus* at 44.13.4, *aecus* on eleven occasions (see Packard i. 252); the form was retained by Heraeus, but I printed *-quu-* consistently in my edition) used the analogizing form.

161. eam: AᶜG; A has *tam*, L *tam*. Kempf read *tantam*: a scribe's eye could have moved from the first *-a-* to the second, but one expects merely the pronoun taking up *uoluptatem* (cf. lines 167–8 *eo animo uitam ... quo eam*), not an indication of the quality of the pleasure to be derived from Simonides' poetry; corruption of *eam* to *tam* is very easy.

ext. 14. *Solon.* Solon was a major figure, both political and literary, in the early history of Athens. Since this *exemplum* is concerned with neither politics nor

Commentary — 155

literature, I say merely that he was archon in 594/3 and died *c.* 560. He is mentioned by V. also at 9. ext. 1, 4.1. ext. 7, 5.3. ext. 3 (lines 161, 224), and 7.2. ext. 2. Cic. *Cato* 26 is V.'s source for the citations in lines 162–3, that for the anecdote that follows cannot be determined.

162. Solon: α; P (and Lupus) has *Solo*. V. uses the nominative also at 9. ext. 1 and 5.3. ext. 3 line 161, and 7.2. ext. 2. At 9. ext. 1 G has *Solon*, AL *Solo*; I printed the former but gave the latter a *fort. recte*. At 5.3. ext. 3 *Solon* is unanimously attested. At 7.2. ext. 2 P (and Lupus) has *Solo legum lator neminem*, α *Solonem*: the latter is clearly the result of a scribe's eye moving from the first *-n-* to the second and *legum lator* will be an addition by Paris; the probability is that V. used the Latin form here, perhaps to avoid *-n n-*, and the same could be the case at 9. ext. 1, though one cannot exclude the possibility that in both passages there has been a haplography of *nn*. These considerations do not apply to our passage and in these circumstances preference should be given to the direct tradition.

162–163. uersibus ... senescere: Cic. *Cato* 26 *uersibus gloriantem uidemus, qui se cotidie aliquid addiscentem dicit senem fieri*. The reference is to Solon fr. 22.7 Diehl (cf. lines 159–60 n.)

γηράσκω δ' αἰεὶ πολλὰ διδασκόμενος.

For other references to the line see Powell on Cic. loc. cit.; add Plut. *Sol.* 2.2 (with γηράσκειν instead of γηράσκω (he has the latter at 31.7).

163. addiscentem: α; thus Cic. loc. cit. P has the *simplex*.

163–166. et supremo ... moriar: there appears to be no other reference to this anecdote.

164. quod: 'in that'. L^c has *quo* (to go with *die*), which Kempf, clearly wrongly, thought possible.

165. fatis ... pressum: for *fatum, -a* 'death' cf. *TLL* vi/1.59.22 ff., citing (66 ff.) also 1.7.6, 8.12, 4.6. ext. 1, 5.1. ext. 4, 7.1.1.

167. ingrederentur: for the imperfect subjunctive in the protasis of a counterfactual conditional, with the pluperfect in the apodosis, cf. K–St ii. 396–7.

ext. 15. *Themistocles*. V. mentions him also at 14. ext. 1, 3.2. ext. 5, 6. ext. 3, 6.5. ext. 2, 9. ext. 2, 7.2. ext. 9.

169–170. V.'s source for Themistocles' learning the names of all Athenian citizens (lines 237–9) is Cic. *Cato* 21 *Themistocles omnium ciuium perceperat nomina*; no other authors refer to the matter.

169. maximarum rerum cura: Themistocles' involement in public affairs in Athens. V. is thinking, presumably, of his role during the Persian invasion in 480–479; he was archon in 493/2.

districtus: A has the correct reading, but the paradosis (LGP) is *destrictus*: the required sense 'distracted' ('preoccupied' SB) is given by *distringere* but not by any of the meanings of *destringere* ('strip', 'scrape', 'unsheathe')'. Elsewhere V. uses *destringere* on eighteen occasions, *distringere* only at 4.3. ext. 1 (where it is transmitted correctly). Confusion between compounds in *de-* and *di-* (e.g. *deligere* and *diligere*, *demittere* and *dimittere* (cf. 14 line 45 n.), *describere* and *discribere* (cf. vol. iii. 547) is common in manuscripts. For *derigere* and *dirigere* (14 line 22) cf. my note on Livy 34.27.6, where read '1532–3'.

170. omnium ... comprehendit: there were *c.* 30,000 Athenian citizens in the early fifth century, so that Themistocles' feat, if authentic, would be comparable to a British politician's remembering the names of about half of his or her constituents.

170–174. per summamque ... adhiberet: for the extensive sources for Themistocles' trial and exile (in the late 470s) see R. Meiggs–A. Andrewes, *Sources for Greek History between the Persian and Peloponnesian Wars, collected and arranged by G. F. Hill* (Oxford, 1951), 349. V's source here is Nepos *Them.* 10.1 (but see next note); Themistocles' acquisition of Persian is mentioned also by Thuc. 1.138.1, Quint. *inst.* 11.2.50, Plut. *Them.* 29.5. V. included Themistocles in his list of those exiled by an ungrateful homeland (5.3. ext. 3, lines 187–92).

171. Xerxem ... deuicerat: at the battle of Salamis in 480. Cf. 5.3. ext. 3 lines 190–1 *quem paulo ante destruxerat*. In fact Artaxerxes had succeeded Xerxes as king (Thuc. 1.137.3); Nepos (*Them.* 9.1) says that most writers make Xerxes still king at the time of Themistocles' arrival, but that he believes Thucydides. Presumably V. followed the majority so as not to destroy the irony of Themistocles fleeing to the man for whose defeat he had been responsible.

AL have *Xerxem*, G *Xerxen*, perhaps correctly. Cf. line 80, 3 lines 7–8 nn.

172. conspectu: α. Later manuscripts (Γ; Torrenius implies some of his have the reading) has *conspectum*. I gave the latter a *fort. recte*, but retained the former as an example of *in* being used with the ablative instead of the expected accusative in reference to a situation which results from the action described. See *TLL* vii/1. 774.57 ff.; they cite from V. 2.6.7, where the direct tradition points to *scaena mimis*, but P has *scaenam mimis* and haplography of *m* is extremely easy, 2.7.15, line 235, where I failed to record that α has *Italia*, 2.8.4, where α has *curia* and I printed Stanger's *curiam*, and, wrongly, 7.3.2, where *referendus* means 'mention'. Shackleton Bailey prints *conspectum* and, on balance, I am now inclined to think he was right (the omission or addition of a final *m* is of course, extremely easy).

173. labore: Kempf wondered whether V. wrote *hoc labore*. He did not: *labore* is used as a synonym for *industria* and is of general application.

173-174. regiis auribus ... adhiberet: an elaborate way of saying that Themistocles addressed the king in Persian, necessitated, presumably, by V.'s having just written *Persico sermone*.

ext. 16. *Cyrus and Mithridates*. V. concludes his long series of non-Roman *exempla* with two from Asia, widely differing in time.

Xenophon *Cyr.* 5.3.46–51 is the earliest mention of Cyrus' knowledge of all his soldiers' names. Of the other passages cited in my *testimonia* apparatus, Pliny *nat.* 25.6, Gell. 17.17.2, and *uir. ill.* 76.1 mention only Mithridates, Pliny *nat.* 7.88 and Quint. *inst.* 11.2.50 both Cyrus and Mithridates (Pliny, from whom Solinus 1.108–9 derives, adds other examples); V. and Pliny derive from a common, unidentifiable, source; cf. Münzer, *Plinius*, 115–17.

175. utriusque industriae: the two achievements of Themistocles related in the previous *exemplum*.

Cyrus: In the *Cyropaedia* Xenophon wrote a 'pseudo-historical account' (thus C. J. Tuplin, *OCD*³ 1629; the term is not used in the rewritten paragraph in the 4th edition (1581–2)) of the life of Cyrus the Great, the founder of the Achaemenid Empire. In 401, the younger Cyrus, in an attempt to depose his elder brother, Artaxerxes II, led the famous expedition described by Xenophon in the *Anabasis*; he was defeated and killed at the battle of Cunaxa.

176. Mithridates: VI of Pontus. He lived from 120 to 63. He built up a huge empire and posed a serious threat to Rome in the first third of the first century BC. Cf. B. C. McGing, *The Foreign Policy of Mithridates VI Eupator, King of Pontus* (Leiden, 1986).

duarum et uiginti: thus α. P has *uiginti duarum*, but *duarum et biginti* in Landulfus Sagax, who used the epitome of Nepotianus (cf. p. 22), eliminates it. *uir. ill.* 76.1 says fifty.

177. linguas ediscendo: A^c L^c; AL have *linguae sediscendo*, G *linguas discendo*. It is most unlikely that anyone would have altered *discendo* to the compound; before V., who uses it only here, *ediscere* is found twice in Plautus, once in *rhet. Her.*, twice in Cicero, once each in Varro, Virgil, and Propertius, and three times in Ovid.

177-178. monitore ... interprete: *monitor* occurs before V. in Terence, Caesar, Sallust, Horace, Ovid, and Livy, *interpres* in the sense of 'translator' in Cicero, Caesar, Sallust, and Livy (*TLL* vii/1.2252.61 ff.).

8 praef. 1. otium ... contrarium: the *industria* about which V. has been talking would not have been described as *negotium*.

quod: α has *quod praecipu(a)e*, corrected in A, by anticipation of *praecipue* in line 2.

1–2. subnecti: cf. 1 line 51 n.

2. quo ... quo: with *otium*.

4. †propriet uitam inertem (the spacing in my edition may have made it appear that I was also obelizing *uitam*): no sense can be made of the transmitted reading (*proprie* G, *propriae* A; *inermem* AG, *inermen* L). A corrector of A added a line over *a*, probably intending *propriam* (later conjectured by Madvig) but omitting to delete *e*. That is easy enough palaeographically, but there seems little point in stressing that it was their own life (as if it might have been that of someone else). Hence a variety of conjectures: *prorsus* (Foertsch), *pro pigra uita* (Thormeyer), *perpetuo* or *pro re publica* Damsté, *morti propiorem* or *perpetuam* (the latter adopted by Shackleton Bailey) Watt. The simplest change to *inermem* is A^c's *inertem* (alternatively *eneruem*), adopted by Watt (who had earlier proposed deletion), and that is what I now print. Thenn's *propriam e uita Mineruam* (*exigant* then means 'drive out' rather than 'spend') is best ignored.

intermissione: the only instance of the word in V.; before him it is used by Cicero, Livy, and Vitruvius.

5. uegetiores: V. uses *uegetus* also at 2.6.2, 3.6.1, 5.7. ext. 1, 7.3.2, 4.4; before him it occurs in Cicero, Catullus, Varro, Horace, and Livy.

1. *Scipio Aemilianus and Laelius*. V.'s source is Cic. *de orat.* 2.22; see also Hor. *sat.* 2.1.71–4; the story probably stood in Lucilius; cf. Leeman–Pinkster–Nelson on the passage of Cicero. The friendship of Aemilianus and Laelius is best attested by Cicero's dialogue *Laelius uel de amicitia* (for the title cf. Gell. 17.5.1), in which Laelius is the principal speaker (the dramatic date is shortly after Scipio's death in 129); see particularly §§ 15 and 103; see also Plut. *TG* 8.5, Gell. loc. cit., Münzer, *RE* xii. 409, Astin, *SA* 81. Cf. 1 line 27 n.

6. par uerae amicitiae clarissimum: V. writes *uerae amicitiae* (the latter misspelt in my edition) rather than the expected *uerorum amicorum* (SB translates 'true friends'), perhaps to avoid the homoioteleuton (one could see the phrase as a combination of *par uerorum amicorum* and *exemplum uerae amicitiae*). Cicero uses *uera amicitia* six times in *Lael.* (22, 32, 58, 59, 64, 91), as well as at *Planc.* 5 (it first occurs at *rhet. Her.*2.35). (*TLL* i. 1897.51 ff.)

Scipio: see 1 line 81 n.

Laelius: C. Laelius (3), son of the consul of 190, whose colleague was L. Cornelius Scipio, the future Asiagenes (cf. 1 line 106 n.). He served as a *legatus* under Scipio at Carthage in 147–146, was praetor in 145, probably governing

Spain in 144, and consul in 140; he was an augur from, probably, before his consulship until his death.

7. iunctum: agreeing with *par*, not, as one would expect, with *Scipio et Laelius*; Pighius' alteration to *iuncti* is quite unjustified. V. mentions him also at 4.7.1, 7, in the former, as here, without *praenomen*, in the latter, wrongly calling him Decimus.

actuosae: 'active'. Before V., who uses it also at 2.1.10, the adjective occurs only at Cic. *orat*. 125, *nat. deor*. 2.110. (*TLL* i. 449.13 ff.).

8. remissioni: A^{c}L^{c}G; AL have *remissionis*, P *animis remissioribus* (my apparatus wrongly has *remissionibus*; *animi remissionibus* is a conjecture of Halm). *remissioni*, even of it is not the transmitted reading preserved by G, is obviously the best explanation of *remissionis*, but *adquiescere* with the dative has the sense of 'obey', 'trust in', occuring before V. only at *bell. Afr.* 10.4 (cf. *TLL* i. 424.8 ff.); I therefore wondered about *remissione*, V. using the ablative to balance *aequali gradu*, but we probably have to do with a syntactical innovation by V., who uses the verb on six other occsasions (2.7 praef., 15, 4.4.11, 7. ext. 2, 5.9.2, 9.12. ext. 1).

9. Caietae: on Caieta (Barrington Atlas 44E3), mod. Gaeta, in southern Latium, see vol. iii. 415. V. mentions it also at 5.3.4 (the index to my edition (p. 858) wrongly cites 1.4.6 (one of the *exempla* missing in the direct tradition), where P has *Caletana* and *Caietana* is the reading of the Mainz edition of 1471; Kempf read the latter and I probably took the entry from his index).

Laurenti: there was no such town as Laurentum; cf. 5 line 33 n. One would not expect Cicero to have made such a mistake and he probably did not: L (the manuscripts descended from the lost Laudensis; cf. Winterbottom–Rouse–Reeve, *Texts and Transmission*, 107–8) has *Lauernium*, which was near Caieta (cf. Cic. *Att.* 7.8.4), and a fragment of *de fato* (4 Ax) has *cum esset apud se ad Lauernium Scipio*. *Laurentum* was no doubt a mistake by V., and the same one was made in the transmission of the *de oratore*.

uagos: AL, corrected in both to *uagas*, the reading of G: manifestly, the wanderers were Scipio and Laelius, not the shells. When this pattern occurs, it is normally the reading of AL which is wrong; the probability is that both *uagos* and *uagas* stood in α and that G and the correctors of AL made the wrong choice.

umbilicos: 'pebbles'. This, the passage of Cicero from which V. derives (cf. 1n.), and Victor *Caes*. 3.11 appear to be the only instances of *umbilicus* in this sense. The word, preserved in P, was corrupted to gibberish in α (*obulicos* A, *obuilicos* LG).

10. lectitasse: cf. 7 line 18 n.

10–11. idque se P. Crassus … praedicauit: Cic. loc. cit. *saepe ex socero meo audiui, cum is diceret socerum suum Laelium …* . The speaker in this passage of the *de oratore* is L. Licinius Crassus (cf. 5 line 13 n.), but Cicero has not given his *praenomen* since the beginning of the book and the mistake is almost certainly V.'s; he had mentioned P. Licinius Crassus Dives at 7.6 (see 7 lines 34–5 n.) and may have had him in mind.

Crassus was married to a daughter of Q. Mucius Scaevola (21; the augur), consul in 117, who was himself married to a daughter of Laelius.

2. *Scaevola*. Another prosopographical error. V.'s source is evidently Cic. *de orat.* 1.217 (from which Quint. *inst.* 11.2.38 also derives), who refers to *P. Scaeuola*, i.e. P. Mucius Scaevola, consul in 133. In the previous *exemplum* V., like Cicero *de orat.* 2.22, did not give the augur's *praenomen* (though he does so at 12.1, 3.8.5, and 5.4.1) and seems not to have realised that Crassus' father-in-law was Quintus.

12. quietae: since this is, effectively (*quiete* L), the transmitted reading and it makes perfect sense, conjectures based on A's (apparent; a corrector deleted it) *quiestis* (*qui ante* or *qui et* Perizonius, *praedictae* Kempf (1854), *qui erat* Halm, *quietis et* Gertz) should be ignored (Shackleton Bailey followed Gertz, a result of his reluctance to accord any authority to G).

13. deuerticulum: V. uses the noun, in a variety of senses, on five occasions. Before him it is found once in Plautus, once in Terence, three times in Cicero, and once in Livy (cf. Oakley iii. 207). Cf. line 125 n.

14. alueo quoque et calculis: Cicero has *duodecim scriptis*, the name of a board game (cf. Leeman–Pinkster–Nelson ad loc.; for a recently discovered fragment of a board see *AnnEpigr* 2014, 111 no. 135); V. evidently feared his readers would find this obscure and therefore talks of 'gaming board and pieces' (SB). In these senses *alueus* occurs elsewhere only in Varro, Vitruvius, Pliny *nat.*, and Suetonius (*TLL* i. 1789.81 ff.), *calculus* before V. at Cic. *phil.* fr. 5 (with reference to *duodecim scripta*) and three times in Ovid (*TLL* iii. 142.49 ff.).

α has *et ad*, by perseveration from the previous line (or, conceivably, from *et ad* at 7 line 171).

15. iura ciuium caerimonias deorum: *asydeton bimembre*. The Venice and Mainz editions of 1471 added *et*, retained by all subsequent editors except Shackleton Bailey and myself. Jim Adams points out to me that *iura ciuium* and *caerimonias deorum* are near-opposites or complements, which frequently stand in asyndeton.

16. †scaelus†: this *uox nihili* is the reading of A, corrected to *scaeuis*, and L, corrected to *scae*, whatever that was meant to mean, with *scaenicis*, clearly a desperate conjecture, in G. Vahlen deleted *scaelus*, almost certainly correctly: it resulted from perseveration from the first syllable of Scaevola's name and dittography of the following *lus-*. He was followed by Halm, Kempf, and Shackleton Bailey. I obelized in order to leave open the possibility that *scaelus* had replaced the original word, but that was unnecessarily cautious (to the conjectures of Eberhard (*serenis*), Foertsch (*intentus*), and Novák (*lasciuiis*), add *suis* (Watt, *Eikasmos* 10 (1999), 245).

ext. 1. *Socrates.* V. returns to Socrates, the subject of 7. ext. 8. The episode is also mentioned by Aelian *u.h.* 12.15, probably deriving from V. (Aelian was a Roman citizen of freedman stock, born in Praeneste; cf. line 20 n.).

18. idque uidit cui ... Socrates: one would expect *Socrates* to precede *cui*: the word order adopted by V. makes the reader momentarily uncertain whom he is talking about.

19. tunc cum: on the distribution of *tum* and *tunc* see Adams, *Informal Latin*, 17; in this case V. may have wanted to avoid *tum cum*.

filiolis: for the dimuntive of a small child cf. *TLL* vi/1.751.37 ff., Adams, op. cit., 260. It is found before V., who uses the feminine at 1.5.3, only in Plautus and Cicero. The coupling with *paruolis*, occurring elsewhere only at Plaut. *Rud.* 39, is striking.

20. Alcibiade: previously mentioned at 1.7. ext. 9, 3.1. ext. 1, 6.9. ext. 4.

uisus: P (and Lupus in A), *risus* α (and Heiric in P); both are possible (for *ridere*, including the passive, 'laugh at' cf. *OLD s.u.* 6a), but Aelian *u.h.* 12.15 has κατελήφθη, which suggests that he was using a text that had *uisus*. Kempf retained *risus* (as did Shackleton Bailey) and referred to the note in his 1854 edition: he there said that κατελήφθη was not inconsistent with *risus* and that the latter could easily have been corrupted to *uisus*. The fact remains that we are dealing with equipollent readings, one of which is closer to κατελήφθη than the other.

ext. 2. *Achilles.* The reference is to Homer *Il.* 9.186

τὸν δ' εὗρον φρένα τερπόμενον φόρμιγγι λιγείῃ.

Homerus is the first word of the *exemplum*, even though it is in fact about Achilles.

22. fides: 'lyre' (*TLL* vi/1.691 ff.: '2. *fides*').

earum: Achilles' hands, not the lyre, of course; there is no real ambiguity.

militare robur leni pacis: chiastic, since the contrast is between *militare* and *pacis*, *robur* and *leni*.

9 tit. eloquentiae: α. P has *eloquentiae et pronuntiatioñ*. The last words are probably an addition by Paris to what was written by the author of the chapter headings (which are not authorial; see p. 28); he was, presumably, motivated by ext. 2, which concerns not so much what Pericles said, but how he did so. The index in P has only *quanta uis eloquentiae*.

praef. 1. etsi ... animaduertimus: V. is presumably thinking of ch. 3 and, perhaps, of 7. ext. 1 (Demosthenes).

Gertz' wish to add *iam* before *animaduertimus* is another example of a conjecture being something which V. could have written, but did not (the omission of *iam* before *anim-* is possible, but not all that likely).

2. propriis exemplis: in a chapter devoted to the subject.

testatiores: the participle of *testor* is used adjectivally, in the sense of 'well attested', by Cicero, Nepos, and Ovid, and by V. also at 14.3 (cf. n. ad loc.). and 4.1.12 (Otón Sobrino (iv. 2181) lists this passage as the only instance in V., classifying 14.3 and 4.1.12 as participial (iv. 2183)).

1. *Valerius*. This episode, referred to by modern scholars as the First Secession of the Plebs, took place in 494 (Varr.). V.'s source is clearly Cicero *Brut.* 54, who has ... *post reges exactos, cum plebes prope ripam Anionis consedisset eumque montem qui sacer appellatus est occupauisset*; *armata* is V.'s own addition. That the secession was ended by Valerius is also stated by Plut. *Pomp.* 13.7. In Livy (2.30.5–32.12), followed by Dio fr. 17, Zon. 7.14.3–10 (DH 6.23–90 is a vastly embroidered amalgamation of the two versions) M'. Valerius Maximus was appointed dictator for a war against the Volsci, Aequi, and Sabines; following its successful completion the plebs seceded and were eventually persuaded to return by Menenius Agrippa; this version probably stood in Piso: cf. *FRHist* 9F24, cited by Livy 2.32.3. See further line 6 n.

In what follows I refer to persons and dates as if they were historical facts; for this early period, of course, that is far from certain.

3. regibus exactis: fifteen years earlier (509 Varr.), on the traditional chronology.

dissidens a patribus: according to Livy (2.31.7–32.12), the secession resulted from the senate's refusal to take any action on debt and their attempt to compel the army to engage in war with the Aequi.

3–4. ripam fluminis Anienis ... appellatur: the Anio (mod. Aniene) rises in the Appennines, flows past Tibur (mod. Tivoli), and joins the Tiber to the north-east of Rome (Barrington Atlas 44C/D2); on the Mons Sacer cf. Oakley iii. 432.

The name varies between *Anio* and *Anien* in the nominative, but in the oblique cases *Anien-* is regular before V. (also at 9.2.1), appearing in Cicero, Virgil, Ovid, and Livy, with *Anion-* only at Ennius *ann. inc.* 603V = 609Sk and Cic. *Brut.* 54, V.'s source here (see above). The likelihood is that V. has altered what stood in Cicero to the normal form, but one cannot exclude the possibility that we should read *Anienis* in Cicero or *Anionis* here. (*TLL* ii. 105.11 ff.). Cf. Skutsch on Ennius loc. cit.

5. a capite ... corporis: although V. was not following Livy's version (see above), his choice of imagery here may have been influenced by Menenius Agrippa's simile at Livy 2.32.9–12.

6. Valeri: α. P has *a Maenenio Agrippa* (*Agrippae* in my apparatus is an error) *ad meliora consilia reuocata est* and Halm suggested reading *Meneni* here; since V. was following Cicero closely, it is very unlikely that he would have departed from him here, or that if he had, a scribe would have known that Cicero was his source and altered *Meneni* to *Valeri*. It is much more likely that Paris remembered that at 4.4.2 V. attributes the reconciliation to Menenius (or was aware of Livy's account or both) and introduced the reference to Menenius. Similarly a twelfth century manuscript, Paris BnF lat. 9688, has *Menenii Agrippae* in the margin. At 3.8. ext. 6 the manuscript has the transmitted *a Parmenione*, with *Antipatro* in the margin; in this case there is no other source which refers to Antipater and it seems likely that the scribe had access to a text of Paris. But if so, he made no further use of it and there is no reason to think that the manuscript contains any transmitted readings differing from α. (At ed. pp. xviii–xix n. 45, which this note otherwise largely repeats, I failed to refer to 4.4.2, as does Shackleton Bailey.)

spes tanti imperii: as if Romans at the beginning of the fifth century had already conceived hopes of a great empire.

7. paene: in this position *paene* must limit *ipso ortu*, not *corruisset*: V. sees the empire as beginning when the Tarquins were expelled.

noua et insolita libertate: Cf. Livy 24.27.5, of the Syracusans, *noua atque insolita libertas*. It is hard to think that V. has deliberately taken over the phrase, though someone, no doubt, will argue that he is comparing Rome after the expulsion of the Tarquins to Syracuse after the murder of Hieronymus. See also Livy 34.49.8 (Flamininus' advice to the Greeks after the defeat of Philip V) *libertate modice utantur: temperatam eam salubrem et singulis et ciuitatibus esse, nimiam et aliis grauem et ipsis qui habeant praecipitem et effrenatam esse.*

8. oratione: 'by a speech'. Gertz' addition of *sua* is not only unnecessary (and, again, palaeographically implausible), but misguided: V.'s subject is the power of speech, and he is saying that it was a speech (not, e.g., the use of force) that brought the crisis to an end.

9. urbem urbi iunxit: the same idea, but with different imagery, as in lines 7–8.

9–10. uerbis ... cesserunt: cf. Cicero's (in)famous line (*carm. frg.* 16) in the *de consulatu suo*

cedant arma togae, concedat laurea laudi.

See also 15.16–17 n.

ira consternatio arma: *asyndeton trimembre*, with two abstract nouns expressing emotions followed by a concrete noun: otherwise V. might have placed the longest word last.

Before V. *consternatio* occurs only in Livy (28.5.5, also with *ira*, 29.6.12, 34.2.6, 37.42.1). V. uses it on nine occasions (also at 1. absol. 3, 4.6.4, 5.8.4, 6.5.3, 7.8.7, 9.3 praef., 7.4, 15.4). (*TLL* iv. 508.13 ff.) Cf. Goodyear's note on Tac. *ann.* 1.39.4.

2. M. Antonius. Antonius (28), grandfather of the triumvir, was consul in 99, and, with L. Licinius Crassus (cf. 5 line 13 n.), one of the two greatest orators of the age. He was one of the victims of the reign of terror instituted by Marius and Cinna on their return to Rome in 87 (for sources see *MRR* ii. 46). The story told by V. is found also in Plut. *Mar.* 44.4–7 and App. *b.c.* 1.72.335; for other sources see *MRR* ii. 49, *s.n.* P. Annius; my testimonia apparatus is defective. Livy 80 was evidently the source of 9.2.2 (see *per.*) and perhaps here too. At 9.2.2 V. says that Marius held Antonius' severed head in his hands while dining.

11. quae: *uerba*.

Marianos Cinnanosque: L. Cornelius Cinna (106) was consul in 87, but was expelled from Rome by his colleague Cn. Octavius. With the help of a legion which was besieging Nola, in the last stages of the Social War, he occupied Rome, where he was joined by Marius, who had fled from Minturnae (cf. 2 lines 35–39) to Africa in 88. Cinna continued as consul for the three following years, in the last of which he was murdered by mutinous troops at Ancona. V. mentions him also at 1.6.10, 2.8.7, 4.3.14, 7.5, 5.3.3, 6.4. For the adjectives cf. 11 line 9 n.

11–12. mucrones ... furentes: as often *mucro*, literally the point of a sword, is used, *pars pro toto*, to refer to the sword as a whole; moreover, as at Cic. *Phil.* 14.6, V. proceeds to attribute an emotion to the swords, rather than to Marius and Cinna. He could have written *quae etiam Marianos Cinnanosque mucrones inhibuerunt: missi enim a saeuissimis ducibus, ciuilis ... furentibus*. See *TLL* viii. 1555.55 ff. (our passage at 1556.50 ff.).

14. cruore: with *uacuos*, not *uibrantes*, of course; there is no way in which punctuation can be used to indicate this. Colometrically, the division is *sermone ... obstupefacti* ('weighted subject') | *destrictos ... gladios* | *uacuos uaginis reddiderunt*.

P. Annius: (17). Not known apart from this episode. He is named also at 9.2.2, saying that Annius brought Antonius' head to Marius; Plut. *Mar.* 44.7, without giving his name, says that Antonius was killed by a military tribune.

The name is preserved in P (and Lupus); α, absurdly, has *Antonius*.

15. in aditu: 'at the entrance' (SB). *in aditu* is Foertsch's emendation of *in ambitu* in α, which makes no sense in the context; Plut. loc. cit. has Ἄννιος ὑπέστη παρὰ τὰς θύρας. Madvig, with one of his less happy ideas, proposed *suauitatis*, deleting *eloquentiae* (the latter is omitted in A, but read by both LG and P; Madvig, of course, knew nothing of L and G and appears not to have appreciated that Paris possessed authority (just as he initially refused to accept that the *codex Spirensis* of Livy possessed authority against the Puteaneus; cf. *Liviana*, 7–8).

expers: 'unaware of' ('out of the range of' SB); Cicero similarly used *expers* with *sermonum, -nis* at *Sull.* 11, *de orat.* 3.45 respectively (*TLL* v/2.1690.28 ff.).

3. Caesar. On V.'s portrayal of Caesar and acceptance of his divinity see *Sileno* 19 (1993), 404–6, Wardle, *CPh* 92 (1997), 323–45. His prosecution of Dolabella is mentioned by Cic. *Brut.* 317, Vell. 2.43.3, Tac. *dial.* 34.4, Suet. *Iul.* 4.1, Plut. *Caes.* 4.1–2, Ascon. 26, 74C, *uir. ill.* 78.2, ps.-Ascon. 194, 234St. V.'s source cannot be determined.

19–20. quam ... columen: for similarly extreme language about Caesar cf. 1.6.13, 8.8, 2.1.10, 3.2.19, 6.8.4, 9.15. For *tam ... quam* / *quam ... tam* 'as much ... as' cf. K–St ii. 457–8 (for the negative with the construction see Adams, *Informal Latin*, 270–1).

20. perfectissimum: cf. 7 line 4 n.

columen: 'peak'. V. uses the word thus also at 4.4.1, 6.4. ext. 2, 9.12.1.

proprie: 'truly' ('aptly' SB); cf. *TLL* x/2.2113.20 ff. (our passage at 52–3).

20–21. in accusatione ... egit: as Asconius (locc. citt.) is at pains to point out, there were two contemporaneous Cn. Cornelii Dolabellae, both defendants (sc. on a charge of *repetundae*). The one accused by Caesar (134) was consul in 81 and governor of Macedonia from 80 to 77; the trial, at which he was acquitted, was probably in the latter year (cf. *MRR* i. 92 n. 4). The other (135) was praetor in 81 and governor of Cilicia in 80 and 79; he was accused by the younger M. Aemilius Scaurus (cf. 1. absol. 10 n.; the reference to a fragment of Scaurus in my testimonia apparatus is erroneous: there are no fragments of his speech) and convicted.

21. C. Cottae: the manuscripts have *L.*, but there is no doubt that the man in question is C. Aurelius Cotta (96), consul in 75 and a noted orator (*ORF* no. 80; Sallust attributed a speech to him (*hist.* 2.47M = 2.43 Ramsey)). I followed Pighius in printing *C.*, while saying that the mistake may have been V.'s, not that of a scribe (Kempf and Shackleton Bailey retain *L.*).

22. si quidem: cf. 1 line 45 n.

†**eloquentiae**† **questa:** the transmitted reading lacks syntax. A corrector of A made the simple change to *eloquentia*. Conjectures in later manuscripts and early editions added *uis* or *laus* and/or changed *questa* to *quaesita* (Perizonius proposed *tum maxima eloquentiae laus quaesita*). None of them, however, succeed in making the clause cohere with *uim facundiae proprie expressit*: that was achieved by Kempf, who added *eloquentia de ui* before *eloquentiae*, i.e. a great orator demonstrated the power of oratory by paying tribute to the eloquence of his opponent (a scribe's eye will have moved from *eloquentia* to *eloquentiae*). Kempf, who was followed by Shackleton Bailey, was certainly on the right lines, but *uis eloquentiae* occurs only in the non-authorial chapter heading (cf. p. 28) and other supplements are possible.

23. adiecerim: 'could add' (SB); a potential subjunctive.

23–24. peregrinandum est: 'I must go abroad' (SB). A pithy and striking way of introducing the *exempla externa*. V. uses *peregrinari* also at 3.4.5 (literally) and 6.9. ext. 1 (metaphorically). Before him the verb is frequent in Cicero, occurring also at *rhet. Her.* 4.63, Caelius ap. Cic. *fam.* 8.1.1, and Sall. *Cat.* 2.8. It is, naturally, extremely frequent in Christian writers.

ext. 1. *Pisistratus.* For the many sources (who do not include Herodotus) for Solon's opposition to Pisistratus' first seizure of power in 561/60 see Rhodes, 201–2; he is wrong, however, to say that this passage, as well as 5.3. ext. 3 (lines 161–9), belongs to the version in which Solon went into exile after Pisistratus' acquisition of power. As Rhodes says, the whole story may well be invention.

25–26. regium imperium ... permitterent: the assembly voted to give Pisistratus a bodyguard (Hdt. 1.59.5, *Ath. pol.* 14.1); no specific power was conferred on him.

26. cum praesertim: for the phrase used in a concessive sense ('even though' SB) cf. *TLL* x/2.867.57 ff. Overall the order *praesertim cum* is considerably more frequent than the reverse, but V., who uses the expression on five occasions, always has the latter (*TLL* art. cit., 23 ff.).

26–27. amantissimus: the superlative of the present participle of *amo* used adjectivally occurs in *rhet. Her.* and frequently in Cicero (*TLL* i. 1958.64 ff.). V. uses it on nine occasions (also at 2.2.1, 4.7. ext. 2, 5.1.1e, 3.2f, 7.3, 6.2.8, 7.3.10, 8.8.).

27. Solon: for the orthography see 7 line 162 n.

27–28. contiones ... disertiores. quo: in the case of all three words a corrupt reading in AL (*contentiones, dissertiores, quod*) has been emended in both manuscripts, with G also having the correct reading on the second and third occasions. (*dissertus* would be the participle of *disserere*: the view of Varro (*ling.* 6.64) and Cicero (*de orat.* 1.240, *diu.* 1.105), followed by many modern scholars ('prob.(ably) fr.(om)' *OLD s.u.*), that *disertus* is derived from *disserere* is probably mistaken; see Ernout–Meillet *s.u.*

28. alioqui: 'in other ways'. Thus later MSS (Kempf says it is in all of those he cites). α has *aliqua*, corrected to *alias* in A; the latter gives the correct sense, but does not explain the corruption. V. uses *alioqui(n)* on twelve occasions and this is the only one where it has been corrupted in transmission.

ext. 2. *Pericles.* V.'s main source here is clearly Cic. *de orat.* 3.138 (see Wisse–Winterbottom–Fantham ad loc.); see also *orat.* 29, *Brut.* 44, 59, Quint. *inst.* 12.10.24, 65. For elements not derived from Cicero see lines 31–2, 37–42 nn. V. mentions Pericles also at 11. ext. 1, 2.6.5, 3.1. ext. 1, 4.3. ext. 1, 5.10. ext. 1, 7.2. ext. 7.

30. felicissimis naturae incrementis: SB translates 'abundant natural advantages'. V. uses *incrementum* on fifteen occasions, in a number of senses, but none of them fit this passage and I am not aware of any parallel for the noun meaning 'advantage'. *TLL* (vii/1.1047.71) classify it under '*i.q. indoles*', citing in addition only Augustine and the *liber praedestinatus*, though Paul. Fest. 94L glosses *indoles* with *incrementum, industria* (perhaps *indoles* and *incrementum* have been transposed). A plant could be described as *felix* if it produced an abundance, but even if *incrementis* could mean 'advantages', it is hard to see how their abundance could be *felicia*. If it means 'character', the adjective is best taken as 'auspicious'.

felicissimis is the reading of A^cG; AL have *felicissimus* and Halm proposed *feliicissimis usus*, with *perpolitus et* (Kempf (1854) implies this is the reading of CD^cEF), which had become the vulgate.

Anaxagora: cf. 7. ext. 6 n.

praeceptore: cf. 11. ext. 1, Cic. *de orat.* 3.138; among Greek writers Anaxagoras is said to have been Pericles' teacher by Plato *Phaedrus* 270A, [Plato], *epist.* 2.311A, [Dem.] 61.45, Plut. *Per.* 4.6 (cf. Stadter ad loc.), 8.1. For *praeceptor* cf. 7 line 80 n.

31–32. liberis ... suo: the claim that Athens under Pericles was in reality a tyranny, not a democracy, originating, no doubt, from his political opponents, was given voice by the comic poets (cf. Plut. *Per.* 3.5, 16.1; cf. 8.4) and encapsulated in Thucydides' famous judgement (2.65.9) ἐγίγνετό τε λόγῳ μὲν δημοκρατία, ἔργῳ δὲ ὑπὸ τοῦ πρώτου ἀνδρὸς ἀρχή. In reality, Pericles could not simply impose his will on the assembly: he had to argue his case on each occasion and his oratorical ability enabled him to do so successfully. The claim is not in Cicero and V.'s immediate source cannot be determined. See also lines 37–42 n.

32. uersauit: 'swayed' ('turned' SB, which is less appropriate); cf. *OLD s.u.* 6b.

33. iucunda ... popularis: Cicero (*de orat.* 1.138) has *populare omnibus et iucundum uideretur*. *popularis* here has the sense of 'pleasing to the people'. Elsewhere V. uses the adjective at 4.1.13, in its political sense, and 4.3.5, where it means 'given to the people'.

34–37. itaque ... praedicabat: Cic. loc. cit. *cuius in labris ueteres comici, etiam cum illi male dicerent ... leporem habitasse dixerunt ... in eorum mentibus qui audissent quasi aculeos quosdam relinqueret*; the ellipses (*quod tum Athenis fieri licebat* and *tantamque in eodem uim fuisse ut*) contain words not taken over or paraphrased by V. See Wisse–Winterbottom–Fantham ad loc.; the notes that follow consist mainly of additions to their commentary.

34. perstringere: cf. 4 lines 12–13 n.

35. hominis: Shackleton Bailey, describing *hominis* as 'scarcely endurable after *uiri*', emended to *omni*: V. is contrasting *potentiam uiri* and *labris hominis*, the power of the politician and the lips of the human being; the expression is somewhat awkward, but it is what he wrote.

melle dulciorem: an addition to Cicero's *leporem*.

habitare: Wisse–Winterbottom–Fantham say that this is a striking metaphor, not previously attested. V., however, is fond of it (see 1. damn. 1, 4.3 praef., 5.5.2, 9.5. ext. 2; cf. p. 18). They rightly say that by using the present, rather than Cicero's perfect, infinitive, V. loses the sense of *lepor* always having been on Pericles' lips.

36. audierant: Cicero has the expected *audissent*, but V., as often in imperial Latin, retains the indicative of the *oratio recta* (cf. K–St ii. 544–5).

37–42. fertur quidam ... tyrannidem gessit: see lines 31–2 n. The anecdote does not appear elsewhere, though Plutarch (*Per.* 7.1) says that when he was young Pericles was regarded as being similar to Pisistratus in both appearance and voice. He was related to Pisistratus by marriage, not blood (see Stadter 64).

39. cauere illum: L^c (A^c no doubt intended the same, but wrote *cauerillum*). α evidently had the strange corruption of *cadauer* (G) or *cadauere* (L) for *cauere*. *cauere* is preserved in P (Paris converted V.'s *oratio obliqua* into direct speech).

ext. 3. *Hegesias.* Head of the Cyrenaic school, founded by Antipater. According to D.L. 2.86, Antipater was the pupil of Aristippus, who was a contemporary of Socrates, and Hegesias belonged to the third generation after Aristippus. It is thus uncertain whether the Ptolemy referred to in line 63 was I Soter (thus my index) or II Philadelphus (thus J. E. King, Loeb edn. of Cic. *Tusc.*, 98 n. 1).

V.'s source is Cic. *Tusc.* 1.83.

43. Cyrenaicum: as in Greek, *Cyrenaeus* is the ethnic of Cyrene, while *Cyrenaicus* normally refers to the philosophical school; cf. *TLL* onom. C 803.13 ff.

44–46. qui sic ... ingeneraret: D.L. loc. cit. calls Hegesias ὁ πεισιθάνατος, though it is unclear whether this was a nickname or just D.L.'s way of referring to the effect of his lectures. The word does not appear in L–S–J (or the Supplement).

repraesentabat ... ingeneraret: on *repraesentare* see 3 lines 17–18 n. *ingenerare* is used by Cicero and Catullus, by V. on six occasions.

10. praef. for pronunciation and correct body language as part of the *officia oratoris* cf. J. Martin, *Antike Rhetorik* (Munich, 1974), 11.

1. conuenienti: A^{c}G; AL have *conueniente*, to which I gave a *fort. recte*. It is impossible to say which represents the paradosis and it would not help much if it were: in the case of Livy, it seems unlikely that he admitted the ablative of a present participle in *-i*, even though it is transmitted at 6.14.13 (cf. vol. iv. 260, Oakley i. 527–8). If V. did write *conuenienti*, he may have been motivated by a desire to have a long vowel balancing *(apt)a*, and the corruption caused by perseveration from *pronuntiatione*.

3. eorum ... horum: the variation, both referring to *homines*, is surprising; V. could, and indeed should, have omitted *horum* and it is somewhat surprising that no one has ever suggested deletion.

3–4. inuadendo ... permulcendos tradendo: V. is not worried by the combination of two gerunds and a gerundive.

1. *Gaius Gracchus.* Although the subject of this *exemplum* is the method used by Gracchus to achieve the right balance in his delivery, V. does not refrain from hostile comments on Gracchus' policies (lines 5–7 *eloquentiae ... maluit*). V. mentions one or both of the Gracchi in twenty-two *exempla*, in nine of which (1.1.1, 7.6, 3.8.6, 6.7.1, 9.5. ext. 4, 7.1, 2, 12.6, 15.1) he does not make a value judgement on them. In the others he is unremittingly condemnatory: 1.4.2 (Paris) *ad res nouas moliendas*; 2.8.7 the murder of Tiberius was a *necessaria uictoria*; 3.2.17 *profusissimis largitionibus fauore populi occupato, rem publicam op-*

pressam teneret ... Gracchum cum scelerata factione quas merebatur poenas persoluere coegit; 4.7.1 *inimicus patriae fuisse Ti. Grachus existimatus est, nec immerito, quia potentiam suam saluti eius praetulerat*; 4.7.2 *C. Gracchi ... conspiratio ... furiosi conatus*; 5.3.2e *qui* (sc. Scipio Nasica) *pestifera Ti. Gracchi manu faucibus oppressam rem publicam strangulari passus non est*; 5.3.2f *C. Gracchi nefarios conatus*; 6.2.3 *Gracchana seditio*; 6.3.1d *statum ciuitatis conati erant conuellere ... rei publicae inimicis*; 6.8.3 *imminentia supplicia*; 7.2.6 *Ti. Gracchum tribunum plebis, agrariam legem promulgare ausum, morte multauit. ... grauissimae seditionis eodem tempore et auctorem et causam*; 9.4.3 *fuerit ille* (sc. C. Gracchus) *seditiosus, bono perierit exemplo*.

It does not seem to have occurred to V. that Caesar, whom he praises without stint (cf. 9.3 n.), had seen himself as an heir to the tradition of the Gracchi.

V.'s source is Cicero *de orat.* 3.225 (see Wisse–Winterbottom–Fantham ad loc.); Gaius' practice is mentioned also by Quint. *inst.* 1.10.27–8, Plut. *TG* 2.6, *mor.* 456A, Gell. 1.11.10–16, Dio fr. 85.2, Amm. 30.4.19.

5–6. propositi ... propositi: on the first occasion the word means 'theme', on the second 'policy'. Gertz thought that the first was a corruption, while Damsté emended the second to *consilii*, but for Latin writers' tolerance of such repetitions see 7 line 148 n.

5. inlustribus: 'well-known'; SB has 'illustrious', which does not fit with the negative judgement which follows. The adjective can mean 'infamous' (cf. *TLL* vii/1.395.65 ff.), but V., in accord with the subsequent contrast, intends it neutrally.

7–8. quotiens apud populum contionatus est: Cicero (loc. cit.) has *cum contionaretur*, P *quotiens contionaretur*. A *contio* was an informal meeting of the people and could also be used to mean a speech before such a meeting. *apud populum* is therefore pleonastic, but there is no reason to doubt that V. wrote it, just as he changed Cicero's *cum* to *quotiens*; it is probably chance that Paris reverted to *contionaretur*, though it is possible that he was acquainted with the passage of Cicero.

8. post se: A^{c}L^{c}G; AL have *posse*, P *prope se* (Cic. loc. cit. *post ipsum*); for *pos* instead of *post* see Adams, *Informal Latin*, 275–6.

9. eburnea: thus also Gellius (1.14.16) in his citation of Cicero; the latter's manuscripts have *eburne(-i)ola*, a hapax, P *eborea*. It cannot be determined whether the diminutive was normalized by V. and Gellius or in the course of transmission of their texts.

modos: 'rhythms'.

9–10. aut nimis remissos excitando: Gellius (1.11.14–15) thought that Cicero was wrong to say that the slave, as required, intensified the rhythm as well as toning it down, on the strange grounds that Gracchus' natural vehemence did not need such stimulation.

11. temperamenti: V. uses the noun also at 4.1.11 and 6.5. ext. 3; before him it occurs only at Cic. *leg.* 3.24.

2. *Hortensius.* Cf. 3 line 22 n. For Hortensius' use of gestures cf. Cic. *Brut.* 303, Quint. *inst.* 11.3.8–9, Gell. 1.5.2. V.'s source cannot be determined.

13. eodem laborando: thus α; P has *eo* and Pighius read *elaborando*, both of which were adopted by Kempf and Shackleton Bailey; I gave the latter a *fort. recte.*

eodem is a case of the attenuated use of *idem* in the sense of *is*: cf. 2.6.7, where P again has *eo*, 9.4.1, where P has *eius*, and 9.13. ext. 3, where Kempf read *eam*; see *TLL* vii/1.205.28 ff. It is most unlikely that *is* would have been corrupted to *idem* on three occasions.

The omission of *e-* would be an easy corruption, but for *laborare* ('work on') used transitively see *TLL* vii/2.808.23 ff.; with a pronoun it is found in Cicero (*fam.* 3.13.1), Seneca, and Pliny *nat.* (*TLL* art. cit. 28 ff.).

14–15. itaque ... concurreretur: cf. 1 line 31 n.

15. oratoris: Halm was clearly wrong to adopt *oratoriis*, found in some later MSS (cf. Torrenius) and first printed by Pighius (in any case, it may well be a corruption rather than a deliberate emendation): V. is talking about the words being spoken by Hortensius, not their being used in oratory.

16. Aesopum: M. Clodius Aesopus (16) was a tragic actor and close friend of Cicero, who mentions him frequently, always by *cognomen* alone; Münzer (*RE* iv. 67) thinks he never used his *gentilicium*, but this is not a necessary conclusion. His son, also Marcus, led a dissolute life: see 9.1.2. He doubtless took the *cognomen* from an Athenian actor of the name (cf. Schol. Aristoph. *Vesp.* 566). For Roscius see 7.7 n.

causas: α; P has *causam*. Both are possible, and the direct tradition should therefore be followed (cf. p. 23).

17. gestus: the entry in my apparatus may seem redundant, since it cites no variant to *gestus*. I included it only to indicate that *petitos ... quantum* was omitted by A and added (not, of course, from Paris) by Lupus in the margin. There is no *saut du même au même* which could explain the omission, which probably resulted from a scribe's skipping two lines in the exemplar. I said 'L^c' because the final letter was written by the corrector in an erasure. It would perhaps be better to print 'gestus ... quantum A^cL(-s L^c in ras.)G : om. A'.

scaenam referrent: α. Kempf suggested *scaena*, Stangl *deferrent*. The former, presumably, thought that V. meant that Aesopus and Roscius reproduced on the stage the gestures they had seen in the forum (cf. *OLD s.u.* 16), the latter, though realising that he meant that they transferred the gestures to the stage, thought that this sense could not be expressed by *referre*. I am, indeed, unaware of a precise parallel, but *referre* is often used with the force of the prefix attenuated, as in the common *referre ad senatum*; cf. Cic. *Pis.* 53 *domum ... rettulisti*: when Livy writes *domum referre* it is either of ambassadors 'reporting back' (3.6.6., 30.37.7, 45.24.11) or (5.20.8) booty); there it is Piso who is going home, but bringing nothing but his face. In our passage Aesopus and Roscius return to the stage, where they belong, with the gestures they have seen in the forum (similarly, in English we say 'bring back home'). Certainly, given the number of linguistic innovations in V. (cf. pp. 10–12), there is no reason to doubt the transmitted reading.

3. *Cicero.* V.'s source is Cic. *Brut.* 277–8, who quotes more of his speech, including *non frons percussa, non femur*; Quint. *inst.* 11.3.123 cites the latter, while at 11.3.155 he paraphrases the sentence quoted by V. with *an ista ... si uera essent, sic a te dicerentur*, together with *tantum abest ut inflammares nostros animos: somnum isto loco uix tenebamus*, for which it is the only source. For other fragments see F. Schoell, *M. Tulli Ciceronis orationum deperditarum fragmenta* (Leipzig, 1917), 399–401. (The speech is strangely omitted by J. W. Crawford, *M. Tullius Cicero: The Lost and Unpublished Orations* (Göttingen, 1984).)

Q. Gallius (6) was plebeian aedile in 67 (*MRR* ii. 144, wrongly citing Quint. *inst.* 11.3.165) and praetor in 65, when he presided at the trial of C. Cornelius (Ascon. p. 62C). It is clear that he was accused of *ambitus* during his campaign for the praetorship. The date of his trial, however, has been disputed, because of an apparent conflict between Asconius p. 88C, who appears to say that the trial rook place after Cicero delivered the *in toga candida* in 64 and *comm. pet.* 19, which can be taken as indicating a date in 66 (*hoc biennio*, but 65 it excluded since Gallius was then in office and immune from prosecution); the matter has formed part of arguments about the authorship of the *commentariolum petitionis*, ostensibly written by Q. Cicero. This is not the place for a detailed discussion of the issues (let alone the *comm. pet.*) and I therefore merely state my belief that Balsdon (*CQ* n.s. 13 (1963), 248–9) and Ramsey (*Historia* 29 (1980), 402–21) were right to think that *comm. pet.* 19 refers to Gallius, aware that a prosecution was likely, engaging Cicero as counsel in 66, but that the trial did not take place until after the consular elections in 64. See also Vonder Mühll, *RE* vii. 672, M. I. Henderson, *JRS* 40 (1950), 11; Marshall's note (300–1) is confusing.

Gallius was clearly acquitted: otherwise Cicero would not have boasted about his speech.

18. nam: for asseverative *nam* (very frequent in V.; cf. Otón Sobrino iii. 1305–7) at the beginning of an *exemplum* cf. 14 line 51.

19. Gallio: P (and Lupus in A); the direct tradition has *Gallo*, an easy corruption.

M. Calidio: (4). Calidius was praetor in 57, when he supported Cicero's restoration; he defended M. Scaurus in 54 and Milo in 52 (Ascon. pp. 20, 34C). He stood unsuccessfully for the consulship in both 51 and 50 (Cic. *Att.* 5.19.3, *fam.* 8.4.1, 9.5). At the meeting of the senate on the first day of 49 he supported Caesar (Caes. *ciu.* 1.2.3), who subsequently put him in charge of Cisalpine Gaul, where he died (Hieron. *chron. s. a.* 57, but saying *bello postea ciuili*).

Cicero's self-quotation in the *Brutus* served to illustrate his point that Calidius, whom he describes (278) as *summus orator*, failed, perhaps deliberately, to stir the emotions of his audience.

For other Calidii mentioned by V. cf. 1 line 90 n.

20–21. testibus … orationis: V. employs an *asyndeton trimembre*, consisting of single words (cf. 7 line 69 n.), immediately followed by three connected phrases governed by *usus*, the first two consisting of adjective + ablative noun, the third of adjective + ablative noun + genitive noun; the asyndeton is crescendo (– ᴗ –, – ᴗ ᴗ –, – ᴗ – ᴗ –), while the first two phrases are of almost equivalent length (ᴗ – – – –, – ᴗ – – ᴗ), the third twice as long as the second (ᴗ – – ᴗ ᴗ – – ᴗ – ᴗ). Cicero (*Brut.* 277) has an asyndeton of no fewer than five members (*chirographa testificationes indicia quaestiones manifestam rem*), while V.'s connected phrases correspond to Cicero's *asyndeton trimembre* (*tam solute egisset tam leniter tam oscitanter*) at the conclusion of his long period.

22. uitium … argumentum: cf. Cic. (278) *uel sanitate uel uitio pro argumento ad diluendum crimen usi sumus*: V. has no doubt that it is a fault.

oratoris … periclitantis: the word order is chiastic. Perizonius' *periclitanti* ignores this; moreover, the personification of *causa*, while not impossible (cf. *TLL* x/1.1449.12 ff.), is not something which should be introduced by conjecture.

23. claudendo: by omitting the rest of the passage quoted by Cicero V. is able to convert its beginning into the punchline.

tu: A (α in my apparatus is an error), confirmed by Cicero loc. cit.: the emphatic pronoun lends weight to Cicero's conclusion, while *tum* (LG, therefore the paradosis) is pointless.

istud: α (*his iŭd* P, corrected by Heiric); Cicero has *istuc*. On the use of *istic*, particularly the neuter singular *istuc*, rather than *iste* and *istud*, see Adams, *Social Variation*, 456–8 (cf. *Informal Latin*, 43): Plautus and Terence appear never to have written *istud*, and *istuc* is the only form attested in Lucilius; the elder Cato, however, has both forms. In the late Republic *istuc* is the only form used in Varro *rust.*, while both occur in *rhet. Her.* and *bell. Afr.* Nepos has only *istud*,

Livy six examples of each. Nepos, the elder Seneca, and V., however, have only *istud*. It thus appears that *istuc* went out of use in the early principate and there is no reason to think that V. did not consciously alter what he found in Cicero (not that *istuc* has ever been proposed in our passage).

23–24. fingeres ... ageres: thus Cicero and P (and Lupus). α has *fingere ... agere*. It is surprising that the corruption was not corrected in either L or G (there is no reason to think that it was connected with that of *tu* to *tum* (see above)).

ext. 1. *Demosthenes.* V.'s source is evidently Cicero *de orat.* 3.213; of the other passages listed in my *testimonia* apparatus, Cic. *orat.* 56 refers only to Demosthenes' statement (without indicating that it was in reply to a question), Plin. *nat.* 7.110, Quint. *inst.* 11.3.6, and ps. (as I should have added) Plut. *mor.* 840D–E, as well as Plin. *epist.* 2.3.10 (cf. 4.5.1), Philostratus *VS* 510, Hier. *epist.* 53.2, only to Aeschines' remark (the younger Pliny cites it in Greek, probably his own, not from a Greek source, as Wisse–Winterbottom–Fantham think; cf. C. Whitton, *Pliny the younger, Epistles book ii* (Cambridge, 2013), 101 and see below).

V., however, varies Cicero's account in two ways. Firstly, Cicero clearly means that when Demosthenes was asked what he regarded as the three most important things in oratory, he replied 'delivery, delivery, delivery' (similarly, Tony Blair, before the British General Election of 1997, said that the three top priorities of a Labour Government would be 'Education, Education, Education'), but V. implies that he was asked the same question three times (see on *interpellatus* below). Secondly, he translates Cicero's *actio* into Greek (see on ἡ ὑπόκρισις below), as with Pliny, no doubt his own (see above and p. 9 n. 33).

25. consentaneum: cf. 1 line 18 n.

cuidam: G. AL have *quidam*, which would, absurdly, mean that the reply was not given by Demosthenes. CDEF have *qui*, which unsurprisingly became the vulgate. It is possible that *cuidam* is a conjecture, not a transmitted reading, and I therefore gave *qui* a *fort. recte* (Foertsch's *qui quidem* (not mentioned in my apparatus) is palaeographically plausible, a scribe's eye moving from *qui* to *qui-*, but *qui quidem ... quidnam* is not something to be attributed to V. by conjecture): *quidam* could have resulted from the following *quidnam*; *cuidam* (adopted by Shackleton Bailey), however, provides a simpler explanation of the corruption, whether it stood in α or only in the source of AL.

26. respondit ἡ ὑπόκρισις: α has *respondit* Η (A; IT LG) ΥΠΟΚΡΙC); P has *hypocrisim rei spondit* (corrected to *respondit*) and Lupus, who had first added IC to ΥΠΟΚΡΙC, wrote Η ΥΠΟΚΡΙCΙΜ in the margin of A (he evidently had a limited knowledge of Greek). There is no doubt that the word order of the direct tradition is correct, the verbs standing at the beginning of both the subordinate and main clauses.

SB wrongly translates ἡ ὑπόκρισις 'the acting', no doubt influenced by Cicero's *actio*: both are the standard words for an orator's delivery (cf. L-S-J *s.u.* II. 1, *TLL* i. 440.18 ff.).

I ought to have put ἡ ὑπόκρισις in inverted commas.

28. Aeschines: this is the only time V. mentions Demosthenes' greatest opponent, who lived from *c.* 397 to *c.* 322; for a convenient summary of his career see G. L. Cawkwell, *OCD*[4] 24–5. The best edition of his three extant speeches (*Against Timarchus, On the Embassy, Against Ctesiphon*) is the Teubner of F. Blass, revised by U. Schindel (Stuttgart, 1978); there is a recent translation by C. Carey (Austin, TX, 2000).

28–30. cum propter ... orationem: in 336 Ctesiphon proposed in the *boule* that Demosthenes be honoured with a crown at the Dionysia for his services to Athens. Aeschines threatened him with prosecution for an illegal proposal, but did not bring the prosecution until six years later, when he failed to secure 20 % of the votes of the jury and thus incurred a fine of 1,000 drachmai and lost the right to bring a similar prosecution in future (cf. M. H. Hansen, Apagoge, Endeixis *and* Ephegesis *against* Kakourgoi, Atimoi *and* Pheugontes (Odense, 1976), 64–6, S. C. Todd, *The Shape of Athenian Law* (Oxford, 1993), 143; A. R. W. Harrison, *The Law of Athens* ii (revised by D. M. MacDowell; Oxford, 1971), 83, argues that in these circumstances the prosecutor became ἄτιμος only until he had paid the fine). He left Athens and spent the rest of his life in Rhodes, where he taught rhetoric. (cf. Plut. *Dem.* 24.2, ps. Plut. *mor.* 840C).

29. rogatu ciuitatis: Cicero has *rogatus a Rhodiis*, by which, presumably, he meant that the request was made by a number of Rhodian citizens; V. converts this into an official request by the Rhodian assembly.

Ctesiphontem: Kempf implies that E and F have the name correctly. *Ct*- was corrupted to *Th*- at an early stage of transmission (thus both Paris and the direct tradition), with further corruption to *Thesispontem* in A and *Thespontem* in L.

Ctesiphon is known only from this episode.

29–30. Demosthenis ... orationem: Demosthenes' speech *On the Crown* (περὶ τοῦ στεφάνου; Dem. 18).

29. deinde: Cicero says that it was on the following day.

34. praedicaret: a correction in G; α has *praediceret. praedicare* 'declare' and *praedicere* 'predict' are often confused in manuscripts (cf. *TLL* x/2.551.62ff.); at Livy 35.39.7 the lost Mainz manuscript read the correct *praediceret*, while the extant manuscripts have *praedicaret*.

34–36. acerrimum ... motus: fourfold phrasal asyndeton (not crescendo); all begin with an adjective or participle, the first and last superlatives (and *ter*-

ribilis is itself superlative in sense, no superlative form being attested) and end with noun phrases, alternating between accusative + genitive and the reverse. There is nothing corresponding in Cicero.

37. quod ... auditur: it is hard to imagine a more absurd conjecture than Damsté's deletion of the clause: V. would never leave his readers to work out the meaning of a paradoxical expression.

The present tenses indicate that V. is talking about Roman readers of Demosthenes, not (or not only) Aeschines' recital of the speech.

11 tit. QVAM ... SINT: α. P has *de effectu artium*, clearly a simplification. The preceding two headings (chs. 9 and 10), like that of ch. 1, also take the form of an indirect question with ellipse of the main verb. Of the remaining chapters, 2, 4, 5, 7, 8, 13, and 14 have *de* + ablative, 3, 6, and 15 *quae* + indicative, the second heading in this chapter (preceding ext. 5; see n. ad loc,) and ch. 12 accusative + infinitive.

1. etiam: to be taken with the sentence as a whole, not just with *effectus* or *effectus artium*.

†**recognosci ... adferret**†: the obelized passage contains three infinitives, with no obvious syntactical conection between them.

I listed no fewer than fourteen (if one includes the readings of A^c and G) attempts to heal the corruption. Shackleton Bailey, mentioning none of the others, adopted that of Perizonius, who substituted *potest* for *posse*, translating 'recognition of the effects of the arts can bring pleasure, ...', i.e. he takes *effectus etiam artium recognosci* as the subject of *potest*. I suspect, however that Perizonius intended both *potest* and *recognosci* to be taken impersonally, with *effectus artium* as the subject of *adferre* ('it is possible for it to be recognized that the effects of arts also bring pleasure'). However that may be, it is hard to believe that V. would have expressed either meaning so obscurely: in the first case he could have placed *potest* after *uoluptatis*, in the second *recognosci potest* before *effectus*.

I can do no more than explicate and comment on the other conjectures listed. Halm read *recognoscendi possunt*, a strange use of the gerundive (presumably that is what Kempf meant by '*soloece Halm*'); Kellerbauer is reported by Halm as altering one letter of the latter's conjecture to produce *recognoscenti*, the dative going with *adferre* and *eos* having to be understood as its object. Wensky changed *posse* to *per se* and *adferre* to *adferet*: as in Shackleton Bailey's interpretation of Perizonius' proposal, *effectus ... recognosci* is the subject of the indicative, while *per se* contrasts with *utiliter*: the word order is acceptable, but it is hard to see why *per se* should have been corrupted to *posse*; Kempf (*NJPhP* 133

(1886), 61) varied Wensky's conjecture with *recognosse* for *recognosci posse* (he adduced *cognosse* at 6.3. ext. 1), again positing an implausible corruption; he also suggested *adferat* as an alternative to *adferet*, which would destroy the parallel to the following three futures. In the same volume of *NJPhP* (797-8) Böhme combined the proposals of Perizonius and Kempf with *recognosse potest*, which produces a more acceptable word order, but again fails to explain the corruption (I inconsistently enclosed the last letter of *potest* in angled brackets, not having done so for Perizonius (or, with *possunt*, for Halm and Kellerbauer). That charge cannot be levelled against the proposals of Gertz (*recognoscere scio posse*) and Heraeus (*recognosse scio*), a scribe's eye having moved, respectively, from the first *sc* to the second and the first *s* to the third: V., however, uses the first person singular sparingly and one hesitates to ascribe it to him by conjecture. Thormeyer's *recognosse possit* is no improvement on Böhme, while Novák, typically more radical, suggested that *oportet quia uidetur* had been omitted between *recognosci* and *posse*. Damsté, again absurdly (cf. 10 line 37 n.), thought that *recognosci posse* belonged to the chapter heading, creating a unique combination of an infinitive with an indirect question (cf. tit. n.). I myself wondered about *recognoscere posse ... adfert*: a scribe would have moved from the first *e* to the next, with subsequent alteration of the remaining *recognosce* to *recognosci*, while *adferre* would have resulted from perseveration from the preceding infinitives.

2. excogitatae: V. uses *excogitare* on thirteen occasions; before him it is found in a comic fragment, *rhet. Her.*, Cicero, who was fond of it, Caesar (twice, though the authenticity of *Gall.* 5.31.5 has been challenged), and Livy (three times). It occurs twice in Tacitus, on both occasions in the *dialogus*.

patebit: G; AL have *patebunt*, resulting from the preceding *excogitatae* and/or the following *reponentur*.

1. *C. Sulpicius Galus and the eclipse of the moon in 168 BC.* For full discussion of this episode see my note on Livy 44.37.5-9. The cross-reference in my *testimonia* apparatus to that on Livy 44.36-42 was not helpful, since the latter includes more than the sources for the eclipse.

V. here follows the version, first found at Cicero *rep.* 1.23 (and subsequently Quint. *inst.* 1.10.47; it is unclear whether it stood in Polybius), in which Galus explains the eclipse the following day. In Livy (loc. cit.; also Pliny *nat.* 2.53, Front. *strat.* 1.12.8) he predicts it. V.'s immediate source is unclear (it was clearly not Cicero).

4. Sulpici Gali: cf. 1 line 13 n. Here P has the correct form of the *cognomen*, altered by Heiric to *Galli*, the reading of the direct tradition (*Sulpici ... omni*, presumably a line in its exemplar, was initially omitted by G but added subsequently; cf. p. 20); in line 10 *Gali* in L is a correction of an original *Gall*, while a corrector of A, together with G, has *Galli*.

4. in omni ... studium: for Galus' learning cf. Cic. *Mur.* 66, *rep.* 1.21–2, *Brut.* 78, *Cato* 49, *off.* 1.19, Plin. *nat.* 2.53, 83, Suet. *uit. Ter.* 4.

recipiendo: 'absorbing' (SB). Gertz quite unnecessarily proposed *percipiendo*, persuading Kempf.

5–6. L. Paulli ... gerentis: L. Aemilius Paullus (114), consul in 182 and 168 (for a full summary of his career see my note on Livy 38.44.11), who brought the Third Macedonian War to an end with the victory at Pydna referred to in lines 14–17. V. has mentioned him on thirteen previous occasions (1.3.4, 5.3, 8.1, 2.7.13, 10.3, 4.3.8, 4.9, 5.1.1d, 8, 10.2, 6.2.3, 7.5.1, 3).

5. Persen: Perseus, the last king of Macedon. He succeeded his father, Philip V, in 179. After his defeat at Pydna he fled to Samothrace, where he surrendered. He was led in Paullus' triumph and imprisoned at Alba Fucens, where he died. See my commentary on Livy books 41–45 *passim*. V. has mentioned him on ten previous occasions (1.5.3, 8.1, 2.2.1, 7.14, 4.3.8, 4.9, 5.1.1c, e, 8, 6.2.3).

Perseus' name appears in manuscripts in a variety of forms; see Neue–Wagener, i. 517–19 (446 for the vocative, always *Perseu*). In V. the evidence is as follows (at 2.2.1 and 5.1.1c the name is ablative in the direct tradition, nominative in Paris; at 6.2.3 the passage is omitted by Paris). The first reading on each occasion is that printed in my edition.

1.5.3 *Perse* GP : *Persae* L : *Persa* AG^c
1.8.1 line 14 *Persen* PN. : *Persam* α
2.2.1 line 112 *Perse* αP
    line 115 *Persen* α : *Perses* P
2.7.14 *Perse* αP
4.3.8 *Perseo* α : *Perse* P
4.4.9 *Perse* αP
5.1.1c *Perse* α : *Perses* P
5.1.1e *Perse* αP
5.1.8 *Persen* GP : *Persem* AL
6.2.3 *Persei* α
8.11.1 *Persen* αP

It thus appears that V. regularly has *Perses* nominative, *Persen* accusative, and *Perse* ablative (6.2.3 is the only instance of the genitive). At 4.3.8 I gave *Perse* a *fort. recte* and probably ought to have printed it.

6. serena: α. P has *sera*, probably an error of transmission (thus Halm), not of Paris himself.

luna defecisset: the eclipse occurred on the night of 21 June 168 (Jul.), *a.d. iii non. Sept.* in the Roman calendar (Livy 44.37.8; the synchronism provides the basis for our knowledge of the Roman calendar at this time; cf. vol. iv. 585); the battle of Pydna took place on the following day.

7. perterritus exercitus noster: thus also Cic. *rep.* 1.23; in Polybius (29.16, from the Suda) both Romans and Macedonians saw the eclipse as foretelling that of Perseus, encouraging the former, dispiriting the latter.

V. uses *perterritus* also at 1.7.7, 8.8; for the distribution of *terrere* and *perterrere* (in republican authors, as in V., the latter overwhelmingly in the past participle) see the table at *TLL* x/1.1782. Here P has the simplex, A *perritus*, L *peritus*: a scribe's eye moved from the first *r* to the second (L restored Latin, but not sense).

8–9. amisisset … misit: in the former AL have *misisset*, in the latter P *dimisit* (Galus sent the army into battle confident: he did not, and did not have the authority to, dismiss them).

9. inclutae: cf. 2 lines 6–7 n.

Paullianae: for other adjectives in *-anus* derived from a *cognomen* cf. *Caesarianus* 1.1.19, 3.2.13, 9.15.5, *Cinnanus* 9.2, 4.7.5, 5.3.3, *Crassianus* 3.4.5, *Flaccianus* 6.3.1c, *Gracchanus* 1.1.1, 6.2.3 (also Paris 5.3.2f), *Sullanus* 6.4.4, 8.2, 7.3.6, 9.15.5. Such adjectives are more commonly derived from the *gentilicium*, notably to indicate the original *gens* in the case of adoption (e.g. P. Cornelius Scipio Aemilianus). *Paullianus* of the Aemilii Paulli is otherwise unattested (though Justinian, *dig.* preface (P. Krueger –T. Mommsen, *Corpus iuris ciuilis* (21st edn., Berlin, 1970), i. 10 = i p. li in Mommsen–Krueger–W. A. J. Watson, *The Digest of Justinian* (Philadelphia, PA, 1985) has *Pauliana responsa* of the jurist Paulus), but it was open to anyone to use the formation.

10. aditum dederunt: 'opened the door to'.

2. *Spurinna*. This *exemplum* is discussed, for different purposes, in two articles by John Ramsey. In *CQ* n.s. 50 (2000), 440–54 he argues, convincingly, that Spurinna's prediction was based on the normal methods of a *haruspex*, and not on astrology, as claimed by F. Cramer, *Astrology in Roman Law and Politics* (Philadelphia, PA, 1954), 77 and M. Molnar, *The Celator* 8.11 (1994), 6–9 (Ramsey and A. L. Licht, *The Comet of 44 BC and Caesar's Funeral Games* (Atlanta, GA, 1997), 138 n. 12) appear to take a more favourable view of Molnar's view); he then seeks to establish the content and date of Spurinna's prophecy. In the second article (in S. Heilen *et al.* (eds.) *In Pursuit of* Wissenschaft (Zurich–New York, 2008), 351–63), he argues that the meeting of Caesar and Spurinna *mane* shows that the senate did not meet at dawn on the Ides of March, as is generally believed (for his earlier view see lines 14–15 n.) and that Mommsen (*StR* iii. 2.920) was wrong to claim that sunrise was the normal time for senate meetings (this is not the place for discussion of the latter argument). Hereafter I cite Ramsey's articles by page number only.

The episode is mentioned also by Plut. *Caes.* 63.1–2, Suet. *Iul.* 81.2, App. *b.c.* 2.149.619 (cf. 153.641), Dio 44.18.4 (Appian and Dio are not mentioned in my *testimonia* apparatus; apart from V. only Suetonius names Spurinna); see lines 20–1 n.

12. Spurinnae: for the limited evidence about Spurinna (no other name is attested) see Ramsey 440 n. 1.

coniectandis: 'divining' (SB). AL have *consectatis*, a corrector of L and G *consectandis*. Halm realised the truth, though V. does not use the verb elsewhere and Suet. *Nero* 6 is the only other instance in classical Latin where it refers to prediction of the future (*TLL* iv. 313.43 ff.). Before V. it occurs in Terence, Livy, Caesar, and Varro.

13–14. praedixerat ... Martiae: V., like all the other sources (see above) makes it clear that the risk to Caesar's life was to last until the end of the Ides of March: Spurinna was not predicting the precise date of his death, as implied by Molnar (see above), and Ramsey (441, 444–5) uses this as a powerful argument against Molnar's position.

proximos triginta dies: Ramsey (445, with n. 23) argues that Spurinna must have given the warning on either 14 or 15 February, depending on whether 44 was a leap year in Caesar's reformed calendar: 13 February, however, is also possible, if the thirty days did not include the day on which Spurinna made the prophecy (and it was not a leap year). As Ramsey proceeds to observe (445–6), Suetonius (loc. cit.) says that Spurinna gave the warning when Caesar was sacrificing and this could have been the occasion, recorded by Cicero *diu.* 1.11, V. 1.6.13, and Suetonius *Iul.* 77, when a sacrificed ox was found to lack a heart, leading Spurinna to say that Caesar should fear for his life. Moreover, Cicero says that the episode occurred on the first occasion on which Caesar sat on a golden chair and wore a purple robe, objects, according to Cicero *Phil.* 2.85, displayed at the *Lupercalia*, a festival celebrated on 15 February. Nevertheless, Ramsey thinks it unlikely that the sacrifice was the occasion for the prophecy, since both V. and Suetonius recount the sacrifice and the prophecy in different places (as far as V. is concerned that is scarcely significant, since he is using the two episodes for different purposes) and Appian (*b.c.* 2.116.488) places the sacrifice on the Ides of March itself and says that it had occurred previously in Spain (Ramsey thinks Suetonius may have been referring to the latter; he thinks it possible (452) either that V.'s formulation represents the amalgamation of two prophecies by Spurinna, one referring only to thirty days, a second specifically to the Ides of March, or that 'because the thirty-day period mentioned in the earlier prophecy by coincidence happened to end on, or close to, the Ides of March, Valerius Maximus, or his source (Livy?), has credited Spurinna with greater foresight than he may deserve').

14–15. eo ... conuenissent: in his first article (452–3) Ramsey thought that this is a mistake by V., since other sources (Nic. Dam. *uit. Caes.* 23.83–4, Suet. *Iul.* 81.4, Plut. *Caes.* 63.8–64.6, App. *b.c.* 2.115.480, Dio 44.17.3) indicate that because of illness, a dream of Calpurnia, and unfavourable sacrificial omens Caesar was initially unwilling to leave his house, eventually going to the senate at the fifth hour (thus Suet. loc. cit.). The senate, Ramsey thought (453) 'had assembled at dawn'. For his later view see introductory note (p. 179).

14. eo: α. P has *eo die* (*quo die* in Landolfus Sagax (cf. p. 22) is not significant, since *dies* does not precede). It is much more likely that *die* was added by Paris, who thought that *eo* alone was obscure following *idus Martias*, than that it was omitted in the direct tradition.

15. Caluini Domiti: Cn. Domitus Calvinus (43) was tribune in 59, when he opposed the triumvirs, praetor in 56, and consul in 53. Now a supporter of Caesar, he was appointed by the latter as *magister equitum* for 43 (the assassination of the dictator, of course, meant that he could not take up the office). He held a second consulship in 40 and was proconsul in Spain from 39 to 36.

α has *Caluini Domiti(i)*, P (and Lupus) *Domiti(i) Caluini*. For the inversion of *nomen* and *cognomen* cf. 7 line 28 n. It is virtually certain that the direct tradition preserves what V. wrote, altered to the normal order by Paris.

ad officium: Ramsey (453) initially took this to refer to the morning *salutatio* ('came to call' SB). He cited, e.g., *TLL* ix/2.519.81, but mentioned that Münzer (*RE* v. 1422) thought that the meeting was occasioned by a sacrifice, perhaps attended by Caesar as *pontifex maximus* and Domitius as a member of the pontifical college (cf. *MRR* ii. 314). Subsequently (353–5) Ramsey adopted Münzer's view (though he cites instead E. Becht, *Regeste über die Zeit von Cäsars Ermordung bis zum Umschwung in der Politik des Antonius* (Freiburg, 1911), 7 n. 2). His first thoughts were preferable: *TLL* cite our passage together with a number of others where *officium* refers to a greeting, including V. 1.7 ext. 6 (again with *ad*) and 5.5.3, while though *officium* occurs in religious contexts (*TLL* ix/2.521.20 ff.), that context is always made clear.

conuenissent: α; P has the singular (adopted by Kempf; SB retains the plural). For *uterque* with a plural verb cf. K–St ii. 22–4. It is far more likely that Paris altered the plural to the singular than that the singular was corrupted in the direct tradition.

16–17. ecquid ... praeterisse: the exchange is best known from Shakespeare's 'The Ides of March are come': 'Ay, Caesar, but not gone'.

16. ecquid: P^c, correcting *et quid*, also the reading of α. *ecquis* was very often written as *etquis* in early manuscripts (cf. *TLL* v/2.37.52 ff.).

scis (idus): α. P has *scis inquit*. Ellipse of a verb of saying is common (cf. K–St ii. 551, vol. ii. 12) and *inquit* is manifestly an addition by Paris (or, conceivably, in transmission). Damsté misguidedly inverted P's word order to put *inquit* in its regular second position.

et: α. P has *at*. Choice is difficult (both Kempf and Shackleton Bailey printed *at*) and one could argue that corruption from the adversative is more likely than the reverse. I preferred, on balance, to follow the direct tradition but gave *at* a *fort. recte*.

17. tamquam: Damsté proposed adding *iam*, plausible enough palaeographically (a scribe's eye moving from one *-am* to another), but totally unnecessary.

ne: *nae* L (and no doubt A before correction); the misspelling is found also in the Vienna MS at Livy 44.22.14 (for asseverative *ne* cf. *Liviana*, 218 n. 4).

19. patriae parentem: the title *parens* (or *pater*) *patriae* was first conferred on Cicero in 63 (though he himself had earlier applied the term to Marius; *Rab. Perd.* 27) and subsequently on Augustus in 2 BC (though it is attested unofficially earlier); cf. Nisbet–Hubbard on Horace *carm*. 1.2.50, S. Weinstock, *Divus Julius* (Oxford, 1970), 200–5).

securitas: Caesar's feeling of security. V. uses the word in this sense also at 1. absol. 13, 6.4.5, 7.1.2, 9.12. ext. 1; before him it occurs only in Cicero. In the sense of 'being safe' (i.e. the English 'security') it is first used by Velleius (2.103.4; in the former sense at 2.89.4); cf. *OLD s.u.*

ext. 1. *Anaxagoras*. On Anaxagoras see 7. ext. 6 n. V.'s source is Cicero *rep.* 1.25 (omitted in my *testimonia* apparatus, thus misleading Shackleton Bailey), from which, no doubt, Quint. *inst.* 1.10.47 also derives. In all these passages Pericles appears to be calming the fears of Athenians in the city; Plutarch (*Per.* 35.2), however, says that it occurred when he had embarked on a trireme (*sc.* in the Piraeus) at the launching of a naval expedition and persuaded the terrified helmsman by putting his cloak over the latter's eyes and asking him if he was frightened by that. The eclipse itself is mentioned by Thuc. 2.28.

20. alienigena: V. uses *alienigenus* on ten occasions; before him it occurs only in Lucretius (five times). The noun *alienigena* is found before V. in Cicero, Varro, Nepos, and no fewer than fifteen times in Livy (cf. my note on 39.3.6). Here the transmitted reading, corrected in L, is *alienigenas*, the result of either dittography of the following *s-* or confusion with the noun.

obscurato ... sole: this partial eclipse of the sun occurred on 3 August 431 (Shackleton Bailey wrongly says 430). See Hornblower on Thuc., loc. cit.

20–21. inusitatis ... angerentur: a city is naturally said to be enveloped (thus SB) in darkness, but *angerentur* introduces a striking personification, though one made easier by the plural form of the name.

solitudine (AL) and *agerentur* (α) (the correct *sollicitudine* and *angerentur* are in A^cG and P respectively) are two easy corruptions which produce Latin but not sense.

22–23. praeceptore suo Anaxagora: cf. 9 line 30 nn.

ext. 2. *Apelles and Lysippus*. For the extensive sources see Ziegler's *testimonia* apparatus on Plut. *Alex*. 4.1–3; cf. Brink's note on Horace, *epist*. 2.1.239. Horace says that Alexander forbad anyone except Lysippus and Apelles to, respectively, cast a statue or paint a portrait of him (thus also Plin. *nat*. 7.125). The Greek sources talk only of Alexander's wishes in the matter (Plut. *Alex*. 4.3, perhaps inadvertently, mentions this only for Lysippus), while of the Latin writers Cicero (*fam*. 5.12.7) says that he particularly (*potissimum*) wanted to be painted by Apelles and sculpted by Lysippus; V. has *tantummodo* rather than *potissimum*, but otherwise uses the same vocabulary as Cicero (which suggests that the latter was V.'s source; the letters *ad familiares* were probably published during the reign of Augustus (cf. Shackleton Bailey, *Cicero: epistulae ad familiares* (Cambridge, 1977), i. 23–4)).

Alexander is mentioned by V. in twenty-one *exempla* (see the index to my edition, pp. 853–4); his portrayal is dicussed in three recent articles: K. Haegemans and K. Stoppie in G. Partoens, G. Roskam, and T. Van Houdt (eds.), *Virtutis imago: Studies on the Conceptualisation and Transformation of an Ancient Ideal* (Leuven, 2004), 145–172, D. Wardle, *AClass* 48 (2005), 141–61, D. Spencer in E. Carney and D. Ogden (eds.), *Philip II and Alexander the Great: Father and Son, Lives and Afterlives* (New York, 2010), 175–191.

26. Apelle: originally of Colophon, Apelles later lived in Ephesus. The most famous painter of antiquity, he is particularly known for his picture of 'Aphrodite rising from the sea', originally painted for the temple of Asclepius on Cos (hence Apelles himself is sometimes described as Coan), but transferred to Rome by Augustus and placed in the temple of *Diuus Iulius* (Plin. *nat*. 35.91, Strabo 14, p. 657C; it was imitated by Botticelli and a number of subsequent artists). See Rossbach, *RE* i. 2689–92 and, with recent bibliography, Hoesch, *NP* i. 829. Cf. lines 32–3, 12 ext. 3 nn.

Lysippo: of Sicyon. Both Lysippus and his less distinguished brother, Lysistratus, worked only in bronze. See Lippold, *RE* xiv. 48–64, Stewart 289–94 and other passages cited in the index (374).

ext. 3. *Alcamenes*. A pupil of Phidias, he was active in the second half of the fifth century; The Suda (*s.n.*) calls him a Lemnian, probably because he came from the Athenian cleruchy established there *c*. 450 (cf. R. Meiggs, *The Athenian*

Empire (Oxford, 1972), 424–5). The statue of Hephaestus is mentioned also by Cic. *nat. deor.* 1.83 and Paus. 1.14.6; the latter says that it stood in the Hephaesteum, next to a statue of Athena. Fragments of the accounts for the statues are preserved in *IG* i³. 472, showing that they were of bronze and that work on them lasted from 421/0 until at least 416/5. See Robert, *RE* i. 1507–8, Malten, *RE* viii. 364, C. Walston, *Alcamenes and the Establishment of the Classical Type in Greek Art* (Cambridge, 1926; pp. 179–81 for the statue of Hephaestus), Pease on Cic., loc. cit., E. B. Harrison, *AJA* 81 (1977), 137–78, 265–87, 411–26, F. Brommer, *Hephaistos* (Mainz, 1978), Stewart 267–9 and other passages cited in the Index (369).

V.'s language reflects that of Cicero (both have *claudicatio* and *leuiter*, Cicero *uestito*, V. *sub ueste*), but V. elaborates Cicero's *non deformis* and *tenet uisentes Athenis* goes well beyond Cicero's *laudamus*. It may be that V., having read Cicero, went to see the statue for himself while in Athens (perhaps en route to Asia with Sex. Pompeius; cf. p. 1).

The *exemplum* is omitted by Paris.

27. Volcanus: the god of fire, syncretized with Hephaestus.

Alcamenis: *Alchiminis* α. Kempf (1854) inplies that F gives the name correctly.; it is somewhat surprising that it was able to do so.

28. perfectissimae: cf. 7 line 4 n.

†praecurrentia†: it makes no sense to say that the *indicia* of Alcamenes' skill 'ran in front', but the transmitted reading went unchallenged until Gertz proposed *occurrentia* or *procurrentia*. The latter was printed by both Kempf and Shackleton Bailey, who translated it as 'outstanding', but there is no parallel for such a meaning. *TLL* x/2.1598.66 ff., cite our passage under the rubric '*apparentes, occurrentes*', together with 6.3 praef. *in medium procurrent*, which is quite different. *occurrenetia*, however, is possible: the corruption could have been caused by haplography of (*e*)*o*, *prae-* being subsequently inserted.

mirantur: later MSS (Kempf (1854) implies CDEF); α has the singular, probably resulting from a scribe's misapprehension that *illud* is nominative.

29–30. stat ... repraesentans: *stans ... repraesentat* A^c. The idea arose from Cicero's *stante*: a manuscript of eight of his philosophical works (Vienna, Österreichische Nationalbibliothek 189 = V) was corrected by Lupus; cf. Rouse in *Texts and Transmission*, 126.

30–31. ut non exprobratum ... significans: *significans* governs both parts of the comparison; Lupus altered *exprobratum* to *exprobrans* (*exprobans* in my apparatus is an error); he subsequently added transposition marks to *exprobrans tamquam*), Kempf *significans* to *significatam*. V. is fond of exact antithesis, but that does not justify imposing it on him by conjecture.

30. tamquam: A^c, an obvious emendation of *tamen quam* (thus also L; G's *tamen tamquam* is almost certainly a conjecture, not a transmitted reading corrupted in the source of AL). Some later manusctipts (cited by Pighius) have *tamen*, adopted by Halm, while Vahlen deleted the words (ascribing the deletion to Halm, *Emendationes Valerianae*, 26; cf. ed. p. xxxvi). The repetition is quite unobjectionable.

31. dei notam: A^c. No doubt A, like L, had *dein tam*, i.e. omitting -*o*-. G's *deitatem* introduces a word used only by Christian writers (*TLL* v/1.513.8 ff.).

ext. 4. *Praxiteles.* Athenian, he was born between 400 and 390 and died between 330 and 325; for his family cf. J. K. Davies, *Athenian Propertied Families* (Oxford, 1971), no. 8334. See Lippold, *RE* xviii. 1786–1808, Stewart, 277–81 and other passages cited in the index (375–6).

V.'s source cannot be determined.

32–33. cuius ... conlocauit: the sculpture of Aphrodite, modelled on Apelles' painting. (cf. line 26 n.).

It is hard to say whether the alliteration in *c*- is deliberate.

32. cuius coniugem: V. does not normally write allusively, but clearly assumes that his readers' will be aware that Aphrodite/Venus was the wife of Hephaestus/Volcanus (cf. Malten, *RE* viii. 354); this, however, seems to be the only explicit reference to the myth in Latin writers (elsewhere Volcanus is the husband of Maia or Vesta; cf. Wissowa, *RuK* 184–6), though Horace *carm.* 1.5.4–8 may allude to it (cf. L. Preller, *Römische Mythologie* (Berlin, 1858), 527).

Praxiteles: P (and Lupus) have the name correctly. A has *Praxitelis*, LG *Praxiteus*. It looks as if α had the latter, resulting from a misreading of -*li*- as *u*-, with A correcting that error. An earlier corruption produced the genitive, perhaps because a scribe thought the name agreed with *cuius*.

marmore: presumably added to distinguish it from Alcamenes' statue of Hephaestus, and perhaps another indication that V. had seen the latter himself. Praxiteles was responsible for the long period of bronze's dominance, though he himself worked equally in both (cf. Stewart, 39, 277).

33–34. propter pulchritudinem ... tutam: this anecdote occurs also at Plin. *nat.* 36.21 (cf. J. Isager, *Pliny on Art and Society* (London–New York, 1991), 153–4) and, at great length, [Lucian] *am.* 15–16; V. is much more reticent. Stewart (op. cit. 279) says 'such erotica, often worked up in verse by Hellenistic and later poets, constitute our major source for the reception of his work in antiquity', but gives no further references.

34–35. quo excusabilior ... incitatus: there are no other references to these episodes.

34. est: LG, and no doubt A before alteration to *esset*. The motive for such an otiose emendation is unclear, but it was perhaps a desire to assimilate it to *miremur* in line 55.

error: A^cL^cG, but in this case clearly the reading of α: *error ... canis* stands in an erasure in A, while L had the nonsensical *aerrore qui*. Halm's *feruor* is totally misguided.

35–37. taurusque ... compulsus: V. takes this story from Livy 41.13.2 (a prodigy report), but while his source is (unusually; see my note ad loc.) explicit, he tells it euphemistically.

35. picti: α (P has *canis pictum canem adlatrauit*). A later manuscript (cited by Torrenius) has *pictae*, to harmonize with the female genitives in lines 34 and 36: a dog, of course, does not need to be sexually aroused in order to bark at another dog.

36. concubitum aeneae uaccae: for *concubitus* as an euphemism for sexual intercourse see my note on Livy 39.11.2, for the genitive *TLL* iv. 100.41 ff.

37. animalia: A^cG; AL have *ania*, a scribe's eye moving from the first *-i-* to the second. See line 38 n.

miremur: 'should we be surprised' (SB).

38. muti ... uideamus: two instances of a corruption in AL (*multis ... uideas*) with the truth in A^cG (cf. p. 17).

lineamentis: 'outlines' (SB). V. uses the word of works of art also at 3.7. ext. 4, 5.4. ext. 1 (cf. *TLL* vii/2.1439.77 ff.). At 7. ext. 7 (n.) it refers to geometrical lines, at 9.14. ext. 2 to physical features. I now print *linea-*, as I did at Livy 21.4.2 (thus the Mainz edition of 1519, though the manuscripts copied from the Puteaneus, not itself extant in this part of book 21, have *linia-*; at 26.41.25, in a passage omitted in the Puteaneus, the lost *codex Spirensis* had *linea-*, the majority of the other Spirensian witnesses *linia-*).

tit. QVAEDAM ... POSSE: as at book 7 ch. 8 and book 9 ch. 13, when V.'s text was divided into chapters (see p. 28), two of the headings were included in one chapter (the heading QVAM MAGNI EFFECTVS ARTIVM SINT does not apply to ext. 5–7). Pighius omitted the heading here.

P has *quae ... possunt*, the form which occurs in the heading to chs. 3, 6, and 15 (see 11 tit. n.); in my apparatus I said '*fort. sic, sed* possint', which wrongly implies that what stands in α was not the original heading; it could still be the case that Paris wrote *quae ... possint*, the same form as in the heading at the beginning of the chapter. Since the headings are not authorial (see p. 28), the matter is of little moment.

ext. 5. *Euphranor.* A Corinthian, though his important paintings were done in Athens, Euphranor was a man of many parts: sculptor in bronze, marble, and reliefs, painter, and writer (Plin. *nat.* 34.50, 35.128). Pliny places his *floruit* in Ol. 104 (364/361), when he produced a painting of the battle of Mantinea (362; Plin. *nat.* 35.129, Paus. 1.3.4), but his works included bronze sculptures of Philip II and Alexander the Great in chariots (Plin. *nat.* 34.78); both, however, may pre-date Philip's death in 336 and do not indicate that Euphranor was active 'at least to ca. 330' (thus Stewart, 287). See Robert, *RE* vi. 1191–4, O. Palagia. *Euphranor* (Leiden, 1980), Stewart, 286–8 and passages cited in the Index (372).

The painting is also mentioned by Eustathius on Hom. *Il.* 1.528–30; see Palagia, op. cit. 54–7. V.'s source cannot be determined.

2. inritam fesso labore: α. Puzzled by *labor* being described as *fessus*, Cornelissen proposed *inrito fessam*, while Kempf wondered about *inritam fessam*. *fessus*, however, is frequently used of things, though this is the first example in prose (cf. *TLL* vi/1.612.3 ff.), and it is not much easier for *ars* to be qualified by the adjective; it should be seen as an epithet transferred from an as yet unexpressed person. SB's 'labour in vain' does not convey the sense of *fesso*.

For *inritus* ('ineffectual') of mental or physical faculties; cf. *TLL* vii/2.435.36 ff. SB translates 'frustrated', taking it in the sense used of persons (*TLL* vii/2.435.64 ff., *OLD s.u.* 4).

4. maiestatis coloribus: the colours that depict the god's majesty. On Euphranor's use of colour cf. Palagia, op. cit. 9.

ext. 6. (*Timanthes*). V.'s source is Cicero *orat.* 74, who, like V., does not name the painter. That is given by Pliny *nat.* 35.73, from another source (cf. ext. 7, 12. ext. 3 nn.); he does not mention Calchas or Ulysses and refers to Menelaus and Agamemnon only as Iphigenia's uncle and father (Livy 45.27.9, in a totally different context, does not even name Iphigenia). Quintilian *inst.* 2.13.13 appears to have combined Cicero and Pliny, and adds that with this picture Timanthes defeated Colotes of Teos. See also Eustathius *Il.*, ed. Van der Walk, iv (Leiden, 1987), 883 lines 18–19. On Timanthes, of Cythnos, cf. Lippold, *RE* viA. 1231–2.

8. quid?: Adams (*Informal Latin*, 149–51) discusses the problem of punctuation when *quid* is used in this way. Kempf, like earlier editors, placed a question mark only after *confessus est* (line 11), but with *nonne* preceding that is clearly wrong. The only alternative to my punctuation, followed by Shackleton Bailey, would be to place the question mark after *pictor*, but *referens* is naturally taken closely with the former. Cf. 5 lines 22–3 n.

luctuosum: before V. the epithet is frequent in Cicero and then occurs once each in *bell. Hisp.* and Sallust and twice in Horace.

8–9. immolatae Iphigeniae sacrificium: for the extensive sources on the sacrifice of Iphigenia at Aulis see my note on Livy loc. cit.

9. referens: for *referre* 'represent' ('portray' SB) of works of art cf. *TLL* xi/2.624.10 ff. Elsewhere, however, the work, not the artist, is the subject. (*OLD s.u.* 18 wrongly classify our passage with those where the verb refers to mentioning in speech or writing (*TLL* xi/2.627.57 ff.)).

Calchantem: the seer.

lamentantem: α has *clamantem Aiacem lamentantem* and Kempf (in his first edition) rightly deleted *clamantem Aiacem*. As he said, (i) *clamantem* is out of place among the adjectives and participle expressing grief (though there is not, as he claimed, a gradation from *tristem* to *maestum* to *lamentantem* to the unexpressible grief of Agamemnon: there is no essential difference in meaning between *maestus* and *tristis*; for grammarians' attempts to distinguish them and a table of their occurrence in different authors see *TLL* viii. 35.43 ff.); (ii) Cicero does not mention Ajax; Kempf argued that the same is true of Paris, but what he says is *Vlixem Menelaum ceteros*, not mentioning Calchas either; (iii) at line 12 V. talks of only one *amicus*.

Kempf thought that the words were added by a *doctus grammaticus* who knew that Timanthes' painting included Ajax (I assume that this is what he meant; what he says is *qui sciret celeberrimum opus inter tabulas Timanthis Aiacem fuisse*). That is unlikely: it will have arisen either from *lamentantem* being corrupted to *clamantem*, the true reading then being restored but without the deletion of *clmantem*, or because someone took *Calchantem ... Vlixen* to be an asyndeton *bimembre* and thought that it should have been followed by another one (*clamantem Aiacem lamentantem Menelaum*).

12. spectantis adfectu: 'by the emotion of the spectator' (SB). Wensky's *spectanti* is not only unnecessary, but produces the awkward meaning 'left to the spectator to be judged by his emotion'; Similarly *affectui* in later manuscripts (DE) produces 'left to the emotion of the spectator to be judged'.

7. (*Nealces*?). As in ext. 6 (n.), V. leaves the painter anonymous. According to Pliny (*nat.* 35.104) he was Nealces, a friend of Aratus of Sicyon (Plut. *Arat.* 13.4–5; cf. Lippold, *RE* xvi. 2105–6), but Dio Chrysostom 63.4–5 (not cited in my *testimonia* apparatus) says that it was Apelles. Plutarch (*mor.* 99B), also leaves him anonymous. V.'s source cannot be determined.

14. pictor equum: L^c, a clearly correct emendation of the transmitted *pictorem cum*. P has *pictor cum equum ab exercitatione uenientem uidisset*, which suggests that Paris' text of V. also had *pictorem cum*. Lupus wrote BR. *cum equum ab exercitatione uenientem uidisset p. a.*, by which he presumably intended that *cum ... uidisset* should precede *praecipuae artis pictor*: I misleadingly implied that he wanted to omit *pictor*.

15. modo non: 'almost'. Before V., who uses it also at 9.2.1, the usage occurs only at Ter. *Phorm.* 68 and Virg. *Aen.* 9.139 (*OLD s.u. modo* 1d wrongly adds Livy 10.24.11, where *modo* and *non* do not go together); cf. *TLL* viii. 1303.80 ff.

15–16. comprehenderat: 'represented'; for the verb used of works of art cf. 3.7. ext. 3, Petr. 88.5, *TLL* iii. 2150.2 ff.

17. materia: 'subject'; for *materia* of works of art cf. *TLL* viii. 461.30 ff.
terebatur: 'was being worn out'; cf. *OLD s.u.* 7.

18, 20. et ueluti, explere: two instances of the truth being preserved in P (and G in the first) with a nonsensical corruption (*eueluti, exemplare*) in, respectively, AL and α.

20–21. adumbrare ... imitatus est: V. appears to be using *adumbrare* as a calque on σκιαγραφεῖν ('paint with the shadows', so as to produce an illusion of solidity at a distance (L–S–J)); cf. *TLL* i. 885.32 ff. Curtius 10.3.14, however, seems to regard *adumbrare* and *imitari* as synonyms and *OLD s.u.* 4 take our passage thus: it seems more likely that Curtius has either misunderstood V. or is deliberately coupling the two verbs in a different way (*TLL* loc. cit. lines 52 ff. classify the passage as a metaphorical use of *adumbrare* = σκιαγραφεῖν).

12 tit. The text and apparatus of my edition do not cohere. G has *esse* after *et disputatorem*, AL before it, and I intended to print the former, while giving the latter a *fort. recte*: if my stemma is correct and G is equipollent to AL, it seems unlikely that a scribe would have altered the former's word order, while the author of the headings (cf. p. 28) may well have been influenced by the order adopted by V. in his preface to the chapter; but if my stemma is wrong and AL represent the paradosis, there is no reason to alter it.

praef. 1. auctorem: 'performer' ('executant' SB). For this use of *auctor* with the genitive cf. *OLD s.u.* 13a, citing Sall. *Cat.* 3.1, Tac. *hist.* 3.2.4 (it is covered by the rubric at *TLL* ii. 1201.20 ff., but they do not cite either the latter passages or ours). A, presumably puzzled by the usage, has *actorem* in both heading and text (a correction in the latter),

1. disputatorem: 'discusser' (SB's 'exponent' is somewhat misleading); Cic. *off.* 1.3 is the only other example of the noun before late antiquity.

2. admoneamur: A^{c}G (it was conjectured by Perizonius); AL have *admoneamus*. In this case (see above), if my stemma is correct, the readings are equipollent and decision is impossible; but if the active is the paradosis, there is again no sufficient reason for altering it.

1. *Scaevola.* V.'s source is Cic. *Balb.* 45, who says, as V. does not, that this is Q. Mucius Scaevola the augur (consul in 117), not the homonymous consul of 95

(see 15.6 n.), who was, in fact, the more distinguished lawyer; cf. 8 lines 14–16, *exemplum* 2 nn.

3. uates: for the noun used in the sense of 'authoritative exponent' cf. *OLD s.u.* 1d, citing only our passage and Plin. *nat.* 11.219 (SB's 'prophet' is misleading).

4. iure praediatorio: 'real estate law' (SB; similarly, he translates *praediator* at Cic. *Att.* 12.14.2 'estate-dealer') is too general. A *praediator* is someone who purchases from the state land held as a surety (Gaius *inst.* 2.61; cf. *TLL* x/2.540.65 ff., for the adjective lines 77 ff., O. Lenel, *Das edictum perpetuum*, 3rd edn. (Leipzig, 1927), 389–90). Apart from Cic. *Balb.* 45 and our passage, *praediatorius* (with *lex*) occurs only at *CIL* ii. 1964 (the *lex Malacitana*) col. 4 lines 51–4 and Suet. *Claud.* 9.2. (*TLL* loc. cit. mention A's *praedicatorio*, a clear corruption, as if it is conceivable that it is correct.)

Furium: (21). Perhaps identical with the N. Furius who was a friend of L. Licinius Crassus (Cic. *de orat.* 3.87); thus Münzer, *RE* vii. 317, Shackleton Bailey, *Onomasticon to Cicero's Speeches* (Stuttgart, 1988), 51, but cf. Leeman–Pinkster–Wisse on Cic. loc. cit.

Cascellium: (1). A. Cascellius, the father of the A. Cascellius mentioned at 6.3.12, apparently *praetor urbanus* during the Triumvirate (cf. *MRR* iii. 50); he himself was a senator and still alive in 73, when his son was a member of the consul's *consilium* (Sherk no. 23 lines 6–7) and is distinguished from him as ὁ υἱός. See Münzer, *RE* iii. 1634, Supp. iii. 236.

quia: Perizonius proposed *qui*, another case of a conjecture producing what V. might have written rather than what he wrote (Kempf printed *quia*, but in his apparatus said of *qui* '*recte, ut uid.*').

5. consultores: in the present sense of 'seeker of advice' the word occurs before V. three times in Cicero (*Mur.* 22, *Balb.* 45, *Tusc.* 5.112) and once in Horace (*sat.* 1.1.10); of a giver of advice it is found in Afranius, four times in Sallust, and in a line of verse (a translation of Hesiod, *Op.* 266) cited by Varro *rust.* 3.2.1; it also appears at Gell. 4.5.5, in a passage said to derive from the *annales maximi* (= *FRHist.* (ii. 22) F6; cf. iii. 7–8, with no mention of Varro; *TLL* iv. 594.20 ff. is misleading).

6. minuebat: later manuscripts (Kempf (1854) cites only A and Γ for *muniebat*); the stem appears as *muni-* in α, the voice as passive in AL (emended by correctors of L and A respectively).

8. professores: The noun is not attested before V., who uses it also at 1.8. ext. 8 (*TLL* x/2.1692.31 ff.).

callide: Cornelissen proposed *candide*, saying that it meant *integre ac uere*, but giving no reasons. The conjecture was not cited by Kempf, presumably because he was unaware of it, but I gave it a *fort. recte* and it was accepted by Shackleton Bailey. He (and Cornelissen) no doubt thought that by referring clients to Furius and Cascellius Scaevola was displaying his honesty, not his cleverness, and that the corruption could easily have been caused by perseveration from *callebant* above. Perhaps, but V. may have meant that Scaevola was displaying his own cleverness by his awareness that Furius and Cascellius had a better knowledge than he of this particular aspect of property law; indeed, the virtual polyptoton of *callebant/callide* may have been deliberate.

ext. 1. *Plato.* V. (it is conceivable but unlikely that an intermediate source was responsible) has here garbled and abbreviated his source (who cannot be determined) to near the point of unintelligibility, in the process, it seems, confusing Eudoxus with Euclid. Plutarch *mor.* 579B–C (from the *de genio Socratis*, a dialogue in which Cephisias, a Theban, narrates the conspiracy which led to the freeing of Thebes from Spartan control in 379 BC; he is here reporting a speech of Simmias, in whose house the conspirators met) says that a group of Delians asked Plato to solve an oracular response telling them to double the altar at Delos (the reference is to the geometrical problem of doubling a cube, involving proportionals; cf., conveniently, G.J. Toomer, *OCD*³ 936; the article has been replaced in the 4th edition). He referred them to Eudoxus (who invented a theory of proportion; cf. Toomer, *OCD*³ 565 (545–6 in the 4th edition, revised by A. Jones) or Helicon. V. probably had little understanding of mathematics.

10–11. conductores: V. converts the Delians who made the request to Plato into contractors.

In that sense *conductor* occurs before V. in Plautus, Cato *agr.*, Cicero, and Caesar, in the sense of 'hirer' in Plautus and Ovid; cf. *TLL* iv. 163.

11. sacrae arae: LG. P (and Lupus in A) has *uiae sacrae*, no doubt an error arising from thinking of the *sacra uia* in Rome (cf. 1 line 127 n.). Kempf, saying that all altars are sacred, and presumably influenced by P's reading, had the strange idea that *sacrae* was an interpolation resulting from dittography of the preceding *-s* and, corrupted, the following *arae*; the pleonasm is slight (and, in any case, not something to which V. was averse).

12. Eucliden: Euclid, the most famous Greek mathematician, in fact lived in the Hellenistic age; cf. Toomer–R. Netz, *OCD*⁴ 544–5.

geometren: α. P has *geometram*, a form used only by late writers (cf. *TLL* vi/2.1907/38 ff.). The accusative in *-en* is found also at Quint. *inst.* 1.10.4.

professioni: in the sense of 'profession' *professio* occurs first in V. and Velleius (1.16.1).

ext. 2. *Philon.* In addition to the arsenal in the Piraeus, the subject of this *exemplum*, Philon, of Eleusis, built the *prostoion* to the Telesterion at Eleusis, completed during the rule of Demetrius of Phalerum, and, probably, was one of those responsible for various works at Delphi in 338. Our detailed knowledge of the arsenal depends on *IG* ii². 1668, which, on the basis of *IG* ii² 505, can be dated to 347/6. See Fabricius, *RE* xx. 56–60.

V.'s source is Cicero *de orat.* 1.62 (but see line 15 n.); of the other sources cited in my *testimonia* apparatus, Strabo 9, p. 395C and Pliny *nat.* 7.125 merely say that Philon was the architect of the arsenal, Vitruvius 7 praef. 12 that he wrote a book about it. I omitted to mention that Philodemus *rhet.* i. 346 appears to refer to Philon's speech.

13. armamentario: before V. the noun occurs in Cicero (*Rab. perd.* 20 as well as *de orat.* 1.62), Varro, and six times in Livy (*TLL* ii. 602.34 ff.).

13–14. est enim ... uisendum: another indication of autopsy (cf. 11. ext. 3 n.); expense cannot itself be seen or visited: V. means that by seeing the arsenal one can imagine how much it cost.

15. institutionis: 'arrangement'; Vitruvius also uses it, three times, of a building; cf. *TLL* vii/1.1996.50 ff.

in theatro: the phrase is not in Cicero; it is unclear whether it was V.'s own addition or whether he found it in another source. It was omitted by G but subsequently added in the margin. It is scarcely conceivable that it was added in the source of AL, though it is possible that it was a variant in α initially not taken up by G or its immediate source. There is no obvious palaeographical reason for the omission, but I wonder whether G remembered the passage of Cicero and deliberately omitted the words (there may have been a manuscript of the *de oratore* at Reims; cf. Winterbottom–Rouse–Reeve, *Texts and Transmission*, 106).

disertissimus: V. attributes eloquence to all Athenians, not just the orators among them.

ext. 3. (*Apelles*). Once again (cf. 11. ext. 6, 7 nn.), the name of the painter, omitted by V., is provided by Pliny (*nat.* 35.85; V.'s source cannot be determined), who adds that Apelles' remark became a proverb (the origin of the English 'let a cobbler stick to his last'; there is no ancient evidence for Rackham's note (Loeb edn., ix. 324) '*ne sutor ultra crepidam*'; see A. Otto, *Die Sprichwörter und sprichwörtlichen Redensarten der Römer* (Leipzig, 1890), 97; cf. Ath. 351A. And as in ext. 1, V.'s brevity means that it would be hard fully to understand what he is saying if we did not have the help of Pliny: he says that the cobbler rebuked Apelles for painting one too few loops on the sandals; Apelles corrected the mistake and on the next day the cobbler made objections to the legs in the picture.

17. moneri se a sutore: Kempf implies that this is the reading of all his renaissance manuscripts except C. AL have the nonsensical *muneris eas ut ore* *suo*: the first four words are merely a matter of faulty word division, with the first vowel corrupted from -*o*- to -*u*-, while *suo* is manifestly the result of perseveration from its preceding occurrence (it is most unlikely that V. would have written *opere suo ... sutore suo* and Pliny talks of just a cobbler, not Apelles' cobbler).

17–18. crepida et ansulis: *crepida* 'sandal' occurs before V. in Cicero, Catullus, Horace, and Livy; V. uses it also at 3.6.1 and 9.1 ext. 4 (*TLL* iv. 1166.70 ff.). Pliny uses *ansa*, found elsewhere in the sense of a 'loop' on a sandal only at Tibullus 1.8.14; this is the first occurrence of *ansula* (*TLL* ii. 123.19 ff., 126.12 ff.).

18. crure: L^{c}G; AL have the nonsensical *cruce*, P *sura*, a poetical word for calf, not found in prose before Curtius (*OLD s.u.*).

plantam: α; P has *plantas*: Pliny writes *crepidam*, which makes it likely that his and V.'s source also had the singular. In any case, preference should naturally be given to the direct tradition (cf. p. 23). *planta*, originally meaning the sole of the foot, but later used for the foot as a whole, occurs in verse from Plautus onwards, in prose only in Varro before V., who uses it only here; Celsus has it on twelve occasions (*TLL* x/1.2321.1 ff.).

13. With the exception of Ap. Claudius Caecus (5) and Hieron (ext. 1), all the long-lived men and women in this chapter are also mentioned by Plin. *nat.* 7.154 (ext. 4–7), 156 (3–4), ext. 1–2, 157 (1–2), 158 (6), and 168 (ext. 3); on these passages see M. Beagon, *The Elder Pliny on the Human Animal* (Oxford, 2005), 358–62, 378. Münzer (*Plinius*, 105–9) argued that, with the exception of *exempla* 6 and ext. 4, Pliny drew not on V. but on their common source, whom he plausibly identifies with Varro. In the introductory notes on individual *exempla* it is to be understood that if I make no reference to it, V.'s source is, or may be, that common source.

praef. This is by far the longest preface in book 8 (elsewhere there are longer ones at book 2 ch. 9, book 4 ch. 4, and book 9 ch. 12, while those at book 5 ch. 5 and book 9 ch. 12 are of the same length), consisting largely (lines 2–8) of one long and complex period (see n. ad loc.; cf. 7 praef. n.), culminating (lines 8–12) in an obsequious expression of V.'s wish for Tiberius' longevity.

1. prouecta: A^{c}G; *prouectam*, -*um* in A and L respectively are the result of perseveration from the preceding accusatives.

1–2. in hoc ... conspecta est: 7.1, 3–4, ext. 5, 9–13.

1. hoc eodem: for *hic idem*, occurring first in Cato *agr.*, cf. *TLL* vii/1.200.62 ff. There is another instance at 9.3.1.

2–8. separatum ... prorogando: the period is constructed thus: the main clause is *separatum ... habeat* (jussive subjunctive); on it depend two final clauses: (i) *ne ... existimetur*, containing a relative clause *cui ... adfuit*, (ii) (with *ut* understood; Gertz wrongly wanted to add *ut* after *simul*) *et simul ... adminicula quaedam dentur*; on *adminicula quaedam*, linked to it by *quibus insistens*, depends a relative final clause *alacriorem ... possit*; there follows a second main clause *tranquillitatem ... confirmet*, containing a relative clause *qua ... fuit* and concluding with the instrumental gerund *prorogando*, governing *salutaris ... terminos* (it might be preferable to punctuate with a semi-colon after *possit*; Shackleton Bailey, while punctuating his text with a comma, translates '... of ancient felicity. And let confidence ...'.

3. titulum: 'heading' (SB); it does not follow that V. himself is responsible for the chapter divisions and *tituli* (cf. p. 28).

ne cui: thus L. A^c (A's reading is unclear) and G have it as one word, presumably under the misapprehension that *cui* is the dative of indefinite *quis*; what a corrector of L intended by *nec ui* is unclear.

4. ornata: A^{c}G; AL have *onata*. Halm conjectured *honorata*, and convinced both Kempf and Shackleton Bailey. He may have been right: as Kempf observed, V. uses *honoratus* in the sense of 'conferring honour' at 14.2, 15.9, 3.8.6, and 5.1. ext. 3; cf. Livy 6.6.8, 27.10.6, *TLL* vi/3.2950.77 ff., Oakley i. 450 (citing our passage as if *honorata* were certain). Nevertheless, *ornata*, involving the addition of only one letter, is a considerably simpler correction, and though V. nowhere else uses *ornatus* of style, there is no reason why he should not have referred to his work, which is certainly ornate, in this way.

simul: cf. lines 2–8 n.

5. adminicula: before V. *adminiculum* occurs in Plautus, Cicero, Varro, and Livy (*TLL* i. 727.56 ff.; cf. Oakley i. 387).

5–6. respectu uetustae felicitatis: 'by contemplation of ancient felicity' (SB). V. is referring to the fact that four of his five Roman male *exempla* lived in the fourth or third centuries BC. The exception is Perperna (*exemplum* 4), who was consul just before the outbreak of the Social War, which was immediately succeeded by the Civil War of the 80s, and died at the beginning of the Civil War between Caesar and Pompey (and his successors). That period was scarcely *uetustus* in the reign of Tiberius, and one doubts whether anyone who lived through it would have talked of his *felicitas*.

7. subinde: SB translates 'ever and anon' ('from then on' *OLD s.u.* 1b), but it is perhaps more likely that V. meant 'immediately' (art. cit. 1a); cf. 15 line 28 n.

fiducia: dett. (Kempf implies all his manuscripts except A). α has *fiduciam*, perhaps the result of a scribe's losing track of the construction of the period.

8. humanae condicionis: V. uses the phrase also at 3.4. ext. 1, 4.7. ext. 2, 6.3.1d, 9.2. ext. 11; before him it occurs at Cic. *Tusc.* 1.15, *nat. deor.* 2.36. *fam.* 6.6.12, and Livy 23.5.11; 'the human condition' is frequent in English.

prorogando: cf. 3 lines 12–13 n.

1. M. Valerius Corv(in)us. Valerius (137) was consul in 348 (in the previous year, as a military tribune, he had defeated a Gaul in single combat; cf. 15.5 n.), 346, 343, 355, 300, and, as suffect consul, 299. V.'s source is Cic. *Cato* 60 (neither has Pliny's statement (*nat.* 7.157) that Corvinus held curule office twenty-one times (cf. Münzer, *Plinius*, 109)), from whom he takes his statement that there were 46 years between Valerius' first and sixth consulships (thus also Pliny); Cicero is omitting the dictator years (333, 324, 309, 301) and counting inclusively; D has *xl et vii* (thus also Pighius from two of his manuscripts; he took V. to be counting exclusively, i.e. 347–300, with the dictator years included), which is probably a dittography of *i* rather than a deliberate alteration (Powell, thinking that Cicero made a mistake of calculation, says that it 'would be odd' for Cicero to have omitted the dictator years: Cicero never shows any awareness of them, doubtless because they had not yet been invented; cf. Oakley i. 104–5).

Valerius' *cognomen* is variously given as *Coruus* and *Coruinus*, the former by the *Fasti Capitolini*, the Chronographer of AD 354, except for 348, the manuscripts of Livy, with the exception of 7.32.15 and 40.3, Tac. *ann.* 1.9.2, and Fest. 458L, the latter by Cicero, loc. cit., the manuscripts of Livy at 7.32.15 and 40, 3, the *Fasti Hydatiani*, V., both here and at 15.5, D.H. 15.1.2, and all other subsequent sources. All this suggests that *Coruus* is correct (thus *MRR*, Oakley); his son, the consul of 312 is called *Coruus* at Festus 458L, but *Coruinus* by the Chronographer of AD 354. See Volkmann, *RE* viiA. 2413–14 (wrongly attributing *Coruus* to Cicero; Shackleton Bailey, apparently unaware of the passage of Cicero, has the notion that V. wrote *Coruinus* because of M. Valerius Messalla Corvinus (consul in 31), somewhat oddly calling him V.'s contemporary), Oakley ii. 30–1 (on similar cases of this variation), 238–9.

9. centesimum annum compleuit: thus also Cicero, loc. cit. Livy (7.26.12) says that Valerius was 23 when elected consul (in *exemplum* 5 V. converts this into being in his twenty-third year). If so, he was 68 when he held office for the last time and lived until 267. In view of the exaggerations in ch. 7 (see lines 6, 155 nn.; see also *exemplum* 2 n. below), the figure should be viewed with suspicion.

11. publicis: G; L (so too, no doubt, A before correction to *rei publicae*) has *solis publicis*, caused by perseveration from *solum*.

11–12. exactissimae: cf. 7 lines 67–8 n.

12. optabile: the adjective, though never common, is found from Plautus onwards (*TLL* viii. 816–17); V. uses it also at 5.1. ext. 6, 6.4. ext. 4, and 9.1. ext. 4.

2. L. Caecilius Metellus. (72). He was consul in 251 and 247, and became *pontifex maximus* in 243; he died in 221. It is, therefore, most improbable that he lived until the age of 100, which would mean that he did not reach the consulship until he was 70. Münzer (*RE* iii. 1203) suggests that he was the son of L. Caecilius Metellus Denter, consul in 284.

Cicero *Cato* 30 appears to be V.'s source, but he says nothing about the length of Metellus' life; that detail, but nothing else, however, is in Pliny *nat.* 7.157; in this case, therefore, it seems that V. has combined Cicero with his and Pliny's common source; cf. Münzer, *Plinius*, 109.

Livy *per.* 19 mentions two of Metellus' actions as *pontifex maximus*, his prevention of the *flamen Martialis*, A. Postumius Albinus, from leaving Rome during his consulship (in 241; see 1.1.2, Livy 37.51.1–2, Tac. *ann.* 3.71.3) and his saving the *sacra* (including the Palladium; cf. Cic. *Scaur.* 54, Plin. *nat.* 7.141, *FRHist* iii. 165) when the temple of Vesta caught fire.

14. quartoque: Perizonius misguidedly proposed *quarto qui*: V. never postpones *qui*. V. is saying two separate things about Metellus, coordinated by *-que*, that he lived for a century and that he fulfilled the duties of the office of *pontifex maximus* for twenty-two years after his second consulship.

14–15. consularia imperia: a unique use of *consulare imperium* as the equivalent of *consulatus*; at 4.1 ext. 8, 6.1.1 it has its normal meaning of '*imperium* of a consul'.

Wensky's conjecture *consulare alterum imperium*, as well as lacking any palaeographical plausibility, is an example of hyper-logical textual criticism (the thought, presumably, that it was only after his second consulship that Metellus became *pontifex maximus*).

3. *Q. Fabius Maximus.* This is the first time the Cunctator appears in book 8; for earlier passages mentioning him see the index to my edition (cf. 1 line 67 n.). His source for the length of the augurate is Livy 30.26.7, reporting Fabius' death in 203, from whom Pliny (*nat.* 7.156; '157' in my apparatus is an error, repeated in the entry for the following *exemplum*) also derives. Pliny (or his manuscripts; Münzer (*Plinius*, 109) took the diference to indicate that Pliny was using another source) gives the figure as 63 (cf. below) V., however, adds that Fabius was already of *robusta aetas* when he became an augur; this is probably not derived from another source, but his own idea, in order to make Fabius, like the subjects of the two previous *exempla*, live for a hundred years. Were he right, Fabius would have been in his 80s and 90s when commanding in the Hannibalic War (his last consulship was in 209, when he recaptured Tarentum).

It can, however, by no means be regarded as certain that Fabius became an augur in 265. As Broughton (*MRR* iii. 88) observes, he must then have been born no later than 280 and probably earlier; he would have held his first consulship, in 233, at a surprisingly late age. What is more, he would have been in his

60s at the times of most of his campaigns against Hannibal and in his 70s in 209 (though Q. Marcius Philippus and L. Aemilius Paullus, the last two commanders in the Third Macedonian War were both in their sixties; cf. my note on Livy 44.17.4).

18. duobus ... annis: Livy has *duos ... annos*, Pliny *(lx)iii annis*. Both the direct tradition and P have *annis*, altered to *annos* in the latter by Mai, while both AL (*ii* G; Kempf (1854) implies that all his later MSS have *duobus*) and P have *duo*. There is thus no doubt that V. used the ablative rather than the accusative of time how long (cf. K–St. i. 260–1 n. 12).

4. *Perperna.* Pliny *nat.* 7.156 also says that Perperna outlived all the members of the senate at the time of his consulship, adding that L. Volusius Saturninus had recently done the same, and all but seven of those he had enrolled in the senate as censor; he also says that Perperna lived to the age of 98 (cf. Münzer, *Plinius*, 109). Dio (41.14.5) reports Perperna's death in 49, claiming that he outlived all the senators of the time of his censorship.

21. M. Perperna: (5). He was consul in 92 and censor in 86 (see below). He was the son of M. Perperna (4), consul in 130, and grandson of M. Perperna (3), a *legatus* sent to the Illyrian king Genthius in 168, arrested by him and released after Genthius' defeat by L. Anicius (Livy 44.27.11.32.1). The name (often, especially in Greek, spelt *Perpenna* (thus P here and both α and P at 3.4.5); cf. Münzer, *RE* xix. 892) is Etruscan and the family, perhaps the *legatus* of 168, must have acquired Roman citizenship early in the second century. At 3.4.5, in a passage riddled with error and confusion, V. claims that after the death of the consul of 130 his father's right to citizenship was challenged and he was forced to return to his former place of residence; see my note on Livy 44.27.11.

21–22. in senatum consul uocauerat: P (and Lupus); the direct tradition has *conuocauerat*, probably the result of an abbreviation of *consul*. For *(in) senatum uocare* cf., e.g., Cic. *fam.* 10.28.2, Livy 22.9.7, 23.2.5, 36.21.7, 39.39.10, 45.1.8; *senatum/patres conuocare* occurs at Livy 2.18.2, 39.39.6, but V. clearly intends a contrast between Perperna's consulship and censorship.

22–23. L. Philippi: L. Marcius (75) Philippus, grandson of the consul of 186 and 169 (see above), was consul in 91, when he strongly opposed the proposals of M. Livius Drusus. He and Perperna must have been acceptable to the regime of Cinna, but he later supported Sulla and in 78 he spoke strongly in the senate against M. Lepidus; see the speech attributed to him by Sallust (*hist.* 1.77M = 67 Ramsey). Cf., conveniently, Badian, *OCD*[4] 897.

23. reliquos uidit: α; Wensky proposed *reliquit uiuos*, another case of something V. could have written (and the posited corruption is quite possible), but did not.

5. *Appius Claudius Caecus.* (91). In my *testimonia* apparatus I did no more than refer globally to the sources cited by Münzer in his entry on Appius at *RE* iii. 2681–5. In the notes which follow I cite all and only those relevant to the matters mentioned by V.; first, though, I summarize Appius' political career (cf., briefly, *OCD*[4] 325; for full discussion and bibliography see Oakley iii. 350–72).

Appius' first office was the censorship of 312–311; he was consul in 307 and 296, an interrex in 298, and praetor in 295, fighting in Etruria, Campania, and Samnium in both 296 and 295; from his *elogium* (*II* xiii/3.79) we know that he also held three military tribunates, a quaestorship, two curule aedileships, a dictatorship, and two other *interregna*, none of which offices are dateable.

Appius does not appear in Pliny (cf. 13 n.), but probably stood in the common source of V. and Pliny.

25. Appi: *Appii* A^cG, *Appio* AL: the latter was caused by anticipation of the following *uero*.

clade: defined in the following clause (*quia ... exegit*).

25–26. infinitum ... exegit: Appius' age when he went blind cannot be determined. All that is certain is that he was blind when he opposed the making of peace with Pyrrhus (see lines 27–9 n.). At 1.1.17 V. says that it was a punishment inflicted on him by Hercules for authorizing, as censor, the transfer of the superintendence of his cult from the Potitii to public slaves; his source was Livy 9.29.11, who attributes it to anonymous writers (*traditur*) and says that Appius became blind *post aliquot annos*; see also D.H. 16.3.1, *uir. ill.* 34.2. Cicero (*Tusc.* 5.112) says that he was blind for many years, during which he held magistracies (thus also Ulpian *dig.* 3.1.1.5; a notable recent instance is David Blunkett, successively Secretary of State for Education and Home Secretary in the British Labour Governments of 1997 and 2001 respectively). He can, however, scarcely have been blind during his military campaigns in 296–295 (see above). Diodorus (20.36.6) has the strange version that at the conclusion of his censorship Appius feigned blindness and remained in his house.

For *infinitus* used hyperbolically to mean 'very large' cf. *OLD s.u.* 3b; the usage is not distinguished at *TLL* vii/1.1425 ff.

26. quattuor ... clientelas: V. takes this from Cic. *Cato* 37. the sons are Ap. Claudius Rufus (316), consul in 268, P. Claudius Pulcher (304), consul in 249 (cf. 1. absol. 4, damn. 4 nn.), C. Claudius Centho (104), consul in 240, and Ti. Claudius Nero (248), the ancestor of the Claudii Nerones and grandfather of

C. and Ti. Claudius Nero (246, 249), consuls in 207 and 202 respectively; see Münzer's stemma at *RE* iii. 2666, Powell on Cic. loc. cit., Oakley iii. 357. The only daughter otherwise known is the Claudia of 1. damn. 4.

For speculation about the nature of Appius' *clientelae* cf. Oakley iii. 369, 670–1; Livy (9.42.4, 46.10–15) indicates that he had strong support among the urban *plebs*.

27. rexisset: Cic. loc. cit. has *regebat*, as the verb of the main clause; its object is only Appius' family and *clientelae*, with no mention of the *res publica*.

27–29. quin etiam ... prohiberet: in 280 the Epirote king Pyrrhus invaded Italy and defeated a Roman army at Heraclea (c. 28 km SSW of Metapontum; Barrington Atlas 45E4). The Romans sent three consulars to Pyrrhus to negotiate the ransom of the prisoners he had taken, but the king released them without ransom and sent them to Rome with Cineas, a Thessalian who was his closest adviser, offering peace terms which would have meant the end of Roman control of southern Italy. The senate was inclined to accept but was dissuaded by Appius' famous speech.

The speech existed in the time of Cicero (*Brut.* 61, *Cato* 16; the latter cites Ennius *ann.* 202–3V = 199–200Sk) and Seneca (*epist.* 114.13), though it is uncertain how far it represented what Appius actually said (cf. Powell on Cic. *Cato* loc. cit.). The episode is mentioned by a large number of other sources (I combine, where necessary correcting them, the lists in Münzer, *RE* iii. 2085, Powell 136, and Oakley iii. 353): *I.I.* xiii/3.79, *FGrH* 839F1.2 (*ineditum Vaticanum*), Cic. *Cael.* 34, *Brut.* 55, *Phil.* 1.11, Livy *per.* 13, Ovid *fast.* 6.203–4, Quint. *inst.* 2.16.7, Plut. *Pyrrh.* 18.1–19.6, *mor.* 794D–E, Suet. *Tib.* 2.1, Pomponius *dig.* 1.2.2.36, App. *Samn.* 10.1–9, Flor. 1.13.20, Ampel. 19.2, *uir. ill.* 34.9, Zon. 8.4.11–12.

See further P. Lévêque, *Pyrrhos* (Paris, 1957), 351–5, P. R. Franke, *CAH* vii^2/2.469–71.

29–30. per se ... peruidere: the alliteration in *p-* and *c-* may be deliberate.

6. *Livia, Terentia, Clodia.* All three are also mentioned by Pliny *nat.* 7.158 (cf. Münzer, *Plinius*, 109, arguing that since Terentia outlived Varro, Pliny here used V. alone), together with four other women, of whom only one, who lived in the reign of Claudius, was of noble birth (two of the others were actresses); *in compluribus* (line 31) perhaps indicates that V. was selecting from a longer list.

32. strictim: 'briefly'; in this sense the adverb occurs before V. (also at 4.1.12 and 6.1.13). in Cicero and Varro. At Plautus *Capt.* 268 it refers to a (literal) close shave.

Liuia Rutili: Rutilius will be P. Rutilius Rufus (34), consul in 105 (the doubt indicated in my index was unjustified), his wife (34; she appears as *Siluia* in P) the sister of M. Livius Drusus (17), consul in 112. Cf. Münzer, *RE* xiii. 899–900 (with an uncharacteristic error referring to Rutilius as consul in 112), Badian, *Studies*, 40.

33. Terentia Ciceronis: Terentia (95) married Cicero at some date before 68, when he first mentions her (*Att.* 1.5.8), perhaps in the early 70s, and she appears to have been influential in his political career. Cicero divorced her in 47 or 46; she is said to have subsequently married both Sallust and M. Valerius Messalla Corvinus (Hier. *adu. Iouin.* 1.48, probably from Seneca (cf. 49, Reitzenstein, *Hermes* 33 (1898), 94). See Weinstock, *RE* vA. 710–16, Badian, *OCD*[4] 1441.

Clodia Ofili: Ofilius (4) was a distinguished jurist and close friend of Caesar (Pomponius *dig.* 1.2.2.44–5), mentioned by Cicero on three occasions during Caesar's dictatorship (*Att.* 13.37.4, *fam.* 7.21, 16.24.1). His name appears as *Ofili* in Pliny loc. cit., but as *Aulifi* in A, *Auli f.* in LG, and *Auli filia* in P (and Lupus); *Auli f(ilia)* is clearly the paradosis, but it is inconceivable that on this occasion V. gave only the wife's name and her filiation. Pighius printed *Aufili* and has been followed by all editors except myself (unfortunately my index lists Clodia as *Aufili uxor*) and Shackleton Bailey. Aufilius, however, is an otherwise unattested *nomen* and the agreement of Cicero and Pliny makes it certain that Münzer (*RE* xvii. 2040) was right to read *Ofili* (though as an alternative he suggested *Ufili* (*Uphilio* occurs in an inscription from Cyprus (*BCH* 51 (1927), 143; Münzer, *RE* xvii. 2041 (no. 6)). Münzer, however, to take account of the MSS readings, prefaced it with *A.*: it is most unlikely that V., not having done so in the case of Rutilius and Cicero, should have added the (otherwise unattested; Cicero refers to him by *nomen* alone) *praenomen*.

Münzer reasonably suggested that Clodia was a niece or granddaughter of Ap. Claudius Pulcher (consul in 79), whose three daughters and one of whose sons called themselves *Clodia / Clodius*.

34. ante amissis: L. A wrongly divided *antea missis*; G's *amissis* no doubt results from a scribe's eye moving from the first *a-* to the second.

ext. 1. *Hieron and Masinissa.* The latter occupies almost the whole of the *exemplum*, Hieron being allotted only seven words.

36. Siciliae ... peruenit: Livy (24.4.4), probably V.'s source, also says that Hieron died in his ninetieth year; according to ps. Lucian (*macr.* 10) he was 92.

At the beginning of the First Punic War Hieron II, (the index to my edition wrongly lists this passage under Hiero I, who lived in the fifth century), king of Syracuse, was allied to Carthage, but Rome's early successes persuaded him to switch sides and in 263 he came to an agreement with Rome and remained a loyal ally until his death in 215, which was followed by Syracuse's defection to

Hannibal. But V.'s *rector Siciliae* is totally misleading: Hieron controlled only Syracuse and a number of towns in its immediate vicinity. See Walbank i. 53–7 (Hieron's rise to power), 66–9, Scullard, *CAH* vii²/2.546.

36–48. The Numidian king Masinissa originally supported Carthage but defected to Rome in 205, a year after his rival Syphax had moved in the opposite direction. During the first half of the second century he was involved in numerous boundary disputes with Carthage, in which the senate consistently took Masinissa's side, and which culminated in the Third Punic War. Masinissa died in 148, the year following the outbreak of the war. See Walsh, *JRS* 55 (1965), 149–60 (the best thing Walsh wrote), Astin, *SA*, 49–51, and my note on Livy 31.11.4–18.

V. says, unusually citing an extant source (he does so again at line 92, but not at first hand; cf. p. 65), that Cicero's *de senectute* is his source for Masinissa's refusal to cover his head because of rain or cold. He is referring to *Cato* 34, but V. has nothing corresponding to Cicero's statement that if Masinissa began a journey on foot, he never mounted a house, if on horseback, he never dismounted. On the other hand, everything else in V. (on Masinissa's age see line 52 n.) finds correspondence not in Cicero, but in Polybius 36.16: the likelihood is that the material was taken over by Livy and that V. combined it with what he read in Cicero and the source on longevity which he shared with Pliny (see above); the latter's influence can be seen in the similarity of *post sextum et nonagesimum annum filium generaret* and Plin. *nat.* 7.61 *post lxxxvi annum generasse filium* (cf. Helm, *RE* viiiA. 104). References to other sources are given in the notes which follow. See Bloomer, 93–6, demolishing Maire's argument that V. here used Diodorus.

36. Masinissa: V. mentions him also at 1.1. ext. 2, 2.10.4, 5.1.1d, 7, 2. ext. 4, 7.2.6, 9.13. ext. 2. The authoritative manuscripts consistently spell his name thus, as, with very few exceptions, do those of Livy; elsewhere *Mass-* sometimes occurs. Those of Polybius have Μασαννάσσης (Büttner-Wobst thought that he wrote Μασαννάσας).

37. hunc modum excessit: i.e. Hieron lived to 89, Masinissa to 90. The latter figure is given explicitly by Pol. 36.16.2, 5, 11, Diod. 32.16 (the whole chapter derives from Polybius), and [Lucian] *macr.* 17; Frontin. *Strat.* 4.3.11 says that he was in his ninetieth year. Cic. loc. cit. makes him 90 in 150, at the time of the dramatic date of the dialogue; cf. lines 39–40 n. (Pliny *nat.* 7.61 has nothing about Masinissa's age at death, as Walbank iii. 676, giving the reference as 'vii. 14.2', claims.) At 5.2. ext. 4 V. makes him live until his hundredth year (it is surprising that no one has ever suggested emending *centesimum* to *nonagesimum*, *xc* being corrupted to *c*).

regni ... spatium: an elaborate alternative to *qui sexaginta annos regnauit*. The same figure is given by Pol. 36.16.2 ('more than 60 years'), Diod.

32.16, and Plin. *nat.* 7.156. The true figure was around 55 years; see Walbank loc. cit.

38–39. Cicero ... scripsit: see above. Apart from those of the grammarians (Nonius Marcellus cites it 58 times) and of Cicero himself at *Att.* 14.21.3, *diu.* 2.3, this is the only explicit ancient reference to the *Cato*; for other works which may have been influenced by it see Powell, 27–30.

39. libro: cf. 15 lines 54–5 n.

39–40. nullo ... potuisse: Cic. *nullo imbri nullo frigore adduci ut capite operto sit* (Masinissa is still alive at the dramatic date of *Cato*; cf. Cic. *quae faciat hodie*, line 37 n.); V. adds *umquam*, elaborates *capite operto sit*, and adds *potuisse*.

39. nullo ... frigore: phrasal asyndeton.

imbri: thus α; P has *imbre*. Both forms of the ablative singular of *imber* are attested from early Latin onwards, but since *imbri* is clearly the transmitted reading in Cicero (see Powell's apparatus) and *imbre* is preferred in late Latin (cf. *TLL* vii/1.421.42 ff.), there is clearly no reason not to follow the direct tradition.

40–43. eundem ferunt ... durasse: Pol. 36.16.2 ὅτε μὲν στῆναι δέοι, στὰς ἐν τοῖς αὐτοῖς ἴχνεσι δι' ἡμέρας ἔμενε, καθεζόμενος <δὲ> πάλιν οὐκ ἠγείρετο. Nothing in Polybius corresponds to *non ante ... fatigasset*, but it could have been added by Livy rather than V.

40–41. in eodem uestigio: number apart, an exact translation of ἐν τοῖς αὐτοῖς ἴχνεσι. *eodem uestigio* occurs at Caes. *Gall.* 4.2.3.

42. ac: α; A^c corrected to *at*, but Masinissa's abilities to both stand and sit still are clearly coordinated, not contrasted.

a sedente: L^cG. AL have *ad sedentem*, which, as A^c realised, is probably a corruption of *as(d)sidentem*, itself resulting from a misapprehension that *agere* preceded. Halm, followed by Kempf, read *ab sedente*, and if G's text is a correction rather than a transmitted reading, that would have made the original corruption easier. The entry for *a* and *ab* in Otón Sobrino's lexicon (i. 1–14) contains, if I am not mistaken, 670 passages, only six of which are instances of *ab* before a consonant (1.6.13, 3.2.4, 8.6, 6.5.1.4, 2.4, 7.2; he also cites 2.2.6, where *ab* is a misprint for *ad*, and 9.7. mil. Rom. 1, where the reading is uncertain; I printed *a*); what is more, in five of these passages *ab* governs a noun (three of them a proper name), in the sixth a pronoun (*se*). While manuscripts cannot always be relied on for this sort of matter, it is most unlikely that the overall statistics are more than marginally wrong, and in these circumstances the introduction of *ab* by conjecture is quite unjustifiable. Cf. 1 line 47 n.

saepe numero: before V., used by Cicero, Caesar, and Sallust; V. may have written it as one word (thus Shackleton Bailey).

43. durasse: 'held out'; before V., the usage occurs in verse in Plautus, Lucretius, and Ovid, but in prose only at Livy 5.2.7 and 6.4 (of the siege of Veii). Cf. *TLL* v/1. 2296.42 ff.

44. noctem diei ... iungendo: cf. Ovid *met.* 11.96, Sen. *contr.* 1 praef. 14 (*TLL* vii/2.685.63 ff.).

45. quo mollius senectutem: the transmitted reading was evidently *quo millius* (A) or *quom illius* (L; *cum illius* A^c). G has *quo minus in senectute*, clearly a conjecture, later manuscripts *quo minus senectute* (Kempf (1854) implies that all those he uses have *quo minus*, all but Γ *senectute*) and this remained the vulgate until C. F. W. Müller (*ZG* 20 (1866), 64) restored the truth by the alteration of one letter (Cornellisen's *mitius* gives an inferior sense and posits a less likely corruption).

46–47. ueneris etiam ... nomen fuit: Pol. 36.16.5 ἔχων ἐνενήκοντ' ἔτη, καθ' ὃν καιρὸν μετήλλαξε τὸν βίον, υἱὸν ἀπέλειπε τεττάρων ἐτῶν, ὄνομα Σθέμβανον, ὃν μετὰ ταῦτα Μικίψης υἱοποιήσατο, πρὸς δὲ τούτοις υἱοὺς ἐννέα. At 5.2. ext. 4 V. gives Masinissa 54 sons.

46. ueneris ... uiguit: Livy (29.23.4), describes the Numidians as sex maniacs (*effusi in uenerem*).

post sextum et octogesimum annum: i.e. 90 minus 4. P has the mathematically nonsensical *xc* (*octogesimum* (*lxxx* G) α and Landolfus Sagax): it is striking that at lines 85 and 93 P again increases a figure by ten, while at line 98 he does so by a hundred; cf. 15 line 36 n.

47. Methymno: Walbank (iii. 676), in an most unusually inaccurate note, does not mention that at Pol. 36.16.5 the sole manuscript (Tours, Bibliothèque municipale 980 = P) has σθεμβανον (*sic*) and says that App. *Lib.* 106.500 and Cic. *Cato* 34 call him Methymnus, Plin. *nat.* 7. 61 Metymannus: Cicero does not mention the boy at all, Appian does not give his name, and in Pliny the manuscripts vary; *Metymannum* is the reading of Detlefsen and it is quite possible that both Polybius and Pliny in fact wrote *Methymnum*.

47–48. terram ... reliquit: Pol. 36.16.7–8, much abbreviated in V; cf. Strabo 17, p. 833C, App. *Lib.* 106.499, Walsh, *JRS* 55, 152–4.

ext. 2. *Gorgias*. One of the leading Sophists, Gorgias lived from *c.* 485 to *c.* 380. He was an important figure in the development of Greek prose style. His *Encomium of Helen* and *Defence of Palamedes* survive; for the fragments of other works see DK ii. 279–306. V.'s source is Cic. *Cato* 13. No other writer mentions this anecdote; for others and sources mentioning Gorgias' age, his pupils, and that he was himself a pupil of Empedocles see Wellmann, *RE* vii. 1598–9, Powell on Cic. loc. cit. (Apollodorus *FGrH* 244F33 = D. L. 8.58). See also Wellmann, op. cit., G. B. Kerferd, *The Sophistic Movement* (Cambridge, 1981), 44–6, 78–82, 95–9, D. A. F. M. Russell, *OCD*[4] 622.

49. Gorgias Leontinus: Cicero has *Leontinus Gorgias*, for which see Leeman–Pinkster on Cic. *de orat.* 1.103, Powell ad loc.; V. changes to the normal word order (so too at 15 line 92).

Isocratis ... uirorum: Cicero mentions only Isocrates (cf. 7. ext. 9 n.). Other pupils attested are Alcidamas of Elea (D.H. *Isoc.* 19, Ath. 592C, Suda *s.nn.* Ἀλκιδάμας, Γοργίας, Δημοσθένης I, Pericles (Suda *s.n.* Γοργίας), Proxenus of Boeotia (Xen. *anab.* 2.6.16), and Polus of Acragas (Suda *s.n.* Γοργίας).

On the orthography of *Isocratis* see 7 line 189 n.

50. sua: Kempf reports Gertz as suggesting *sua senex*, which both produces an extraordinary word order and posits a very implausible omission; I wonder, therefore, whether he in fact proposed *senex sua*, which would avoid those objections but is totally unnecessary.

51–52. nihil ... accusem: Cic. '*nihil habeo*' inquit '*quod accusem*'. For (*non, nihil*) *habere quod* 'to have (no) reason to' cf. K–St ii. 278.

52–53. aut longius aut beatius: in ext. 4–7 V. proceeds to give seven examples of an allegedly longer life; he ought to have written *longo tractu aetatis beatius*.

53–54. neque in hoc ... illo reliquit: he had nothing in his first hundred years to complain about and made no complaints thereafter.

ext. 3. *Xenophilus.* Xenophilus' age is given as 105 by Pliny *nat.* 7.168 and [Lucian] *macr.* 18, the latter also citing Aristoxenus as his source. DL 8.16, 46, Iamblichus *Pyth.* 251, and Suda *s.n.* Ἀριστόξενος mention him in connection with Aristoxenus, saying, respectively, that the latter cited a saying of Xenophilus, saw him, was the source of information about the last group of Pythagoreans in southern Italy, and was his pupil (these references are given by Ziegler, *RE* ixA. 1566). Xenophilus' life will have spanned the greater part, if not the whole, of the fourth century BC.

55. Xenophilus: P (and Lupus) have the extraordinary error, whether of Paris or in the course of transmission (as Halm thought, printing Xenophilus in Paris) Xeno philosophus.

Chalcidensis: from Chalcidice, not Euboean Chalcis; see DL 8.46, Iamb. loc. cit., though both speak of him as a Chalcidian ἀπὸ Θράκης (cf. Arist. *pol.* 1274b24).

56. Aristoxenus musicus: Aristoxenus, from Tarentum, was the most important Greek musical theorist, who also wrote works of philosophy, history, and biography. He lived from *c.* 370 until some time after 322; see von Jan, *RE* ii. 1057–65, A. D. Barker, *OCD*[4] 163–4.

According to Pliny and Lucian (locc. citt.) Xenophilus too was a *musicus*.

ext. 4. *Arganthonius; Pollio.* V.'s source for lines 83–7 *auctores* is Cic. *Cato* 69, to which he adds the citation from Pollio (= *FRHist* 56F1) in the rest of the *exemplum*; there is no reason to doubt that V. read Pollio at first hand (thus Bloomer, 144–5).

Herodotus (1.163.2) says that Arganthonius, the king of Tartessus, lived for 120 years; other writers (Plin. *nat.* 7.154, App. *Ib.* 63.267, [Lucian] *macr.* 10, Phlegon *FGrH* 257F37(V), misinterpreting Anacreon fr. 8 Diehl = 361 Page (cf. 7 lines 159–60 n.) give him 150 years (Censorinus 17.3 claims that this is Herodotus' figure), while Silius 3.396–8 makes him reign for 300 years). Cf. Münzer, *Plinius*, 105–8, arguing that Pliny combined V. and Varro.

See Powell on Cic. loc. cit., Drummond, *FRHist* iii. 521. The latter, as usual, demonstrates his extraordinary bibliographical knowledge, but strangely does not refer to Powell's note (and does not mention Silius).

58. Gaditanus: for the mistaken identification of Gades, a Phoenician colony (mod. Cádiz) with Tartessus (Cicero refers to both) see Drummond, loc. cit.

58–59. quam diu ... foret: 'reigned for so long a period that to have lived that long would be more than enough to produce satiety' (SB). *etiam* (which he does not translate), *ad satietatem*, and *abunde* are pleonastic in the extreme; perhaps V. is deliberately using far more than enough words to convey his meaning. Gertz transposed *ad satietatem* and *uixisse*, so that *etiam* goes with *uixisse* ('even to have lived'): that produces much better Latin, but it is not what V. wrote. (Damsté, typically, deleted *ad satietatem*).

60. cuius ... auctores: V. strengthens Cicero's *ut scriptum uideo*.

61. Asinius etiam Pollio: on Pollio, consul in 40, and his historical work see Drummond, *FRHist* i. 430–45.

non minima ... stili: 'not the least part of Roman literature' (SB). Cf. Gallus fr. 145 Hollis (*Fragments of Roman Poetry c. 20 BC–AD 20*, Oxford, 2007, 224), Virg. *Aen.* 2.6, 10.427, P. J. Parsons and R. G. M. Nisbet, *JRS* 69 (1979), 141.

61–62. tertio ... libro: V. cites four fragments of otherwise lost Roman historians: the others are 1.7.6 Coelius Antipater *FRHist* 15F49b (from Cicero), 4.3.2 Munatius Rufus *FRHist* 37F1, and 4.4.11 Aemilius Scaurus *FRHist* 18F1. The last, like our passage, has a book number.

62. centum ... annos: perhaps a deliberate compromise between 120 and 150; Drummond (*FRHist* iii. 521) thinks that Pollio was 'implicitly engaging' with Varro's argument that high lifetime figures were calculated on the basis of 'years' that were in fact the length of a month (cf. Lact. *inst.* 2.12.21–2).

62–63. neruosae uiuacitatis: 'vigorous longevity' (SB). A striking example of linguistic innovation. *neruosus* in this sense does not occur before this passage; in the sense of 'sinewy' it refers to parts of the body at Catull. 67.27 and Lucr. 4.461, to style at Cic. *Brut.* 121. For *uiuacitas* cf. 7 line 41 n.

ext. 5. *Ethiopians, Indians, Epimenides.* V. cites separate sources for the three items and I therefore deal with them in the notes that follow.

64. consummationem: cf. 7 lines 48–9 n. Here it means 'accumulation' (*TLL* iv. 595.12 ff.).

65. Herodotus: 3.23.1. This is the only occasion on which V. mentions him.

uicesimum: cf. line 46 n. My apparatus is somewhat obscure: A has *xxmum*, LG *xx*; P has *xxx annos* and Lupus added a third *x* to A's reading.

66. Ctesias idem: α has the nonsensical *et Eseias quidem*, I wrongly ascribed the truth to '*dett.*'. In fact *Ctesias* appears first in the Aldine edition of 1502, *idem* in the Milan edition of 1508,[106] Ctesias of Cnidus (*FGrH* 688; unfortunately Jacoby missed our passage) was a doctor at the court of Artaxerxes II, who succeeded to the Persian throne in 405. His principal work was τὰ Περσικά in 23 books; our passage comes from the single book of τὰ Ἰνδικά and he also wrote a Περίοδος in three books.

Epimenides Cnosius: Epimenides was a legendary figure about whom nothing can be known for certain. The 157 years attributed to him by Theopompus (see below) and Phlegon of Tralles (*FGrH* 257F38) is almost doubled by the 299 which DL 1.111 says was the figure given by the Cretans themselves; Xenophanes (DK 21F20) made it 154. The story of his purification of Athens from the pollution caused by the murder of the associates of Cylon, first found in *Ath. Pol.* 1, is variously dated to the end of the seventh or beginning of the sixth century (see Rhodes 81, 83), but Plato (*leg.* 642D) puts him in Athens shortly before the Persian Wars. If the latter is right, Epimenides could have been the author of the *Theogony* attributed to him, but the other works under his name (see *FGrH* 457) are clearly forgeries. See further Münzer, *Plinius*, 105 n. 1, 159–50, Kern, *RE*vi. 173–8, Jacoby, *FGrH* iiib, Text, 308–15, Noten, 190–200.

A and P have *Cnosius*, A^c and G *Gnosius*, and L has *Onosius*. This suggests that *Cn-* represents the paradosis, but while both forms are attested elsewhere, Livy is the only Latin writer before V. to mention Cnossos and *Gn-* is transmitted at both 37.60.3 and 42.51.7: hence my *fort. recte* for *Gnosius*.

---

[106] Thus the BL catalogue (there is no date in the edition itself); cf. M. Crab, *Schede umanistiche* 26 (2012), 111–18, *BiblH&R* 75 (2013), 294. Schullian (*CTC* v. 302; but cf. p. 375, accepting the date of 1509–11) thought that since it did not contain the *exempla* missing in the direct tradition, it may in fact be earlier than the first Aldine, published in 1502 (cf. ed., p. xxxiv). The argument lacks force: they had first been included in the Mainz edition of 1471, but not in most subsequent incunables (cf. p. 19). Coler, in his Frankfurt edition of 1601, credited *Ctesias idem* to 'Edit. Venet.', by which he presumably meant the Venice reprint of the Milan edition, published later in 1508 (the Aldine of that year, like that of 1502, has *quidem*); cf. Crab, opp. citt.

Theopompus: *FGrH* 115F68b (I omitted to give the reference in my testimonia apparatus); 68a is *Paroemiographi Graeci* i. 309, adding that Epimenides was asleep for 57 of these years (πεντήκοντα καί is an addition by Meursius on the basis of DL 1.109), 68c Pliny *nat.* 7.154. Theopompus of Chios (from which he was twice exiled) was, with Xenophon and Ephorus, one of the most important historians of the fourth century BC. He wrote the *Hellenica* (twelve books), a continuation of Thucydides covering the years 411 to 394 and, his principal work, the *Philippica* (58 books), of which *FGrH* contains no fewer than 373 fragments. See particularly G. S. Shrimpton, *Theopompus the Historian* (Montreal, 1991), M. A. Flower, *Theopompus of Chios: History and Rhetoric in the Fourth Century* (Oxford, 1994).

ext. 6–7. *Epii, Dandon, King of Latmos.* Pliny *nat.* 7.154–5 (my testimonia apparatus refers only to 154) similarly cites Hellanicus, Damastes, Alexander, and Xenophon.

ext. 6. 68. Hellanicus: *FGrH* 4F195. Hellanicus of Lesbos (*c.* 480–395), a leading figure in fifth century Greek historiography, wrote the first Atthis, as well as works of mythography, ethnography, and chronology. Cf. Gudeman, *RE* viii. 104–55, P. E. Harding, *OCD*⁴ 655.

Epiorum ... est: in Homer the Ἐπειοί are the original inhabitants of Elis. Ephorus (*FGrH* 70F115, from Strabo 8, pp. 357–8C) says that Aetolus was expelled from Elis to Aetolia by the king of the Epii, naming the country after himself. He subsequently invaded Elis, defeated the Epii and took possession of their land. There is no evidence for a people called Epii in Aetolia in historical times and the natural assumption is that the reference to Aetolia was an erroneous comment by V. or his source (Pliny has *quosdam in Aetolia Epiorum*). Furthermore, *est* is absent in α and was added by A^c: it could, though, have easily been omitted in copying from a manuscript which abbreviated *est* to *ē* (cf. Lindsay, *Notae Latinae*, 69, observing that it is an ancient abbreviation). I continue, though, to wonder (but no more) whether *quae pars Aetoliae* originates from a gloss, added by someone who remembered what Pliny had written. The original gloss could have been just *pars Aetoliae*; someone thought it was part of the text and added *quae* and *est*, the latter being subsequently omitted.

68–69. ducenos: AL; G has *ducentenos*, later manuscripts (Kempf says just 'dett.'; in 1854 he printed *ducentos*, with no entry in his apparatus) read *ducentos*, while P has *ccc* (cf. line 46 n.). The distributive could be regarded as hypercorrect, but there is no good reason to depart from the reading of the oldest MSS; G's reading is an analogizing form found in some later writers (cf. *TLL* v/1.2143.33 ff.); one cannot exclude the possibility that it was a variant in the archetype.

69. Damastes: *FGrH* 5F5. Damastes of Sigeum was a pupil of Hellanicus who wrote works of both history and ethno-geography (Suda; T1); only eleven fragments survive.

69–70. Litorium: in the manuscripts of Pliny his name appears as *Pictor(-e-, -i-)um*; there is no other mention of him. Damastes was no doubt seeking to improve on his teacher's far-fetched story.

70. maximarum ... praecipuae: chiasmus.

ext. 7. 72. Alexander: *FGrH* 273F17. Alexander Polyhistor of Miletus. He was captured, presumably during the Mithridatic Wars of the 80s, and came to Rome as the slave of a Cornelius Lentulus; he was subsequently freed by Sulla (Suda; T1), thus taking the name Cornelius. He was a prolific writer, largely of geographical works containing a large amount of paradoxography. Iulius Hyginus was his pupil (Suet. *gramm.* 20; T3; cf. *FRHist* i. 475).

de Illyrico tractu: it is unclear whether this is a translation of the title given to the work by Alexander or merely a description of its contents.

73. Dandonem: again (cf. line 99 n.), there is no other mention of him. The form of the name (*dant donam* AL, *Danthonam* G) is guaranteed by the agreement of P and the manuscripts of Pliny.

74. Xenophon ... περίπλους: Xenophon of Lampsacus (not in *FGrH*) lived in the late second and/or early first centuries BC: he referred to the destruction of Carthage (Plin. *nat.* 6.199) and was used by Alexander Polyhistor (*FGrH* 273F72). In view of the latter, it is likely that the citation of Xenophon derives ultimately from Alexander. Pliny cites Xenophon also at *nat.* 4.95 and 6.200, and lists him as a source for books 3, 5, and 6. He is also cited by Solin. 56.12. Cf. Gisinger, *RE* ixA. 2051–5.

I should not have said that περίπλους is found in later MSS; Kempf (1854) does not cite it from any of those he used. It was first printed by Pighius, though as two words.

legitur: V. presumably means that the citation is from Xenophon's work entitled περίπλους, but there seems to be no parallel for the use of *legere* to indicate a title (the passage is not cited in *TLL s.u.*). SB translates literally 'is read', which is not helpful; it is scarcely likely that V. means that the work is extant (in any case, how would he have known?).

75. insulae ... Latmiorum: α; P has *Lamiorum*, the MSS of Pliny *Lutm(-in-)iorum*, which has been variously emended (to *Latmiorum* by Salmasius). The agreement, initial vowel apart, of α and the MSS of Pliny eliminates *Lamiorum*; in any case, the ethnic of Lamia is Λαμιεύς; nor is Lamia (Barrington Atlas 55C3) an island, though it is near the Malian Gulf and it could have been claimed that it was once an island. Latmus lay a little east of Miletus, at the foot of the mountain of the same name (Barrinton Atlas 61F2) and near a large lake (mod.

Bala Gölü); it too could have been said to have originally been an island. There is no toponym beginning *Lutm-* and whatever is read in Pliny, there is no reason to depart from the transmitted reading in V. (cf. Gisinger, art. cit. 2053).

76. parum benigne acceptus: 'harshly treated' (SB). *benigne accipere* is first found in Livy (cf. *TLL* iv. 1905.32 ff.), but this ironic negative formulation appears to be unique.

quoque: 'in addition', going with the whole clause: no one else who lived for 600 years has been mentioned.

14 praef. V. says, at some length, that he is not concerned with theorizing about glory, only with examples of desire for it. On glory in ancient philosophers see U. Knoche, *Philologus* 89 (1934), 102–23, A. D. Leeman, *Gloria* (Rotterdam, 1949; in Dutch, with an extensive English summary on pp. 177–90), chs. 3–4 (pp. 25–122), dealing, respectively, with Hellenistic philosophers before Posidonius and Posidonius himself.

Cicero wrote a work *de gloria* (for the jejune fragments see O. Plasberg in the Teubner edition of Cicero, *Cato* and *Laelius*, 88–90), which V. may well have used; cf. p. 243.

V. has spoken of *gloria* on sixty-two occasions, and will do so ten further times in ch. 15 and book 9 (see Otón Sobrino ii. 843–5).

1. cuius sit habitus: 'what is its character'.

2. melius a uirtute neglegatur: the Epicurean view; cf. Cic. *Pis.* 56, with Nisbet's note, Livy 22.39.9.

4. animaduerterunt: A^c. AL have *animaduerterentur* (divided in different ways), G *animaduerterent*: the passive is clearly wrong (the subject continues to be *ii*) and the imperfect subjunctive inexplicable. I now wonder whether V. wrote *animaduerterint*, the subjunctive being generalizing ('whatever they observed') and the tense (one would expect the pluperfect) influenced by *uiderint* above.

4–5. factis ... facta sua: 'who did what'.

5. propriis: can be taken as either 'appropriate' (thus SB) or 'individual'.

1. *Scipio Africanus and Ennius.* V.'s source is Cic. *Arch.* 22; to the other sources listed in my *testimonia* apparatus add Hier. *chron.* a.Abr. 1852. The *exemplum* consists of one long and less than perspicacious period (see lines 8–13 n.).

7. superior Africanus: thus Cic. loc. cit. V.'s many references to the elder Scipio are listed in the index to my edition (p. 862); he calls him *superior Africanus* also at 2.7.12, 10.2, 3.5.1, 4.2.3, 5.3, 5.3.2b, 4.2, 6.7, 6.6.4, 9.2, 7.3.3, 9.8.1 (cf. 2.10.4). This is the first occasion in book 8 that V. mentions him explicitly, though he does so allusively at 1. damn. 1.

7–8. Enni … uoluit : the tomb of the Scipios, still extant, lies on the Via Appia, between the Servian and Aurelian walls; see Zevi, *LTUR* iv. 281–5. In the version of Valerius Antias Scipio was buried at Liternum (Livy 38.52.8), but at 38.56.3–4 Livy says that according to some writers he was buried in Rome and adds that there are three statues in the tomb of the Scipios, said to be of Africanus, his brother Lucius (cf. 1 line 106 n.), and Ennius. Like Livy and the other early sources, V. does not say that Ennius was buried there; that appears first in schol. Bob. on Cic. *Arch.* 22 (p. 178 St.) and Hier. loc. cit. (The above largely repeats what I wrote in my note on Livy 38.56.4.)

8–13. non quidem … dignior: the three clauses depending on *quam diu* (*Romanum … floreret, et Africa … subiecta, totiusque … possideret*) limit *eorum … non posse*, though at first glance the reader might well imagine that they are indirect questions depending on *non quidem ignarus*.

10. totiusque … possideret: for Rome as the *caput orbis terrarum / mundi*, first attested in Livy (1.16.7, 21.30.10, the latter put in the mouth of Hannibal) and Ovid, cf. *TLL* iii. 426.29 ff. Taken literally, the claim that the Capitoline occupied the highest point in the Roman empire is absurd.

11–12. si tamen … accessisset: AL. *sed … accessisse* is a correction in A and G has *se … accessisse*. The reading of AL is not only unexceptionable but clearly right and the correction seems strange. It is possible, however, that G preserves the paradosis, which survived as a variant in the source of AL, to be adopted by A^c with *se* altered to *sed*.

12. Homerico … praeconio: cf. Sil. 13.793–7, Suda *s.u.* Ἔννιος. V. is probably alluding to Ennius' claim that Homer had appeared to him in a dream, saying that the latter's soul had passed into his (*ann.* 1–11Sk = 1, 5–6, 10–15, 69V; for other *testimonia* see Skutsch, 150–3); Horace (*epist.* 2.1.50) called Ennius an *alter Homerus*. V. may also be alluding to Cic. *fam.* 5.12.7 (the letter to Lucceius). V. judges Ennius by the standards of his age; cf. Hor. *epist.* 2.1.51–2, Vell. 1.17, H. Prinzen, *Ennius im Urteil der Antike* (Stuttgart–Weimar, 1998), 342–5 (Prinzen's book was the subject of one of Harry Jocelyn's last reviews, published posthumously in *JRS* 90 (2000), 217–18).

For *praeconium* in the sense of publicly expressed praise, also used thus by V. at 3.2.22 and 5.1. ext. 1, cf. *TLL* x/2.2504.53 ff.

2. *D. Iunius Brutus and Accius.* V.'s source is Cic. *Arch.* 27 (cf. schol. Bob. ad loc. (p. 179 Stangl)); Cicero also mentions Brutus' friendship with Accius at *Brut.* 107; Pliny *nat.* 36.26 refers to his temple.

14. honoratus animus: for the active sense of *honoratus* ('disposition to honour' SB) cf. 13 line 5 n.

Accium: L. Accius, playwright and scholar, lived from 170 to *c.* 86; see H. D. Jocelyn–G. Manuwald, *OCD*⁴ 3, E. Stärk in Suerbaum 158–66.

D. Bruti: D. Iunius Brutus Callaicus (57), consul in 138, with command prorogued in 137 and 136. He defeated the Lusitani and Callaeci (the latter name survives in the modern Spanish region of Galicia), took the *cognomen* Callaicus, and celebrated a triumph (cf. *MRR* i. 483, 485, 487).

15–16. uersibus: A^c added *eius* before, later manuscripts (DEF) after *uersibus*. The omission is easy in either position, a scribe's eye moving from one *-us* ro another, but *eius* is easily understood from *cuius*. Schol. Bob., loc. cit., says that they were Saturnians.

16. templorum ... consecrauerat: the temple of Mars in the Circus Flaminius, designed by Hermodorus of Salamis; see Nepos *FRHist* 45F11 and for further details and bibliography commentary ad loc. (iii. 502).

This appears to be the only instance in prose of *templa* referring to a single temple (cf., e.g., Virg. *Aen.* 6.19, 41, Ovid, *fast.* 4.159); for such 'poetic plurals' cf. K–St i. 82–5, H–S 16–18. Perhaps V. thought it appropriate in the context.

3. *Pompey and Theophanes.* V.'s source is Cic. *Arch.* 24 (cf. lines 17–20 n.). For Strabo 13, p. 617C see lines 25–6 n.

17. Pompeius ... Magnus: this is the first mention of Pompey in book 8 (he reappears at 15.8–9); for other references to him see the index to my edition (pp. 878–9).

17–20. Theophanen ... prosecutus: *Theophanen ... donauit* reproduces Cicero exactly, but nothing corresponds to *beneficium ... prosecutus*, while V. omits what Cicero says about the approving shouts of Pompey's soldiers.

17–18. Theophanen ... suarum: Strabo, loc. cit., says that Theophanes was both a historian and a Mitylenean politician. He mentions Theophanes' friendship with Pompey and the assistance Theophanes gave him, but not that he wrote about his achievements. For other references to him see *FGrH* 188T1–10 (in 48 he served as Pompey's *praefectus fabrum*: T8); add *CRAI* 1969, 42–64, *Chiron* 22 (1992), 377–82. His historical work appears to have dealt only with the Third Mithridatic War (*FGrH* 188F1–7).

18. Mitylenaeum: the original form of the name was Μυτιλήνη(α), but Μιτυλήνη is found in inscriptions from *c.* 300 BC; manuscripts of Latin authors (who prefer *-nae*) vary and it is impossible to determine what they wrote on any particular occasion. At 6.5. ext. 1 *Mity-* is transmitted, here α has *Mity-*, P *Myti-*, while at 9.11.4, where Paris has no mention of the city, α (AG; L is defective at this point) has *Myti-*.

19. testata: 'well attested' (not 'well publicized' (SB)). *accurata* and *testata* limit *oratione* in different ways, but for V. 's use of *testatus* adjectivally see 9 line 2 n. Perizonius' *recitata* (omitting *et*) and Gertz' *exacta* are both unnecessary and implausible in themselves.

21. incohareth: 'initiating' (SB).

4. *Sulla.* Sulla's use of a signet ring engraved with the surrender of Jugurtha is also mentioned by Pliny *nat.* 37.9, Plut. *Sull.* 3.8–9, *Mar.* 10.8, *mor.* 806D; for a coin of Faustus Sulla commemorating it see *RRC* no. 426.1. Sallust (*Iug.* 102–13) narrates in detail Sulla's part in the events that led to the capture of Jugurtha, but says nothing about the signet ring. V.'s immediate source cannot be determined.

22. L. ... Sulla: cf. 6 line 9 n.

etsi ... direxit: V. thus indicates the transition from the first three *exempla*, all of which derive from Cicero *pro Archia*, to those which do not concern literary figures and derive from other sources.

22–23. Iugurthae ... perducti: Marius had been elected consul for 107 and succeeded to the command of the war against Jugurtha, which had begun in 111; the events referred to took place in 105. Bocchus, the king of Mauretania, had joined Jugurtha, whose daughter was one of his many wives, in the winter of 108/7 (Sall. *Iug.* 80); their forces were defeated by Marius in 106 (Sall. *Iug.* 101) and Jugurtha was captured in 105.

α has the nonsensical *perducto* (and G the additional corruption *Iugurtha*), by perserveration from the preceding ablatives); *perducti* is the reading of two manuscripts cited by Torrenius.

23. tam: added by A^c: the omission will have been caused by a scribe's eye moving from (*tande*)*m* to *ta*(*m*). Heraeus (*Philologus* 59 (1900), 434) suggested inserting *adeo* before *adseruit* (equally plausible palaeographically), adducing the placing of *adeo* after an adverb at 9.3. ext. 3: I should have given him a *fort. recte*.

24–25. et quantus<quantus> postea: Perizonius' supplement, positing the easiest of haplographies, provides by far the simplest alternative to the transmitted reading (*quantusquantus* occurs in Plautus, Terence, Lucretius, and Cicero). Pighius retained the latter, placing an exclamation mark after it, but that produces an abruptness totally alien to V., not much imroved by Gertz' addition of *ita*; Kempf (1854; in 1888 he obelized, suggesting *et quantuscumque postea*) merely punctuated with a comma after *postea*, most implausibly arguing that *et tantus quantus postea erat* is to be understood. There is no need to discuss the other proposals (*en* for *et* Halm, *qui tantus* Gertz, *euasit tunc* after *postea* Novák).

5. *The freedman and Metellus Scipio.* There is no other evidence for this episode. V. may have learnt of it orally.

26. gloriosum: cf. line 71 n.

Scipionem: Q. Caecilius Metellus Scipio Nasica (99). He was the son of P. Cornelius Scipio Nasica, probably praetor in 94 or 93 (cf. Broughton, *MRR* ii. 16 n. 2), and grandson of P. Cornelius Scipio Nasica, consul in 111 and Caecilia Metella, daughter of Q. Caecilius Metellus Macedonicus (cf. 5 lines 3–4 n.), but was adopted, perhaps posthumously, by Q. Caecilius Metellus Pius, consul in 80. Despite this pedigree, he, together with P. Plautius Hypsaeus, had the support of Clodius in the abortive consular elections for 52. After the murder of Clodius, however, Pompey, now sole consul, married Metellus Scipio's daughter and secured his acquittal on a charge of *ambitus* (see 9.5.3). In the civil war he commanded the centre of Pompey's army at Pharsalus in 48; after the battle he fled to Africa and assumed command of the Pompeian forces; defeated by Caesar at Thapsus in 46, he committed suicide while attempting to escape by sea (see 3.2.13). The present episode, if historical, will have taken placce in 47. For other anecdotes involving him see 3.8.7, 9.1.8 (the latter's authenticity, accepted by Syme, *RR* 40, in a devastating assessment of Scipio, is highly dubious). See further Münzer, *RE* iii.1224–8 (with stemma).

27. T. Labienus: (6). A *popularis* tribune in 63, Labienus served as a *legatus pro praetore* (perhaps an indication that he had held the praetorship by 59) under Caesar throughout his Gallic campaigns, but joined Pompey in January 49 (Cic. *Att.* 7.11.1; cf. Hirt. *Gall.* 8.52.3) and served under him until the battle of Pharsalus in 48; he escaped to Africa, serving under Scipio until the defeat at Thapsus; he fled to Spain and was killed at Munda in 45. See further Münzer, *RE* xii. 260–70.

28. aureas armillas: as in lines 32–3 *argenteis armillis*, the emphasis is on the adjective: Scipio intended to give the *eques* armlets, the only question being whether they should be of gold or silver.

29. qui ... seruisset: it is unclear whether he had been manumitted by his master and soon enrolled in Scipio's army or was a slave given freedom by Scipio himself. Genuine or not, the sentiment typifies the attitude of the Pompeian leaders (cf. Broughton, *MRR* ii. 341, concerning Labienus himself).

29–30. ex praeda Gallica: i.e. gold given to Labienus by Caesar from the booty acquired in Gaul.

30–31. habebis ... diuitis: i.e. Labienus had so much gold he could give it away easily.

31. id accepit: heard Scipio's words, not received the gold, of course.

32. demisit: A^c; *dimisit* α: he hung his head, not got rid of it. For the confusion see 7 line 169 n; see also 15 line 82 n.

33. donat', alacer: Gertz suggested adding *accepto dono* before *alacer*: the omission is explicable, a scribe's eye moving from the first *a-* to the next, but totally unnecessary, as well as spoiling the effect of the brief main clause. (Kempf added *bene* to his report of the conjecture, but did not print it; for this practice (and worse) by Conway and Walters in their OCTs of Livy cf. *Liviana*, 11).

gaudio abiit: *gaudium excepit* P. My apparatus, following that of Kempf, wrongly implies that P has *gaudio excepit*.

tanta humilitas: somebody serving in the cavalry, even if an ex-slave, is scarcely the most humble of men.

6. *C. Fabius Pictor.* V.'s source for Fabius' paintings is unclear: of the first five passages cited in my *testimonia* apparatus, Cic. *Tusc.* 1.4 mentions Fabius, but not Salus or Iunius, Plin. *nat.* 35.19 Fabius and Salus, but not Iunius, Livy 9.43.25 and 10.1.9 Iunius and Salus, but not Fabius, while D.H. 16.3.2 refers only to wall paintings in general.

35. illa: *sc. gloria.*

a claris: *alacris* α. The anagrammatic corruption is easy in itself, but is here assisted by perseveration from *alacer* in line 33.

humillimis: in line 33 *humilitas* refers to the person seeking *gloria*, here to its source. As with the former, V. is carried away by his own rhetoric: painting murals may not have been the most appropriate activity for a patrician, but it was not the lowest imaginable; cf. line 39 *sordido*.

36. quid sibi uoluit: 'what was C. Fabius about?' (SB). For *quid uelle* with the dative of personal pronouns cf., e.g., Cic. *Cato* 66, Livy 3.67.6, K–St i. 324.

C. Fabius: C. Fabius Pictor (122; the *cognomen* is attested only by Pliny loc. cit) was almost certainly the father of the consuls of 269 and 266 and grandfather of Rome's first historian (*FRHist* 1); for the possibility that he is to be identified with C. Fabius Ambustus (*mag. eq.* 315) see Oakley iii. 292–3, *FRHist* i. 163 n. 10.

36–37. aede Salutis quam C. Iunius dedicauerat: C. Iunius Bubulcus Brutus (62), was consul in 317, 313, and 311. It was presumably in the last year that he vowed the temple of Salus, the contract for which he let as censor in 307 (Livy 9.43.25) and which he dedicated as dictator in 302 (Livy 10.1.9). Pliny gives the date of the murals as *a.u.c.* 450 = 304 BC, presumably derived ultimately from Fabius' inscription (cf. Münzer, *RE* vi. 1835). For the temple, situated on the Quirinal, see Coarelli, *LTUR* iv. 229–30; it was destroyed by fire during the reign of Claudius (Pliny loc. cit.). On the development of the cult of abstract deities in this period cf. D. Miano, *Monimenta* (Rome, 2011).

37. inscripsit: (A^cL^cG; *inscribit* AL, *inscribsit* L^c). P has *nomen suum scripsit*, omitting *iis*: my apparatus is misleading.

38. familiae: *familia* can refer to those under the *potestas* of one *pater familias*, to those closely related, or, as here to the *gens Fabia*, to the *gens* as a whole; cf. Livy 2.49.1, 3.12.2, 6.40.3; at 38.58.3 it refers to the Cornelii Scipiones, as contrasted to the *gens Cornelia* (at 38.55.2 it is unclear which is meant); cf. Caes. fr. ap. Suet *Iul.* 6.1 *cuius gentis familia est nostra*, contrasting the Iulii Caesares with the *gens Iulia* as a whole.

consulatibus et sacerdotiis: later MSS (Kempf (1854) implies E and F for the former, just F for the latter); *consularibus et sacerdotibus* α. With *triumphis*, rather than *triumphatoribus*, following, that is certainly what V. ought to have written and he probably did: but I would not exclude the possibility that he in fact wrote *consulibus et sacerdotibus*.

38–39. celeberrimae: A^c; α has *celeberrimum*, caused by anticipation of the three words ending in -*um* in the following sentence.

39. deerat: later manuscripts (cf. Torrenius), an obvious emendation of α's *dederat*.

sordido: cf. line 35 n.

qualemcumque: 'for what it was worth'; for the depreciatory use of *qualiscumque* cf. *OLD s.u.* 1c (SB's 'whatever its nature' misses the point'; at lines 64–5 his 'whatever may be thought of' is appropriate).

40–42. uidelicet ... solueretur: other transitions to *exempla externa* involving a close connection between the last Roman and first foreign *exemplum* occur in book 1 ch. 1 and book 5 ch. 4. Since it forms part of the preceding sentence, it was impossible to avoid putting Phidias into the Roman *exempla*.

Phidias of Athens, the most famous of all ancient sculptors, was active from c. 470 until the 420s; see Stewart 257. V. is referring to the chryselephantine statue of Athena Parthenos on the Acropolis (see Stewart 257–63). Of the four passages cited in my *testimonia* apparatus, Cic. *de orat.* 2.73 merely mentions the statue, *orat.* 234 says that removal of the shield would result in the destruction of the whole work, but has nothing about its containing a self-portrait, *Tusc.* 1.34 the self-portrait but not the consequences of removing it; similarly Plut. *Per.* 31.3, adding that it also contained a portrait of Pericles. V.'s version derives from a Hellenistic invention, found also at [Arist.] *mir. ausc.* 846a, *mund.* 399b, Dio Chrys 12.6. Apul. *mund.* 32; Ampel. 8.10 substitutes Daedalus for Phidias. See E. Preisshofen, *JDAI* 89 (1974), 50–69; cf. Stewart 259, Stadter 294.

qua ... solueretur is a relative final clause.

ext. 1. *Themistocles.* Cf. 7 ext. 15 n. The story in lines 43–8 is mentioned by Plutarch on no fewer than six occasions (*Them.* 3.4, *Thes.* 6.9, *mor.* 84B, 92C,

184F–185A, 800 B); V.'s source cannot be determined; in lines 48–50 the source is Cic. *Arch.* 20.

43–44. sed melius ... aemulatus: Fabius, the subject of the previous sentence, of course, not Phidias.

43. aliena imitatione: 'imitation of a foreigner'; for the use of an adjective in place of an objective genitive cf. K–St i. 212–13.

44. uirtutum: α. P has *uirtutis*, printed by Kempf. One expects the singular, but V. uses the plural frequently (Otón Sobrino iv. 2308; see also lines 48–50 n. below) and while corruption from the singular could be explained as anticipation of the following *agitatum*, that is not a sufficient reason to depart from the direct tradition. Shackleton Bailey, retaining *uirtutum*, translates 'great achievements', but there seems to be no parallel for its meaning 'virtuous deeds'.

44–45. noctes inquietas exigentem ... eo tempore in publico uersaretur: the latter phrase explains the former: because of his insomnia Themistocles went for walks through Athens in the middle of the night.

45. quid ita eo tempore: for such redundant uses of *ita* cf. *TLL* vii/2.527.433 ff., but without any examples with *quid* (normally *quid ita* stands as an independent direct question 'how so?' (cf. *OLD s.u.* 16). I have played with the idea that *eo tempore* is an early (P also has *quid ita eo tempore*) gloss on *ita*.

46. de somno excitant: α. P has *exagitant*, which is merely abbreviation, influenced by *agitatus* (Paris makes *Themistocles* the subject of the sentence)

46–48. Marathon ... incitabat: i.e. the fame Miltiades had acquired by his victory over Darius at Marathon inspired Themistocles to his victories over Xerxes at Artemisium and Salamis.

47–48. ad ... incitabat: Perizonius' correction of the transmitted *et ... incitabant*, which makes no sense (and is not improved by A^c's (apparent) alteration of *inlustranda* to *illum inlustrando*.

48–50. Cic. *Arch.* 20 has *dixisse aiunt, cum ex eo quaereretur quod acroama aut cuius uocem libentissime audiret, eius a quo sua uirtus optime praedicaretur*. *uirtutes* is the reading of P; α has *artes*, printed by both Kempf and Shackleton Bailey. Cicero's *uirtus* almost guarantees *uirtutes* in V. (the change of *praedicaretur* to *canentur* (P has *referrentur*) is of a quite different order). Moreover, the theme of the *exemplum* is Themistocles' desire for recognition of his moral virtues, not his skills; α's reading in line 44 and P's here can be said to support each other, providing effective ring composition.

50. gloriosam: SB translates 'vainglorious': V. then means that he almost criticized Themistocles for boasting. That makes excellent sense and is probably right. Nevertheless, V. uses *gloriosus* on nine other occasions and in none of them does it mean 'boastful'; at 7. ext. 12, 2.2.3, 7.6, 3.4.2, 5.4. ext. 3, 7.1, 6.4. ext. 4, and 9.3.4 it means 'glorious', at 14.5 'eager for glory' (Otón Sobrino (ii. 846) misleadingly classifies both the latter passage and ours under the rubric 'ansioso de gloria, engreido' (i.e. he takes *gloriosam* as 'boastful'). I wonder, therefore, whether V. means that he almost said that the pleasure Themistocles took in his glory was glorious in itself. The formulation would result from the fact that Latin does not have a concept equivalent to English pride.[107]

ext. 2. *Alexander.* Cf. 11 ext. 2 n. The anecdote occurs also at Plut. *mor.* 466D and Aelian *VH* 4.29. Sen. *suas.* 1.5 and Juv. 10.168, also cited in my *testimonia* apparatus, are two of a number of allusions to it, for which see Mayor's note on the latter. V.'s source cannot be determined.

51. nam: cf. 11 line 26 n.

insatiabile laudis: for *insatiabilis* + genitive cf. Sen. *contr.* 1.8.8, *dial.* 11.11.1, K–St i. 442.

Anaxarcho: Anaxarchus of Abdera, whose gruesome death V. related at 3.3. ext. 4, was an adherent of the philosophy of Democritus and teacher of the sceptic Pyrron. He accompanied Alexander on his eastern campaigns. Cf. Kaerst, *RE* i. 2080.

52. Democriti: cf. 7. ext. 4 n.

innumerabiles mundos: on the doctrine of innumerable worlds, propounded by both Leucippus and Democritus, cf. Kirk–Raven 416–19.

53. ne: α has *nec* (Kempf (1854) implies that *ne* is the reading of F). In earlier Latin *nec ... quidem* must be interpreted as separate words ('and not ... indeed') and if that is not possible (as it is not here), emendation to *ne* cannot be avoided (see my note on Livy 33.30.4; for *nec = ne ... quidem* see that on 31.22.7). There are, however, a number of cases of *nec ... quidem* in authors of near to V.'s time (Vitruvius, Velleius, Columella, and the elder Seneca (cf. K–St ii. 45, H–S 450) and it may be that the usage had become accepted (Woodman rejects *nec* at Vell. 2.67.1; see his note ad loc.). Hence my *fort. recte*.

54. †gloriae†: the transmitted reading is impossible: *possessio* goes with *quae* and refers to the known world. Perizonius deleted *gloriae* and he may have

---

[107] I take the opportunity to record that many years ago the (then) Department of Greek and Latin at Manchester was asked by Manchester City Football Club to provide them with a Latin motto translating 'Pride in Battle'. The request was passed to me and I said that the only thing I could think of was *superbia in proelio*, but that this did not really convey the required sense, since *superbia* implied arrogance. Nevertheless, the Club accepted it and until recently it appeared on the players' shirts and a wide variety of merchandise (I much regret that I did not ask for royalties).

been right: G has it before *possessio* and if that represents the paradosis, it could have resulted from a scribe's eye returning to *gloriae* before *paene* in line 70. Gertz proposed *hominis gloriae possessio*, taking, so Kempf reports, *gloriae* as equivalent to *gloriae cupiditati*, which I fail to understand. Kempf himself suggested transposing *gloriae* to precede *cupiditati* at the beginning of *exemplum* 3: he presumably thought that a scribe's eye would have moved from the first *-ae* to the next: *gloriae* there, however, spoils the effect of *in capessenda laude* (lines 55–6) and is not something to be introduced by conjecture; nor is the juxtaposirion of a dative and a genitive with the same termination. Shackleton Bailey prints a (new; it is not one of those discussed in his 2003 article; cf. p. 28) conjecture of his own, adding *auido* before *gloriae*: he presumably thought that it was omitted because a scribe's eye moved from (*possessi*)*o* to (*auid*)*o*. That is not impossible, though, again, the interlaced word order is not something that should be introduced by conjecture and, in any case, it is by no means sufficiently probable to be placed in the text.

ext. 3. 55–61. *Aristotle and Theodectes*. Theodectes, from Phaselis in Lycia, was both an orator and a writer on rhetoric; he also composed tragedies and verse riddles. He is said to have been a pupil of Isocrates, Plato, and Aristotle (see below) and to have died at the age of 41 (Suda *s.n.*).

This is the only full statement of the belief, almost certainly mistaken, that Theodectes' work on rhetoric, called τὰ Θεοδέκτεια at Arist. *rhet.* 1410b3, was in fact by Aristotle; see also [Arist.] *rhet. ad Alex.* 1421a38, anon., *Rhetores Graeci* (ed. Spengel), i. 454 (cf. schol. Dem. *Olymp.* 2 53d Dilts), Quint. *inst.* 2.15.10; it may be that it lies behind the statement that Theodectes was a pupil of Aristotle (also Cic. *orat.* 122; cf. Ath. 13.566E). The work is ascribed to Theodectes himself, without any expression of doubt, at Cic. *orat.* 172, 194, 218, D.H. *comp.* 2, *Dem.* 48. The origin of the error was probably Aristotle's reference to τὰ Θεοδέκτεια and the fact that he composed a τέχνης τῆς Θεοδέκτου συναγωγή (DL 5.24, V. Rose, *Aristotelis qui ferebantur librorum fragmenta* (Leipzig, 1886), pp. 13, 71).

See Solmsen, *RE* vA. 1722–34.

56. Theodecti: LGP^c; P (and Lupus; *Theodenti* A) have *-ae*, which is not a possible transcription of -ει. At line 59 P has *Theodecti* for *-tis*, but that may an error in the course of the transmission of Paris.

57. pro suis: P; om. α. The phrase is essential to the whole episode (Aristotle is not merely asking Theodectes to publish the work) and the omission in the direct tradition was caused by a scribe moving from (*quo*)*s* to (*sui*)*s*. But Kempf and Shackleton Bailey should not have printed it as a supplement: it was not a conjecture by Paris (see p. 23).

58. planius: Shackleton Bailey (1996, 182) observing that 'Aristotle is not likely to have implied that his treatment of these matters had lacked clarity' proposed *plenius* (and printed it in his edition). V., however, had not himself read Aristotle's *Rhetoric* and was drawing on a source that ascribed Theodectes' work to Aristotle; even if that source did not make Aristotle say that Theodectes' exposition was clearer, V. could well have done so himself. One cannot, though, exclude the possibility that Aristotle did indeed say what V. attributes to him, meaning that his discussion was more detailed and hence less clear than that that of Theodectes.

60–61. dignum ... traderentur: someone who said that was himself in need of moral instruction. The implication is that Arisotle should not have himself undertaken works of moral philosophy: in fact, Aristotle's ethical works do not recommend specific courses of action.

62–67. This passage serves as a transition to the two *exempla* which follow: *ceterum ... adsequantur* (lines 62–4) contrast Aristotle with writers who do not refrain from putting their name on books professing contempt for glory, while in the sentence which follows V. says that their hypocrisy is far preferable to those who commit criminal acts in order to perpetuate their name. It would perhaps have been better if the passage had been made part of ext. 4.

63–64. quoniam ... adsequentur: V. somewhat bizarrely implies that those who professed to despise glory should have published their books anonymously or under a pseudonym.

63. ipsis: Shackleton Bailey prints <*iis*> *ipsis*, proposed without argument at 1996, 183. Such a corruption would be extremely easy, a scribe's eye moving from *ii*- to *i*-, but the conjecture is quite unnecessary: 'those very volumes' (thus SB) is in no way superior to 'the volumes themselves'.

64. eleuant: cf. 5 line 27 n.

usurpatione memoriae: 'laying claim to (not 'use of' (SB)) remembrance'

64–66. memoriae adsequantur ... memoriam adsequerentur: deliberate polyptoton.

64–65. qualiscumque: cf. line 39 n.

66. innotescere: a rare word before Christian writers and this is its only occurrence in V.; before and contemporaneously with him it is found only at Ovid *am.* 3.12.7, Livy 22.61.4, and twice in Phaedrus.

ext. 4. *Pausanias*. The fullest account of Pausanias' murder of Philip II, the subject of 1.8. ext. 9, is Diod. 16.93–4; see also Arist. *pol.* 1311b2, Plut. *Alex.* 10.6, Just. 9.6.4–7.14, Zon. 4.9; POxy. 1798 (an anonymous work about Alexander) fr. 1 concerns Philip's funeral. Pausanias' question and the answer are in Diodorus (16.94.1; see line 69 n.), but V. has nothing of the homosexuality and deep drinking that are at the centre of the differing accounts of Diodorus and Justin (euphemistically alluded to by Aristotle and Plutarch); his immediate source cannot be determined.

68. Pausanias: a very common name in Macedon; cf. *LGPN* iv. 276–7. Diodorus' story begins (16.93.4) with Philip transferring his affections from one Pausanias to another.

69. Hermoclen: not otherwise known. Diodorus (16.94.1) calls him Hermocrates, a sophist. No contemporary sophist of the name is known (for one *c.* 200 cf. Münscher, *RE* viii. 888–9) and C. B. Welles (Loeb edn. of Diodorus, viii. 99 n. 1) suggests he is the grammarian who taught Callimachus (cf. Funaioli, *RE* viii. 887–8).

70. si ... occidisset: AL. The clause is omitted in G, a scribe's eye moving from one *-disset* to the next (*saut du même au même* from one pluperfect subjunctive to another is very common).

aliquem inlustrem uirum: Diod. τὸν τὰ μέγιστα πράξαντα.

72. tam enim: A^c, correcting α's *tamen*, an easy enough corruption.

Philippus uirtute: *sc. se*: it may have been failure to realise this that led to the corruption to *uirtutem* in AL, though it could have been caused simply by anticipation of the following accusative; it was certainly the reason for A^c's *uirtute fuerat*.

ext. 5. (*Herpstratus*). In my *testimonia* apparatus I referred only to Plaumann, *RE* viii. 1145, who himself cites *Forschungen in Ephesos* i (Vienna, 1906), 262 nos. 338 ff. (in fact 262–3, nos. 338–55) for a complete collection of references to the fire. I list them in chronological order (an asterisk indicates those which refer only to the fire, not the arsonist): *Arist. *mete.* 371a32–4, *Cic. *nat. deor.* 2.69, *diu.* 1.47, Strabo 14, p. 640C, Curt. 1.1*, Jos. *Ap.* 2.131, *Plut. *Alex.* 3.3, Gell. 2.6.18, Lucian 55.22, *Clem. *protr.* 4.53, Solin. 40.2–4, *Arnob. *nat.* 6.23, Greg. Nyss. Migne 45.265, Ioann. Chrys. Migne 62.9, *Zon. 4.8. V.'s source cannot be determined.

The episode occurred in 356 and was synchronised by Timaeus with the birth of Alexander (Cic. *nat. deor.* loc. cit. = *FGrH* 566F150a; cf. Jacoby ad loc. (*FGrH* iiib, Kommentar, 592); the synchronism is also given by Cic. *diu.*, Curt., Plut., Solin., and Zon. locc. citt.

74. illa: for *ille* pointing forward see *TLL* vii/1.347.82 ff.

74–75. Dianae Ephesiae templum: on the temple see A. Bammer, *Das Heiligtum der Artemis von Ephesos* (Graz, 1984).

76. disiceretur: the use of *disicere* to mean 'spread abroad' is unique (cf. *TLL* v/1.1383.13 ff); F has *diffunderetur*, which perhaps originated as a gloss rather than a variant reading.

α's *dissiceretur* is a mistaken orthography frequently found in manuscripts. It may have been caused by confusion with *dissecare*; cf. *TLL* v/1.1381.52 ff.

eculeo impositus: cf. ch. 4 n. The *ec(qu-)uleus* was an instrument of torture in the form of a horse, used as a rack; it is first mentioned, on a number of occasions, by Cicero. Cf. Hitzig, *RE* v. 1931–2, *TLL* v/2.730.54 ff.

77–79. ac bene ... comprehendisset: there is an understood apodosis meaning 'and they would have succeeded'; cf. my note on Livy 32.25.8 and those listed in vol. iii. 594, iv. 798, *s.uu.* 'conditional clause(s), apodosis understood'.

76–77. decreto ... abolendo: 'in abolishing by decree'; *decreto* and *abolendo* do not go together (Damsté's *decreto suo* is totally unnecessary).

AL have *in abolendo*. Kempf and Gertz (independently, apparently) suggested *in aeternum abolendo* (a scribe's eye would have moved from the first *-a* to the next); Damsté proposed transposing *in* to precede *historiis* (*comprehendere* 'include' is used with both the plain ablative and *in*; cf. *TLL* iii. 2047.51 ff.). The likelihood is that *in* resulted either from perseveration from *(hom)in(is)* or anticipation of *in(genium)*.

77. Theopompi: cf. 13 line 95 n.

Theopompi magnae facundiae ingenium: 'Theopompus' eloquent genius' (SB). A striking expression, a combination of *Theopompi ingenium* and *Theopompi, uiri magnae facundiae*.

The passage constitutes *FGrH* 115F395 bis (see vol. iiib, Noten, 398).

78–79. eum ... comprehendisset: i.e. he gave the arsonist's name, mentioned only by Strabo 14, p. 640C, Aelian *n.a.* 6.40 (who is not explicit, merely listing him as one of the enemies of te gods), and Solin. 40.3.

15 tit. contigerunt: α; P has *contigerint*. For the indicative cf. chs. 3, 6 titt.; the subjunctive was influenced by the *tituli* to chs. 9–11 (on the syntax of the *tituli* cf. 11 tit. n.).

praef. 2–3. aeque †praemiorum ... iudicanda†: my edition wrongly placed the first obelos before *aeque*, which is not in doubt (though Perizonius proposed *aequa*, not mentioned in my apparatus).

L^c and G have *uirtutis* (conjectured by Ascensius), AL *uirtutes* (not reported in my apparatus), A^c *uirtus*. My apparatus wrongly implies that G has *operum*, conjectured independently by Madvig and Foertsch: it in fact has *honorum*; ope-

rum is clearly correct: V.'s theme is the rewards that rightly resulted from deeds; *praemiorum uirtutis* and *operum* correspond to both *magnifica merito* in line 2 and, in inverse order, *industrie appeti* and *exsolui grate* in line 4. It is likely that *operum* was first corrupted to *onerum* (thus L; mention of burdens is clearly out of place), a change of only one letter, and that *honerum* (A was an emendation to *honorum* not fully carried through.

uirtutes lacks syntax and the genitive is beyond question.

Like both Kempf and Shackleton Bailey I now think that Ascensius was right to emend *iudicanda* to *iucunda*: *contemplatio* is not something about which one makes a judgement and the corruption is easy enough (the conjectures of Blaum *honorum adpetitus ... iudicanda* and Gertz *iucunda iudicanda* are objectionable in themselves: *honorum appetitus* means 'desire for honours', while the required sense would be 'way they sought honours', and Gertz proposal involves a jingle which should not be introduced by conjecture).

4. cum: Gertz is reported by Kempf as suggesting *et cum*: *et* would have no reference and I wonder if he meant *cum et*.

industrie appeti et exsolui grate: chiasmus. Although there is no doubt about any of them, three words out of five are corrupt in some or all of the authoritative manuscripts: *industrie* and *grate* are found only in later manuscripts (Kempf (1854) implies CEFΓ for the former, CEF for the latter), *appeti* in L^c and G.

4–7. uerum ... tribuuntur: V. is explaining, in an obsequious and contorted way, that the *exempla* that follow do not include Augustus or Tiberius: for those who can look forward to posthumous deification (he was not to know that Tiberius would not become *diuus*) earthly honours, however great, are less than they deserve.

5. Augustam domum: as at 2.8.7 V. means the actual house, not the imperial family (surprisingly no other author uses the phrase). The reference must be to the house of Augustus on the Palatine (cf. Iacopi, *LTUR* ii. 46–8); on the so-called *domus Tiberiana*, probably initiated by Tiberius but not in existence when V. wrote (in any case, Tiberius lived in Capri from AD 27), cf. Krause, *LTUR* ii. 189–97.

beneficentissimum: *beneficus* is a rare word (though Cicero uses it on eighteen occasions), occurring only here in V. The superlative *beneficissimus* occurs only at Cato *orat.* 180 = 137 Cugusi, *beneficentissimus* also at Cic. *nat. deor.* 2.64, *Lael.* 51.

honoratissimum: the superlative occurs earlier only at Plaut. *Capt.* 278, Cic. *fam.* 3.10.9, and five times in Livy (2.15.1, 3.58.2, 67.8, 5.14.5, 27.10.6); V. uses it also at 4.5. ext. 2.

6. cui: A^c; α has *cuius*, by anticipation of the following *ascensus*.

1. *Scipio Africanus.*

8–11. V. here conflates the election of the elder Africanus to the consulship of 205 with that of Aemilanus for 147, mentioned at lines 28–9 (see n. ad loc.; for other confusions of the two see 2.4.3, 5.1.7); in neither case, however, does any other source say that the army sent a letter to the senate demanding the election, though Appian (*Lib.* 109.517) says that the army believed that only Aemilianus could capture Carthage and that many wrote home in this vein (cf. Astin, *SA* 64; Pighius transposed *quod ... poposcerunt* (my apparatus wrongly says *quod ... admonuit*) to follow *fecit* in line 41). Livy (28.38.7–10) says that the turn-out for the election of Africanus was higher than at any other during the Hannibalic War and records the belief that Scipio would bring the war to an end (cf. Coelius Antipater *FRHist* 15F30 and commentary ad loc.).

8. citerior legitimo tempore: before the *lex Villia annalis* of 180 there was no minimum age for magistracies prescribed by law, though the *lex Villia* enshrined in law what had become customary during the previous twenty years (cf. my notes on Livy 31.4.7, 40.44.1; for a very young consul see *exemplum* 5). Africanus was born between 237 and 234 (cf. Henze, *RE* iv. 1463, Walbank, ii. 199) and hence was between 27 and 30 at the time of the elections for 205. In 148, however, Aemilianus' age was the central issue (he was born in 185 or 184, and the minimuum age for holding the consulship was 42 or 43 (see my note on Livy 40.44.1), though it is possible that the *lex Villia* prescribed an age two years younger for patricians (cf. Badian, *Studies,* 140–56). See Astin, *SA* 61–9.

10–11. toga ... arma: cf. 9 lines 9–10 n.

13. maiore ... sunt: 14.1, 2.10.2, 3.7.1e, 4.1.6.

13–16. itaque quod ... Capitolium est: at 4.1.6 V., in a passage taken almost verbatim from Livy 38.56.12, says that Scipio refused to allow his statues to be placed *in comitio, in rostris, in curia, in ipsa denique Iouis optimi maximi cella*; Livy continues *prohibuisse ne decerneretur ut imago sua triumphali ornatu e templo Iouis optimi maximi exiret,* but V. has *uoluerunt imaginem eius triumphali ornatu indutam Capitolinis puluinaribus adplicare.*

In Livy this forms part of an *oratio obliqua* speech attributed to Ti. Sempronius Gracchus, father of the Gracchi, who was tribune of the plebs at the time (187). As I said in my note on the passage it 'constitutes virtual proof that the speech of Gracchus was composed at the time of Caesar's dictatorship, doubtless to attack Caesar for accepting honours which Scipio had declined' (I meant a speech in *oratio recta* utilized by Livy). Livy, and if he too used the word, the author of the speech, must have intended *imago* as mere variation for *statua,* though if Scipio had vetoed the placing of a statue in the temple of Jupiter Optimus Maximus, he would not have also needed to veto a proposal about what was to be done with it; V. perhaps realised this and hence wrote *uoluerunt*; *Capitolinis puluinaribus adplicare* is just elaboration of *exiret*.

Unless V. had forgotten what he wrote at 4.1.6, he must mean that the practice of bringing Scipio's statue out from the temple at funerals of members of the *gens Cornelia* was a later development, and he was no doubt right; Scullard (*SA* 21) thought the practice had been instituted by Scipio Aemilianus; the placing of the statue in the temple may have occurred soon after Africanus' death: *quod ... adiciam* (*capit adiciam* A^c, *capita dicam* AL, *capit dicam* G), that is to say, contrasts this honour with those conferred in Africanus' lifetime (*in uita*), and not, as *prima facie* appears to be the case, with those which *maiore ex parte iam relata sunt*.

See further the whole of my note on Livy 38.56.12–13.

13. quod ... capit: 'I will add an extraordinary one which he still receives to this day' (SB).

hodieque occurs before V. only at Livy 42.34.3 (if one accepts the reading of the *editio princeps*; see my note ad loc.), Vitruvius, and Velleius. V. uses it also at 2.2.6, 4.4.2, 5.6.21, and 7.2. ext. 2.

For *capere* in the sense of 'obtain, receive' cf. *TLL* iii. 328.30 ff. (our passage at 51 ff.), *OLD s.u.* 13b. Otón Sobrino (i. 275) wrongly glosses our passage as 'destacar'.

15. funus ... gentis: i.e. the funeral of a member of the *gens Cornelia*; in English we speak of a 'family funeral'. App. *Ib*. 23.89, the only other evidence for the practice, talks just of processions.

The transmitted *munus* was corrected by Pighius.

2. *Cato. uir. ill.* 47.9 is the only other evidence for Cato's statue in the *curia*.

What V. says in lines 18–21 refers to Cato's statue being in the senate house, which he has not explicitly mentioned, not to its being brought out for funerals.

16. tam hercule quam: 'so to be sure' (SB).

curia: Eberhard's addition of *e* is demonstrably wrong. For the plain ablative in prose from Livy onwards, particularly common with compound verbs, see K–St i. 361–3; cf. 1.1.10 *plaustro descenderent*, 4.5.3 *templo descendit*; for conjectures which make *curia* nominative see next note.

16–17. superioris Catonis ... †illius ad cuius†: to the conjectures listed in my apparatus add Shackleton Bailey (in his edition) *superiori Catoni cuius effigies ad illius* (mentioned, but without discussion, in (2003)).

illius ad cuius makes no sense and none of the many conjectures is convincing enough to be placed in the text. Of later manuscripts C omitted *ad cuius*, leaving *illius generis officia* without syntax, while E has *eius* in place of *cuius*, so that *illius*, impossibly, has to be taken with *superioris Catonis*; my apparatus wrongly implies that it had *ad eius* in place of *illius ad cuius*; for D see below. Later Eberhard proposed deleting *cuius*; so too Faranda (666 n. 133), but with *huius* for *illius*: that would make perfect sense, but the corruption is hard to explain.

The same is true of most conjectures in the age of print. Pighius changed *superioris Catonis* to the dative, placing a colon after it, adding *unde* before *effigies*, and changing *cuius* to *eiusdem*. Vorst read *effigiei:* (my apparatus omits the colon) *unde ad eius*, saying that this is the reading of a Brandenburg manuscript, in fact D (cf. Kempf (1854), 73–4, 81–2; in his apparatus (1854, 664) Kempf wrongly implies that D reads *effigies unde ad cuius*[108]); *effigiei* is dative, balancing *illi*, which Vorst strangely took to refer to *imaginem* (line 14) rather than to Scipio himself, *curia* nominative, balancing *Capitolium*); similarly Kempf (1854) suggested *effigiei, quae illinc ad huius* (or *eius*). Halm (1854; '1874' in my apparatus is a misprint) proposed *cuius effigies illinc ad huius*, Madvig *unius ad huius*, Gertz *superiori soli Catoni: inde enim effigies illius ad huius*, Kempf *superiori Catoni* (or retention of the genitive with *imagini* understood), Novák *superiori Catoni cuius inde effigies ad huius*; Damsté, understanding *imagini*, transposed *effigies illius* to precede *officia*. Shackleton Bailey read *superiori Catoni, cuius effigies ad illius*: the transposition is ingenious, but the total process of corruption involved very complex.

18–19. omnibus numeris uirtutis: 'every kind of virtue' (SB); cf. 4 line 1 n. V. may have had in mind Livy's character sketch of Cato at 39.40.4–12.

20. consilio ... Carthago deleta est: after his return from an embassy to Carthage in 153 Cato famously ended every speech in the senate by saying that Carthage must be destroyed (Diod. 34/35.33.3, Vell. 1.13.1, Plin. *nat*. 15.74, Plut. *Cato mai*. 27.2, App. *Lib*. 69.315, Flor. 1.31.4, *uir. ill*. 47.8). The precise words Cato used cannot be determined. Of the Latin sources Velleius says only *perpetuus diruendae eius auctor*, Pliny *clamaret ... Carthaginem delendam*, Florus *delendam esse Carthaginem ... pronuntiabat*, and *uir. ill. Carthaginem delendam censuit*. The often quoted *ceterum censeo Carthaginem esse delendam* was an invention of the nineteenth century; see S. Thürlemann, *Gymnasium* 81 (1974), 465–75 (I recall Eduard Fraenkel once saying that Cato did not use this formulation). Cf. Astin, *Cato*, 127 n. 71, Powell on Cic. *Cato* 18.

Scipionis: Aemilianus, of course. At lines 10–11 *Scipionem* is Africanus, but there is no confusion here (cf. lines 8–11 n.): all V.'s readers knew perfectly

---

[108] I am grateful to Kurt Heydeck, of the Staatsbibliothek Berlin, for confirming the reading of D.

well that it was Aemilianus who destroyed Carthage in 146, and V. says so explicitly at 2.7.1.

3. *Scipio Nasica.* For the many sources (the earliest are Cic. *har. resp.* 27, *Brut.* 79, *fin.* 5.64) concerning the bringing of the Magna Mater to Rome in 205 see Münzer, *RE* iv. 1495; the fullest account, probably V.'s source, is Livy 29.10.4–11.8, 14.5–14. Cf. D. Magie, *Roman Rule in Asia Minor* (Princeton, NJ, 1950), ii. 769–70, F. Bömer, *P. Ouidius Naso, Die Fasten* (Heidelberg, 1957–8), ii. 237, T. Köves, *Historia* xii (1963), 321–47, and my note on Livy 34.3.8. V. also mentions the episode at 7.5.2, confusing Scipiones Nasicae of four generations, this Nasica, his son, consul in 162 and 155, his grandson, consul in 138 (the murderer of Tiberius Gracchus), and his great-grandson, consul in 111; cf. *Sileno*, 406–7.

21. specimen: 'example' (SB); cf. *OLD s.u.* 2.
in: 'in the case of ' (SB). The preposition, omitted in α, was correctly added by A^c, (*in* is easily omitted after *-is*, but 4.7.2 *in eadem domo ... oboriuntur*, adduced by Kempf, is different).
Scipione ... Nasica: (350). Publius, the son of Cn. Cornelius Scipio Calvus (cf. line 74 n.) and cousin of Africanus. He was curule aedile in 197, praetor in 194, and consul in 191; he is last heard of in 171 (Livy 43.2.5).
22. manibus et penatibus: Livy (29.14.10–14) says that Nasica met the ship carrying the sacred stone of Pessinus called the Great Mother (Livy 29.11.7) and received it from the priests accompanying it; he then gave it to a group of leading *matronae* who, carrying it in turn, took it to Rome and placed it in the temple of Victoria on the Palatine: Nasica did not take it to his own house, as *penatibus* implies.
nondum quaestorii: α has *quaestori*, which A^c altered to the genitive. That remained the vulgate until Kempf, in 1854, restored the paradosis, taking it be a contraction of *quaestorii*. *nondum quaestoris* would convey the sense of 'was not yet a quaestor'), but Livy (29.14.8) has *nondum quaestorium*: I preferred, however, to print the normal form, as did Shackleton Bailey.
22–24. Pythii ... praestarentur: following the discovery of a Sibylline oracle saying that a foreign enemy could be expelled from Italy and defeated if the *mater Idaea* was brought from Pessinus to Rome, the senate despatched an embassy to Attalus of Pergamum (Livy 29.10.4–11.4); on their way, they visited the Delphic oracle and were given the response that Attalus would enable them to fulfil their mission and that when they had brought the goddess to Rome, they should arrange for her to be received by Rome's *uir optimus*.
22–23. Pessinunte: Pessinus in Phrygia (Barrington Atlas 62G3) was an independent temple state within the Attalid kingdom; cf. Ruge, *RE* xix. 1104–13,

Magie, loc. cit. According to Varro *ling.* 6.15 Attalus had the stone at Pergamum and himself gave it to the envoys, and this version is preferred by Magie (he adds that there is no mention of Pessinus in Ovid's account at *fasti* 4.255 ff.: the name, of course, was intractable in dactylic verse).

23. deam: Kellerbauer proposed *matrem Idaeam*: *matrem* could have been omitted because a scribe's eye moved from (*accersita*)*m* to (*matre*)*m* and corruption of *Idaeam* is certainly possible, but with *matri deum* following one would not expect V. to have written *matrem* here, even though one might have preferred him to have said *matrem deum* here and *deae* in the causal clause.

24–26. Apart from his frequent use of *age* (20 instances; cf. Otón Sobrino i. 113), the only other passage where V. addresses the reader in the second person is 2.2.3.

25. morum principatu: cf. 5.6.2, Cic. *orat.* 56, Nep. *Att.* 5.4, all with the genitive (of definition; cf. Pinkster, 1023–4), *TLL* x/2.1302.14 ff.

4. *Scipio Aemilianus.* V.'s source(s) cannot be determined.

27–28. tradunt ... commemoranda: Aemilianum: after Africanus and Nasica. They, however, were born Cornelii Scipiones, Aemilianus became one by adoption (cf. 1 lines 114–15 n.).

27. subinde: 'time and again' (*OLD s.u.* 2a); cf. 13 line 7 n.

28. populus ... fecit: on Aemilianus' election to the consulship of 147 despite the provisions of the *lex Villia annalis*, being at least five years younger than the minimum age and not having held the praetorship (the law was suspended for a year, in order to allow his election) see Astin, *SA* 61–7; he lists the large number of other sources at p. 61 n. 1. Cf. lines 8–11 n.

candidato aedilitatis: α; P (and Lupus) has *aedilicio*. Before V., Cicero (*Mur.* 57, 62, 68, *Att.* 4.15.7, 18.3, *Q. fr.* 2.15.4, 16.2), Sallust (*hist.* 2.45M = 2.41 Ramsey), and Livy (10.15.8) use *candidatus* with an adjective denoting the office sought, but V. has *praeturae candidatus* at 5.2.7 and 6.9.14 and *candidatus* with the genitive of the name of the office occurs at Ascon. pp. 85, 88C, Sen. *benef.* 7.28.2, and Suet. *Tib.* 42.2, *Claud.* 40.2, *Vesp.* 2.3. There is clearly no reason to depart from the direct tradition. (*TLL* iii. 238.16 ff.).

28–30. eundem ... reduxit: for Aemilianus' election to a second consulship, for 134, see Astin, *SA* 135. In, probably, 151 a law had been passed banning re-election to the consulship, a reaction to the election of M. Claudius Marcellus to a third consulship, for 152; see Livy *per.* 56, Mommsen, *StR* i³. 521 n. 1. Appian *Ib.* 84.363–4 wrongly says that Aemilianus was still under the minimum age, but is no doubt right that he had again to be given an exemption; Cicero (*rep.* 6.11) is also mistaken, saying that he was elected in his absence. No other source says that Aemilianus was supporting his nephew's candidacy for the quaestorship. For other references to the second consulship see Astin, loc. cit., n. 1.

29. Q. Fabi ... filii: Q. Fabius Maximus Aemilianus (109), consul in 145, was also the natural son of Aemilius Paullus (cf. lines 39–40 n.), adopted into the Fabii (probably by Q. Fabius Maximus (105), praetor in 181); his son was Q. Fabius Maximus Allobrogicus (110), consul in 115.

30–31. eidem ... dedit: for the assignation of the command against Carthage by the people see Livy *per.* 51, App. *Lib.* 112.533, Astin, *SA* 67; there is no other evidence concerning the assignation of the Spanish command in 134.

31. †neque ... senatori†: the transmitted text clearly lacks a second *neque* and, in all probability, an adjective, balancing *ambitioso*, to go with *senatori*. A^c added *neque* after *ciui* and wrote *necuiquam ambitioso senatori* in the margin; L^c has *neque cuiquam bioso* (my apparatus is wrong). *necuiquam* is not Latin and the fact that both correctors wrote it or something like it suggests that it was a variant in the exemplar of A and L, and was a mistake for *nequaqum*, which would make perfect sense ('in no way a favour-seeking senator'), though it is not very likely to have been corrupted to *neque ciui*. Kempf (1854) was on the right lines with *neque ciui ambitioso neque apud populum gratioso senatori* (thus Halm, but without *ad populum*, which spoils the balance): a scribe's eye would have moved from the first *-tioso* to the second. Foertsch proposed *neque ciuili neque ambitioso* (the movement would then have been from the first *neque* to the second), but V. is scarcely likely to have said that Aemilianus was a senator who did not behave as a citizen should (and as some emperors did; cf. A. Wallace-Hadrill, *JRS* 72 (1982), 32–48). Gertz wanted to add *contigerunt* after Kempf's conjecture as emended by Halm, but *dedit* is easily understood, even if *haec* refers to everything that precedes, not just to the assignment of provinces by popular vote.

32. uitae ... cursus: i.e. he made no attempt to curry favour with the people; a conspicuous example is his statement to a *contio* that he regarded Tiberius Gracchus as having been *iure caesus* and, in response to protests from the crowd, *taceant quibus Italia nouerca est* and *non efficietis ut solutos uerear quos adligatos adduxi* (6.2.3; for other passages citing one or both of these utterances see Astin, *SA* 264–6).

32–33. mors ... insidiis: Scipio was found dead in bed in 129, the day after a *contio* involving a bitter clash with supporters of Gracchus; there were claims that he had been murdered. See Astin, *SA* 240–1, with citation of the extensive evidence.

5. *M. Valerius Corv(in)us.* On Valerius see 13.1 n. V.'s source is Livy 7.26.1–10 (349; Peter wrongly made the passage fragment 12 of Claudius Quadrigarius; see Oakley ad loc., *FRHist* i. 192), 12 (election as consul for the following year; other sources are listed at *MRR* i. 129–30 (missing our passage for the combat and citing 13.1 as 12.1)).

35–36. coruum propugnatorem subicientes: cf. Livy 7.26.5, saying that the bird attacked the Gaul's mouth and eyes; V. summarizes with *propugnatorem*. The noun occurs only in prose, from Cicero onwards (*TLL* x/2.2137 ff.); V. uses it also at 1.8.1, 3.8. ext. 2, 5.1. ext. 4, and 7.4.2.

36. tertium ... ingresso: Livy has *tres et uiginti natum annos*, while V. makes him 22 (24 in P: *cum esset xxiiii annorum*; cf. 13 line 46 n.). As Oakley (ii. 250) observes, this is the only instance in the second pentad where Livy gives the age of a magistrate.

37. uetustae ... gens: cf. p. 1. *uetustae originis optimi nominis* is an asyndeton *bimembre*.

nominis: α (Shackleton Bailey wrongly says 'A *corr.*') has *hominis*, corrected by Perizonius. V. cannot mean that Valerius was an excellent name and Shackleton Bailey well translates 'reputation' ('famosa' Faranda; cf. *OLD s.u.* 11), but with *cognomen* following V. could have chosen a better word. The *cognomen*, moreover, was used only by the hero's son (cf. 13.1 n.), not all Valerii.

38. summo ... ornamento: the six consulships of Corvus, the supreme achievement of the Valerii.

subiungit: 'attaches' (SB); V. means that the Valerii talk of Corvus' election to his first consulship at so young an age in the context of his six tenures of the office (*tam celeritate quam principio*).

α has *subiungitur*, corrected by Pighius; cf. 12 line 6 n.

6. *Q. Mucius Scaevola*. Scaevola the *pontifex* (22), consul in 95; it is much disputed whether his governorship of Asia followed his consulship or his praetorship (98 at the latest; cf. Badian, *Athenaeum* n.s. 34 (1956), 105 n. 4); see Broughton, *MRR* iii. 145–6, T. C. Brennan, *The Praetorship in the Roman Republic* (New York, 2000), 549–52 (this is not the place to add to the discussion). For the sources (V.'s cannot be determined) on Scaevola's governorship, aimed principally at curbing the behaviour of the *publicani* (cf. Brennan, op. cit., 550) see *MRR* ii. 7.

40. ne Q. quidem: V. similarly has a *praenomen* between *ne* and *quidem* at 3.1.2, 5, 6.3.3; cf. Cic. *Phil.* 2.17, 10.11, *Brut.* 269, *off.* 2.58, Nep. *Att.* 6.4, Tac. *dial.* 40.3, Devine–Stephens, 272, *TLL* ix/1.334.39 ff.; there are, strikingly, no examples in the whole of Livy (nor of *praenomen* plus *nomen* or *cognomen*).

quem ... L. Crassus habuit: in fact in all his offices except the tribunate (Cic. *Brut.* 161).

40–41. Crassus ... consulatu ... gloria ... qui Asiam: all these words are corrupted in AL, with the correct reading in one or more of A^cL^cG.

41–43. senatus ... proponeret: i.e the senate attached Scaevola's edict to the *senatus consultum* giving instructions to governors of Asia (*Scaeuolam = edictum Scaeuolae*). Cicero made use of the edict as governor of Cilicia in 51–50 (*Att.* 6.1.15).

42–43. formam officii: 'model of administration' (SB). for *forma* in this sense cf. Cic. *rep.* 2.22, *TLL* vi/1.1085.17 ff. Cornelissen and Gertz, independently, proposed *normam*, used in this sense by V. at 4.3.5, and it was adopted by Kempf. Another case of what V. could have written, but did not.

7. Marius. The story is told also by Plutarch *Marius* 3.2–5; Marius' service under Aemilianus at Numantia is mentioned by Velleius 2.9.4; V.'s source cannot be determined. Cf. 2.3 n.

44. illi: Kempf read *uni*, comparing *exemplum* 9: he was, I take it, referring to *duarum syllabarum* (line 67), not *in uno* (line 63). The resulting sense is excellent, providing a contrast with the following *septem* and *duo*, and he persuaded Shackleton Bailey. In itself, though, *illi* is unexceptionable and it could be said that if V. intended such a contrast, he could have made it more effective by placing *inhaerent* ('lie embedded in' SB) before *septem*. But I ought at least to have given *uni* a *fort. recte*. Cf. line 48 n.

septem C. Mari consulatus: 107, 104–100, 86.

44–45. duo ... triumphi: over Jugurtha in 104 and the Cimbri and Teutones (see below) in 101.

45–46. cum ... mereret: in 134 or 133; cf. lines 29–31 n.

46. Numantiam: on Numantia (Barrington Atlas 25C4) see A. Schulten, *Numantia* (Munich, 1913–31), on the Numantine War (144 or 143 to 133) H. Simon, *Roms Kriege in Spanien* (Frankfurt, 1962), 143–91, Harris, *CAH* viii². 134–6.

equestria stipendia mereret: a minimum of ten years cavalry service, commencing at the age of 17, was a pre-requisite of candidature for political office; cf. Mommsen, *StR* i³. 505. Marius was born, at the latest, in 156 (cf. Weynand, *RE* Supp. vi. 1367) and so was at least 22 in 134.

47. si ... accidisset: as in English 'if anything happens to', a euphemism for death; cf. *TLL* i. 292.84 ff.

illi: Halm's *ipsi* is totally misguided: *illi* represents *tibi* in *oratio recta*.

48. se supra ipsum: *supra*, which sometimes follows its object, goes with *se*, and *ipsum* is Marius. *supra* indicates that Marius was dining to Aemilianus' left (cf. my note on Livy 39.43.9).

uel: 'maybe'; cf. *OLD s.u.* 5a. Plutarch *Mar.*3.5 has τάχα δὲ τοῦτον.

50. certius ... potest: cf. 1 line 31 n.; here the alternatives include the verbs as well as the comparatives themselves.

accenderit: Γ. α has *acciderit*; the corruption, easy enough in itself, resulted from perseveration from *accidisset* in line 68 (neither of these factors applies to Torrenius' *acuerit*).

50–53. illa ... libauerit: the libations are also mentioned by Plut. *Mar.* 27.9. V. may have been thinking of the libations poured to the *genius Augusti* at banquets, both public and private, authorized by a *senatus consultum* of 30 (Dio 51.19.7) and mentioned by Hor. *carm.* 4.5.33–5 and Ovid *fast.* 2.637–8; cf. L. R. Taylor, *The Divinity of the Roman Emperor* (Middletown, CT, 1931), 151, 181–3.

52. Cimbros ab eo deletos: at the battle of Vercellae (mod. Vercelli; Barrington Atlas 39C3) on 30 July (Varr.) 101; see *MRR* i. 570. The Cimbri were a Germanic tribe who, together with the Teutones and the Ambrones, had left their homeland in Denmark and, after inflicting a series of defeats on Roman armies elsewhere, entered Italy in 102; cf., conveniently, O. P. F. Brogan–J. F. Drinkwater, *OCD*[4] 317–18.

8. *Pompey.* In my *testimonia* apparatus I referred only to Miltner, *RE* xxi. 2063 ff. for the multitude of sources for the five honours conferred on Pompey. It remains impractical to cite them individually, but I here give references to *MRR* for each one separately. V.'s source(s) cannot be determined.

54–55. hinc ... obstrepuntur: α. Torrenius aded *in* before *litterarum*, while Madvig altered *obstrepuntur* to the active. The latter was adopted by both Kempf and Shackleton Bailey, who translates 'assault our ears'. V. is thus made to say that when we read about Pompey's honours, they are accompanied by the noise of favour or hostility. That, however, implies that the reading experience is unpleasant, which is a rather stange way of introducing the topic. With the transmitted reading *obstrepuntur* means 'are overwhelmed by' (cf. *TLL* ix/2.248.55 ff.) and V. is complaining that the facts, instead of speaking for themselves, are drowned out by flattery or hostility. For the plain ablative of works of literature cf. 13 line 39, K–St i. 354.

V. is right to stress the polarization of attitudes towards Pompey. For Livy see Tacitus' famous words put in the mouth of the historian Cremutius Cordus *Cn. Pompeium tantis laudibus tulit ut Pompeianum eum Augustus appellaret* (*ann.* 4.34.2). Sallust was hostile, as one would expect of a *popularis* tribune of the year 52, though no fragment of the *historiae* refers to any of the honours mentioned by V; cf. Syme, *Sallust*, 194, 201–2, 212. Unfavorable treatment was no doubt to be found in the works of Caesar's friends Oppius and Balbus (*FRHist* 40, 41; see i. 380–4), praise in those of Theophanes (see 14 lines 17–21 n.) and the freedman M'. Otacilius Pitholaus (*FRHist* 29; see i. 333–4).

55–57. eques Romanus ... missus est: Pompey received proconsular *imperium* to command against Sertorius in 77; for sources see *MRR* ii. 90.

55–56. eques Romanus: Pompey's father, Cn. Pompeius Strabo, consul in 89, had enobled the family (they are not descended from Q. Pompeius, consul in 141; see Miltner, *RE* xxi. 2050, with the stemma at 2051–2), but sons of senators remained members of the equestrian centuries until they had achieved office.

56. Sertorium: Q. Sertorius (3) was praetor in 83, when he went to his province of Hispania Citerior; he maintained the Marian cause there until 72, when he was murdered by his officers.

56–57. pari imperio ... ciuitatis: Q. Caecilius Metellus Pius (98) was consul in 80 and proconsul of Hispania Ulterior from 79 to 71. Since he and Pompey had separate provinces, there was, as usual in Spain, no clash of *imperia*, though Pius and Pompey collaborated harmoniously in 75 and 74 (cf. *MRR* ii.98, 104).

Pio Metello: for the inversion of *nomen* and *cognomen* cf. 7 line 28 n.

57–58. nondum ... triumphauit: from Africa in 79, despite Sulla's initial opposition, and from Spain in 71 (*MRR* ii. 84, 124)

57. ullum honorem: P has *honorem curulem*, printed by Kempf and Shackleton Bailey (both, as usual, putting it in angled brackets, giving the misleading impression that it is the equivalent of a supplement of the age of print; cf. p. 23) and to which I gave a *fort. recte*. In fact Pompey had not held any magistracy, curule or not, but the omission is easy, a scribe's eye moving from the first *-em* to the next and the mistake could have been made by V., not Paris. There is no obvious reason for the latter to have added it, but cf. p. 23.

auspicatus: *auspicari* in the sense of 'embark on' does not occur before *CIL* xii. 4333, line 25 (AD 11), Vell. 2.101.3, and V., who also uses it thus at 4.4.1 and 5.4.4

58. initia ... cepit: Pompey's first consulship in 70 (*MRR* ii. 126).

58–59. tertium ... gessit: in 52 (*MRR* ii. 233–4); see now Ramsey, *Historia* 65 (2016), 298–324.

59–60. de Mithridate ... triumphum: in 61 (*MRR* ii. 181).

59. Mithridate: cf. 7 lines 246–7 n. Pompey defeated him in 66 and he fled to the Crimea. He was killed, at his own wish, by a bodyguard in 63.

Tigrane: king of Armenia and Mithridates' son-in-law; he surrendered to Pompey in 66 but was allowed to keep Armenia, losing his other possessions.

59–60. multis ... gentibus: cf. *I.I.* xiii/1.85, 566 (the exact form of the entry is uncertain).

60. praedonibus: Pompey defeated the pirates in 67 (*MRR* ii. 146).

9. *Catulus.* V.'s source is Cic. *Manil.* 59; Sall. *hist.* 5.24M = 20 Ramsey refers to the episode, which is also related by Vell. 2.32.1, Plut. *Pomp.* 25.10, and Dio 36.36a.

It occurred at a *contio* held in 66 to debate the law proposed by the tribune C. Manilius, conferring the command against Mithridates on Pompey; the law was supported by Cicero in his speech *pro lege Manilia*.

61. Q. etiam Catulum: Q. Lutatius Catulus (8), consul in 78 and censor in 65.
  ad sidera: for the hyperbole cf. *OLD s.u.* 7b.
  62. euexit: for *euehere* in similar contexts cf. Hor. *carm.* 1.1.6, *TLL* v/2.1008.31 ff.
    62–63. si in uno ... perseuerasset: Cic. *si in uno Cn. Pompeio omnia poneretis.*
  62. in uno: A^c; AL omit *in*, easily done beween *si* and *uno*, while G has *uiuo*, probably inspired by *absumpto illo* in line 64.
  64. in te: taking up *in quo*. Some of those present may have known (or remembered in the first case) that of Catulus' only two (homonymous) consular ancestors his father, consul in 102, had, together with Marius, been victorious at the battle of Vercellae in 101 (cf. line 53 n.), while the consul of 242 had defeated the Carthaginian fleet at the battle of the Aegates Isles, thus putting an end to the First Punic War. Catulus himself had defeated M. Aemilius Lepidus in civil war in 77 (cf. *MRR* ii. 90).
  66. duarum ... inclusum: V. could have written just *duabus syllabis* (SB translates 'in two syllables').
    spatio: the time it took to shout *in te* (cf. *OLD s.u.* 8c).

10. *The younger Cato.* On Cato cf. 7.2 n. In 58 a law of Clodius, who wanted him out of Rome, appointed Cato to annex Cyprus and restore Byzantine exiles; he returned to Rome in 56; cf. *MRR* ii. 198, 211. The episode is also related by Vell. 2.45.5 and Plut. *Cato min.* 39.1–2; V.'s source cannot be determined.

67. ex Cypro cum regia pecunia: Cyprus had been under Ptolemaic control since 294. In 80 the Alexandrines installed Ptolemy, the younger brother of Ptolemy XII Auletes as king of Cyprus. Cato offered him the priesthood of the temple of Aphrodite at Paphos (Plut. *Cato min.* 35.1), but he decided to commit suicide; at 9.4. ext. 1 V. says that he planned to drown himself together with all his money, but could not bring himself to do so; he eventually took poison. See Volkmann, *RE* xxiii. 1755–6.
  68. Tiberis: later MSS (D^{c}EF); α has *urbis*, retained by Kempf. *ripa urbis*, as he admitted (1854), was unparalleled (Latin, unlike modern languages, does not use *ripa* to mean the area near a river ('Left Bank')). The corruption, though surprising, is by no means inexplicable. (Shackleton Bailey printed *Tiberis* and his apparatus shows that he intended to do so, but translates 'the city's waterside': perhaps he changed his mind after completing his translation, but failed to alter the latter.)

11. *L. Marcius.* The choice of Marcius to command the remnants of the armies of P. and Cn. Cornelius Scipio after their defeats and deaths is related by Livy 25.37.5–6, presumably V.'s source; he is also mentioned at 1.6.2 and 2.7.15 (on the latter cf. lines 73, 75 nn.). These events occurred in 211 but are placed by Livy in the consular year 212; cf. Walbank ii. 8.

72. praecipuum: for the ellipse of a part of *esse* in subordinate clauses cf. K–St i. 12, H–S 431–2 (A^c added *sit*).

L. Marci: (101). Almost certainly Septimus, not Septimius (thus *MRR* i. 275, 300); see my note on Livy 32.2.5. For his service under Scipio Africanus in 206 see *MRR* i. 300.

Gertz proposed *Marcius*, and this was adopted by both Kempf and Shackleton Bailey. *L. Marcius* is then the subject and *praecipuum ... exemplum* the predicate, while with the transmitted reading the meaning is 'L. Marcius' example of unusual honour is preeminent'; the former is the more natural Latin and the omission of *-us* could have resulted from a scribe's eye moving from *-i-* to *i-*; it deserved a *fort. recte*, but I continue to think that it is another conjecture producing what V. ought to have written rather than what he in fact wrote.

73. equitem Romanum: thus also Livy 25.37.2, 5, Frontin. *strat.* 2.6.2, 10.2; at 2.7.15 (cf. line 75 n.), however, V. calls him a *tribunus militum*, Cic. *Balb.* 34, in the context of a treaty he concluded with Gades in 206 (mentioned by Livy only at 32.2.5), *primi pili centurio*. At 2.7.15 V.'s source is clearly Livy 26.2.1–4 and he has forgotten what Livy wrote at 25.37; when he got to our passage, he forgot what he had written earlier. Cicero is confused, apparently thinking that Marcius made the treaty with Gades soon after the defeat of the Scipios (though it is not impossible that the confusion is due to an an annalist whom Cicero had read).

73–74. duo exercitus ... lacerati: see Livy 25.32–6. The Scipios were faced by three Carthaginian armies, commanded, respectively, by Hannibal's brother Hasdrubal, Hasdrubal the son of Gisgo, and Mago.

73. P. et Cn. Scipionum: Publius Cornelius Scipio (330), the father of Africanus, was consul in 218, Cn. Cornelius Scipio Calvus (345), the father of the consul of 191 (see line 21 n.), in 222. V. mentions one or both at 1.6.2, 2.7.15, 3.7.1, 4.4.10–11, 5.4.2, 6.6. ext. 1, 9.11. ext. 1, 4.

75. nullum ... relinquebat: 'there was no room for popularity-mongering' (SB). Nor did he do himself any favours when he wrote to the senate describing himself as a propraetor (2.7.15, Livy 26.2.1).

12. *Sulpicia.* She is mentioned also by Pliny *nat.* 7.120 and Solin. 1.126, the building of a temple to Venus Verticordia by Ovid, *fasti* 4.157–60. The temple, situated at the south-west end of the Circus Maximus, was dedicated in 114, following the trial of three Vestal Virgins for having sexual relations with men; see Coarelli, *LTUR* v. 119.

The detail of V.'s account indicates that he was using a learned source, most likely Varro.

76–77. Sulpicia ... uxor: Ser. Sulpicius Paterculus (81) was, in all probability, the brother of C. Sulpicius Paterculus (80), consul in 258. Her husband was Q. Fulvius Flaccus (59), consul in 237, 224, 212, and 209, one of the most important commanders in the Hannibalic War. M. Torelli, *Lavinio e Roma* (Rome, 1984), 80–1, followed by Coarelli, loc. cit., implausibly identifies Sulpicia's husband with his son (61), consul in 179 and censor in 174. He was the man who while censor stripped the temple of Juno Lacinia of its roof (Livy 42.3, 28.11–12), a most unsuitable husband for a lady of such high virtue; there are, moreover, no Sulpicii Paterculi attested other than the consul of 258 and Sulpicia's father. She is probably to be identified with the mother-in-law of Sp. Postumius Albinus, consul in 186 (cf. vol. iii. 236).

ext. In these final *externa exempla* of book 8 V. first returns to two figures who featured earlier in the book (7. ext. 2, 13. ext. 2), proceeds to a mythological person, and concludes, as in the Roman *exempla*, with a woman.

ext. 1. *Pythagoras.*

82–83. ceterum ... transgrediemur: V. makes this apology because the Roman *exempla* have been of oustanding individuals and he does not want to suggests that they are outshone by the Greeks who follow.

82. deminutione: A^c; α has *diminutione. deminuo* and *deminutione* are the correct forms (cf. Varr. *ling.* 5.172), but MSS vary between *de-* and *di-* (cf. 7 line 169, 14 line 32 nn.).

83. transgrediemur: for the future cf. 9.1. ext. 1; later manuscripts (cf. Torrenius) have *transgrediamur*.

83–86. Pythagorae ... dixisse: V.'s source is Cic. *nat. deor.* 1.10; for the manifold references, none earlier than Cicero, to Pythagoras' followers regarding him as infallible see Pease ad loc.; he suggests that Cicero learnt of their practice from P. Nigidius Figulus.

84. deducere nefas: A^cL^cG, corrupted in AL to *deducerent fas*. The corruption is intelligible; had it been to *deducere fas*, one would have said that a scribe's eye had moved from one *e* to the next.

86. schola tenus: 'extending no further than the school' (SB).

86–91. V.'s source here cannot be determined.

87. Crotoniatae: cf. 7 lines 75–9 n.

ipsorum AL: G has *eorum*. For *ipse* of the subject of the main clause, in contrast to *suus* in the subordinate clause, cf. H–S 176.

89. †tam frequentem†: an insoluble crux. Not only is the transmitted reading senseless, but, as is clear from *urbium* in line 86, *post mortem* in line 89, and *illa urbs uiguit* in line 90, which clearly refers to the decline of Metapontum (cf. 7 lines 78–9 n.) V. is talking about Metapontum and must have mentioned its citizens explicitly and in a way that balanced *Crotoniatae* in line 87 (Morel's conjecture (*PhW* 1929, 527), implausible enough in any case, can therefore be excluded). Madvig, typically, was the first to diagnose the problem (*tam frequenter*, found, Kempf (1854) implies, in all his later manuscripts, was the vulgate), but his proposal to replace *tam frequentem* by *Metapontini* involves the strangest of corruptions. Somewhat more plausibly, Gertz changed *tam frequentem* to *iam praesentem*, adding *Metapontini* before it and *eius* after *domum* (presumably to make it clear that *domum* did not go with *Cereris*, but there is no real ambiguity), and this, apart from *eius*, was printed by Shackleton Bailey; Novák, building on Gertz' conjecture, proposed *Metapontini uiuum iam frequenter ... domum <eius>*: in both cases the omission could have been caused by the loss of a line in a manuscript of late antiquity. The plural verb, of course, presents no difficulty, following both a collective noun (cf. K–St i. 22) and a plural in apposition. I have wondered about adding *Metapontinorum* after *ciuitas*.

domum: see previous note.

90. †quaque †: the last passage in book 8 where I felt constrained to use the obelos. 'and where' makes no sense and Pighius read *quantumque*, whatever he thought that meant, Vorst *quamdiuque*, Perizonius *quumque*, Kempf *quoadque* (adopted by Shackleton Bailey), while Novák, retaining *quaque*, added *aetate* after *uiguit* (I wonder if Kempf misreported the conjecture, made to him privately: the separation of *quaque* from *aetate* would be unmotivated, but omission of *aetate* after *quaque* could be explained by a scribe's moving from one *-e* to the next). *quamdiuque* and *quoadque* both provide the required sense; V. uses *quamdiu* at 13. ext. 4, 14.1, and 6.5. ext. 1 (in the first and third with a preceding *tam diu*, so that it must be printed as two words), *quoad* meaning 'while' at 4.3. ext. 3 and 7.7.3 (and very frequently meaning 'until'). Neither provides a particularly easy explanation of the corruption, but *quoadque* is closer to the paradosis and if forced to make a choice, I would print it.

ext. 2. *Gorgias*. This practice of Gorgias is first mentioned by Plato *Gorg.* 447C; Cicero refers to it on three occasions, *de orat.* 1.103, 3.129, and *fin.* 2.1. All use similar language, but only the last two share *ausus* and *in conuentu* with V., the first and third have *primus(m)*, the second *princeps*, while the first has *de quibus quisque*, the second, with V., *qua de re quique*, the third *qua de re quis*. The statue is mentioned only at *de orat.* 3.129 (for other sources see lines 94–5 n.). V. is thus closest to the latter, but he had probably read all three passages.

92. Gorgiae Leontino ... praestanti: G^cP. α had *Leontini* (thus AL, *Fleontini* G, so it seems); A^c altered *praestanti* to the genitive to agree with *Leontini*. Since Cicero has *cui ... soli*, there can be no doubt that the indirect tradition preserves what V. wrote; the corruption was caused by the ambiguity of *Gorgiae* and the fact that one expects *statua* to be constructed with the genitive of the person concerned. The dative conveys the sense of 'in honour of'.

For the word order see 13 line 49 n.

93. in conuentu: 'at a gathering' (SB). AL have *ei* before *in*, deleted by A^c amd omitted in G. There is no obvious explanation for the interpolation and no reason to connect it with the corruption discussed in the previous note.

94–95. For the statue of Gorgias see. K. A. Morgan, *CQ* 44 (1994), 375–86, Wisse–Winterbottom–Fantham, 126–7.

Other sources for the statue at Delphi are Hermippus fr. 63 Wehrli, Pliny *nat.* 33.83, Paus. 10.18.7, Dio Chrys. 37.28, Philostr. *VS* 9.4; apart from Pausanias, who says it was gilded, all, like Cicero and V., say it was made of solid gold. There is no reason to reject the consensus.

V. says that the statue was dedicated by *Graecia*, i.e. it was a common dedication by a number of Greek states, and this is implied by Cicero; that is was a dedication in honour of Gorgias is also implied by Dio Chrysostom and Philostratus. An epigram, however, inscribed on the base of a statue of Gorgias at Olympia (*Inscr.Olymp.* 293), dedicated by his great-nephew Eumolpus and mentioned by Paus. 6.17.7–8, shows that Hermippus, Pliny, and Pausanias were right to say that Gorgias dedicated it himself.

in templo Delphici Apollinis is V.'s interpretation, doubtless correct, of *Delphis* in Cicero.

94–95. posuit ... gens: omitted by G, leaving a space smaller than would have been required for the words (the omission, therefore, was not caused by *saut du même au même* from *(aur)o* to *(summ)o*).

ext. 3. *Amphiaraus.* On the shrine and oracle of Amphiaraus at Oropus see my note on Livy 45.37.12 (it was visited by L. Aemilius Paullus during his archaeological tour of Grece after his victory over Perseus in 168), to which add a reference to Pease's note on Cic. *diu.* 1.88, who is V.'s source. Strabo 9, p. 399C and Paus. 1.34.2, cited in my *testimonia* apparatus, are only two of the many writers who mention the shrine, the earliest Herodotus 1.52, 92.2, 8.134.2; see Bethe, *RE* i. 1893–7. Amphiaraus was a legendary figure who was said to have been swallowed up by the earth while taking part in the expedition of the Seven against Thebes (cf. Bethe, *RE* i. 1891).

96. incubuit: 'devoted itself '; cf. *OLD s.u.* 6a.

97. condicionemque ... redigendo: 'and function ... converting' (SB).

98. instituendo: for *instituere* with accusative and infinitive cf. K–St i. 693, citing, as well as our passage, Virg. *Aen.* 6.142, Vell. 2.6.3, and Suet. *Aug.* 31.4.

98–99. Pythicae ... Dodonae ... Hammonis: *uariatio* between adjective, locative, and genitive (Morel (loc. cit., line 130) proposed *Dodonaeo*).

Pythicae cortinae: the tripod, shaped like a cauldron, on which the Delphic priestess sat; the word is first attested at Ennius *ann.* 9V = *trag.* 365–6 Jocelyn, used, according to Varro *ling.* 7.48, because the space between earth and sky resembled it.

99. aheno Dodonae: Dodona, in Epirus (Barrington Atlas 54C2; cf. N. G. L. Hammond, *Epirus* (Oxford, 1967), 169–71), was the site of the oldest oracle in Greece. For the use of a gong at Dodona see A. B. Cook, *JHS* 22 (1902), 5–28, esp. pp. 21–2, arguing that its original function was apotropaic but it came to be used for oracular purposes; cf. Kern, *RE* v. 1262, Pease on Cic. *diu.* 1.3. For inscribed lead plates found at Dodona cf. *REG* 129 (2016), 476 nos. 281–4. See also p. 243.

aheno is Pighius' correction of *Athenae* in α. For the substantive cf. *TLL* i. 1444.51 ff.; *ahenum* is the older form and the corruption suggests that it was transmitted thus. It is possible, though, that V. wrote *aeno* or *aheneo*.

Hammonis fonti: Zeus/Jupiter Hammon (normally thus in Latin, Ἄμμων in Greek) is the Egyptian god Amen-Râ, whose oracle, the Ammonium, was at Siwah, in the Libyan desert; it was famously consulted by Alexander. Its spring was said to vary in temperature throughout the day and night (Hdt. 4.181, Lucr. 6.848–78, Diod. 17.50, Arr. *anab.* 3.4.2, Curt. 4.7.22, Plin. *nat.* 22.228, Mela 1.39): it is in fact constant at *c.* 28C. See Pietschmann, *RE* i. 1853–60, Pease on Cic. *diu.* 1.3, *nat. deor.* 1.82.

α has *fronti*, eventually corrected by Pighius.

ext. 4. *Berenice.* The final *exemplum* of book 8 presents a complex prosopographical problem. I first make the following additions to the sources listed in my *testimonia* apparatus: the scholion on Pindar *Ol.* 7 is Aristotle fr. 569 Rose; add Philostratus *gymn.* 17, Choricius 7.11. V.'s source cannot be determined.

No other source gives the woman's name as Berenice: Pausanias 5.6.7, Philostratus, and Aelian *u.h.* 10.1 have Pherenice, and Berenice is probably a mistake by V., who knew it as the name of a number of women of the Ptolemaic dynasty; one cannot, though, exclude the possibility that the the error occurred in the course of transmission (no one has ever proposed reading *Pherenices*). For other Rhodian women called Pherenice see *LGPN* i. 457.

The fragment of Aristotle, from the scholion on Pindar *Ol.* 7, written in honour of Diagoras of Rhodes, Olympic boxing victor in 464, is the ultimate source of all the other evidence; it says that the sons of Diagoras' daughters were Eucles, whose father was Callianax, and Peisirhodos; one of his daughters was Callipateira, and it was she who was eventually allowed to watch the games, having said that her father, brothers, and nephew Eucles, as well as her own son Peisirhodos, had been Olympic victors. As Boeckh (*Pindari opera quae supersunt* ii. 2 (Leipzig, 1821), 166) realised, Aristotle must in fact have said that Pherenice was the mother of Peisirhodos, Callipateira of Eucles; later writers transferred the honour of having been the only woman admitted to the games from Callipatreia to Pherenice, V., corrupting her name and making her the mother of Eucles. Pausanias 6.7.2 correctly makes Eucles the son of Callipatreia and says, without giving her name, that it was Peisirhodos whose mother accompanied him to the Olympic games, posing as his trainer, where he was victorious in the boys' boxing (similarly Philostratus loc. cit.). Cf. Kroll, *RE* xix. 2033–4 (the article on Eucles (*RE* vi. 1054 (14)), cited by Shackleton Bailey, does not discuss the problem).

100–101. cui soli ... permissum est: women were prohibited from watching all competitions, not just those associated with *gymnasia*; cf. Paus. 5.6.7–8; at 6.20.9 he says that the ban did not apply to παρθένοι. Cf. S. G. Miller, *Ancient Greek Athletics* (New Haven, CT–London, 2004, 150–1). The ban was instituted, of course, because the competitors were naked (cf. Miller, op. cit., 11–14.).

101. ad Olympia: P has *Olympiae*, an apparently unique case of *adducere* with the dative of a toponym (Halm suggested emending to *Olympiam* or *ad Olympia*).

102. ingressurum: P (and Lupus); α has *ingressu*, presumably the result of a scribe's eye moving from the first *u* to the second, with subsequent deletion of *m*.

Olympionice: the Latin form is found before V. at Cic. *inu.* 2.144, *Flacc.* 31, and *Tusc.* 1.111.

102–103. fratribus ... adsecutis: Aristotle gives their names as Damagetos, Dorieus, and Acusilaos.

Appendix

Corrections to Teubner edition

I list here, in addition to three items in the Preface, (i) the errors and omissions in my edition mentioned in the commentary, whether in the text (the text in this volume has been corrected accordingly), *testimonia* ('T'), *apparatus criticus* ('App.'), or Index; (ii) alterations to the *apparatus criticus* to make it cohere with changes of mind indicated in the commentary. Unless stated, references are to the line numbers of the edition.

p. xxxiv n. 4. See M. Crab, *BiblH&R* 75 (2013), 291–318.
p. xl. Under 'Shackleton Bailey' for '678' read '67'.
p. xli. Under 'Vahlen, *GPS*', in line 3 after '*Schriften,*' add 'i,'.
1.2–3. App.: under 'A^c' delete '…'.
1.4–10. T: delete stop after '*ad*'.
1.4. App.: after the semi-colon add '*fort.* P *scribendum*'.
1.16–17 App.: add '*fort.* ultima senectutis suae oratione'.
1.44. App.: for '*C. Torr.*' read '*P. Pighius*'.
1.102–110. T: for '388–9' read '589'.
1.112. App.: read 'in opprimendis A^c : opprimendis α, *fort. recte*'.
1.125–135. T: read '**136–147**'.
1.152–153. App.: after '*Watt*' add '(1995)'.
1.175–180. T: for '120' read '220'.
1.186. App.: delete entry.
1.210. App.: under *P* read 'Areopagitarum'.
2.8–9. App.: read 'a … coactus α : sed iussus Calpurnius domum demoliri *P*'.
2.11. App.: add 'in formulam Shackleton Bailey'.
3.9. Text: read 'Androgynem'.
4.13. App.: for '*Halm*' read '*Kempf*'.
6.7. Under 'dignus hac' delete '*P*'.
6.10–16. T: after '574,' add '576,'.
7.7–13. T: add '*Livy* 39.40.12'.
7.9. Text: read 'capitali'.
7.16–20. T: for '20' read '18' and add separate entry '**18–20**', listing sources cited in commentary ad loc.
7.54. App.: for '*1878*' read '*1877*'.
7.109–130. T: add '*Cic. fin.* 5.87'.
7.116. App.: add at end ', *fort. recte*'.
7.120–121. Read 'effusam per Mariam *Achelis* (*CQ* 1911, 112)'.
7.154. App.: add 'effecit α : efficit *Watt* (*Latomus* 2001, 937)'.
7.185. App.: read 'uilissimum'.
7.189. App.: after 'G^c' add '*P*'.
7.213–221. T: delete '*adde Cic. sen.* 22'.
7.222–224. T: add 'Simonides fr. xxviii Page'.
8.8. Text: read 'amicitiae'.
8.11. App.: read 'animis remissioribus *P* : remissionibus *Halm*'.
9.8. App.: in line 2 read 'Agrippa'.

9.15–25. T: add sources listed at *MRR* ii.49, under 'P. Annius'.
9.26–33. T: Delete reference to a fragment of Scaurus.
10.34. App.: read 'tu *A*'.
10.35. App.: add 'qui quidem *Foertsch (1864)*'.
11.18–29. T: add '*App. b.c.* 2.149.619 (*cf.* 153.641), Dio 44.18.4'.
11.30–36. T: add '*Cic. rep.* 1.25'.
11.44. App.: under *A*ᶜ read 'exprobrans' (*bis*).
11.47–50. T: add '*AP* 16.167, Ath. 590F–591A' and read '49.13–16'.
11.56–57. Text: read 'lineamentis'.
11 tit. (before *exemplum* 5). T: read 'P (*fort.* possint scripsit Paris)'.
11.19–29. T: add '*Dio Chrys.* 63.4–5'.
12 tit. Text: read 'AVCTOREM ET DISPVTATOREM ESSE'.
13.25–28, 29–33. T: for '157' read '156'.
13.93. App.: read 'xxmum (xxxmum *A*ᶜ) *A* : xx *LG* : xxx annos *P*'.
13.95. T: add 'Theopompus *FGrH* 115F68b'.
13.97–109. T: read '154–5'.
13.106: App.: read 'περίπλους *Pighius, sed duo uerba*'.
14.9–18. T: add '*Hier. chron.* a.Abr. 1852'.
14.46–47. App.: read 'gaudium excepit *P*'.
14.53. App.: read 'nomen suum scribsit (scripsit *P*ᶜ) *P*'.
14.104–111. T: see sources listed in commentary.
15.3. Text: read, without obeloi, 'aeque praemiorum uirtutis atque operum contemplatio iucunda'.
15.3–4. App.: read 'aeque ... honorum ... iudicanda *G*'; after first '*sic, sed*' add 'uirtutes *AL*' and delete '(*honorum*)' on both occasions; after second '*sic, sed*' add 'aequa *Perizonius*'.
15.13–14. App.: for 'admonuit' read 'poposcerunt'.
15.25. App.: in second line read 'illius ad eius *dett.*'. In sixth line read '(1854)'.
15.46. App.: under '*L*ᶜ' read 'neque cuiquam bioso'.
15.139–144. T: add 'Hdt. 1.52, 92.2, 8.134.2; cf. Bethe, *RE* i. 1893–7'.
15.143. App.: add 'Dodonae α : Dodonae<o> *Morel* (*PhW* 1929, 527)'.
15.145–149. T: after 'inscr. B' add '= Aristotle fr. 569 Rose'; add Philostratus *gymn.* 17, Choricius p. 103 Foerster–Richsteig.

Index nominum

p. 858. Caieta: delete '1.4.6'.
p. 861. Clodia: read 'Ofili'.
p. 862. P. Cornelius Scipio Africanus: read '2.1.10'; P. Cornelius Scipio Africanus Aemilianus: add '8.8.1'.
p. 865. Q. Fabius Maximus Rullianus, Q. Fabius Maximus Verrucosus: move '8.1.absol.9' from the latter to the former.
p. 867. P. Furius: for '4.7.6; 9.13.3' read '8.1.damn.2'.
p. 868. Hiero I, II: move '8.13.ext. 1' from the former to the latter.
p. 880. Ptolomaeus I, II: in the former add '?' before '8.9.ext. 3', in the latter add ', ?8.9.ext. 3' after '4.3.9'.
p. 881. P. Rutilius Rufus: delete '?'.

Addenda

p. 8. Add '14 ? Cic. *De gloria*.'

p. 38. In apparatus add '6 Catonem *AG* : Porcium Catonem *PA*ᶜ, *fort. recte* : Porcius M. Catonem *L*

p. 100. **6–7.** AG have *M. Catonem*, L *Porcius M. Catonem*, Paris (and Lupus in A) *M. Porcium Catonem*. The latter could be right, the omission of *Porcium* being caused by a scribe's eye's moving from *M.* to *-m* (L's *Porcius* would be a gloss). But of the other fifteen occasions when V. mentions the younger Cato (see 7.2 n.), only at 2.10.7–8, 3.4.6, and 7.5.6 does he use his *nomen* and an addition by Paris is equally likely.

p. 238. **100. Aheno Dodonae:** change stop at end to comma and add 'R. C. T. Parker, *ZPE* 194 (2015), 111–14, *G&R* 63 (2016), 69–90, J. Mendéz Dosoma, *ZPE* 197 (2016), 119–39'.

Indexes

General

The names of Romans are followed by an indication of the date of their consulship(s) or, if they did not reach the consulship, the highest office(s) they held. Figures in brackets indicate a date (BC unless stated). Modern scholars are included only for general remarks about them, not for individual conjectures. See also the Index to my Teubner edition (the text and apparatus in this volume are not indexed). 'Rome', 'Romans', and 'Italy' are omitted.

Abdera 145, 217
Academy 146
L. Accius 211
Acropolis, Athenian 215
actors 137
Acusilaos 239
adultery 85–6, 104
T. Aebutius Parrus (*pr.* 178)
Aegates Isles, battle of 233
Aelian 161
L. Aelius Seianus (*cos.* AD 31) 2, 4
M. Aemilius Lepidus (*cos.* 78) 197, 233
M. Aemilius Lepidus (*cos.* 46, 42) 102, 111
M'. Aemilius Lepidus (*cos.* 66) 120
Mam. Aemilius Lepidus Livianus (*cos.* 77) 120
M. Aemilius Lepidus Porcina (*cos.* 137) 93
L. Aemilius Paullus (*cos.* 182, 168) 84, 178–9, 197, 228, 237
M. Aemilius Scaurus (*cos.* 115) 83, 116–18, 127
M. Aemilius Scaurus (*pr.* 56) 77, 83, 165, 173
Aeschines 175
Aetolia, Aetolus 207
Africa 84, 125, 164, 213
Agamemnon 187–8
M. Agrius, Agrii 113
Ajax 188
Alba Fucens 178
Alba Longa 67
Alcamenes 183–5
Alcibiades 161
Alcidamas 204
Alexander the Great 2–3, 30, 183, 187, 217, 238
Alexander Polyhistor 207–8

Alexander, name of slaves 113
Alsium 93
Ambrones 231
Amphiarius 237–8
ampliatio 84
Anaxagoras 137, 148, 182–3
Anaxarchus 217
Ancona 164
Anio, river 162
P. Annius (*tr. mil.* 87) 165
T. Annius Milo (*pr.* 55) 173
Antiochus III 88
Antipater, Macedonian 163
Antipater, founder of Cyrenaic school 169
C. Antonius (*cos.* 63) 128
C. Antonius (*pr.* 44) 71
M. Antonius (*cos.* 99) 90, 114, 117, 164–5
M. Antonius (*cos.* 44, 34) 111, 164
Apamea, peace of 89
Apelles 183, 192
Aphrodite 183, 185; temple of at Paphos 233
C. Appuleius Decianus (*tr. pl.* 98) 89–90
L. Appuleius Saturninus (*tr. pl.* 103, 100, 99) 89–90, 116, 125
P. Aquillius (*iiiuir nocturnus*) 92
C. Aquillius Gallus (*pr.* 66) 103
L. Aquillius Gallus (*pr.* 176) 103
Aratus 188
Arausio 117
arbiter and *iudex* 100–1
Archias 136
Archimedes 137, 148–9
Archytas 144
Areopagus 97

Arganthonius 205
Aricia 107
Arion 144
Aristippus 169
Aristobulus II 72
Aristonicus 136
Aristotle 218–19
Aristoxenus 204
Artaxeres I 156
Artaxerxes II 157, 206
Armenia 232
Artemis, temple of at Ephesus 220–1
Artemisium, battle of 216
arx 99
Asclepius 183
Asia, province of 2–3, 96, 229–30
C. Asinius Pollio (*cos.* 40) 9, 205
C. Ateius Capito (*cos.* AD 5) 91
Athena, statue of 184; Athena Parthenos, statue of 215
Athens, Athenians 146, 192, 206
A. Atilius Cal(i)atinus 82
M. Atilius Regulus (*cos.* 294) 82
P. Atinius 113
Attalus I 226–7
Attalus III 136
Atthis 207
auguraculum 99
augurs 99
Augustus, Emperor (Octavian) 3, 30, 85, 97, 100, 111, 182–3, 222
Aulis 187
C. Aurelius Cotta (*cos.* 75) 127, 166
L. Aurelius Cotta (*cos.* 144) 83–4
C. Aurelius Scaurus (*pr.* 186) 83
M. Aurelius Scaurus (*cos. suff.* 108) 83

Berenice 238–9
Blair, Tony 174
Blunkett, David 198
Bocchus 212
Boeotia 204
Bona Dea scandal 121
Bononia 85–6
Byzantium 233

Caecilia Metella 213
L. Caecilius Metellus (*cos.* 251, 247) 195
L. Caecilius Metellus Calvus (*cos.* 142) 115
L. Caecilius Metellus Denter (*cos.* 304) 196
Q. Caecilius Metellus Macedonicus (*cos.* 143) 115, 122, 213
Q. Caecilius Metellus Pius (*cos.* 80) 117, 119, 213, 232
Q. Caecilius Metellus Pius Scipio Nasica (*cos.* 52) 135, 213
Caelian Hill 99
Caieta 159
Calchas 187–8
M. Calidius (*pr.* 57) 173
Calidius, of Bononia 85–6
Callaeci 211
Callianax 239
Callimachus 220
Callipateira 239
Calpurnia 77, 181
L. Calpurnius Bestia (*cos.* 111) 127
P. Calpurnius Lanarius 99
C. Calpurnius Piso (*cos.* 67) 118
L. Calpurnius Piso (*cos.* 112) 77–8
L. Calpurnius Piso (*pr.* 74) 77
L. Calpurnius Piso (*cos.* 58) 77–8
calumnia 104
Campania 125
C. Canuleius 89
Capitoline hill 210
Capri 222
Capua 117
Carfania, Cafranii, Carfanii 110
Carneades 137, 146–7
Carthage 84, 158, 200–1, 208, 225–6, 228, 233
A. Cascellius (senator) 190–1
A. Cascellius (*pr.*) 190
L. Cassius Hemina 5
C. Cassius Longinus (*pr.* 44) 97
L. Cassius Longinus (*cos.* 107) 78
L. Cassius Longinus Ravilla (*cos.* 127) 93
cavalry service 230
Centumcellae 93
Ceos 2–3, 153
Cephisias 191
Chalcidice, Chalcis 204
Chaldaeans 140
Chios 207
Chrysippus 137, 147, 151–2

Cilicia 122, 165, 230
Cimbri 116, 230–1
Cineas 199
Circus Flaminius 211
Circus Maximus 235
Cisalpine Gaul 173
Civil wars 128, 194
Claudia 90
Claudii 77, 91
Ap. Claudius Caecus (*cos.* 307, 296) 73, 193, 198–9
C. Claudius Centho (*cos.* 240) 198
T. (?Ti.) Claudius Centumalus 99
M. Claudius Marcellus (*cos.* 222, 215, 214, 210, 208) 148–9
M. Claudius Marcellus (*cos.* 166, 155, 152) 227
M. Claudius Marcellus (*leg.* 102, 90, ?*pr.*) 118
M. Claudius Marcellus (*aed. cur.* 91) 118
C. Claudius Nero (*cos.* 207) 199
Ti. Claudius Nero 198–9
Ti. Claudius Nero (*cos.* 202) 199
Ti. Claudius Nero (*pr.* 42) 71
Ap. Claudius Pulcher (*cos.* 79) 200
C. Claudius Pulcher (*cos.* 92) 77–8
C. Claudius Pulcher (*pr.* 56) 77
P. Claudius Pulcher (*cos.* 249) 74–5, 90–1, 198
Q. Claudius Quadrigarius 5
Ap. Claudius Rufus (*cos.* 268) 198
Clazomenae 148
Cleanthes 137, 152–3
Clodia, wife of Ofilius 199–200
M. Clodius Aesopus 171–2
P. Clodius Pulcher (*tr. pl.* 58, *aed. cur.* 56) 71, 77, 121, 200, 213, 233
Cloelii 86–7
Cnidus 206
Cnossus 206
L. Coelius Antipater 5
Colophon 183
Colotes 187
Cominii 118
comitia tributa 79–80
Cornelii Scipiones 215; tomb of 210
C. Cornelius (*tr. pl.* 67) 118–121, 172
L. Cornelius Balbus 231
L. Cornelius Cinna (*cos.* 87–84) 164, 197

Cn. Cornelius Dolabella (*cos.* 81) 165
Cn. Cornelius Dolabella (*pr.* 81) 165
P. Cornelius Dolabella (*cos. suff.* 44) 96–7
Cornelius Lentulus, owner of Alexander Polyhistor 208
P. Cornelius Lentulus Spinther (*pro qu. pro pr.* 43) 96
Cornelius Nepos 5, 9
P. Cornelius Scipio (*cos.* 218) 234
P. Cornelius Scipio, son of Africanus 84
P. Cornelius Scipio Aemilianus (*cos.* 147, 134) 84, 115, 135, 158, 223–8
P. Cornelius Scipio Africanus (*cos.* 205, 194) 84, 88–9, 127, 149, 209, 223–7
L. Cornelius Scipio Asiagenes (*cos.* 190) 88–9, 210
Cn. Cornelius Scipio Calvus (*cos.* 222) 226, 234
P. Cornelius Scipio Nasica (*cos.* 191) 88, 226–7, 234
P. Cornelius Scipio Nasica (*cos.* 162, 155) 226
P. Cornelius Scipio Nasica (*cos.* 138) 226
P. Cornelius Scipio Nasica (*cos.* 111) 226
P. Cornelius Scipio Nasica (*pr.* 94 or 93) 213
L. Cornelius Sisenna (*pr.* 78) 72, 128
L. Cornelius Sulla (*cos.* 88, 80) 117, 125, 136–7, 197, 208, 212
Corsica 76
Cos 183
C. Cosconius 80–1
M. Cosconius (*pr.* 135) 81
Crete 141
Croton 141, 236
crucifixion 114
Ctesias 206
Ctesiphon 175
Curiatii 67
Cylon 206
Cyprus 233
Cyrenaic school 169
Cyrus, the Great 137, 157; the younger 157
Cythnos 187

Daedalus 215
Damagetos 239
Damastes 207–8
Dandon 208
Darius I 216

Delos 191
Delphi 192, 238
Demetrius, of Phalerum 191
Democritus 137, 145–6, 217
Demosthenes 137–9, 174–6
Diagoras 239
dictator years 195
Dionysia 175
Diuus Iulius, temple of 183
Dodona 238
Cn. Domitius Calvinus (*cos.* 53) 181
domus Augusti, Tiberiana 222
domus publica 121
Dorieus 239
duodecim scripta 160

Echecrates 144
eclipses, moon 177–9, sun 182
eculeus 221
Egypt 140–3
Elea 204
Eleusis 191
Elis 207
Q. Ennius 210
Epameinon 145
Ephesus 183, 220–1
Ephorus 207
Epii 207
Epimenides 206–7 206
Epirus 238
L. Equitius (*tr. pl.* 99) 89
Ethiopians 206
Eucles 239
Euclid, Eudoxus 191
Euphranor 186–7
Eurytus 142
exempla, exemplarity 5

Q. Fabius Maximus (*pr.* 181) 228
Q. Fabius Maximus Aemilianus (*cos.* 145) 228
Q. Fabius Maximus Allobrogicus (*cos.* 115) 228
Q. Fabius Maximus Rullianus (*cos.* 322, 310, 308, 297, 295) 79, 82,
Q. Fabius Maximus Verrucosus (*cos.* 233, 228, 215, 214, 209) 102, 149, 196–7
C. Fabius Pictor (?= C. Fabius Ambustus (*mag. eq.* 315) 214–16

C. Fabius Pictor (*cos.* 269) 214
N. Fabius Pictor (*cos.* 266) 214
Q. Fabius Pictor (*leg.* 216) 214
Fannia 105–7
C. Fannius (*cos.* 122) 105
Cn. Fannius 105
Faventia 117
First Punic War 233
M. Flavius (*tr. pl.* ?327, 323) 78–9
?Q. Flavius (*tr. pl.* 327) 78–9
C. Flavius Fimbria (*cos.* 104) 116
formula 101
Fraenkel, Eduard 225
Q. Fulvius Flaccus (*cos.* 237, 224, 212, 209) 235
Q. Fulvius Flaccus (*cos.* 179) 235
Ser. Fulvius Flaccus (?*pr.* 135) 114
C. Fundanius Fundulus (*cos.* 243) 74, 91
N.(?) Furius 190–1
P. Furius (*tr. pl.* 99) 89–90

A. Gabinus (*cos.* 58) 71–2
Gabinius Sisenna 72
Gades 205, 234
Q. Gallius (*aed. pl.* 67) 172
Gaul 213
genius Augusti, libations to 231
gens, gens Cornelia, Fabia, Iulia 215; *gens Cornelia* 224; *gens Valeria* 1, 229
glory 209
Gorgias 203–4, 236–7
M. Gratidius (*praef.* 102) 116
Greek dialects 136
Griffin, M. T. 120

Hammon, oracle of 238
Hannibal 30, 201, 234
Hannibalic War 196
Hasdrubal, brother of Hannibal 234; son of Gisgo 234
Hegesias 169
Heiric of Auxerre 20, 177
Hellanicus 207–8
hellebore 147
Hephaestion 3
Hephaestus, statue of 184–5
Heraclea, battle of 199
Heraclides of Byzantium 88–9

Hermocles, Hermocrates 220
Hermodorus 211
Herodotus 206
Herpstratus 220–1
Hieron II 193, 200–1
Hieronymus 163
Historia de preliis Alexandri Magni 22
Homer 210
Honos and *Virtus*, temple of 99
M. (?P.) Horatius 67–69
Hortensia 111
Q. Hortensius Hortalus (*cos.* 69) 111, 119, 171

Ianuarius Nepotianus 19, 22–3, 26–7
Ides of March 179–81
Illyria 76
Indians 206
Interamna Nahars 121
interdictio bonorum 124
Iophon 153
Iphigenia 187
Isauri 122
Isocrates 137, 150–1, 218
Italica 127
iudex 106; see also *arbiter*
iudicium populi 69, 75, 90–1, 93
Iulii Caesares 215
C. Iulius Caesar (*cos.* 59, 48, 46–44) 9, 71–2, 77, 100, 111, 121, 165–6, 170, 179–82, 213, 223
Sex. Iulius Caesar (*cos.* 90) 118
C. Iulius Hyginus 5, 7
Iulius Paris 19–23, 26
M. Iunius Brutus (*pr.* 44) 97
D. Iunius Brutus Callaicus (*cos.* 138) 211
C. Iunius Bubulcus Brutus (*cos.* 317, 313, 311) 214
L. Iunius Pullus (*cos.* 249) 91
Iuventii 102
M. Iuventius Laterensis (*pr.* 51) 101–2
M'. Iuventius Thalna (*cos.* 163) 102

Jenkins, Roy 138
Jugurtha 212, 230
Jupiter Optimus Maximus, temple of 223

Kempf, C. 15, 22, 26–8

T. Labienus (*tr. pl.* 63, ?*pr.*) 213
C. Laelius (*cos.* 140) 73, 115, 158–9
D. Laelius 73
D. Laelius (*leg.* ?76) 73
D. Laelius (*tr. pl.* 54) 73
Lamia 208
Lampsacus 207
Landolfus Sagax 22
Latmus 208
Lavinium, Laurentum 122, 159
Lemnos 183
Lesbos 207
Leucippus 145, 217
lex Calpurnia 84
lex Cassia tabellaria 93
lex Cornelia de sicariis 87
lex Iulia de adulteriis coercendis 85–6
lex Iulia repetundarum 83
lex Plautia iudiciaria 127
lex Pompeia de parricidiis 87
lex Seruilia Caepionis, Glauciae 80–1, 127
lex Titia agraria 90
lex Varia 127–8
lex Villia annalis 223, 227
A. Licinius Archias 136
Licinius Bucco 110, 123
L. Licinius Crassus (*cos.* 95) 105, 117–18, 160, 190, 229–30
M. Licinius Crassus (*cos.* 70, 55) 123
M. Licinius Crassus Agelastus (*pr.* 127 or 126)
P. Licinius Crassus Dives Mucianus (*cos.* 131) 123, 135–6, 160
C. Licinius Hoplomachus 123–4
L. Licinius Lucullus (*cos.* 74) 119
C. Licinius Stolo (*cos.* 364 or 361) 124
Litorius 208
Livia, wife of Augustus 2–4
Livia, wife of P. Rutilius Rufus 199–200
C. Livius Drusus 134
M. Livius Drusus (*cos.* 112) 100, 134, 200
M. Livius Drusus (*tr. pl.* 91) 100, 116–17, 197
M. Livius Drusus Aemilianus (*cos.* 147) 134
L. Livius Salinator (*leg.* 81) 99
Livy 9, 231
Cn. Lollius (*iiiuir nocturnus* ?241) 91–2
Luca, conference of 71
L. Lucceius (*pr.* 67) 210
C. Lucilius 158

Lupus, Servatus 19–21, 148, 184
Lusitani 69, 211
Q. Lutatius Catulus (*cos.* 242) 233
Q. Lutatius Catulus (*cos.* 102) 137, 233
Q. Lutatius Catulus (*cos.* 78) 119, 232–3
Lycia 218
Lysistratus 183

Macedonia 165
Maesia 108
Magi 140
Magna Mater 226–7
Magnesia, battle of 88–9
Mago 234
Maia 185
maiestas 91
Malian Guf 208
Manchester City Football Club 217 n. 107
C. Manilius (*tr. pl.* 66) 118, 233
Marathon, battle of 216
Marcia, Marcius, Marcius Hortalus (*pr.* AD 25) 112
L. Marcius Philippus (*cos.* 91) 117, 197
Q. Marcius Philippus (*cos.* 186, 169) 197
L. Marcius Septimus (*leg.* 206; ?210–207) 234
Maria, Mareotis, lake 143
C. Marius (*cos.* 107, 104–100, 86) 89–90, 105–7, 116–18, 125, 164–5, 182, 212, 230–1, 233
Mars, temple of 211
Masinissa 201–3
Mauretania 212
Melissa 147
C. Memmius (*pr.* ?104) 116
C. Memmius (*pr.* 58) 71
C. Memmius (*tr. pl.* 54), 71
L. Memmius 127
Menelaus 187
Menenius Agrippa 162–3
Mentor 147
Metapontum 141–2, 199, 236
Methymnus 203M
Miletus 208
Miltiades 216
Minturnae 105, 164
Mithridates VI 89, 137, 157, 232–3
Mithridatic Wars 208, 211

Mitylene 211
Mons Sacer 162
P. Mucius Scaevola (*cos.* 133) 160
Q. Mucius Scaevola (*cos.*117) 105, 160, 189, 191
Q. Mucius Scaevola (*cos.* 95) 189, 229–30
M. Mulvius (*iiiuir nocturnus* ?241) 91–2
L. Mummius (*cos.* 146) 127
Munda, battle of 213

Nealces 188
Neanthes 145
Nicostrate 153
P. Nigidius Figulus (*pr.* 58) 235
Nola 164
C. Norbanus (*cos.* 83) 116–117
Numantine War 84, 115, 230
Numidians 203

Cn. Octavius (*cos.* 87)
Ofilius 200
Olympic games 141
L. Opimius (*cos.* 121) 81
Oppian Hill 99
C. Oppius 231
Orestes 97
Oropus 146, 237
Ostia 93
Otacilia 101–4
M'. Otacilius Crassus (*cos.* 263, 246) 102
T. Otacilius Crassus (*cos.* 261) 102
T. Otacilius Crassus (*pr.* 217, 214) 102
M'. Otacilius Pitholaus 231

Palatine Hill 99, 226
Palladium 196
Paphos 233
parens patrae 182
Paris, of Troy 188
parricidium 68
pater familias 215
patria potestas 126, 215
Pausanias, Macedonian 219
Peisirhodos 239
Pergamum 136, 226–7
Pericles 167–8, 204
Peripatetic school 146
M. Perperna (*leg.* 168) 197

M. Perperna (*cos.* 130) 197
M. Perperna (*cos.* 92) 194
Perseus 178, 237
Persian invasion of Greece 156, 206
Pessinus 226–7
Phalerum 191
Pharsalus, battle of 213
Phaselis 218
Phidias 183, 215–16
Philip II 187, 219
Philip V 178
Philippus, name of slaves 114
Philolaus 142
Philon 191
Phlius 144
Pighius, S. V. 24–5
pilleum 125
Piraeus 182, 191
pirate war 232
Pisistratus 166–8
Plataea, battle of 153
Plato 137, 142–5, 150, 191, 218
P. Plautius Hypsaeus (*pr.*) 213
Polus 204
Polybius 74
Polycrates 139
Q. Pompeius (*cos.* 141) 115, 232
Sex. Pompeius (*cos.* AD 14) 1–3, 184
Cn. Pompeius Magnus (*cos.* 70, 55, 52) 72–3, 127, 135, 211, 213, 231–3
Q. Pompeius Rufus (*cos.* 88) 127
Cn. Pompeius Strabo (*cos.* 89) 232
Pomponius Rufus 7
L. Pontius Aquila (*tr. pl.* 45) 135
Pontius Lupus 135
C. Popillius Laenas (*cos.* 172) 126
M. Popillius Laenas (*cos.* 359, 356, ?354, 350, 348) 95, 126
M. Popillius Laenas (*cos.* 316) 95, 126
M. Popillius Laenas (*cos.* 173) 95, 126
M. Popillius Laenas (*cos.* 139) 95, 126
M. Popillius Laenas (*leg. pro pr.*) 95
M. Porcius Cato (*cos.* 195) 30, 69–70, 130–1, 146, 224–5; *Origines* 70
M. Porcius Cato (*tr. pl.* 99) 100
M. Porcius Cato (*pr.* 54) 30, 100, 132, 233
M. Porcius Cato Salonianus 132

Sp. Postumius Albinus (*cos.* 186) 235
Praeneste 161
Praxiteles 185
proconsulare imperium 97
prouocatio 68
Proxenus 204
Ptolemy I Soter, II Philadelphus 169
Ptolemy XII Auletes 71, 233; his brother 233
Publicia 134
Publilia (second wife of Cicero) 134
Publilius (senator) 134
C. Publilius (*qu.* 146) 134
Volero Publilius (*tr. pl.* 472–471) 134
Q. Publilius Philo (*cos.* 339, 327, 320, 315) 134
Pullius (*tr. pl.* 248) 74
Pydna, battle of 178–9
Pyrrhus 199
Pyrron 217
Pythagoras 137, 139–42, 150, 235–6; Pythagoreans 204

quaestiones perpetuae 127
P. Quinctius 137
L. Quinctius Flamininus (*cos.* 192) 94

L. Reginus (*tr. pl.* 103) 117
repetundae 71–2, 83
Rhodes 117, 175, 239
Q. Roscius Gallus 136–7, 171–2
Rusticius Helpidius Domnulus 21
P. Rutilius Rufus (*cos.* 105) 199

sacra uia 92, 191
Salamis 211; battle of 156, 216
C. Sallustius Crispus (*pr.* 46) 200, 231
Salonia 132
Salus, temple of 214
salutatio 181
Samnium 82
Samothrace 178
Sardinia 76
Sceptics 217
Schnetz, J. 19
Schottus, Andreas 18
C. Scribonius Curio (*pr. c.* 121) 115
L. Scribonius Libo (*tr. pl.* 149) 69

M. Scribonius Libo Drusus (?*pr.* AD 16) 4, 69
Secession of Plebs, first 162
C. Sempronius Gracchus (*tr. pl.* 123–122) 81, 134, 168, 170–1, 223
Ti. Sempronius Gracchus (*cos.* 238) 91
Ti. Sempronius Gracchus (*cos.* 177, 163) 95, 223
Ti. Sempronius Gracchus (*tr. pl.* 133) 169–70, 223, 228
Sentinum 109
Q. Sertorius (*pr.* 83) 127, 232
Cn. Servilius Caepio (*cos.* 141) 93, 115
Q. Servilius Caepio (*cos.* 140) 115
Q. Servilius Caepio (*cos.* 106) 117
P. Servilius Geminus (*cos.* 252, 248) 122
C. Servilius Glaucia (*pr.* 100) 89–90, 116, 125
P. Servilius Isauricus (*cos.* 48) 111
P. Servilius Pulex Geminus (*cos.* 202) 122
P. Servilius Vatia (*cos.* 79) 122
Seven against Thebes 238
L. Sextius (*cos.* 366) 125
L. Sextius (*iiiuir nocturnus* ?241) 91–2
Shackleton Bailey, D. R. 27–8
Sicyon 146, 183, 188
Sigeum 208
Simmias 191
Simonides 137, 153–4
Smyrna 96–7
Social War 128, 164, 194
Socrates 137, 142, 145, 150, 161, 169
Solon 137, 154–5
Sophocles 137, 153–4
Sophron 142
Sora 82
Spain 69, 84, 213, 228, 232
Sparta 141, 191
stipulatio 103
Stoa 146–7, 152
Sucro 127
Sulpicia 235
Ser. Sulpicius Galba (*pr.* 151) 69, 130–1
C. Sulpicius Galus (*cos.* 166) 70, 177–9
C. Sulpicius Paterculus (*cos.* 258) 235
Ser. Sulpicius Paterculus 235
P. Sulpicius Rufus (*tr. pl.* 88) 117
Sybaris 142
Syme, R. 120

Syphax 201
Syracuse 148–9, 163, 200–1
Syria 71, 96

Tarentum 142, 196, 204
Tarquins 163
Tarracina 86–7
Tarraco 86
Tartessus 205
Taurus, mts. 88–9
Telesterion, at Eleusis 191
Teos 2187
Terentia, wife of Cicero 199–200
M. Terentius Varro (*pr.* after 77) 5, 133, 205, 235
M. Terentius Varro Lucullus (*cos.* 73) 119
Teutones 230–1
Thapsus, battle of 213
Thebes 191
Themistocles 137, 155–6, 215–17
Theodectes 218–19
Theoderic 21
Theophanes 211, 231
Theopompus 207
Third Macedonian War 197
Third Punic War 201
Thucydides 207
Tiber, river 77
Tiberius, Emperor 1, 3–4, 72, 112, 194, 222
Tibur 162
Tigranes 232
Timaeus, Pythagorean 144
Timaeus, of Tauromenium 220
Timanthes 187–8
C. Titinius 105–6
Q. Titinius 105
L. Titius (*pr.*) 109
M. Titius (*cos. suff.* 31)
Sex. Titius (*tr. pl.* 462 109
Sex. Titius (*tr. pl.* 99) 90
Titius Probus 21
C. Titius Rufus (*pr.* 50) 109
torture 113
Traube, L. 19
C. Trebonius (*cos. suff.* 45) 96
triumuiri nocturni 92
Tuccia 75–7

M. Tullius Cicero 9, 68, 71–2, 83, 89–90, 96, 101, 118, 121, 136–7, 171–4, 182, 184, 200, 230, 233
Q. Tullius Cicero (*pr.* 62) 172

Ulysses 187

C. Valerius (*aed. cur.* 328; ? = C. Valerius Potitus, *cos.* 331) 79
Valerius Antias 79, 210
M. Valerius Corv(in)us (*cos.* 348, 346, 343, 335, 300, *cos. suff.* 299) 195, 228–9
M'. Valerius Maximus (*dict.* 494) 162
Valerius Maximus, status 1; legal knowledge 1, 69; and Sex. Pompeius 2–3, 184; ?visit to Athens 184, 192
Facta et dicta memorabilia 5–6; sources 6–9, V.'s use of his sources 79, 151, 174; language and style 9–14, 159. 205; chapter divisions and headings 28–9; authorial statements 85; prefaces 193; *exempla externa*, transitions to 215; address of reader in second person 227; manuscripts 5, 15–23; editions 19, 24–28
M. Valerius Messalla Corvinus (*cos.* 31) 200

C. Valerius Tappo (*tr. pl.* 188) 1
L. Valerius Tappo (*pr.* 192) 1
Valerius Valentinus 81
Q. Varius Hybrida 127
Velleius Paterculus 9
Venus 185; Venus Verticordia, temple of 235
Vercellae, battle of 233
Vesta 185
Vestal virgins, trial of 235
uia Appia 210
uia Laurentina, Ostiensis 123
Vibo Valentia 81
Victoria, temple of 226
P. Villius (*iiiuir nocturnus*) 92
?C. Visellius Ruga (*aed. pl.* 491) 102
C. Visellius Varro (?*tr. pl.* 69, ?*aed. cur.* 59) 101–3
Volcanus 184
L. Volusius Saturninus (*cos. suff.* AD 3) 197

Xenophilus 204
Xenophon 207
Xenophon of Lampsacus 207–8
Xerxes I 145, 156, 216

Zeno 147, 152

Language and Style

See also pp. 9–14.

ablative, without *e(x)* 224; of works of literature 231
adjective, instead of objective genitive 216
adjectives in *-anus* derived from a *cognomen* 179
alliteration 69, 76, 102, 185
anaphora 129
antithesis 75, 126, 137, 184
asyndeton 140, 143, 160, 164, 173, 175, 202, 229

chiasmus 71, 161, 173, 208, 222
combination of expressions 151, 221
conditional clause, counterfactual, tenses in 155; understood apodosis 221

dative of disadvantage 104
dubitatio comparatiua 74–5, 152

ellipse 154, 181, 234

gerund, instead of present participle 153

nomen and *cognomen* inverted 135, 181, 232

oratio obliqua, tenses in 126, 168–9

periods 129, 142–3, 193–4
personification 182
pleonasm 205
poetic plural 211
polyptoton 86, 191

repetition 152, 170
ring composition 150

subjunctive, potential 85, 166

word order 166, 204, 213, 230, 237; see also chiasmus, Wackernagel's Law

zeugma 121, 140

Authors and Passages

A. Literary

For practical reasons references to Valerius himself are excluded.

Academicorum philosophorum index
  Herculanensis 143
Accius *trag.* 569 110
Aelian fr. (ed. Domingo-Forasté) 113 122
n.a. 6.40 221
u.h. 4.20 145–6
29 217
10.1 238
12.15 161
Alcidamas *ap.* Aristotle *rhet.* 1398b15 248
Alexander Polyhistor *FGrH* 273F17, 72 208
Ammianus 29.2.19 96
30.4.19 170
Ampelius 8.10 215
19.2 199
26.2 125
Anacreon fr. 361 Page 205
anon. *Rhetores Graeci* (ed. Spengel) i.454 218
Appian *b.c.* 1.33.148 89
37.166, 38.169 128
57.262 125
60.271 106
72.335 164
2.115.480 181
116.488, 149.619, 153.641 180
4.32.135–34.146 111–12
Celt. 1.8 78
Ib. 38.153 127
63.267 205
84.363–4 227
Ill. 60.249–54 69–70
Lib. 69.315 225
106.499–500

109.517 223
112.533 228
Mith. 95.435 73
Samn. 10.1–9 199
Apollodorus *FGrH* 244F33 203
46 151
51 146
Apuleius *mund.* 32 215
Aristotle *fr.* (ed. Rose) pp. 13, 71 218
fr. 569 238–9
mete. 371a32–4
pol. 1274b24 204
1311b2 219
rhet. 1398b15 248
1410b3 218
[Aristotle] *mir. ausc.* 846a, *mund.* 399b 215
rhet. ad Alex. 1421a38 218
Arnobius *nat.* 6.23 220
Arrian *anab.* 3.4.2
Asconius (ed. Clark) *Corn.* 118–120
pp. 20, 34 173
22 127–8
26, 74 165
62, 85, 88 172, 227
ps. Asconius (ed. Stangl) pp. 194, 234 165
Athenaeus 217B 144
217E 145
351A 192
566E 218
592C 204
Ath. pol. 1 206
14.1 166
Augustine *anim.* 3.4.5 138
ciu. 8.11 145

bellum Africum 10.4 159
bellum Alexandrinum 5.3 152

Caelius *ap.* Cic. *fam.* 8.1.1 166
Caesar *ciu.* 1.2.3 173
3.111.1 149
Gall. 1.12.7 78
4.2.3 202
5.31.5 177
44.2 149
ap. Suet. *Iul.* 6.1
Caper *gramm.* 7.94 141
Cato *agr.* 33 144
orat. 180 222
origines FRHist 5T13, 87–93, 106–7 70
Catullus 16.5–6 81
67.27 205
Celsus 1.2.6, 8.1.6 144
Censorinus 15.3 146, 152
17.3 205
Choricius 7.11 238
32.14 145
chronographer of AD 354 195
Cicero *ac.* 2.118 149
Arch. 20 216
22 209
27 210
Att. 1.1.1 103
5.8 200
4.15.7, 18.3 227
5.9.1 152
19.3 173
7.8.4 159
12.14.2 190
13.37.4 200
14.21.3 202
15.1a.2 118
Balb. 34 234
45 189–90
51 123
54 81
Brut. 44, 59 167
54 162–3
55, 61 199
66 214
78 178
79 226
81 83

89–90 69
107 210
121 205
122 115
168 106, 116
192 138
264 101
269 229
277–8 172–3
303 171
317 165
Cael. 34 199
69 103
70 102
carm. frg. 16 164
Cato 13 144–5, 151, 203
16 199
18 25
21 155
22 124, 153
26 150, 155
30 196
33 145
34 201, 203
37 198
38 131
49 178
69 205
Corn. (frs., ed. Puccioni) 1 fr. 61 118, 120
de gloria 209
de iure ciuili (ed. C.F.W. Müller) fr. 2 133
de orat. 1.57 118
62 192
103 204, 236
171 131
187 149
217 160
260–1 138
2.22 158, 160
48 90
73 215
89, 107, 109, 164, 200–3 116
154 141
265, 285 77
3.45 165
87 190
129 236
137, 139 141

138 167–8
213 174
225 170
diu. 1.3 238
11 180
47 220
79 37
88 237
2.3 202
94 152
dom. 47 78
123 122
127 77
132 120
fam. 3.10.9 222
4.6.1 70
5.12.2 128
7 183, 210
6.6.12 194
7.21 200
8.4.1, 9.5 173
9.2.11 118
10.28.2 197
32.3 136
16.23.2 122
24.1 200
fat. 19 107
fr. 4 (Ax) 159
fin. 2.1 236
3.7 132
61 108
5.3 138
4 142
50 148
64 226
87 140, 142, 144–5
Flacc. 31 239
77 89
Font. 23 115
24 116–17
26 116
38 83
41 128
har. resp. 12 77
27 226
in Clodium et Curionem 74
inu. 1.49 109
80 115

2.78–9 67–9
144 239
Lael. 158
22, 32, 58–9, 64, 91 158
13 141
21 70
51 222
leg. 1.11 137
2.14, 31 90
3.24 171
Manil. 59 232
Mil. 7 67–8
Mur. 22 190
57, 62, 68 227
58 83
66 178
nat. deor. 1.10 235
79 137
82 238
83 184
2.36 194
64 222
69 220
110 159
off. 1.3 189
19 178
23 86
2.15 107
49 116
58 229
144 144
3.66 99–100
orat. 21 118
29 167
38 138
56 174, 227
74 187
122, 172, 194, 218 218
125 159
234 118, 215
or. frg. VIII 18 84
part. 104–5 116
Phil. 1.11 199
2.12 122
17, 10.11 229
85 180
5.16 78
14.6 164

phil. frg. 5 160
Pis. 6 120
13 78
20 76
53 172
56 209
Planc. 5 158
58 102
p. red. in sen. 11 86
25, 37 122
Q. fr. 2.15.4, 16.2 227
3.2.1, 5.8 71
3.7.5 140
Q. Rosc. 137
5 122
Quinct. 8 84
77 137
Rab. perd. 20 192
24–5 89–90
27 182
rep. 1.12 141
21–2 178
23 177, 179
25 182
2.23, 52 108
3.6 146
7 141
6.11 227
Scaur. 54 196
Sest. 20, 26 78
130 122
S. Rosc. 64–5 86–7
71 87
110 83
Sull. 11 165
46 116
Tusc. 1.4 214
15 194
27 108
34 215
38 141
81 123
83 169
111 239
4.2 141
71 102
5.9–10 141
104 145

108 123
112 134, 190, 198
115 148
Verr. 2.1.51 83
128 105
2.23 67, 104
65 83
3.77 102
86 146
211 122
4.51 146
131 148
[Q. Cicero] *comm. Pet.* 19 172
Claudian 18.475 75
Clement *protr.* 4.53
strom. 1.61 141
Coelius *FRHist* 15F30 223
49b 205
Columella 4.15.2 94
6.5.7 94
Ctesias *FGrH* 688 206
culex 226 93
Curtius 1.1 220
4.7.22 238
8.4 132
10.3.14 189

Demosthenes 18 175
[Demosthenes] 61.45 167
digest 1.2.2.36 199
44–5 200
3.1.1.5 110, 198
19.1.38.1 134
44.17.3 181
48.9.1, 9.9 pr. 87
Dio Cassius fr. 17 162
85.2 170
95.3 89
36.18.1, 19.1 73
36a 232
38–40 119
39.56.5 72
61 71
41.14.5 197
45.16.1–2 122
46.5.4 102
51.19.7 231
53.32.5 97

54.46.1 2
Dio Chrysostom 12.6 215
37.28 237
63.4–5 188
Diodorus 13.103.4 153
16.93–4 219–20
17.50 238
20.36.6 198
32.16 201–2
34/35.33.3 225
Diogenes Laertius 1.12 141
109 207
111 206
2.7 148
86 169
3.2–3 145
6 142
4.63–4 147
65 146
5.24 218
7.84 151
168 152
8.16, 46 204
58 203
9.34 145
36 145–6
Dionysius of Halicarnassus 2.69 75
3.13–18 67
27.1, 30.4, 31.1 68
6.23–90 162
15.1.2 195
16.3.1 198
2 214
20.8.1 82
comp. 2, Dem. 48 218
Isoc. 19 204
Duris *FGrH* 76F72 145

Ennius *ann.* 1, 5–6, 10–15, 69V = 1–11Sk 210
9V = *trag.* 365–6 Jocelyn
81V = 235Sk 122
202–3V = 199–200Sk 199
incert. 603V = 609Sk 163
Ephorus *FGrH* 70F115 207
Epimenides *FGrH* 457 206
Euripides *didasc.* 153
Eusebius *PE* 14.8.13 147

Eustathius on Hom. *Il.* 1.528–30, ed. Van der Walk iv. 883 lines 18–19 187

Fasti Capitolini, Hydatiani 195
Festus (ed. Lindsay) 120 142
458 195
496 81
512 103
Florus 1.13.20 199
31.4 225
2.6.1 128
Frontinus *strat.* 1.12.8 177
2.6.2, 10.2 234
4.3.11 201

Gaius *inst.* 2.61 190
Gallus fr. 145 Hollis 205
Gellius 1.5.2 171
11.10–16 170
2.6.18 220
4.5.5 190
5.9.2 138
14.17 97
10.6 90–1
12.7 96–7
17.15 147
17.2 157
19.11.4 94
ap. FRHist 5F27, 41, 77b, 78, 97, 103 70
Gorgias 203
Grattius 233 139
Gregory of Nyssa 45.265 Migne 220

Hermippus fr. 63 Wehrli 237
Herodotus 1.52, 92 238
59.5 166
63.2 205
3.23.1 206
4.181 238
7.119, 8.120 145
8.134.2 238
Hesiod *Op.* 266 190
Hieronymus *adu. Iouin.* 1.48 200
chron. s. a. 57 173
epist. 53.2 174
historia Augusta Heliog. 26.4 94
Pert. 12.6 94
Homer *Il.* 9.186 161

Horace *ars* 183 136
carm. 1.1.6 233
4.5.33–5 231
epist. 1.15.34 94
1.19.4 111
2.1.50 –2 210
239 183
epod. 11.13 103
sat. 1.110 190
2.1.71–4 158
5.40 94

Iamblichus *Pyth.* 251 204
Isocrates 11 (*Busiris*).28 140
12 (*Panathenaikos*) 151
267–70 151

John Chrysostom 62.9 Migne 220
Josephus *AJ* 14.92 72
Ap. 2.131 220
Justin 9.6.4–7.14 219
20.4.7 141
Justinian *inst.* 4.18.6 87
Juvenal 10.168 217

Lactantius *inst.* 5.14.3–5 146
Livy 1.24–26 67
26.4–9 68
31.2 106
2.15.1 222
18.2 197
30.5–32.12 162
49.1 215
3.6.6 172
12.2 215
36.7 102
39.8 124
58.2 70, 222
67.6 214
8 222
4.2.11 150
43.8 134
5.2.7 203
9 97
6.4 203
11.12 84
14.5 222
20.8 172

6.6.8 194
14.3 169
26.7 84
34–42 125
40.3 215
7.5.6 106
16.9 125–6
26.1–10 228–9
26.12, 32.15, 40.3 195
8.22.3 78
37.8 79
9.17.1 91
42.4, 46.10–15 199
42.6, 43.1 82
43.25 214
10.1.9 214
15.8 227
27.1, 30.4, 31.12 109
per. 13 199
19 74, 90–1, 196
20 75–6
21.4.2 186
46.1 106
22.9.7 197
13.6 82
35.3 95
39.9 209
53.4 83
61.4 219
12 142
23.2.7 197
5.11 194
9.7 98
14.13 82
19.5 101
24.4.4 200
16.8, 32.19 125
27.5 163
34.8–11 148
43.8 106
25.2.7 106
15.6 142
31.9–10 148–9
32–6 234
37.2, 5–6 234
26.2.1–4 234
41.25 186
27.10.6 194, 222

19.9 123
51.3 142
28.5.5 164
38.7–10 223
29.6.12 164
10.4–11.8, 14.5–14 226
23.4 203
30.26.5 196
37.7 172
31.4.7 223
7.1 142
32.2.5 234
23.6 125
33.6.8 101
30.4 217
10 135
34.2.6 164
3.8 226
11 126
5.9 135
28.6 154
49.8 163
54.8 84
58.1 103
35.12.18, 42.12 144
36.21.7 197
25.6 86
37.5.6 149
35.10 89
40.3 206
42.1 164
42.1 164
45.14 89
51.1–2 196
57.7 86
59.2 88
60.3 206
38.3.11 145
18.9 112
30.5, 36.8 106
38.4 89
44.11 178
51.5 75
52.8, 56.3–4 210
53.7 89
54.2 110
55.2 125, 215
56.12–13 223–4

58.3 215
59.1–2 88
60 72
39.3.6 182
9.2 126
11.2 73, 186
39.6, 10 197
40–41 130–1
40.4–12 69, 130, 225
41.5 95
42.8–43.4 94, 114
40.37.4 95
43.2–3 95
43.9 230
44.1 223
54.4 70
41.9.10 95
13.2 186
42.3, 28.11–12 235
7.8 150
34.3 224
51.7 206
44.13.4 154
22.14 182
27.6, 37.5, 8 70
37.5–9 177–8
45.1.8 197
16.4 95
24.11 172
37.12 237
39.9 124
41.6 73
44.19 125
per. 47 146
48 134
49 69
51 228
epit. Oxyrh. 55 83
per. 56 227
91 97
103 121
131 147
Lucan 4.100 141
Lucian *de morte peregr.* 22 220
[Lucian] *am.* 15–16 185
macr. 10 200, 205
17 201
18 204

19 152
20 151
24 153
Lucilius (ed. Marx) 1307 81
Lucretius 4.461 205
6.848–78 238

Macrobius *Sat.* 3.14.13 136
Manilius 2.140 139
Marmor Parium s. a. 406/5 153
Munatius Rufus *FRHist* 37F1 205

Naevius *com.* 65 94
Nepos *Att.* 5.4 227
6.4 229
Cato 3.1 131
Chabr. 3.4, *Iph.* 3.3 128
Phoc. 2.4 93
Them. 9.1, 10.1 156
FRHist 45F11 211
Nicolaus of Damascus *uita Caes.* 23.83–4 181
Nonius Marcellus 202

Obsequens 46 90
Olympiodorus *uita Platonis* p. 2 145
Orosius 4.11.5–9 91
21.10 69
5.15.24 78
19.5 125
Ovid *am.* 3.12.7 219
fast. 2.637–8 231
4.64 142
157–60 211, 235
255 ff. 227
6.203–4 199
met. 11.96 203
Pont. 4.1.1–2, 5.33–8, 15.3–4, 41–2 2
4.16.47 116
trist. 5.5.22 76

Pausanias 1.3.4 187
14.6 184
34.2 237
5.6.7–8 238–9
6.7.2 239
17.7–8 237
19.1 142

20.9 239
10.18.7 237
Petronius 88.4 147
5 189
Philodemus *rhet.* 1.346 192
Philostratus *gymn.* 17 238–9
VS 9.4 237
510 174
Phlegon *FGrH* 257F37(V) 205
38 206
Piso *FRHist* 9F24 162
Plato *Hipp. mai.* 283A 148
leg. 642D 206
Phaedrus 270A 167
Prot. 343A
Symp. 216D 150
Theaet. 149A–151D
[Plato] *epist.* 2.311A 167
Plautus *Capt.* 278 222
Most. 41 78
Persa 407 78
Rud. 39 161
461 152
652 103
Truc. 230 67
Pliny *epist.* 2.3.10 174
17.2 123
4.5.1 174
5.6.10 68
7.29.3 78
9.21.4 103
nat. 2.22 107
53 177–8
83 178
4.95 208
6.199–200 208
7.61 201, 203
88 157
110 174
120 235
125 148, 183, 192
141 196
154–8, 168 193, 196–7, 199–201, 204–5
8.180 94
213 128
11.219 190
12.82 107
15.74 225

17.2 103
19.37 107
22.228 238
25.6 157
51 147
28.21 75–6
161, 189 94
31.11 109
83 237
33.133 123
34.50, 78 187
35.19 214
73, 128–9
85 192
91 183
104 188
36.21 185
26 210
Plutarch *Alex.* 3.3 220
4.1–3 183
10.6 219
Arat. 13.4–5 188
Caes. 4.1–2 165
63.1–2 180
63.8–64.6 181
Cato mai. 22.6–7 146
27.2 225
Cato min. 19.1 132
35.1, 39.1–2 233
Cic. 5.3 137
Dem. 6.4, 11.1 138
24.2 175
Mar. 3.2–5 230
27.9 231
28 106
35.7 125
37.12, 38.2 106
38.3–6 105, 107
44.7 164–5
Marc. 19.8–12 148
mor. 84B, 92C 215
99B 188
184F–185A, 800B 216
456A 170
466D 217
579B–C 191
794D–E 199
Per. 3.5, 7.1, 8.4, 16.1 168

4.6, 8.1 167
16.7 148
31.3 215
35.2 182
Pomp. 13.7 162
25.10 232
71 87
Pyrrh. 18.1–19.6 199
Sert. 7.3 99
Sol. 2.2 155
Sull. 10.1 106
62.2 137
TG 2.6 170
Them. 3.4 215
29.5 156
Thes. 6.9 215
[Plutarch] *mor.* 840C 175
840D–E 174
844E–F 138
Pollio *FRHist* 56F1 205
Polybius 1.52.3 74
2.39.1 141
8.5–6 148
21.43.6 89
29.16 179
36.16 201–3
Pompeius Trogus *prol.* 6 128
Porphyry *VP* 6 140
prolegomena philosophiae Platonicae (ed. Westerink) p. 7 144
Propertius 3.7.24 67

Quadrigarius fr. 12 Peter 228
Quintilian *decl.* 286 68
271 87
342 103
351 84
inst. 1.1.6 111
10.4 191
13 150
17 145
27–8 170
47 177, 182
11.5 138
12 136
2.13.13 187
15.10 218
16.7 199

4.1.14 84
5.7.5 122
11, 39 141
8.5.35 109
6.7 118
9.1.2 109
10.3.30, 54 138
5.18 94
11.2.38 160
50 135, 156
3.6 174
8-9 171
11.3, 123,155 172
12.1.19 141
3.9, 11.23 131
10.24, 65 167

rhet. Her. 2.33 115
3.25 158
4.23 86
63 166

Sallust Cat. 2.8 166
3.1 189
51.30 102
hist. (ed. Maurenbacher) 1.77 197
95-6 99
2.16 103
45 227
47 166
3.20 75
4.27 110
5.24 232
Iug. 27.3, 30.4-34.1 116
63.2 106
80, 101 212
Satyrus ap. uita Soph. 13 153
Scaurus FRHist 18F1 205
scholia Aristophanes Vesp. 566 171
scholia Bobiensia Cic. p. 85St 115
90 74
95 89
178 210
scholia Demosthenes Olymp. 2.53d Dilts 218
scholia Pindar Ol. 7 238-9
Seneca benef. 7.28.2
contr. 1 praef. 14 203
8.8 217

dial. 11.11.1
epist. 44.3 152
79.3 107
82.17 87
114.13 199
nat. 2.4.1 124
5.18.16 122
suas. 1.5 217
Silius Italicus 3.396-8 205
13.793-7 210
14.676 148
Simonides (ed. Page) fr. xxviii 154
Sisenna FRHist 26F31 127
Solinus 1.108-9 157
126 235
40.2-4 220-1
56.12 208
Solon (ed. Diehl) fr. 22.7 155
Sophocles O.C. 153
Statius Achill. 1.937 132
silu. 3 praef. 1 124
126 235
Strabo 8, p. 357-8C
9, p. 395 192
p. 399 237
14, p. 640 220-1
p. 657 183
17, p. 833 203
Suda s.n. Ἀλκιδάμας, Ἀριστόξενος, Γοργίας, Δημοσθένης 204
Ἔννιος 210
Ἰοφῶν 153
Κλεάνθης 152
Πλάτων 144
Suetonius Aug. 31.4 238
Cal. 36 102
Claud. 9.2 190
40.2 227
gramm. 20 208
Iul. 4.1 165
6.1 215
77, 81.2 180
81.4 181
Nero 6 180
Tib. 2.1 199
3 90
11.4 3
42.2 227

57.2 2
Vesp. 2.3 227
3 147
uita Ter. 4 178

Tacitus *ann.* 1.9.2 195
14.1 23, 97
19.3 68
76.2 97
2.27–32 4, 69
38 112
61.2 4
3.58.2 97
71.3 196
4.34.2 73, 231
36.3 103
6.14.1 2
12.41.1, 59.1 97
13.21.3, 52.1 97
dial. 34.4 165
40.3 229
hist. 3.2.4 189
Terence *Eun.* 276 124
Haut. 104 147
Phorm. 68 189
theologia arithmeticae p. 40 140
Theophanes *FGrH* 188T1–10, F1–7 211
Theopompus *FGrH* 115F68 207
F395 bis 221
Thucydides 1.137.3, 138.1 156
2.28 182
65.9 168
Tibullus 1.8.14 193
tragica incerta 179 103
Tzetzes *chil.* 2.136–49 148

Varro *ling.* 6.15 227
64 167
7.48 238
74 116
96 103
rust. 2.5.4 94
3.2.1 190

ap. Gell. 3.10.2 73
Velius Longus *gramm.* 7.74 141
Velleius Paterculus 1.10.1 106
13.1 225
16.1 191
17 210
2.6.3 238
9.4 230
10.1 93
11.1, 19 106
32.1 232
43.3 165
45.5 233
67.1 217
100.3–5 3
101.3 232
103.4 182
Victor *Caes.* 3.11 159
Virgil *Aen.* 2.6, 10.427 205
6.19, 41 211
142 238
9.139 189
de uiris illustribus 34.2 198
9 199
47.8–9 224–5
69.2 125
76.1 157
78.2 165
uita Aristotelis Marciana (ed. Rose) p. 428 145
uita Platonis p. 7 145
uita Sophoclis 13–14 153
Vitruvius 7 praef. 12 192

Xenophanes DK 21F20 206
Xenophon, *Anab.*, *Cyr.* 157
Cyr. 5.3.46–51 157

Zonaras 4.8 220
9 219
7.14.3–10 162
8.4.11–12 199
9.5.5 148

B. Inscriptions, Papyri and Coins

Chiron 22 (1992), 377–82 211
CIL ii. 1964 190
xi. 5783 108
CRAI 1969, 42–64

IG i³. 472 184
ii². 505, 1668 192
1471 2
v/1. 1432.36 116
I.I. xiii/3. 79 198

ILLRP 991 87
Inscr.Olymp. 293 237

POxy 1798 219

RRC 260, 332 87
RS 1.47–8 84
7.3 83

s.c. de Pisone patre 96 136
Sherk 23 190

Latin

Entries in this Index refer to notes dealing with matters of Latinity. References to notes dealing with matters of substance will be found in the General Index.
The words listed on pp. 9–14 are not indexed.

a, ab 78, 202
abscidere, abscindere 112
absoluere 104
acceptum (re)ferre 107
acies (oculorum) 134
actor 135
actuosus 159
actus 139
adducere 100
adigere 100, 239
adlatrare 110
adminiculum 194
adquiescere + dat. 159
adumbrare 189
aedilis 79
aetas 134
age 227
agitatio 145
a(h)en(e)um 238
alienigenus 182
alter ... alter 68
alueus 160
amantisimus 167
ambustus 95
animosus 106
Anio 163

ansa, ansula 193
Areopagus 97–8
armamentarium 192
auctor 189
auspicari 'embark on' 232
aut 78

bellum sociale 128
beneficus 222
benigne accipere 209
bucco 110

calculus 160
calumnia 104, 111
candidatus 227
capere 'obtain', 'receive' 224
causae dictio 75
citerior 151
colorare 102
columen 165
commercium libidinis 102
commodare 107
comprehendere, of works of art 189
concidere 93
concubitus 186
conductor 191

confodere 84
coniectare 180
consanguineus 69
consentaneus 71
consideranter 98
consternatio 164
consulare imperium 196
consultor 190
consummatio 138, 206
contio 170
crepida 193
cribrum 76
cuias 122
cum, inuersum 72
cumulus 129
Cyrenaeus, Cyrenaicus 169

damnare 104, 106
deesse, superesse 133
deformiter 78
de industria 106
deligere, diligere; demittere, dimittere;
    describere, discribere 156, 213
deminutio 235
de(di-)rigere 156
destrictus 103
destringere, distringere 156
deuerticulum 91
dilatare 144
disertus 167
disicere 221
dispergere 144
disputator 189
domesticus 129
dum 80, 122, 128, 132, 143
duramentun 130
durare 'hold out' 203

edictum 101
ediscere 157
eleuare 122
emancipare 126
equidem 124
euidenter 84
excessus 108
excogitare 177
ex facili 145
exigere 140

expensum ferre 102
expers 165
explorare 82
expresse 138
extrahere 152

facere in 94
fatum 155
feneratrix 103
fessus 187
flagrare, flagrantissimus, fragrare 132
flectere 152
flexuosus 144
fomentum 73
fortis 68
fragor 85
frons 103
fructuosus 148
fulmen 118

geometres, -ra 191
gloriosus 216–17
gratiosus 90

habere + perfect participle 132
habitare 18, 89, 168
haurire 69, 152
hic idem 193
hoc / eo / eodem / quodam loci 108
hodieque 224
homines 85
honoratus 194, 210, 222
humana condicio 194

iactura 91
idem = is 171
ille pointing forward 220
imber 202
imperium 'order' 149
impius, impie, impietas 68
impudicus 106
impugnare 84
in + abl. instead of acc. 156
inanis 103
incestum 121
inclutus 100
incommodum 1135
in conspectu 106

incrementum 167
incursus 92
infinitus 199
ingenerare 169
iniquus 154
iniuria 75, 91
inritus 187
institutio 192
intermissio 158
in senatum uocare, senatum / patres conuocare 197
instituere + acc. and inf. 238
intemperantia 86
interpellare 134
interpres 157
interuentus 72
inuerecundus 103
irrumpere 149
istic 173–4
iudicialis 121

laborare 171
laboriosus 146
latratus 110
lectitare 132
legere 208
liberare 86
liberos, heredem tollere 124
libidinosus 102
librare 69
lineamentum 149, 186
(in) loco 122
luctuosus 187

machinator, machinatio, machinamentum 149
maestus 188
magna, maior Graecia 141–2
manare 107
materia, of works of art 189
miles + gen. 146
Mity(yti)len(a)e 211
modo non 189
modus, motus 109
monitor 157
morum principatus 227
mucro 164

nam, asseverative 173
namque 73
ne, asseverative 182
ne ... quidem, nec ... quidem 217, 229
neruosus 205
nocte, noctu 86
nominare 133
nubes 76
numerus 113, 136

officium 181
omasum 94
operatus 146
orbis terrarum 144
ostentare 125

patientia 139
percitus 72
perfectus 130
perinde ac 114
perrogare 128
Perseus 178
perstringere 115
peruicax 150
pestifer 129
planta 193
ponere, promere 136
popularis 168
pos(t) 170
praeceptor 143
praeconium 210
praecurrere 184
praediator(ius) 190
praedicare, praedicere 175
praedictum 101
praeproperus 74
pro causal 67
professio 191
professor 190
propugnator 229
prorogare 111
prosternere 90
prouentus 73
puerulus 94

quaestio 99
quantulus 150
quantusquantus 212

quid ita 216
quid ... nonne 121, 187
quid uelle + pronoun 214
quod si 103

referre 138, 172, 188
relegare 98
rerum natura 77
repraesentare 111
reus 76
roborare 129

saepe numero 202
securitas 182
sequi 112
si quid accidit 230
si quidem 75, 122
sorbere 140
stipendium 118
strictim 199
subinde 194
subnectere 79
suppliciter 78

sura 193
sustinere + inf. 98

tam ... quam / quam ... tam 'as well as' 165
temperamentum 171
tempestas of disease 102
templa 211
terrere, perterrere 179
testatus 162, 211–12
tristis 71, 188
trux uoltus 73

uates 190
uegetus 158
uel 'maybe'
uerecundia 108
uicissitudo 124
uir + gen. 70
uiuacitas 152, 205
uiuax 133
umbilicus 159
umbo 121
uterque + plural verb 181

Greek

ἀνθύπατος 97
Ἄρειος πάγος, Ἀρειόπαγος, Ἀρειόπαγίτης 97

βαδίζειν 122

δολοφονεῖν 99

Μυτι(ιτυ)λήνη(α) 211

σκιαγραφεῖν 189

τρόπος 109

ὑπόκρισις 174–5

www.ingramcontent.com/pod-product-compliance
Lightning Source LLC
Chambersburg PA
CBHW031803220426
43662CB00007B/506